Enterprise Compensation Management with SAP® ERP HCM

 PRESS

SAP PRESS is a joint initiative of SAP and Galileo Press. The know-how offered by SAP specialists combined with the expertise of the Galileo Press publishing house offers the reader expert books in the field. SAP PRESS features first-hand information and expert advice, and provides useful skills for professional decision-making.

SAP PRESS offers a variety of books on technical and business related topics for the SAP user. For further information, please visit our website: *www.sap-press.com.*

Stefan Kauf and Viktoria Papadopoulou
Creating Forms in SAP ERP HCM
2009, 231 pp.
978-1-59229-282-0

Jeremy Masters and Christos Kotsakis
Implementing Employee and Manager Self-Services
In SAP ERP HCM
2008, 431 pp.
978-1-59229-188-5

Martin Esch, Anja Junold
Authorizations in SAP ERP HCM
2008, 336 pp.
978-1-59229-165-6

Satish Badgi
Configuring US Benefits with SAP
2007, 75 pp.
978-1-59229-164-9

Jeremy Masters and Christos Kotsakis

Enterprise Compensation Management with SAP® ERP HCM

Galileo Press

Bonn • Boston

Galileo Press is named after the Italian physicist, mathematician and philosopher Galileo Galilei (1564–1642). He is known as one of the founders of modern science and an advocate of our contemporary, heliocentric worldview. His words *Eppur se muove* (And yet it moves) have become legendary. The Galileo Press logo depicts Jupiter orbited by the four Galilean moons, which were discovered by Galileo in 1610.

Editor Jenifer Niles
Copyeditor Michael Beady
Cover Design Jill Winitzer
Photo Credit Image Copyright Regien Paassen. Used under license from Shutterstock.com
Layout Design Vera Brauner
Production Editor Kelly O'Callaghan
Assistant Production Editor Graham Geary
Typesetting Publishers' Design and Production Services, Inc.
Printed and bound in Canada

ISBN 978-1-59229-207-3

© 2010 by Galileo Press Inc., Boston (MA)

1st Edition 2010

Library of Congress Cataloging-in-Publication Data
Masters, Jeremy.
  Enterprise compensation management with SAP ERP HCM / Jeremy Masters,
Christos Kotsakis. -- 1st ed.
       p. cm.
  Includes index.
  ISBN-13: 978-1-59229-207-3 (alk. paper)
  ISBN-10: 1-59229-207-0 (alk. paper)
  1. SAP ERP. 2. Integrated software. 3. Personnel management. I. Kotsakis, Christos. II. Title.
  QA76.76.I57M363 2010
  005.5'7--dc22
2009028811

Contents at a Glance

Contents

7 Business Add-Ins (BAdIs) 201

9　Authorization Management 253

10　Job Pricing 279

Foreword

At Colgate-Palmolive, we strive to be effective and efficient in everything we do as we work to fulfill our vision to be the best global consumer products company. Colgate, with operations in more than 200 countries and territories, is focused on serving consumers in four core categories—Oral Care, Personal Care, Home Care and premium Pet Nutrition.

One of the most important factors behind our continued success is the quality of our people and their personal commitment to our business priorities. Colgate people are talented, well trained, and globally diverse. To retain our people and of course, to attract new candidates and future leaders, we provide a climate that promotes personal development, opportunity for advancement, and financial rewards. We maintain a competitive compensation strategy that is in line with our "pay for performance" philosophy because we want our people to feel a connection between motivating work, good performance, and rewards and recognition.

Last year, as part of our overall strategy to empower leaders at all levels to develop and coach their people, we implemented elements of SAP's Enterprise Compensation Management (ECM). This implementation will help further our goal of bringing the tools and information to the desktop of our managers, allowing them to make better, and more informed people decisions.

The ECM implementation project was truly global in scope — with over eighty countries represented on the team — and included annual salary recommendations (merit, adjustment, mandated increases and growth promotion) as well as our corporate-wide annual bonus plan.

Looking at our success factors, it was critical for us to integrate with our other HR processes such as our performance management system, have in-country team experts on the ground with global and regional teams driving the process, and globally standardized data fields.

From respecting local business practices to accommodating legal and statutory requirements, localizing even a global process — such as salary recommendations —

presented several challenges. The handling of government-mandated increases in Italy, Spain, and Belgium, for example, needed a fully integrated solution that would comply with all legal obligations. Local compensation programs and practices were also important considerations in our design since it impacted our change management program and organizational readiness assessment.

The technology provided us a vehicle to deliver a validated system comprehensive enough to meet Colgate's unique business requirements. The team supporting this technology sought innovative technical solutions and offline workarounds, when necessary, to deliver processes that could accommodate country-specific requirements, while reinforcing our global standards.

As we look ahead and continue to deploy new and enhanced compensation functionality, we will look for solutions that put our people — our greatest asset and most important competitive advantage — at the forefront.

Trish DeBlasio
Worldwide Director of Compensation
Colgate-Palmolive Company

Preface

Strategically managing compensation within an enterprise is one of the most important HCM initiatives with the largest impact on the success of a company. Administering compensation holistically and consistently — throughout the enterprise — has become increasingly important as companies try to optimize compensation models that reward and retain employees and streamline compensation spending — often one of the largest operating expenses a company has.

As technology has improved, so have the tools that are available to Human Resources (HR) organizations. Tools, such as SAP ERP HCM Enterprise Compensation Management (ECM), enable the strategic aspects of compensation management by integrating talent management processes and enabling companies to tie compensation with employees' performance and the company's overall corporate strategy.

As part of our series on talent management, we have written this book to address both the functional and technical needs of any ECM implementation. Throughout the book, we provide examples and Best Practices on common business requirements for compensation matters. In some cases, we have expanded the content to include functionality that extends beyond the standard solution to show what enhancements are possible within the SAP NetWeaver platform. Considerations for a successful global rollout of ECM are also discussed.

This book was written as a complete reference to cover the compensation processes typically performed by organizations and the associated applications within SAP that deliver them. We dedicated a chapter to lessons learned from past ECM implementations and highlighted recommended approaches and solutions to address key gaps within the functionality.

This book is targeted to both customers and consultants who are implementing ECM or considering its implementation. If you have comments or questions relating to ECM or the contents within the book, feel free to contact the authors by email at *jmasters@worklogix.com* or *christos.kotsakis@emedianet.com*.

Acknowledgments

This project draws inspiration from the effort and support of many individuals. Without these family members, friends, and colleagues, this book would not have been possible.

We would like to dedicate this book to our parents for their years of support, their dedication to our growth, and the valuable wisdom they have shared to make us who we are today. We owe a huge debt of gratitude to Clark and Judith Masters and Nicholas and Effy Kotsakis.

We owe the utmost thanks to our families, who have supported us during the writing of this book. Juad and Nicholas Masters and Paola, Nicholas, and Michael Kotsakis — thank you for your love and patience throughout this project.

We would also like to thank our colleagues who have dedicated countless amounts of hours to the success of key initiatives. Without their dedication to solving seemingly impossible problems, we would have never achieved the successes that we have. We owe big thanks to Venkat Challa, Rinaldo Condo, Matt Miller, John Wunderlich, Brad Chilcoat, Vidyasagar Guntur, Jimmy Kalivas, Michel Chamoun, Rhamut Jaffari, Patrick Rabbat, Song Park, Andrea Mascher, Kristina Hoock, Nish Pangali, and Karen Heatwole.

And thank you to our friends at Galileo Press for their guidance, patience, and support. We would especially like to thank Jenifer Niles, who made this book possible and encouraged us to get the words onto the printed page (again).

We hope you find this book a useful resource for your Enterprise Compensation Management implementation.

Sincerely,

Jeremy Masters & **Christos Kotsakis**
New York, NY
August 2009

Enterprise Compensation Management (ECM) lets companies align their workforce with the company's corporate strategy through fair and rewarding compensation practices, which also help attract and retain key employees. This book explains how to implement and support compensation management using SAP ERP HCM ECM functionality, including leveraging self-service components to optimize the processes related to administering compensation. This chapter gets us started with an introduction to the book, its target audience, and the layout.

1 Introduction

Today's volatile business environment creates a dynamic employment market that is characterized by both reductions and growth in workforces. Companies across the globe have become increasingly aware of business conditions and continue to focus efforts on effectively sourcing and managing their workforce. As business conditions fluctuate, companies are challenged to maintain high morale, manage change, and retain key employees. These challenges directly affect a company's ability to succeed.

Compensation is a prominent component of workforce management, so you need to manage and optimize compensation spending effectively, and ensure that the design of your compensation models tie performance to your corporate strategy. And to remain competitive within your industry, you need to focus on retaining high-performing, "key" employees — especially in difficult business climates.

To address these challenges, companies have been implementing ECM. By utilizing an ECM solution to optimize employee compensation at an *enterprise* level, companies have been able to achieve greater workforce effectiveness, better execution of pay-for-performance strategies, increased productivity, and substantial fiscal savings.

In addition, through the implementation of ECM, companies can align their employees with the organization's goals and strategic objectives to have a direct impact on the company's bottom line. Through a strategic implementation of

ECM, companies have been achieving greater workforce effectiveness by moving to a pay-for-performance culture, gaining efficiencies by harmonizing compensation processes, and improving budgetary controls to support financial audits and increased regulatory compliance.

1.1   Target Audience

This book is written for Human Resource (HR) professionals, Information Technology (IT) professionals, and SAP ERP HCM consultants interested in understanding the steps needed to deliver and operationally support a successful ECM implementation using the latest SAP® versions.

Project and program managers of ECM implementations will also find this book helpful, as we share insights about what "went right" and what "could have gone better" in past implementations. We expect that the information in this book will resonate with project managers and project team members alike.

1.2   Book Layout

We organized the book in a logical sequence to help you both explore the components of SAP ERP HCM ECM and assist in its implementation. The book begins with an introduction to general compensation processes and progresses to the SAP configuration and implementation specifics. The first part of the book provides an overview of compensation processes and discusses aspects of ECM functionality while the remainder of the book addresses more technical topics, including the configuration and development capabilities required for a successful implementation. The book concludes with lessons learned from other ECM implementations and a resources chapter that contains useful information for your project team's reference.

Let's take a quick look at what is covered in each chapter:

Chapter 2, Compensation Management Overview, presents a high-level overview of the processes within compensation management. The chapter breaks down the processes and discusses the elements that make up each process. Important topics such as pay-for-performance and salary benchmarking are covered.

Chapter 3, Baseline Configuration and Infotypes, provides a view into the basic configuration and related infotypes that are introduced by implementing SAP ECM. Concepts such as compensation areas, compensation plans, compensation reviews, and compensation review items are reviewed and examples are provided.

Chapter 4, Compensation Budgeting, covers the budgeting process and the tools that are available to effectively manage and support both monetary and nonmonetary budgets. The budgeting cycle is covered — from preparation to initialization to maintenance to closure. Standard integration with Personnel Cost Planning (PCP) and custom alternatives are also addressed.

Chapter 5, Process Administration, discusses the administration of ECM components, including compensation planning, compensation record status changes, and activation steps. Attention is also given to lessons learned from previous implementations.

Chapter 6, Self-Service, discusses the functionality and use of self-service applications that enable the delivery and administration of compensation through the SAP Portal. Supporting R/3 and iView configuration is also covered.

Chapter 7, Business Add-Ins (BAdIs), focuses on the functionality that can be provided through ECM BAdIs). An explanation of each BAdI is covered by BAdI group. The BAdI groups discussed include Compensation Planning and Administration, Long-term Incentives, Job Pricing, and Statements.

Chapter 8, Advanced Topics and Additional Enhancements, discusses advanced topics that need to be addressed in a typical ECM implementation such as on-cycle growth and organizational promotions during the compensation cycle, off-cycle increases, and second-level approval of proposed compensation recommendations.

Chapter 9, Authorization Management, reviews the important topic of authorizations. Both standard backend authorizations and SAP Portal authorizations are discussed. Attention is placed on structural authorizations and when and where structural authorizations should be implemented. Standard-delivered roles are also discussed.

Chapter 10, Job Pricing, discusses the Job Pricing functionality within ECM. The chapter covers all SAP Job Pricing functionalities, including the process of setting up vendors, participating in salary surveys, importing market data from surveys, analyzing market data, and updating pay structures.

Chapter 11, Integration Components, provides a perspective on the integration points between ECM and other components within SAP ERP HCM. Components discussed include Personnel Administration (PA), Organizational Management (OM), Personnel Cost Planning (PCP), Performance Management, and Payroll.

Chapter 12, Global Considerations, discusses topics that need to be considered during a global implementation of ECM, including global employees, currencies, budgeting, proration, and mandated/general increases.

Chapter 13, Reporting, highlights the standard reporting capability that is provided within ECM. The chapter also provides an overview of the reports available through the implementation of SAP Business Warehouse (BW).

Chapter 14, Lessons Learned, reviews lessons learned from previous ECM implementations. The chapter is divided into four sections, including general lessons learned, compensation process, change management, and system implementation.

Chapter 15, Resources, reviews helpful resources for your ECM implementation, including where to find answers to common problems either online or the SAP network.

1.3   Product Releases

Although many of the concepts and configuration elements apply to all versions of ECM, this book is based on the latest version of SAP ERP. (At the time of this book's writing, the latest version of SAP ERP 6.0 is with enhancement package 4). Although customers using ECM can benefit from the contents of this book, because the core functionality has not fundamentally changed from its original version (available from 4.7 Enterprise, Extension Set 2.0).

1.4   Summary

This book serves as a comprehensive guide for understanding and implementing SAP ERP HCM ECM functionality. The book highlights important compensation process constructs, key implementation components, and provides Best Practices for implementation. We hope you enjoy the book.

Compensation administration enables managers, Human Resources (HR) professionals, and Compensation professionals to quickly and effectively complete the compensation process using self-service applications. The evolution of compensation administration practices has enabled companies to better position and execute their pay-for-performance strategies while reducing the cost of administering compensation recommendations. This chapter explores the administration and application of compensation processes during the annual cycle and while off cycle as well.

2 Compensation Management Overview

In this chapter, we will provide a high-level overview of the processes within compensation management. Compensation management represents one of the most critical parts of the HR function today, because employee retention and recruitment strategies are closely aligned to a company's compensation offerings. Although some may call it cliché, a sound pay-for-performance philosophy still makes a profound impact within any organization — especially in more competitive industries. The work done within the Compensation department provides the competitive advantage for companies willing to apply policies and pay that are fair and commensurate with experience and performance.

To ensure the company's pay practices are equitable and consistent, most companies adopt and administer an annual process to allow Compensation and management to evaluate and adjust employees' pay. We will first discuss the annual compensation process (e.g., your annual merit and bonus programs) in detail and then delve into year-round events such as off-cycle increases. The annual compensation process is the most visible to managers and HR professionals, because it typically affects the largest employee population. The manager's role within the overall process will be highlighted, because the manager is becoming more integral to its successful application.

2.1 Compensation Planning Overview

Compensation planning is an integrated process that ties many processes together, allowing managers, HR professionals, and compensation professionals to effectively execute the compensation strategy while adhering to defined policies. A complete compensation solution can facilitate the administration of fixed pay, variable pay, and long-term incentives, but to effectively administer these plans, the solution has to bridge together performance management, salary benchmarking, and payroll processing, which we will discuss later.

Definitions of fixed pay, variable pay, and long-term incentives are listed in Table 2.1, along with a short description and examples.

Compensation Element	Description	Examples
Fixed Pay	Represents the periodic (e.g., weekly, bi-weekly, semimonthly, monthly) form of payment from an employer to the employee.	Salary, Base Salary, Base Pay/Base Rate, and Lump Sum Payment.
Variable Pay (also called Short-term Incentives)	Represents compensation usually tied to employee or company performance measured against pre-defined targets.	Bonuses, Profit Sharing, Deferred Compensation, or Commissions.
Long-term Incentives	Represents compensation usually tied to long-term company performance, typically, over a three year period or more.	Stock Options, such as Nonqualified Stock Options and Incentive Stock Options. Restricted Stock, such as Stock Appreciation Rights (SARS), Phantom Stock Plans, or Performance-based Plans.

Table 2.1 Definition of Compensation Elements Fixed Pay, Variable Pay, and Long-term Incentives

These three types of compensation provide a "total compensation" picture for employees within the company. Your company may not use all three types — perhaps only one or two. And although companies typically deliver some form of fixed pay to its employees, short-term and long-term incentives are subject to the compensation practices within each company. Typically, these practices mirror industry trends in an effort to remain competitive, particularly the use of variable pay and long-term incentives, which have proven effective instruments in attracting and retaining employees.

Your annual compensation process may or may not include all of these compensation components. Although base pay is typically discretionary in nature, variable pay and long-term incentives can be partly or fully formulaic (and nondiscretionary) based on company or department achievement against achievement targets. If there are discretionary components to the design of these plans, then the compensation planning process may include them. Today, manager discretion is frequently used to administer variable pay and long-term incentives in addition to department or company metrics.

In Figure 2.1 you can see the high-level compensation planning process typically administered on an annual basis. Salary benchmarking against market data — typically performed in the fall — marks the beginning of the cycle, because internal pay practices are married to external data from surveys. From this, guidelines and salary ranges are established, and budgets for compensation planning purposes are created and approved. Planning occurs with managers, HR, and Compensation involvement. Recommendations are adjusted and approved by senior leaders during the calibration process. Compensation results are communicated through online statements, and payments are issued via normal payroll processing.

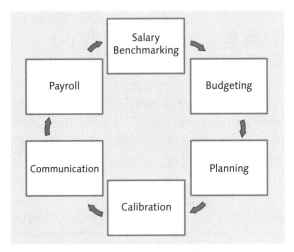

Figure 2.1 Processes within the Annual Compensation Cycle

Each process within the cycle has its own unique challenges and opportunities, so we will review each of them, beginning with the *salary benchmarking* process, to help you understand how they fit into the overall compensation planning cycle.

> **Note**
>
> Although most companies administer fixed pay annually, there are some companies that administer compensation based on a service anniversary or some other predefined date or event. In some cases, it is required by contract or by government mandate — as is the case with several European Union countries, including Italy, Spain, and Belgium.

2.2   Salary Benchmarking

Every company approaches salary benchmarking differently. It largely depends on the way your company has set up its pay structures and its overall pay philosophy. Salary benchmarking is also referred to as job pricing or market analysis, which is covered in Chapter 10, Job Pricing. The analysis inherent within the process ensures that employees are being paid fairly for the work they perform and the value they bring to the company.

The way it works is that certain key jobs within your company's job catalog are benchmarked against the prevailing market rate by qualitative measures such as job ranking, grading, and classification or by quantitative methods such as a point-factor comparison. The participation in salary surveys for these benchmark jobs allows vendors such as Mercer, Towers Perrin, and Watson Wyatt to conduct a thorough analysis by industry, company size, revenue size, etc. This "scope" data is paramount to understanding how employers with similar companies pay their employees competitively.

Survey results from these vendors enable the Compensation department to understand how other companies are paying for employees with the same skill sets. The process of salary benchmarking ends with updates being made to the pay structure. Although the process of salary benchmarking can be done at any time, it is typically completed annually (survey submission in the spring and survey/market analysis in the fall). Having said that, management can decide to request evaluations of specific jobs if retention is becoming an issue or if it has become increasingly difficult to recruit and hire for key positions. In this case, individual analysis can be performed at the job level regardless of results from an available survey.

Let's look at the process in finer detail.

2.2.1 Determining Which Jobs to Evaluate

The Compensation department starts the benchmarking process by selecting which jobs need to be evaluated and compared against market rates. These jobs usually represent key positions within the company and can even be correlated to positions that give the company a competitive advantage. Not all jobs will fall into this category, but you should benchmark as many jobs as possible to ensure that you are paying employees appropriately.

One factor you should consider when selecting which jobs to benchmark is the current market conditions and industry trends. It is critical in determining which jobs to evaluate and how to interpret the results. For example, if you are having difficulty attracting and retaining a specific skill set (let's say an IT Analysts to support your Supply Chain function), you should focus more attention on those jobs and the availability of resources in that area. You may also want to conduct those salary surveys more often or pay a higher salary than what is represented from the market data. When selecting jobs for evaluation, you should always consider the job being evaluated and not the employee or employees holding that job. This will provide a more unbiased evaluation.

2.2.2 Update and Extract Job Data

Once the jobs have been selected for evaluation, you should be sure that the job descriptions are updated to represent the current roles and responsibilities. And, because these benchmarked jobs set the value to the job (and not the employees that are currently doing the job), it is helpful to have a clear picture of the duties that must be performed by employees that hold that job through the use of clear job descriptions.

After your job descriptions have been updated, an extract of the jobs and their descriptions should be sent to the salary survey provider for any surveys your company wishes to participate in.

2.2.3 Selecting Providers for Survey Participation and Analysis

Your company can use one or more providers of salary survey data. Be sure to spend time evaluating the providers to ensure that they are reputable and use proven methods to gather and analyze compensation data. You want to use providers who cover the industry your company is in and who can provide data on enough jobs to be cost-effective. For example, a telecommunications company will want to select a provider that conducts surveys focused within the telecommunications industry, because the market data from these surveys will be relevant to their industry.

Compensation departments also like to limit the number of providers they use because it is easier to obtain survey data and keeps a finite number of contracts in place with the survey vendors. Selected providers will offer salary survey data they have collected based on your company's geography, industry, and size (i.e., what Compensation professionals refer to as "scope").

Depending on the date of the survey data, you may need to age the data from the effective date of the survey to the current date or a date in the future. This ensures that the data is always "fresh," despite the data being several months (even years) old. Once you have clean data, you can use it to develop your salary structure and budgets.

2.2.4 Updating Salary Structures and Developing the Budget

You can take the data from salary surveys and import it into Excel for further analysis or into a market job pricing tool, such as SAP's Job Pricing functionality. Once the data is reviewed, the compensation department can update pay structures. In some cases, they will have several jobs to update or create revised pay structures for. But before updating the pay structures from the market analysis there are several decisions you need to make:

- How many pay grades are needed in your salary structure?
- How do you want to apply your pay philosophy to the market reference salary?
- What should the distance between the grades be?
- How many pay grade levels do you want per grade?

▸ How wide should the levels be (i.e., should grades be "banded")?

Once your data is reviewed and compared to the current pay structures, your new pay structures can be updated to reflect any desired changes.

In addition to implementing new pay structure changes based on market data analysis, you need to perform the compensation *budgeting process* in preparation for the annual administration and planning process.

2.3   Budgeting

The budgeting process involves the analysis and preparation of budgets for all compensation components being planned. You need separate budgets for the fixed pay, variable pay, and long-term incentive elements of your compensation program. Budgets are typically not shared across components, because they are based on different measures and accrued based on a separate set of assumptions or timelines; however, within one element, you can associate one budget to multiple compensation vehicles. For example, if a merit increase is given as a lump sum, it would be deducted from the overall merit budget even though it has not been applied against the employee's base pay. (A lump-sum increase is a one-time payment given in lieu of — or in addition to — an increase to an employee's base pay/rate.)

Your budgeting can be implemented using a "top-down" or "bottom-up" approach. The available mechanics for applying these approaches within the SAP system are discussed in Chapter 4, Compensation Budgeting. For now, at a high level, the Compensation team delivers a set of budget percentages to apply to a predefined group or groups of employees sharing similar compensation practices. These budgets can be delivered based on geography, business function, or organizational structure (among others). For ease of administration, budgeting based on the organizational structure is typically the easiest to implement, because the roll-up by organization (i.e., reporting structure) makes the most sense to planning and approving managers. In highly matrixed organizations, administering and keeping to a budget proves more difficult because employees can be spread across the organization. So reporting on budgeting must be robust for managers, HR, and compensation professionals for there to be transparency throughout the planning process. Budgets should be reportable based on organizational structure roll-up, country roll-up, and function roll-up at a minimum.

After the budgeting process is complete, compensation planning can begin. So let's move on to *compensation planning* and the integral components for making it a powerful process for compensation administration.

2.4   Compensation Planning

At the start of every annual compensation cycle, compensation plans are reviewed and can be adjusted if design changes occur. Strategic changes within a plan or policy design, or changes due to government mandates will necessitate updates to the system to accommodate this new functionality.

Common updates include changes to plan eligibility and guidelines. You can expect the latter case to change each year, because guidelines fluctuate with the market conditions and individual performance scores. Eligibility, however, is typically steadier and only changes through a significant change in compensation strategy. For example, hourly union employees in the United States or tariff employees in Germany may not be eligible for discretionary merit increases because their base pay is predetermined based on agreed upon step progressions within their respective contracts. Or, as another example, sales employees may not be eligible for the typical annual corporate bonus plan because they are eligible for a distinct sales bonus plan that is commission based. Whether it's a change to your eligibility rules or an update to your plan guidelines, your system needs the necessary configuration to support these changes. Obviously, this must happen before the planning worksheet opens for managers. (Plan configuration and the technical components that support it are discussed in Chapter 3, Baseline Configuration and Infotypes.)

But let's first discuss *eligibility* in detail, because this is one of the primary drivers within compensation planning.

2.4.1 Eligibility

Eligibility allows you to determine which employees are permitted to participate in a compensation plan. Eligibility rules are established to provide the filtering mechanism needed for the system to distinguish who is eligible and who is not. These rules are based on specific criteria that the employee has to meet to be considered eligible.

For example, eligibility could be based on an employee type such as salaried versus hourly, permanent versus temporary, union versus nonunion, and executive versus nonexecutive. Eligibility could also include more specific employee attributes such as years of service, grade level, and hire date. As long as eligibility is equitable and nondiscriminatory, the company can establish whatever rules make sense for the organization.

From your compensation department perspective, it is critical to identify the employees who are eligible for the various compensation plans and to validate that the criterion used correctly captures the targeted employee population. The last thing any compensation department wants is to realize that a select group of employees has not been planned for due to some incorrect eligibility logic. So, during the testing phase of your project, you need to be sure that all test scenarios are validated by the compensation team to ensure all eligible employee groups are available within the compensation planning worksheet

From a manager's standpoint, only eligible employees are planned for on the SAP portal. Typically, online documentation and email communications assist managers in understanding which employee populations are eligible for which compensations plans and the reasoning behind each. So remember that managers need a clear picture of the eligibility rules for each compensation plan, because it will help them understand how the eligibility rules work, and empower them to deliver a consistent message about the compensation policies and strategies to all employees within the company.

> **Note**
>
> It is important from a change management perspective to clearly articulate the eligibility rules for each of your compensation plans to employees and managers. For example, managers who plan on the SAP portal and have access to the long-term incentive program may wonder why they are not eligible for the plan. This could cause some unwanted pushback from the group you are depending on for a smooth process. In these cases, proper change management is needed to ready the organization and its line management for this type of situation.
>
> The days of exclusive compensation plans for upper management are slowly coming to an end. With recent market trends (and with some "big" government intervention), compensation programs for senior management are being exposed, or at least, becoming more transparent to the rest of the organization.

In addition to eligibility, plan *guidelines* are subject to change based on policy decisions made from the Compensation team.

2.4.2 Guidelines

Guidelines provide managers with default recommendations during the planning process. Guidelines can take into consideration many factors including performance ratings, compa-ratio, and specific target achievements. Guidelines can be either a set percentage or amount, such as 3% or US $1,000, or a set range, such as 2% to 4% and US $500 to US $1,500. Guidelines can either be pre-populated within the worksheet, or available as a display to managers for decision support. Guidelines serve to accelerate the planning process for managers because they can provide their own recommendations while considering the suggestions. As with eligibility, your compensation department needs to review guideline configurations before every planning cycle opens to verify that they meet current plan requirements.

Typically, guidelines are set within a matrix. Two- or three-dimensional matrices can be established to suggest the guideline default based on some underlying employee information. Figure 2.2 shows one of the more typical two-dimensional matrices — Performance versus Quartile. In this example, the guidelines are percentage based and include a mix of minimum, maximum, and default values. An employee receiving an "Exceeds Expectations" rating on their performance appraisal and having a salary within the third quartile will have a guideline with a minimum of 4% and a maximum of 5%. An employee receiving a "Does Not Meet

Expectations" rating on their performance appraisal and having a salary within the same third quartile will have a default guideline of 0%. This doesn't mean that the manager cannot recommend an increase to salary. However, recommending a salary increase for an employee with low performance would need to be justified to management and the compensation team, because the pay-for-performance philosophy would be violated.

		Quartile					
		Below Minimum	1st Quartile	2nd Quartile	3rd Quartile	4th Quartile	Above Minimum
Performance Rating	Significantly Exceeds Expectations	10% - 12%	10% - 12%	8% - 10%	6% - 8%	4% - 6%	4%
	Exceeds Expectations	6% - 7%	6% - 7%	5% - 6%	4% - 5%	3% - 4%	3%
	Meets Expectations	4% - 5%	4% - 5%	3% - 4%	2% - 3%	2%	0%
	Does Not Meet Expectations	0%	0%	0%	0%	0%	0%

Figure 2.2 Example 2009 Guideline Matrix for an Asian Country: Performance Rating and Quartile

Another popular matrix is performance versus compa-ratio. Other guidelines could be based on seniority, grade level, or employee type. These types of factors are more typically found in variable pay or long-term incentive plans. A bonus plan, for example, could have guidelines based on job or employee grade level. A long-term incentive program could be based on adjusted service dates or span of control (department, division, business unit responsibility, etc.).

2.4.3 Proration

Although an employee may be eligible for a compensation plan, he may only be eligible for a portion of the time period for which the plan covers. Proration is used to apply these rules. Depending on how your Compensation group thinks of applying proration, proration can be applied against the guideline during planning time. Alternatively, managers may be asked to plan without thinking of proration, or proration can be applied after the fact manually or programmatically based on set rules.

As with eligibility and guidelines, your Compensation department needs to review proration rules before every planning cycle to verify that they meet the plan requirements. Changes in proration rules need to be communicated to managers and HR professionals so that they can answer questions asked by employees. The concept of proration is sometimes foreign to employees (and even to managers!), so it's important to educate those involved in the process on what proration is and why it exists.

After eligibility, guidelines, and proration rules have been established within the system, the compensation planning worksheet can be opened for managers and HR professionals, which we will discuss next.

2.4.4 Planning and Review

Compensation planning typically involves manager or HR professional assistance. As self-service delivery becomes more commonplace within the marketplace, more and more managers are planning for their direct reports via an online process. Spreadsheets are quickly being replaced with online functionality. HR professionals — such as HR business partners, HR mangers, and HR generalists — continue to support the process, but now in a more automated fashion. Planning, which is typically accessed within a portal environment, is now given to a variety of users including:

▸ Managers (including Executives);

▸ Proxies or Delegates for Managers;

▸ HR professionals, including HR Business Partners, HR Mangers, or HR Generalists; and

▸ Compensation Specialists.

For the successful delivery of compensation planning on the portal, the right level of support is needed from those driving the process to its completion. Managers who have questions about certain aspects of the planning process should be able to turn to their HR support and the compensation team in times of need. Due to the typical short planning window available for managers on the portal, it is absolutely crucial that the right amount of assistance is provided quickly so that all roadblocks can be removed. The typical portal planning process lasts 2 - 3 weeks for managers (with another few weeks available for HR and compensation staff), so timely responsiveness is critical for managers during this planning and review period.

The planning approval process itself can follow a more linear or more collaborative scenario, depending on the philosophy of your compensation group. In the more linear/sequential scenario, managers who plan online submit their recommendations for their direct reports to their manager. The "one-up" manager then reviews and either approves, rejects, or edits and approves the recommendations. All managers up the organization will follow a similar process, whereby they are reviewing recommendations that have been planned for and reviewed by all underlying managers. The approval process ensures that all managers up-the-chain are contributing to the process. You should be sure that any change to a recommendation from a higher-level manager is communicated to the affected managers below. All too often, planning managers are not aware of higher-level manager changes to employee recommendations and become blindsided during the delivery of the compensation statement later in the process.

Planning can also be performed in a looser, more collaborative format, whereby managers discuss their recommendations with other managers within the department and input recommendations without a set approval path. In this scenario, there is no real approval or rejection function, because recommendations have already been vetted and agreed upon at various levels of the organization through informal discussions. Although some organizations may find this unacceptable from a compliance perspective, the collaboration achieved and time-efficiencies earned make this option attractive.

After manager planning and higher-level manager review (in whatever scenario chosen), a *calibration* process is conducted after recommendations have been collected from line management.

2.5   Calibration

Most companies introduce calibration into their compensation management process using a variety of methods. Some companies delegate the process to each function, allowing managers to approve recommendations at each level and then have an HR review to ensure recommendations are in line with guidelines and within budget. Other organizations drive the calibration process across functions by having HR or the compensation department drive higher-level calibration to review high performers and key positions. Regardless of your implementation, it is a critical part of the process to ensure that compensation strategies and policies have been applied correctly and that budgets have been adhered to.

Before conducting calibration sessions, your compensation department will first need to generate reports for each department and roll up the totals either by function or by organization. These reports typically list all relevant compensation data needed to review and calibrate the recommendations. Some examples of important data for eligible employees include:

▸ Position and Organizational Information

▸ Current Base Salary/Rate

▸ Time in Position

▸ Performance Rating(s)

▸ Current and New Compa-ratio

▸ Current and New Quartile

▸ Recommendations

▸ Budget Data (Total and Spent)

▸ Guidelines

Once the reports have been generated and formatted, the compensation department sets up meetings with senior-level management and HR to review the proposed recommendations and budget roll-ups. During these meetings, employees are compared against their peers. Close attention is paid to high performers that represent a flight risk to the company.

Reports on the portal can also be used during this process but may become prohibitive depending on the size of the manager's span of control. Viewing and analyzing the planning data for a large section of the organization may not be possible due to slow performance on the portal. If data can be accessed quickly (for example, within a data warehouse), then calibration can include online reports and analysis. Otherwise, it's best to work within a familiar environment (e.g., Excel) and record changes quickly. Although this means rekeying the changes into the system at a later date, the real-time option may not be available to you.

2.5.1 Realizing Calibration Objectives

During the calibration meetings, the following objectives should be considered:

- Reviewing proposed recommendations to ensure that employees are being fairly compensated across the organization;
- Identifying recommendations that are outside of the proposed range allowed by the compensation guidelines;
- Determining if unused budgets can be reallocated to properly compensate high performers and employees with high flight risk;
- Reviewing merit increases that are targeted toward moving employees to the midpoint of the salary grade; and
- if applicable, reviewing promotions and other recommendations such as adjustments and lump-sum payments.

2.5.2 Revising Proposed Recommendations

Once calibration is complete, the Compensation department may need to make revisions to the recommendations in the system. Each update must be entered through the portal. This activity can be accomplished by redistributing the revised recommendations back to the managers and having the managers themselves input the changes into the system. If this approach is adopted, the Compensation department will often review the changes to ensure that they have been applied correctly. Depending on the number of changes, it might make more sense for the compensation department to apply the changes in the system themselves. If this approach is adopted, the compensation department is responsible for communicating the revisions to the managers of the affected employees.

Once you have conducted calibration and the recommendations have been adjusted where necessary, you need to update the *payroll* system, which we will discuss next.

2.6 Payroll

Once all recommendations are made active in the system, payroll is updated to reflect the new compensation, whether it be a salary increase, a bonus payment, or a stock or option grant. This process — known as "activation" within the SAP system — is discussed in detail in Chapter 5, Process Administration. Activation makes the approved recommendations "real" by creating the payroll-relevant records within the system.

Regardless of whether or not you use SAP Payroll, creating the necessary infotypes or files for payroll calculations is a crucial step in the process, because it will actualize the compensation recommendations and affect payroll processing.

But before the employee sees the new salary, bonus, etc., in their paycheck (or shares/options in their brokerage account), it's important to give managers enough time to communicate these changes directly to the employee.

2.7   Employee and Manager Review

Once the compensation administration process is completed and the proposed recommendations are approved and activated for payroll, your managers can begin to communicate the results to employees. This is an opportunity for managers to discuss and strengthen the company's pay-for-performance strategy. A face-to-face meeting between the manager and employee allows discussion over the employee's performance ratings and resulting compensation.

Managers prepare for this part of the process by printing out a compensation statement for each employee. The statement provides the formal communication to an employee detailing how the compensation was determined and applied. Explanations on the statement can include proration, guidelines, and specifics on promotions, or government-mandated increases. Your statements can also be branded with the company logo and offer some words of encouragement and thanks to the employee for their contributions to the company. Once this is done, your annual compensation process is complete. But there may be some processes to deal with in regard to *off-cycle increases*, so let's look at these next.

2.8   Off-Cycle Increases

In addition to the annual process, your compensation department should have ongoing work throughout the year to support employees and uphold the compensation principles of the organization thoughtfully, consistently, and fairly. In many instances, employees' salary or total compensation must be looked at again (outside of the annual process) to ensure that employees' are being paid fairly internally and competitively compared to your competitors.

Some examples of off-cycle increases include the following:

- Promotions
- Change in Position with Salary Change
- Change in Salary
- Adjustments (e.g., Market Adjustment)
- General Increases (e.g., Step Progressions)

> **Note**
>
> Although not as common, the compensation team also needs to manage any demotions or downgrades that occur due to employee issues or reduction in employee responsibilities. This type of compensation action deserves special attention because employees typically react negatively when they learn about a reduction in base salary. So the compensation department and HR should work together with the manager to ensure that the demotion/downgrade is communicated under the right context.

The approval process for off-cycle increases is typically handled through a formal routing procedure. In a standard scenario, a promotion or change in salary is administered through the portal form (or through a paper form offline). A set group of approvers is established based on predefined business rules. The approvers usually include the one-up manager (the employee's manager's manager) and HR or the Compensation department, depending on the transaction. The approval may need senior-level management approval if, for example, it involves a highly compensated employee or a member of the senior management or executive team.

There are a host of technologies to support this process, which is discussed in Chapter 8, Advanced Topics, including discussion on off-cycle increases and some ideas on how SAP customers commonly implement them.

2.9   Summary

In this chapter, we reviewed common annual compensation administration practices. We covered processes including salary benchmarking, budgeting, planning/

review, calibration, activation and, finally, employee communication. Having a solid knowledge of baseline compensation processes facilitates a more effective application of SAP functionality available within ECM.

We also explored administering and applying off-cycle increases throughout the year, because it is the compensation department's duty to ensure that employees are paid equitably throughout the entire year (and not just during annual planning time). There are occasions when employees' pay must be examined and adjusted to ensure fairness in compensation practices across the organization.

In the next chapter, we will discuss the basics of SAP ERP HCM ECM functionality from a more technical perspective. We will focus on the core components of the module including compensation plans, compensation reviews, and compensation review items.

Enterprise Compensation Management (ECM) functionality provides a robust framework on which to administer global compensation programs. The technology supporting this framework allows for a level of extensibility necessary to deliver innovative solutions for global corporations. In this chapter, we discuss the baseline ECM solution, including configuration and infotypes.

3   Baseline Configuration and Infotypes

The functionality within ECM allows customers to configure solutions to meet their specific business requirements. Several infotypes — including Infotype 0758 (Compensation Program), 0759 (Compensation Progress), 0760 (Compensation Eligibility Override), and 0761 (Long-term Incentive Granting) — form the backbone of the compensation functionality. Along with a solid and highly extensible configuration framework, SAP also provides Business Add-Ins (BAdIs) throughout the functionality to supplement the configuration where necessary. (BAdIs are discussed in detail in Chapter 7, Business Add-Ins).

In this chapter, we will review the standard configuration and infotypes necessary to deliver and support a robust compensation solution using ECM. We will first cover the framework components such as compensation areas, compensation plans, compensation reviews, and compensation review items to understand the baseline of the core functionality. We will then cover important topics such as eligibility, guidelines, and proration, and specific LTI plan components including vesting, exercising, and life events.

3.1   Building Blocks

This section addresses the basic constructs and core configuration included in the ECM solution. The compensation area, compensation plan, compensation review, and compensation review items are described in context to give you a better appreciation for how they support the functionality. Before we discuss the building blocks, however, let's first look at how to activate ECM.

3.1.1 ECM Activation

ECM must be activated within the system before you can utilize the functionality. This is important if you are a current customer using Compensation Management (application component PA-CM) and if you are implementing any compensation functionality in SAP for the first time. By activating ECM the transactions, infotypes, and transactions within ECM become available.

wrong should be EC

The activation switch for ECM is configured within the Implementation Guide (IMG) under the following path: PERSONNEL MANAGEMENT • ENTERPRISE COMPENSATION MANAGEMENT • GLOBAL SETTINGS • ACTIVATE ENTERPRISE COMPENSATION MANAGEMENT. You can also access the table directly with Transaction SM30 by viewing Table T77S0, Group HRECM, and Semantic Abbreviation ECMON. Figure 3.1 shows this configuration.

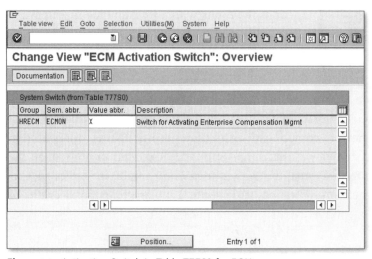

Figure 3.1 Activation Switch in Table T77S0 for ECM

In the standard system, the entry is blank. You need to provide the X entry to activate the functionality.

Now let's review compensation areas and their use within ECM.

3.1.2 Compensation Area

The *compensation area* is a key configuration element that groups together employees who have similar compensation attributes such as eligibility and guidelines. The compensation area is typically set along geographic lines, but can also be configured to support alternate configurations including by business unit and functional area. If configured by geography, the two-digit country International Organization for Standardization (ISO) code is commonly used to group employees. Usually, this is better than using SAP's country grouping (entity MOLGA), because sometimes country grouping is not granular enough to support the nuances for entities within all country groupings. A good example is Puerto Rico, which may have separate and distinct compensation practices to the United States. Although employees in the United States and Puerto Rico are under the same country grouping (MOLGA=10), compensation areas US and PR could be defined to differentiate them.

It is important to note that employees can be assigned to more than one compensation area at the same time. For example, an employee could be assigned to compensation area WW (Worldwide) and compensation area US (United States). You might want this if you have a compensation program that is global (e.g., bonus), but need to have another way to categorize employees by country/geography for another program (e.g., merit). The time constraint on the infotype is 2 (Record May Include Gaps with No Overlaps) meaning that multiple records can be created and saved on the same employee over the same period of time.

Compensation areas are used throughout ECM, and are found in Infotypes 0758, 0759, and 0760. Figure 3.2 shows the compensation area in the first position on the screen for Infotype 0758. Compensation area — along with the first and second compensation program groupings — defines the macro-eligibility of an employee for compensation plan purposes. Eligibility is covered later in this chapter.

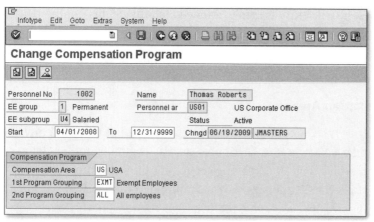

Figure 3.2 Infotype 0758 (Compensation Program)

Compensation areas are configured within the IMG under the following path: PERSONNEL MANAGEMENT • ENTERPRISE COMPENSATION MANAGEMENT • COMPENSATION ADMINISTRATION • DEFINE COMPENSATION AREAS. You can also access the table directly in Transaction SM30 from Table view V_T71ADM01. Figure 3.3 shows this configuration with three entries: DE (for Germany), US (for the United States), and WW (for Worldwide).

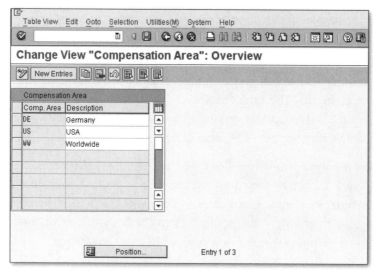

Figure 3.3 Configuration of Compensation Areas

Compensation areas default to Infotype 0758 based on Feature CARGP. Within this feature, you can make a decision on any of the following fields: Country Grouping (MOLGA), Company Code (BUKRS), Personnel Area (WERKS), Employee Group (PERSG), Employee Subgroup (PERSK), Personnel Subarea (BTRTL), Organizational Unit (ORGEH), Work Contract (ANSVH), Job (STELL), Region (State, Province, County (REGIO)), Planned Compensation Type (CPIND), Pay Scale Type (TRFAR), Pay Scale Area (TRFGB), ES grouping for collective agreement provision (TRFKZ), Pay Scale Group (TRFGR), Pay Scale Level (TRFST), Compensation Area (CAREA), First Compensation Program Grouping (CPGR1), and Second Compensation Program Grouping (CPGR2).

Figure 3.4 shows an example of configuration for Feature CARGP. The feature for compensation areas defaulting is configured within the IMG under the following path: PERSONNEL MANAGEMENT • ENTERPRISE COMPENSATION MANAGEMENT • COMPENSATION ADMINISTRATION • DEFINE COMPENSATION AREA FEATURE. You can also access the feature directly with Transaction PE03.

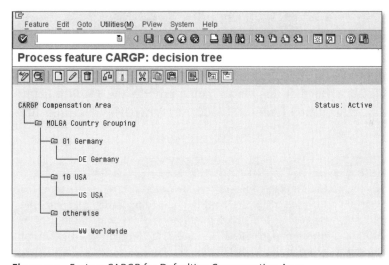

Figure 3.4 Feature CARGP for Defaulting Compensation Area

Now let's look at more of the building blocks within ECM, beginning with the compensation plan.

3.1.3 Compensation Plan

A *compensation plan* is a key entity within ECM that links guidelines, eligibility rules, and activation logic together. Each compensation plan is assigned one compensation category that dictates which infotype record should be updated or created when the compensation process is completed and the recommendations are activated. The available compensation categories are listed in Table 3.1 with the infotypes updated/created and common examples of how they are used.

Compensation Category	Compensation Category	Infotypes Updated or Created During Activation	Example Plan
1	Salary Adjustment	0008 (Basic Pay)	Merit
2	Regular Bonus	0015 (One-time Payments)	Bonus
3	Off-cycle Bonus	0267 (Off-cycle One-time Payments	Spot Bonus
4	LTI Grant	0761	Stock

Table 3.1 Compensation Categories

Only one category can be defined for a compensation plan. If multiple infotypes need to be updated or created during the activation process, the BAdI for Activation can be used. The Activation BAdI HRECM00_ACTIVATION is discussed more in Chapter 7.

> **Note**
>
> The four-character compensation plan code impacts the order of tabs on the compensation planning worksheet. If three plans are used during compensation planning, the order (from left to right) is dictated by this alphanumeric code of the compensation plan. For example, a naming convention of 1MER, 2BNS, and 3EQY would make the tabs of the worksheet ordered (left to right) as Merit, Bonus, and Equity.

Compensation plans are configured within the IMG under the following path: PERSONNEL MANAGEMENT • ENTERPRISE COMPENSATION MANAGEMENT • COMPENSATION ADMINISTRATION • COMPENSATION PLANS AND REVIEWS • DEFINE COMPENSATION PLANS. You can also access the table directly with Transaction SM30 from

Table view V_T71ADM02. Figure 3.5 shows the compensation plan code, text, and linked compensation category.

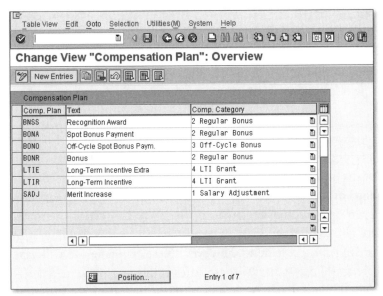

Figure 3.5 Configuration of Compensation Plans with Compensation Category

Compensation plans are important as well because eligibility, guidelines, and rounding rules are all tied together within the configuration. Wage types (including the calculation base) are also identified within each plan in the configuration, which we will discuss in detail later in the chapter.

For now we'll discuss the compensation review.

3.1.4 Compensation Review

The *compensation review* groups compensation plans together for planning during a set time period. You can think of a compensation review as an "umbrella" for compensation plans. On the portal, managers plan on the compensation planning worksheet based on the available compensation reviews, which is a concept created to support the online compensation planning process.

The compensation review is comprised of a review period and a selection period. A *review period* is the period in which planning managers can plan and submit recommendations using Manager Self-Service (MSS) (compensation planning iView). If not specified, no restrictions apply and the compensation review dropdown (on the planning iView) is always available to managers. For example, a review period for an annual review may begin on January 18 and end a few weeks later, say on February 12, of a given year. Typically, manager planning lasts 2 - 3 weeks, but this depends on your compensation practices. Additional weeks may be needed for compensation and (HR) to follow up and calibrate. If done on the portal, this review window would need to be lengthened to support these calibration activities.

The *selection period* is the period in which the system retrieves the set of objects (organizational units, positions, and employees) for compensation planning on the portal. If you enter the same date in both the start and end fields, the selection of employees is made as of that key date. If both dates are left blank, you must indicate that the review is an "anytime" review using the Anytime Review checkbox. (This is common for any compensation items requiring year-long availability, such as spot bonus awards.) For most reviews, however, the selection period will have a *begin* and *end* date specified. Typically, these dates coincide — in some way — with your review period. This depends on your business requirements, including whether or not you decide to implement a "freeze" period. If a freeze is established for your planning, the selection start date should coincide with the start date of your freeze. If you decide not to implement a freeze, the start date for the selection period can be any date in the future (perhaps a day after the compensation planning worksheet closes, i.e., the day after the review period end date).

The preceding guidelines are for your reference only. You should thoroughly test the configuration performed in these activities. The catch here is that some of this testing is dependent on the actual system date. You need to be creative on how you test this because your system date will never mimic the date of planning (until actual production time)! This could mean that you use different dates to test during your formal project testing and then have to change your configuration ahead of deployment once you have completed testing.

Compensation reviews are configured within the IMG under the following path: PERSONNEL MANAGEMENT • ENTERPRISE COMPENSATION MANAGEMENT • COMPENSATION ADMINISTRATION • COMPENSATION PLANS AND REVIEWS • DEFINE COMPENSATION REVIEWS. You can also access the table directly with Transaction SM30 from

Table view V_T71ADM08. Figure 3.6 shows the compensation review with the Anytime Review checkbox, the review period, and the selection period.

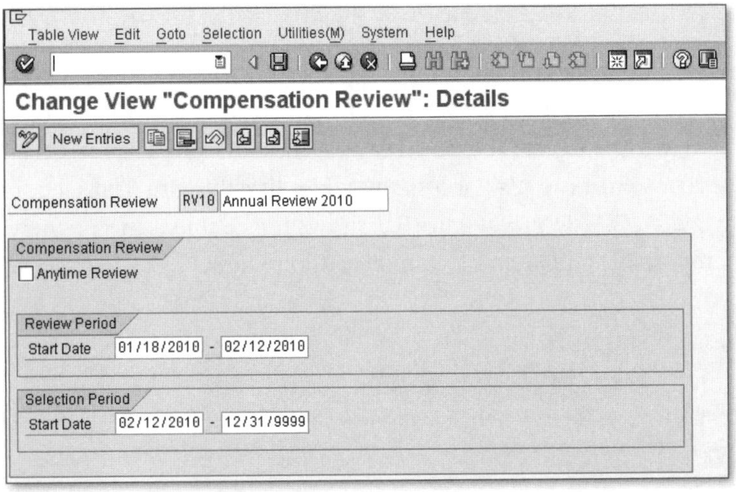

Figure 3.6 Configuration of Compensation Review

Due to the time-relevant data stored within a compensation review, compensation review configuration must be performed each year as part of the annual compensation configuration checklist. Another yearly checklist activity is the configuration of compensation review items, which are discussed next.

3.1.5 Compensation Review Item

The *compensation review item* is one of the most significant pieces of data within all of ECM. The compensation review item — which is formulated by a unique combination of a compensation plan and compensation review — is also the subtype that is recorded on an employee's Infotype 0759 record. The compensation review item is what most professionals regard as the "recommendation" (which then becomes the applied merit adjustment, bonus payment, or LTI grant after approval and activation). In addition, the compensation review item is compensation area–dependent, which provides a lot of flexibility when defining its attributes.

You must associate a compensation review item with a compensation plan and a compensation review. You cannot associate two different compensation review items with the same plan and the same review. You also cannot associate two different compensation review items to the same plan but different reviews. The combination of plan and review cannot be used for more than one review item. The system has controls to check this and prevents you from saving any configuration otherwise.

Compensation review items are configured within the IMG under the following path: Personnel Management • Enterprise Compensation Management • Compensation Administration • Compensation Plans and Reviews • Define Compensation Review Items. You can also access the table directly with Transaction SM30 from Table view V_T71ADM09. Figure 3.7 shows the compensation review item linked to a compensation plan and a compensation review.

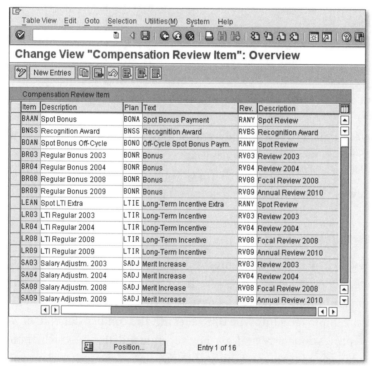

Figure 3.7 Configuration of Compensation Review Items

The attributes of compensation review items drive much of the compensation functionality including eligibility, guidelines, effective dates, budgeting, activation, and much more. The attributes of compensation review items are configured within the IMG under the following path: Personnel Management • Enterprise

COMPENSATION MANAGEMENT • COMPENSATION ADMINISTRATION • COMPENSATION PLANS AND REVIEWS • ASSIGN COMPENSATION REVIEW ITEM ATTRIBUTES. You can also access the table directly with Transaction SM30 from Table view V_T71ADM10. Figure 3.8 shows the compensation review item with all of its attributes.

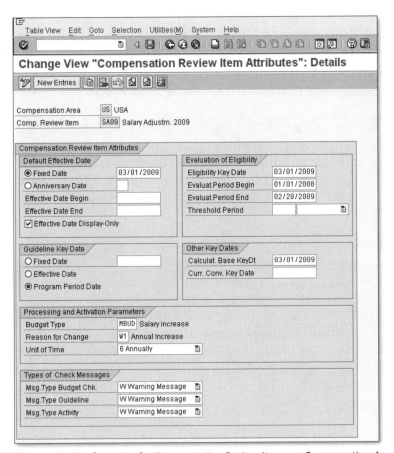

Figure 3.8 Configuration for Compensation Review Item per Compensation Area

The compensation review item drives the default effective date of the compensation element. You can influence the effective date of the Infotype 0759 record based on the configuration in this table. The effective date can either be based on a fixed date or an anniversary date. If the default effective date is based on an employee's anniversary date, the effective date period begin and end dates are required. The system checks whether Infotype 0041 (Date Specifications) contains a record with the specified date type as of the period begin date. If not available, the period begin date is used as the default effective date, otherwise the earliest anniversary date within the effective date period is used. If, however, the effective date period does not include any anniversary dates, the default effective date is used instead.

In addition, if the Effective Date is Display-Only checkbox is selected the effective date cannot be edited on the planning worksheet. This prevents portal users from changing the effective date at the individual level. Except for anytime awards such as a spot bonus, you typically configure this field to be display only.

> **Note**
>
> The effective date is only defaulted into Infotype 0759 when using the portal planning worksheet. For those creating or updating Infotype 0759 directly via Transaction PA30 on the employee record, no defaulting is performed. You must be very careful when creating records in the backend due to this fact because eligibility and guidelines may be impacted based on the effective date actually used.

The logic for effective date defaulting for compensation review items can be overridden based on the Effective Date BAdI, HRECM00_EFFDATE. Chapter 7, BAdIs, describes this functionality in more detail.

Eligibility is also defined at the compensation review item level. Within the Evaluation of Eligibility section, the following parameters are available:

- Eligibility Key Date
- Evaluation Period Begin
- Evaluation Period End
- Threshold Period

An Eligibility Key Date is required for all plans except the anytime reviews. The Evaluation Period Begin, Evaluation Period End, and Threshold Period are all optional. If the Evaluation Period Begin and Evaluation Period End are left empty, the evaluation period is the Eligibility Key Date. If the Eligibility Key Date is set to 01/01/2010 for the 2010 salary review, employees hired after this date would be excluded from the review. You can also set an evaluation period using the Evaluation Period Begin and Evaluation Period End dates. The Threshold Period specifies the required minimum length of the program period for an employee to be eligible. If this field is populated, the system checks whether the longest consecutive assignment is at least as long as the threshold period specified. If the field is left empty, an employee is eligible as soon as he belongs to a compensation program containing the plan for at least one day during the evaluation period. That evaluation period can either be from the Evaluation Period Begin to the Evaluation Period End or simply based on the Eligibility Key Date.

Guidelines are also defined within the compensation review item attributes. The guideline key date can be defined based on one of three choices:

▶ Fixed Date

▶ Effective Date

▶ Program Period Date

If the key date for guideline evaluation should be based on a fixed date, the Fixed Date radio button should be checked and the appropriate date should be input. You cannot save this option without specifying an explicit date.

With the Effective Date option, the guideline is evaluated based on the effective date of the compensation review item. If this is selected, no date can be input into the Fixed Date field.

Finally, the guideline can be evaluated based on the Program Period Date. In this case the guideline is evaluated for each program period interval separately, then prorated and aggregated. The end date of the program period interval is used as a key date for guidelines.

There are two other important dates configured against the compensation review. The Calculation Base Key Date provides the date for evaluating the calculation basis for an employee. If left blank, the system uses the effective date of the compensation review item. If more complex logic is needed for the calculation basis or calculation base key date, BAdI HRECM00_CALCBASE (Calculation Base) can be used.

The other important date is the date of currency conversion. The Currency Conversion Key Date specifies the key date for any currency conversions occurring during the compensation process. The currency conversion uses standard Table TCURR (Currency Exchange Rates) maintained within the Treasury component. The standard conversion type M is used for conversion purposes within ECM.

More information on currency and exchange rates can be found in Chapter 12, Global Considerations.

In the Processing and Activation Parameters section, the budget type, reason for change, and time unit are specified. From a budgeting perspective, adding the appropriate budget type at this compensation review item links the budgeting piece into the solution. If left blank, the compensation review item will not reference any budget during or after planning occurs.

A reason for change can be specified on the compensation review item. This configuration is optional, but, if specified, a reason for change is created during the activation process for Infotypes 0008, 0015, and 0267. For LTI plans, a reason for change is not available (as this field does not exist on Infotype 0761).

The Unit of Time is vitally important to all non-LTI processes because it defines the time unit used as reference for the calculation base salary and period-based salary adjustments. This is the time unit that Infotype 0759 uses to calculate the calculation basis. In merit plans for the United States, for example, this value is typically defined as annually, because most managers and employees think of compensation in terms of annual salary. In Europe and other places, a monthly time unit for merit might make more sense because managers and employees think of compensation more in terms of monthly pay.

The time unit recorded in this field impacts the activation process as well. For example, an hourly time unit indicates that a merit adjustment is against an hourly wage. The activation routine uses this information as it updates Infotype 0008.

> **Note**
>
> Through a series of enhancements, hourly wage earners can be planned against an annual salary. If you decide to enhance this, there are a few considerations including budgeting and rounding. With respect to budgeting, you must ensure that the enhancement does not adversely affect the initialization and maintenance of the budget. For rounding, the precision of an adjustment may become compromised when annualizing (during the formation of the calculation basis) and de-annualizing (during activation). Both impacts should be discussed with the Compensation team to mitigate risk and provide the best solution possible.

The last piece of the compensation review item attributes concerns messaging on the portal. The following check messages are available:

▸ Message Type for Budget Check — Indicates that the manager has exceeded the allocation of one or more of his budget units.

▸ Message Type for Guideline — Indicates that the manager has specified an amount that is below or above the minimum and maximum amounts set in the guidelines.

▸ Message Type for Activity — Indicates that the manager is trying to plan for an employee who is inactive on the effective date of the compensation process.

In all three checks, you can either specify a hard error (Error Message), a soft warning (Warning Message), or no alert at all (No Message). A hard error prevents the manager from saving and submitting the recommendation while the soft warning renders a message but does not prevent further processing.

If additional messages need to be incorporated into the planning worksheet, the BAdI HRECM00_CONSISTENCY (Define Additional Check Criteria) can be used to define customer-specific consistency checks. These checks can be used to generate error messages based on your specific business requirements. See Chapter 7 for more on this BAdI.

Now that we've seen how important the compensation review item is, let's turn our attention to eligibility and how it is defined in the system.

3.2 Eligibility

Eligibility within ECM is defined on two levels: macro- and micro-eligibility. Macro-eligibility refers to the high-level criteria an employee needs to fulfill to participate in a compensation plan. An employee is macro-eligible for a compensation plan if the plan is part of his compensation program for at least one day of the evaluation period (see Section 3.1.5, Compensation Review Item, Figure 3.8). Micro-eligibility is at a finer level, which considers eligibility variants, eligibility groupings, and appraisal rules. Eligibility variants are linked to compensation plans later in the configuration.

Let's discuss macro-eligibility. To do this, we must first discuss a compensation program.

3.2.1 Compensation Program

A *compensation program* is a set of compensation plans assigned to a combination of first and second compensation program groupings within a particular compensation area. Each macro-eligible employee must have a valid Infotype 0758 on their personnel record (refer back to Figure 3.2 for a screenshot of this infotype).

The compensation program is composed of three elements:

► Compensation Area

► First Compensation Program Grouping

► Second Compensation Program Grouping

Note

Infotype 0758 is similar in look and functionality to Infotype 0171 (General Benefits Information). Both infotypes have similar concepts of an "area" and first and second program groupings. Although the infotype infrastructure is similar, there is no integration between the two.

The *first compensation program grouping* is a four-character code that describes a logical employee grouping. Some example entries are:

► Executives

► Exempt Employees

► Others

► Workers

First program groupings are configured within the IMG under the path: PERSONNEL MANAGEMENT • ENTERPRISE COMPENSATION MANAGEMENT • COMPENSATION ADMINISTRATION • COMPENSATION PROGRAMS • DEFINE FIRST COMPENSATION PROGRAM GROUPINGS. You can also access the table directly with Transaction SM30 from Table view V_T71ADM05. Figure 3.9 shows the list of first compensation program groupings.

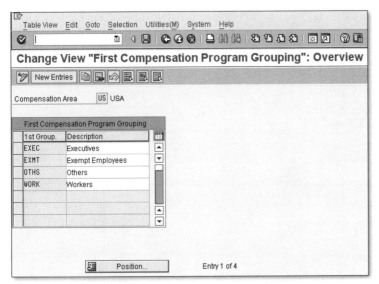

Figure 3.9 Configuration for First Compensation Program Grouping

Defaulting for the first compensation program grouping on Infotype 0758 is achieved via Feature CP1GP. Within this feature, you can make a decision on any of the following fields: Country Grouping (MOLGA), Company Code (BUKRS), Personnel Area (WERKS), Employee Group (PERSG), Employee Subgroup (PERSK), Personnel Subarea (BTRTL), Organizational Unit (ORGEH), Work Contract (ANSVH), Job (STELL), Region (State, Province, County (REGIO)), Planned Compensation Type (CPIND), Pay Scale Type (TRFAR), Pay Scale Area (TRFGB), ES Grouping for Collective Agreement Provision (TRFKZ), Pay Scale Group (TRFGR), Pay Scale Level (TRFST), Compensation Area (CAREA), First Compensation Program Grouping (CPGR1), and Second Compensation Program Grouping (CPGR2).

Figure 3.10 shows an example of the configuration for Feature CP1GP. This feature is configured within the IMG under the following path: PERSONNEL MANAGEMENT • ENTERPRISE COMPENSATION MANAGEMENT • COMPENSATION ADMINISTRATION • COMPENSATION PROGRAMS • DEFINE FIRST COMPENSATION PROGRAM GROUPING FEATURE. You can also access the feature directly with Transaction PE03.

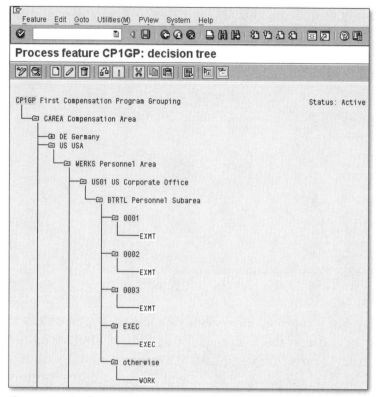

Figure 3.10 Configuration for Feature CP1GP (First Compensation Program Grouping)

Most decisions are based on employee group, employee subgroup, personnel area, and personnel subarea. In cases where the standard feature cannot determine the default grouping, you can implement BAdI HRECM00_CP1GP (Determine First Compensation Program Grouping). If you do implement this BAdI, the logic will fully replace the feature configuration.

The *second compensation program grouping* is similar to the first compensation program grouping. If no further breakdown is needed for your employee population, you can simply use a generic term such as ALL (All Employees) as a catch-all grouping for all employees. Because the second compensation program grouping is a required field in Infotype 0758, you must provide a value for all employees.

Like the first compensation program grouping, the second compensation program grouping is a four-character code that describes a logical employee grouping. Some example entries are:

- Salaried
- Hourly
- Full-time
- Part-time

Second program groupings are configured within the IMG under the path: Personnel Management • Enterprise Compensation Management • Compensation Administration • Compensation Programs • Define Second Compensation Program Groupings. You can also access the table directly with Transaction SM30 from Table view V_T71ADM06. Figure 3.11 shows the list of second compensation program groupings.

Figure 3.11 Configuration for Second Compensation Program Grouping

Defaulting for the second compensation program grouping in Infotype 0758 is achieved via Feature CP2GP. Within this feature, you can make a decision on any of the following fields: Country Grouping (MOLGA), Company Code (BUKRS), Personnel Area (WERKS), Employee Group (PERSG), Employee Subgroup (PERSK), Personnel Subarea (BTRTL), Organizational Unit (ORGEH), Work Contract (ANSVH), Job (STELL), Region (State, Province, County (REGIO)), Planned Compensation Type (CPIND), Pay Scale Type (TRFAR), Pay Scale Area (TRFGB), ES Grouping for

Collective Agreement Provision (TRFKZ), Pay Scale Group (TRFGR), Pay Scale Level (TRFST), Compensation Area (CAREA), First Compensation Program Grouping (CPGR1), and Second Compensation Program Grouping (CPGR2).

Figure 3.12 shows an example of the configuration for Feature CP2GP. This feature is configured within the IMG under the following path: PERSONNEL MANAGEMENT • ENTERPRISE COMPENSATION MANAGEMENT • COMPENSATION ADMINISTRATION • COMPENSATION PROGRAMS • DEFINE SECOND COMPENSATION PROGRAM GROUPING FEATURE. You can also access the feature directly with Transaction PE03.

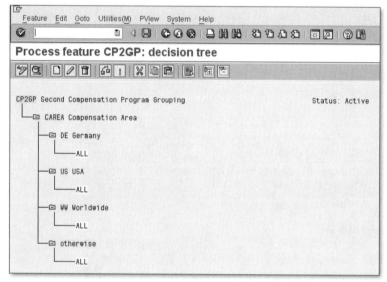

Figure 3.12 Configuration for Feature CP2GP (Second Compensation Program Grouping)

Most decisions are based on employee group, employee subgroup, personnel area, and personnel subarea. In cases where the standard feature cannot determine the default grouping, you can implement BAdI HRECM00_CP2GP (Determine Second Compensation Program Grouping). If you do implement this BAdI, the logic will fully replace the feature configuration.

The compensation area and compensation program groupings come together in Infotype 0758. This is where the macro-eligibility is stored for an employee. The configuration to support the macro-eligibility is performed within the IMG path: PERSONNEL MANAGEMENT • ENTERPRISE COMPENSATION MANAGEMENT • COMPENSATION ADMINISTRATION • COMPENSATION PROGRAMS • DEFINE COMPENSATION PRO-

GRAMS. You can also access the table directly with Transaction SM30 from Table view V_T71ADM07. Figure 3.13 shows a list of compensation plans eligible for a particular compensation program (for those employees who have Infotype 0758 with compensation area set to U.S., first compensation program grouping set to EXMT (Exempt Employees), and first compensation program grouping set to ALL (All Employees) within the time period for that compensation plan).

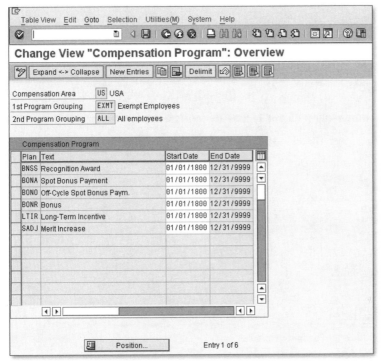

Figure 3.13 Configuration for Compensation Program

That wraps up macro-eligibility, so let's turn to micro-eligibility. With micro-eligibility, variants, groupings, and rules must be established.

3.2.2 Eligibility Variant

An *eligibility variant* — sometimes called an eligibility rule variant — enables you to define different rules according to employee groups (known as eligibility groupings) and then apply those rules to a compensation plan.

At a minimum, you will most likely have a variant for each compensation plan. For example, your bonus and merit plans might each have their own variant. These variants are important (along with the eligibility groupings) to provide robust flexibility in defining complex eligibility logic against your compensation plans.

Eligibility variants are configured within the IMG under the path: PERSONNEL MANAGEMENT • ENTERPRISE COMPENSATION MANAGEMENT • COMPENSATION ADMINISTRATION • ELIGIBILITY • DEFINE ELIGIBILITY RULE VARIANTS. You can also access the table directly with Transaction SM30 from Table view V_T71ADM11. Figure 3.14 shows a list of eligibility variants.

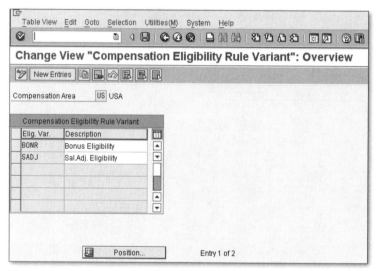

Figure 3.14 Configuration for Eligibility Variants

Now let's discuss eligibility groupings, which are used — in combination with eligibility variants — to define micro-level eligibility.

3.2.3 Eligibility Grouping

An *eligibility grouping* is a set of employees with common characteristics, grouped together to determine whether or not they are eligible for a particular compensation plan.

Eligibility groupings are configured within the IMG under the path: PERSONNEL MANAGEMENT • ENTERPRISE COMPENSATION MANAGEMENT • COMPENSATION ADMIN-

ISTRATION • ELIGIBILITY • DEFINE ELIGIBILITY GROUPINGS. You can also access the table directly with Transaction SM30 from Table view V_T71ADM12. Figure 3.15 shows a list of eligibility groupings.

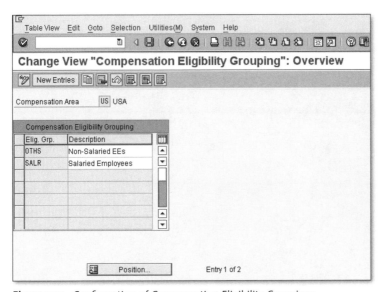

Figure 3.15 Configuration of Compensation Eligibility Groupings

Some examples of eligibility groupings include:

▶ Executives

▶ Salaried

▶ Hourly

▶ Contractors

Eligibility groupings are determined throughout the compensation processes at runtime for eligibility determination based on Feature CELGP (Compensation Eligibility Grouping). This feature is configured within the IMG under the path: PERSONNEL MANAGEMENT • ENTERPRISE COMPENSATION MANAGEMENT • COMPENSATION ADMINISTRATION • ELIGIBILITY • DEFINE ELIGIBILITY GROUPING FEATURE. You can also access the feature directly with Transaction PE03, and Figure 3.16 shows the configuration for Feature CELGP.

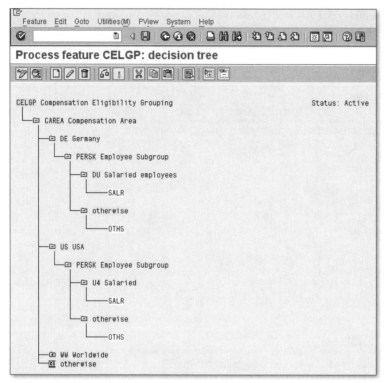

Figure 3.16 Configuration for Feature CELGP

Within this feature, you can make a decision on any of the following fields: Country Grouping (MOLGA), Company Code (BUKRS), Personnel Area (WERKS), Employee Group (PERSG), Employee Subgroup (PERSK), Personnel Subarea (BTRTL), Organizational Unit (ORGEH), Work Contract (ANSVH), Job (STELL), Region (State, Province, County (REGIO)), Planned Compensation Type (CPIND), Pay Scale Type (TRFAR), Pay Scale Area (TRFGB), ES Grouping for Collective Agreement Provision (TRFKZ), Pay Scale Group (TRFGR), Pay Scale Level (TRFST), Compensation Area (CAREA), First Compensation Program Grouping (CPGR1), and Second Compensation Program Grouping (CPGR2). Beginning in SAP ERP 6.0, Enhancement Package 3, Compensation Plan (CPLAN) is also available.

In cases where the standard feature cannot determine the default eligibility grouping, you can implement BAdI HRECM00_ELIGP (Determine Eligibility Grouping).

Using the export parameter PROCESS_STANDARD allows you to process logic using the standard feature for any criteria you do not wish to use your BAdI logic for.

3.2.4 Appraisal Rule

Appraisal rules allow you to specify whether or not the existence of an appraisal (or a minimum or maximum rating from one) impacts an employee's eligibility for a compensation plan.

Appraisal rules are configured within the IMG path: PERSONNEL MANAGEMENT • ENTERPRISE COMPENSATION MANAGEMENT • COMPENSATION ADMINISTRATION • ELIGIBILITY • DEFINE APPRAISAL RULES. You can also access the table directly with Transaction SM30 from Table view V_T71ADM14.

Figure 3.17 shows an example appraisal rule. In this example, appraisal rule ZMRT (Merit Appraisal Rule) is configured within a minimum appraisal result of 1.000. This means that any employee who has an appraisal rating lower than 1.000 is considered ineligible for this compensation plan.

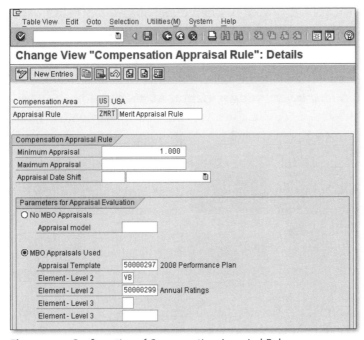

Figure 3.17 Configuration of Compensation Appraisal Rule

The appraisal rule can be integrated with either the old performance management functionality (using appraisal models) or the new performance management functionality (using MbO appraisals). In our example, appraisal template ID 50000297 (2008 Performance Plan) is referenced from the new performance management component. In this setup, the appraisal rating is retrieved via the VB element (or criteria group) 50000299 (Annual Ratings) using the FAPP (Final Appraisal) column.

You can also set the key date for the appraisal evaluation earlier. The Appraisal Date Shift is the key date for eligibility checks based on the original eligibility key date minus the period specified. If left blank, the key date for eligibility checks is used as normal.

Now let's discuss eligibility rules, which are the culmination of micro-eligibility.

3.2.5   Eligibility Rules

Eligibility rules specify micro-eligibility criteria based on a combination of compensation area, eligibility variant, and eligibility grouping. These micro-eligibility checks can be established based on your business requirements. SAP delivers several common criteria that can comprise an overall eligibility rule.

Figure 3.18 shows a screenshot of eligibility rules configuration. Eligibility rules are configured within the IMG under the path: PERSONNEL MANAGEMENT • ENTERPRISE COMPENSATION MANAGEMENT • COMPENSATION ADMINISTRATION • ELIGIBILITY • DEFINE ELIGIBILITY RULES. You can also access the table directly with Transaction SM30 from Table view V_T71ADM13.

The following criteria are available for micro-eligibility within the eligibility rule:

▸ **Minimum Service** — Defines the minimum service needed before an employee can be eligible. If the Calculation Process field is not specified, the Seniority Calculation method SENI is used.

▸ **Salary** — Defines the minimum percentage in range, maximum percentage in range, minimum compa-ratio, and maximum compa-ratio an employee needs before he can be eligible.

▸ **Minimum Working Hours** — Defines the minimum number of working hours an employee needs before he can be eligible.

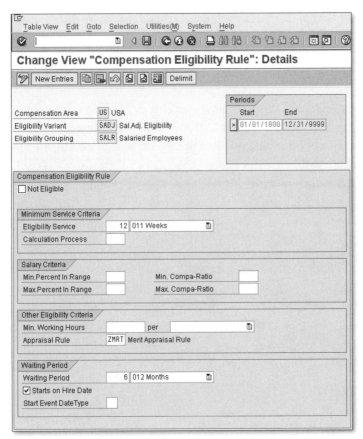

Figure 3.18 Configuration for Compensation Eligibility Rule

- **Appraisal Rule** — Defines the specific appraisal rule used to determine if an employee is eligible.

- **Waiting Period** — Defines the waiting period before an employee can be eligible. The Starts on Hire Date checkbox should be selected if you want the waiting period to start as of the employee's hire date. However, if you want to use a customer-specific date, you can use the Start Event Date Type checkbox. If this indicator is set (and the waiting period is blank), the employee only has to be hired to be eligible.

In the event that the preceding criteria do not satisfy your business requirements, BAdI HRECM00_ELIGIBILITY (Determine Eligibility) can be used to determine further micro-eligibility based on customer-specific criteria. For more information on this BAdI, see Chapter 7.

3.2.6 Eligibility Override

Eligibility can also be overridden at the employee level at any time in the planning process using Infotype 0760 (see Figure 3.19). An employee ordinarily eligible for a compensation plan can be made ineligible or vice versa. If made eligible, an employee can be made eligible for the entire time span of the infotype record, unless the Eligibility Date is populated. In this case, eligibility commences as of this date instead of the begin date of the infotype record.

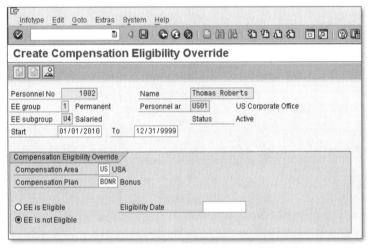

Figure 3.19 Compensation Eligibility Override Infotype (0760)

Now that we have covered eligibility from a macro- and micro- perspective, let's discuss guidelines.

3.3   Guidelines

Guidelines allow you to provide default, minimum, or maximum amounts; percentages; or numbers for recommendations based on configured criteria. Guidelines can be based on a wide variety of elements including performance ratings, compa-ratio, and position in range. The standard configuration can permit up to three of these "dimensions." Most companies base guidelines only off one or two dimensions — two of the most popular guidelines are performance ratings and compa-ratio.

As with eligibility, guidelines have variants and groupings with features and BAdIs to support them. Let's review guideline variants first.

3.3.1   Guideline Variant

A *guideline variant* — sometimes called a guideline rule variant — enables you to define different guideline rules according to employee groups (known as guideline groupings) and then apply those rules to a compensation plan.

As with eligibility, at a minimum you will most likely have a variant for each compensation plan. For example, your bonus plan and merit plan might each have their own variant. These variants are important (along with the guideline groupings) to provide robust flexibility in defining complex guidelines for your compensation plans.

Guideline variants are configured within the IMG under the path: PERSONNEL MANAGEMENT • ENTERPRISE COMPENSATION MANAGEMENT • COMPENSATION ADMINISTRATION • GUIDELINES • DEFINE GUIDELINE VARIANTS. You can also access the table directly with Transaction SM30 from Table view V_T71ADM15. Figure 3.20 shows a list of guideline variants.

Now let's look at guideline groupings, which are used — in combination with guidelines variants — to define guidelines for eligible employees.

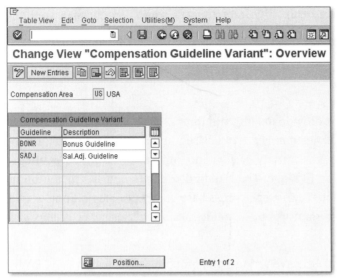

Figure 3.20 Configuration for Guideline Variants

3.3.2 Guideline Grouping

A *guideline grouping* is a set of employees with common characteristics, grouped together to administer guideline rules for a particular compensation plan.

Guideline groupings are configured within the IMG under the path: Personnel Management • Enterprise Compensation Management • Compensation Administration • Guidelines • Define Guideline Groupings. You can also access the table directly with Transaction SM30 from Table view V_T71ADM16. Figure 3.21 shows a list of guideline groupings.

Some examples of guideline groupings include:

- Executives
- Salaried
- Hourly
- Expatriates

Guideline groupings are determined throughout the compensation processes at runtime for guideline determination based on Feature CGDGP. This feature is configured within the IMG under the path: Personnel Management • Enterprise

COMPENSATION MANAGEMENT • COMPENSATION ADMINISTRATION • GUIDELINES • DEFINE GUIDELINE GROUPING FEATURE. You can also access the feature directly with Transaction PE03. Figure 3.22 shows a list of guideline groupings based on Feature CGDCP.

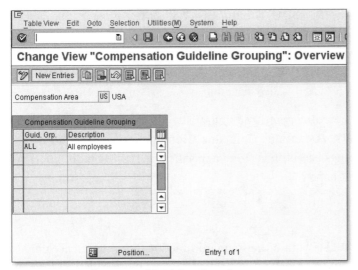

Figure 3.21 Configuration of Guideline Groupings

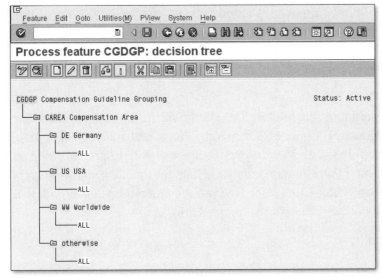

Figure 3.22 Configuration of Compensation Guideline Feature (CGDCP)

Within this feature, you can make decisions on any of the following fields: Country Grouping (MOLGA), Company Code (BUKRS), Personnel Area (WERKS), Employee Group (PERSG), Employee Subgroup (PERSK), Personnel Subarea (BTRTL), Organizational Unit (ORGEH), Work Contract (ANSVH), Job (STELL), Region (State, Province, County (REGIO)), Planned Compensation Type (CPIND), Pay Scale Type (TRFAR), Pay Scale Area (TRFGB), ES Grouping for Collective Agreement Provision (TRFKZ), Pay Scale Group (TRFGR), Pay Scale Level (TRFST), Compensation Area (CAREA), First Compensation Program Grouping (CPGR1), and Second Compensation Program Grouping (CPGR2). Beginning in SAP ERP 6.0, Enhancement Package 3, Compensation Plan (CPLAN) is also available.

In the event that the preceding criteria do not satisfy your business requirements, BAdI HRECM00_GDEGP (Determine Guideline Grouping) can be used to determine guideline groupings based on customer-specific criteria. For more information on this BAdI, see Chapter 7.

3.3.3 Proration

Proration rules are available within the standard functionality to influence guidelines. Standard proration in SAP affects guidelines — not the calculation basis or the recommendation entered by the manager. If your business requirements call for proration of the calculation base, you can use the BAdI HRECM00_CALCBASE (Calculation Base) for this purpose. If your business requirements call for proration of the recommendation entered by the manager, you need to make an enhancement to the compensation planning worksheet. (This scenario is not covered in this book, but you may want to seek consulting assistance if you have to implement it.)

For standard proration of guidelines, SAP allows you to prorate the guideline based on days or months. Figure 3.23 shows the Proration Based on Days option versus the Proration Based on Months option. If you choose to prorate based on months, you can enter the minimum number of days for rounding up the program period and the evaluation period, respectively. If the minimum number of days is not specified, the number of months is rounded down.

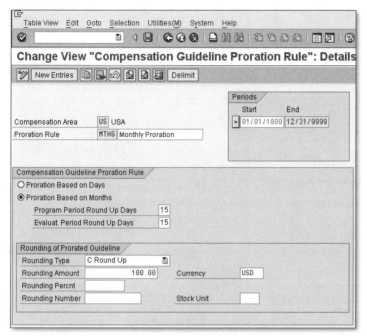

Figure 3.23 Configuration of the Guideline Proration Rule

If you want to round, you can specify a rule for rounding the prorated guideline amount, percentage, or number. You must specify either a currency (if you have opted for a guideline amount) or a stock unit (if you have opted for a guideline number).

Proration rules are configured within the IMG via: Personnel Management • Enterprise Compensation Management • Compensation Administration • Guidelines • Define Guideline Proration Rules. You can also access the table directly with Transaction SM30 from Table view V_T71ADM18.

For many customers, the standard proration configuration does not fully support their business requirements. If this is the case, BAdI HRECM00_GUIDELINE (Determine Guideline) can be used to prorate the guideline based on customer-specific needs. Method EVALUATE_GDL_CONTRIB within this BAdI is where proration of the standard guideline can be manipulated. Often, a custom table is built and referenced to support the calculation of the proration. For more information on this BAdI, see Chapter 7.

3.3.4 Guideline Matrix

A matrix is built within the configuration to support guidelines. Based on the number of dimensions needed to meet your requirements, your matrix will be one-, two-, or three-dimensional. The matrix can also support a guideline in the form of a percentage, number, or amount. This percentage, number or amount can be provided as default, minimum, or maximum.

A matrix dimension method is needed for each dimension. Figure 3.24 shows the standard matrix methods. Matrix dimension methods are configured within the IMG via: PERSONNEL MANAGEMENT • ENTERPRISE COMPENSATION MANAGEMENT • COMPENSATION ADMINISTRATION • GUIDELINES • MATRIX • DEFINE METHODS FOR MATRIX DIMENSIONS. You can also access the table directly with Transaction SM30 from Table view V_T71ADM21.

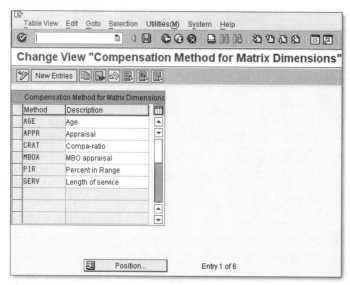

Figure 3.24 Configuration Method for Matrix Dimensions

Each of these methods become a filter for BAdI HRECM00_MATRIX_SEGM (Methods for Matrix Dimensions). This BAdI is vital for calculating guidelines because it contains the logic to retrieve the relevant data for evaluation. For example, standard implementation HRECM00_MATR_MBOAPPR (Matrix dimension method: MBO Appraisal) calls on standard function module HRHAP_PA_ECM_PERFOR-

MANCE_GET to retrieve the employee's appraisal rating from their appraisal stored in the new Performance Management component. Other implementations are available to retrieve data including compa-ratio, percent in range, age, and length of service. The available BAdI HRECM00_MATRIX_SEGM implementations can be found within the IMG under the path: Personnel Management • Enterprise Compensation Management • Compensation Administration • Guidelines • Matrix • Business Add-In: Methods for Matrix Dimensions. Figure 3.25 lists the standard implementations.

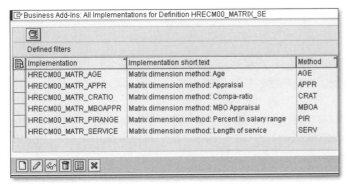

Figure 3.25 Available Standard Implementations for BAdI HRECM00_MATRIX_SEGM

For each method used within your guideline, you may need to define some required parameters. This depends on the method chosen. For example, the matrix dimension method for MbO appraisals needs to reference a specific appraisal template (VA), criteria group (VB), or criterion (VC) to know where to retrieve the rating from within the appraisal document.

Matrix dimensions are configured within the IMG via the path: Personnel Management • Enterprise Compensation Management • Compensation Administration • Guidelines • Matrix • Define Matrix Dimensions. You can also access the table directly with Transaction SM30 from Table view V_T71ADM20.

In Figure 3.26, matrix dimension ZRTG (Performance rating) uses matrix dimension method MBOA to return the appraisal result from method parameter VA50000730. This method parameter is specific to this dimension method because it requires an appraisal template, criteria group, or criterion. Other methods — such as compa-ratio — do not need parameters because they are predefined calculations.

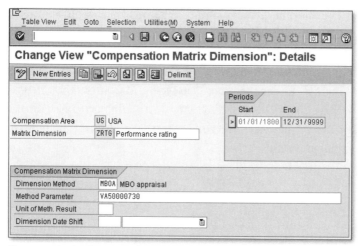

Figure 3.26 Configuration for Compensation Matrix Dimension Using Method MBOA

Once you have defined each of your matrix dimensions, you must configure the segments needed within the dimension. Figure 3.27 shows Matrix Dimension ZRTG with four segments:

▶ 0001 for FM — Fails to Meet

▶ 0002 for MM — Meets Mosts

▶ 0003 for MA — Meets All

▶ 0004 for RE — Regularly Exceeds

Each segment has a minimum and maximum result. The values depend on the dimension itself. You must include values from the full range of possible results. In the example, the appraisal result always returns a value of 1, 2, 3, or 4. If the employee's appraisal rating is a 3, then Segment 0003 (MA - Meets All) is used as the segment for this matrix dimension.

Matrix dimension segments are configured within the IMG under the path: PER-SONNEL MANAGEMENT • ENTERPRISE COMPENSATION MANAGEMENT • COMPENSATION ADMINISTRATION • GUIDELINES • MATRIX • DEFINE MATRIX DIMENSION SEGMENTS. You can also access the table directly with Transaction SM30 from Table view V_T71ADM22.

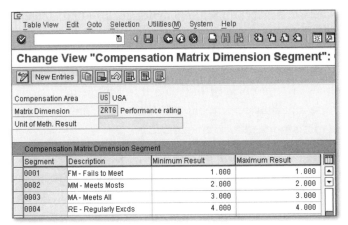

Figure 3.27 Configuration for Matrix Dimension Segments

Once you have defined all of your segments, you must define your guideline matrix. Figure 3.28 shows an example guideline matrix ZSAL with two dimensions — one for performance rating and one for compa-ratio.

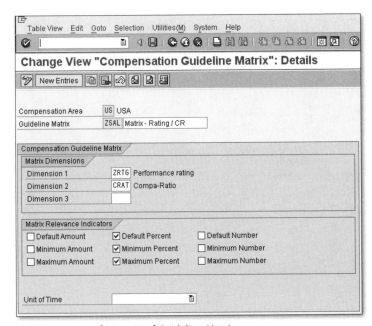

Figure 3.28 Configuration of Guideline Matrix

The guideline matrix is where you select up to three dimensions and the default, minimum, and maximum indicators for amount, percentage, and number guidelines. The number guideline can only be used for LTI plans. You can specify both amount and percent guidelines within the same matrix but this is not common. Typically, percent guidelines are the norm in the majority of implementations. Many companies simply use a default percent but others like to define an upper and lower limit using the minimum and maximum percent.

Guideline matrices are configured within the IMG via path: PERSONNEL MANAGEMENT • ENTERPRISE COMPENSATION MANAGEMENT • COMPENSATION ADMINISTRATION • GUIDELINES • MATRIX • DEFINE GUIDELINE MATRICES. You can also access the table directly with Transaction SM30 from Table view V_T71ADM19.

Once the matrix is defined, the values for the matrix must be populated with the actual guideline values. Figure 3.29 shows example guideline matrix ZSAL. This guideline matrix is a two-dimensional matrix with performance rating for Dimension 1 and compa-ratio for Dimension 2.

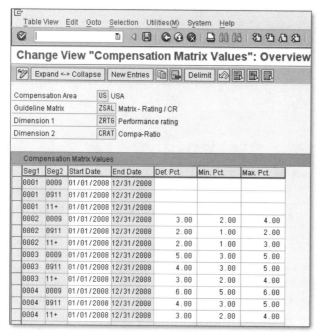

Figure 3.29 Configuration for Matrix Values

Because the matrix was previously indicated as being relevant for default, minimum, and maximum percentages, those columns are available for input only.

Guideline matrix values are configured via the IMG path: Personnel Management • Enterprise Compensation Management • Compensation Administration • Guidelines • Matrix • Assign Matrix Values. You can also access the table directly with Transaction SM30 from Table view V_T71ADM23.

In the previous example, an employee with Segment 0003 (MA - Meets All) for Dimension 1 and Segment 11+ (meaning he has a compa-ratio over 1.1) for Dimension 2 will have a default percent of 3%, a minimum of 2%, and a maximum of 4%.

> **Note**
>
> As of SAP ERP 6.0 enhancement package 4, you can perform mass adjustments to configuration values within a matrix, effective on a specified key date. This is particularly helpful for those guidelines that increment by a set percentage or amount each year.

Now that we have defined the matrix values, we can discuss the guideline rule and how the matrix configuration is linked to a compensation plan.

3.3.5   Guidelines

After defining the matrix dimensions, dimension segments, matrix (or matrices), and the values for each matrix, you can incorporate all of this into a guideline. The guideline is dependent on a combination of compensation area, guideline grouping, and guideline variant. Similar to eligibility rules, the guideline is the culmination of the configuration where it "all comes together."

Within each guideline, you can specify a guideline matrix and a proration rule. You can also define default amounts, percentages, and relevant numbers that can be applied without regard to a matrix. If you enter explicit guideline values here, the system will not accept a guideline matrix. If guidelines are needed, either a guideline matrix or the explicit configuration must be provided. If guidelines are not needed, both the guideline matrix and guideline values can be left blank. Figure 3.30 shows an example guideline with a guideline matrix and proration rule.

Guidelines are configured via the IMG path: Personnel Management • Enterprise Compensation Management • Compensation Administration • Guidelines • Define Guidelines. You can also access the table directly with Transaction SM30 from Table view V_T71ADM17.

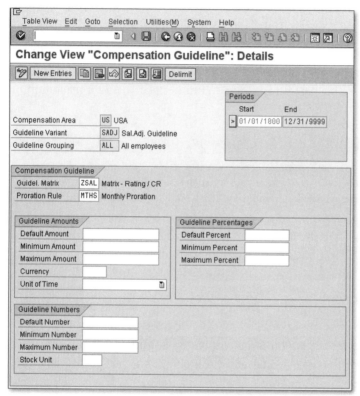

Figure 3.30 Configuration for Compensation Guidelines

In the event that the matrix and guideline configuration do not satisfy your business requirements, BAdI HRECM00_GUIDELINE (Determine Guideline) can be used to establish more complex guidelines based on customer-specific criteria. For more information on this BAdI, see Chapter 7.

Now let's turn back to compensation plans, where we can link the eligibility rules and guidelines to the plan.

3.4 Compensation Plan Attributes

Assigning compensation plan attributes — such as eligibility variants, guideline variants, and payroll data — is critical to the definition of compensation programs within ECM. In the following section, we cover the necessary plan-level attributes.

3.4.1 Plan Attributes

For each compensation plan, attributes such as eligibility variant, guideline variant, and rounding rule are specified. Both the eligibility and guideline variants are optional fields. For merit plans, a rounding rule can be established for both salaried and hourly employees. For bonus plans, only one general rounding rule can be applied. For LTI plans, rounding rules are not relevant. Each rounding rule can specify the rounding type as Round Down, Round Up/Down, or Round Up. The rounding amount is specified along with a reference currency. Beginning with SAP ERP 6.0 enhancement package 4, rounding formulas are available. Rounding formulas provide currency-dependent rounding rules. Using this new functionality, you can have rounding rules based on an employee's specific currency — even across the same compensation plan and compensation area.

In addition, a cost item from the Personnel Cost Planning (PCP) and Simulation component (PA-CP) can be specified against the compensation plan. This cost item is used within the employee data collection. For more information on integration with PCP and Simulation, see Chapter 11, Integration Components.

Compensation plan attributes are configured within the IMG under the path: PERSONNEL MANAGEMENT • ENTERPRISE COMPENSATION MANAGEMENT • COMPENSATION ADMINISTRATION • PLAN ATTRIBUTES • ASSIGN COMPENSATION PLAN ATTRIBUTES. You can also access the table directly with Transaction SM30 from Table view V_T71ADM03.

Figure 3.31 shows the example compensation plan SADJ (Merit Increase) with eligibility variant SADJ (Sal.Adj. Eligibility) and guideline variant SADJ (Sal.Adj. Guideline). The rounding rule for salaried employees is to round up to the nearest 10 units and for hourly employees is to round up to the nearest .01 unit.

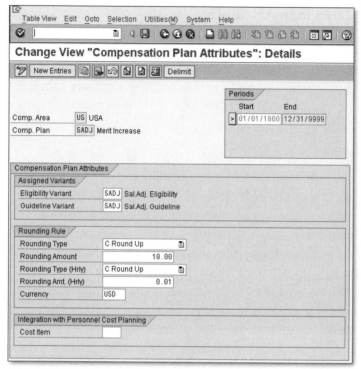

Figure 3.31 Configuration of Compensation Plan Attributes

Next, we'll look at the necessary payroll configurations at the compensation plan level.

3.4.2 Plan Payroll Data

Payroll data per country grouping and compensation area must be specified for each compensation plan. There are two main payroll-relevant wages: the compensation component wage and the calculation base wage.

Compensation plan payroll data are configured within the IMG under the path: PERSONNEL MANAGEMENT • ENTERPRISE COMPENSATION MANAGEMENT • COMPENSATION ADMINISTRATION • PLAN ATTRIBUTES • ASSIGN COMPENSATION PLAN PAYROLL DATA. You can also access the table directly with Transaction SM30 from Table view V_T71ADM04. Figure 3.32 shows an example configuration for a merit plan with compensation component wage as 9003 (Basic Pay) and the calculation base wage as CSAL (Compensation Management Salary).

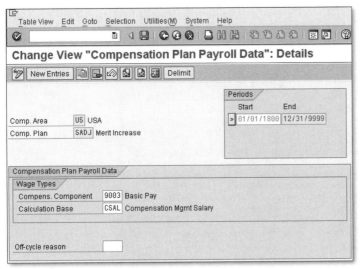

Figure 3.32 Configuration for Compensation Plan Payroll Data

The wage type for Compensation Component specifies which wage type is updated during the activation of the compensation process record (Infotype 0759). This field is optional for merit plans, required for bonus plans, and not relevant for LTI plans. If left blank for merit plans, the wage type in the first position on Infotype 0008 is updated. If more complex rules are needed, the BAdI HRECM00_ACTIVA-TION (Activation) can be used to enhance the activation logic. For more information on this BAdI, see Chapter 7, BAdIs.

For the calculation base, a valuation wage type should be specified. SAP provides standard-delivered wage type CSAL (Compensation Management Salary) as the default. For salaried employees, you typically assign a valuation wage type. The CSAL wage type is tied to one or more base wage types based on the wages identified within Table T539J. This valuation configuration is performed in Table view V_T539J. You can access this table via Transaction SM30. Figure 3.33 shows this table view with the list of valuation wage types including CSAL (Compensation Management Salary).

Although not common, the calculation base can be left blank. If no calculation base wage type is provided, the compensation can only be specified as a flat amount, not as a percentage. For hourly employees, no calculation base wage type is used by the system. The calculation base is calculated based on the sum of all wage types read from Infotype 0008.

Mod.	Valuated	Wage Type Lo	No	Start Date	End Date	Base WT	Wage Type Lo	Percen
ANSAL	ASAL	Annual salary	1	01/01/1800	12/31/9999	M001	Hourly Rate	100.0
ANSAL	ASAL	Annual salary	2	01/01/1800	12/31/9999	M002	Payscale Salary	100.0
ANSAL	ASAL	Annual salary	3	01/01/1800	12/31/9999	M003	Pay Period Sala	100.0
ANSAL	ASAL	Annual salary	4	01/01/1800	12/31/9999	M004	Pension/Retiree	100.0
ANSAL	ASAL	Annual salary	5	01/01/1800	12/31/9999	MF02	Pay Period Adj.	100.0
ANSAL	ASAL	Annual salary	6	01/01/1800	12/31/9999	MF04	Hourly Adj. Basi	100.0
ANSAL	ASAL	Annual salary	7	01/01/1800	12/31/9999	9003	Basic Pay	100.0
ANSAL	ASAL	Annual salary	8	01/01/1800	12/31/9999	9001	Hourly Pay	100.0
ANSAL	BSAL	Benefit-based s	1	01/01/1800	12/31/9999	M001	Hourly Rate	100.0
ANSAL	BSAL	Benefit-based s	2	01/01/1800	12/31/9999	M002	Payscale Salary	100.0
ANSAL	BSAL	Benefit-based s	3	01/01/1800	12/31/9999	M003	Pay Period Sala	100.0
ANSAL	BSAL	Benefit-based s	4	01/01/1800	12/31/9999	M004	Pension/Retiree	100.0
ANSAL	BSAL	Benefit-based s	5	01/01/1800	12/31/9999	9003	Basic Pay	100.0
ANSAL	CSAL	Compensation t	1	01/01/1900	12/31/9999	M001	Hourly Rate	100.0
ANSAL	CSAL	Compensation t	2	01/01/1900	12/31/9999	M002	Payscale Salary	100.0
ANSAL	CSAL	Compensation t	3	01/01/1900	12/31/9999	M003	Pay Period Sala	100.0
ANSAL	CSAL	Compensation t	4	01/01/1900	12/31/9999	9003	Basic Pay	100.0
ANSAL	CSAL	Compensation t	5	01/01/1900	12/31/9999	9001	Hourly Pay	100.0
ANSAL	NSAL	Annual salary (p	1	01/01/1800	12/31/9999	ASAL	Annual salary	100.0
ANSAL	NSAL	Annual salary (p	2	01/01/1800	12/31/9999	CHNG		100.0

Figure 3.33 Valuation Wage Type Definition Including CSAL

When the preceding configuration is complete, merit and bonus records can be created for eligible employees. Infotype 0759 stores the recommendations data collected during manager planning. Infotype 0759 can also be manually created by administrators using standard Transaction PA30. However, not all of the system controls are leveraged from the configuration using Transaction PA30. A good example of this is rounding. Rounding rules are automatically applied during manager planning on the portal, but need to be applied manually when using Transaction PA30 with the Round amount button. Figure 3.34 shows an example infotype record.

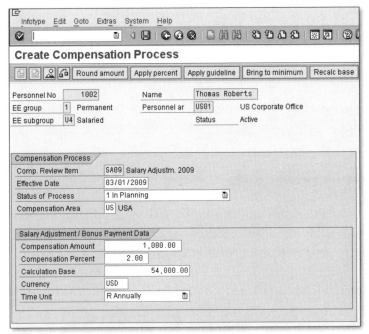

Figure 3.34 Infotype 0759 (Compensation Process)

Other functions within this infotype record include the following:

▶ **Apply percent** — calculates the Compensation Amount based on the percent entered in the Compensation Percent field

▶ **Apply guideline** — applies the guideline based on the configured guideline rules, taking into consideration proration rules

▶ **Bring to minimum** — raises an employee's salary to the minimum of his salary range if he is below minimum

▶ **Recalculate base** — recalculates the Calculation Base

> **Note**
>
> Clicking the Check button in 0759 performs a consistency check. Warning and error messages related to eligibility, guidelines, and salary range are checked.

Infotype 0759 represents the core planning infotype within ECM. It is also the basis for much of the security authorization because the compensation review item saved on this infotype is used within security profiles. (The compensation review item is also the subtype of this infotype.) For more information on security, see Chapter 9, Authorization Management.

The statuses on Infotype 0759 drive the process from beginning to end. The entire compensation process is covered in Chapter 5, Process Administration.

This concludes our discussion of compensation plans. Now let's turn our attention to the LTI functionality.

3.5   Long Term Incentives (LTIs)

Offering LTIs represents a significant investment for compensating your employees. Even if you are a publicly traded company, you may or may not have an established LTI plan for your employees. Some companies have LTI plans that are eligible for a relatively small group of employees and are tracked manually (in spreadsheets, for example) due to their sensitive nature.

> **Note**
>
> SAP's LTI functionality is based on stock units not currency value. Although not supported by SAP, some companies configure their LTI plan as a bonus plan as a workaround for this. By doing so, you can plan on currency value (whether that be dollars, Euros, pounds, etc.) as opposed to shares or options.
>
> In this chapter, we only cover the standard functionality of planning in stock units. If planning in currency value is something of interest to you, you may want to seek outside consulting assistance.

Most companies have a third-party stock administrator that manages the exercising of options, the storage of outstanding shares granted, and the financial reporting associated with stock plan accounting. This vendor works with your company to ensure grants, outstanding shares, and exercised options are kept current and within governmental laws and regulations.

So let's look at the various LTI-related elements needed for supporting LTI plans within SAP.

3.5.1 Stock Unit

A stock unit must be defined in the system to use the ECM functionality for LTI. Each stock unit is identified as a four-character field with an associated description. A security ID number — available from the SAP Treasury component — can be associated to the security (optionally). Figure 3.35 shows the stock unit CSTK (Company Stock) configured.

Stock units are configured within the IMG under the path: PERSONNEL MANAGEMENT • ENTERPRISE COMPENSATION MANAGEMENT • GLOBAL SETTINGS • STOCK UNITS • DEFINE STOCK UNITS. You can also access the table directly with Transaction SM30 from Table view V_T71LTI05.

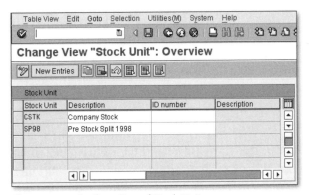

Figure 3.35 Configuration of Stock Units

Conversion of stock units — discussed more in Chapter 5 — provides a mechanism for identifying stock splits if they occur. In addition to specifying the stock unit being converted from and to, the split ratio must be identified. Rounding rules for stock conversion are also available. Stock unit conversion rules are configured within the IMG under the path: PERSONNEL MANAGEMENT • ENTERPRISE COMPENSATION MANAGEMENT • GLOBAL SETTINGS • STOCK UNITS • DEFINE STOCK UNIT CONVERSION RULES. You can also access the table directly with Transaction SM30 from Table view V_T71LTI06. Figure 3.36 shows a 3-to-1 stock split from stock unit SP98 to stock CSTK where no rounding rules have been specified.

Additional configuration including vesting, exercising, and life events are needed to set up LTI plans. Let's discuss vesting first.

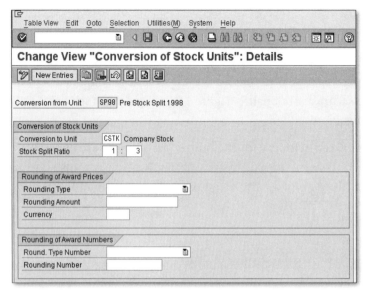

Figure 3.36 Configuration of Stock Unit Conversion

3.5.2 Vesting

Vesting refers to the period between the vesting date and the expiry date, when employees are allowed to exercise all or a portion of their options. Vesting rules are established in the system to represent different vesting arrangements. Vesting rules are configured within the IMG under the path: PERSONNEL MANAGEMENT • ENTERPRISE COMPENSATION MANAGEMENT • LONG-TERM INCENTIVE PLANS • VESTING • DEFINE VESTING RULES. You can also access the table directly with Transaction SM30 from Table view V_T71LTI07. Figure 3.37 shows vesting rules VE01 (Cliff vesting) and VE02 (Gradual vesting).

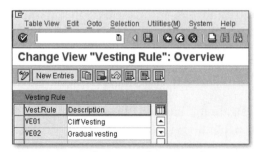

Figure 3.37 Configuration of Vesting Rules

Vesting schedules define when (and to what extent) employees can exercise their options. Vesting schedules are typically based on a cliff or gradual vesting arrangement. With cliff vesting, *all* granted options become available after reaching a given time period (let's say three years). With gradual vesting, a percentage of the award is available for exercise after a specific period of time until all options are vested.

Vesting schedules are configured within the IMG under the path: PERSONNEL MANAGEMENT • ENTERPRISE COMPENSATION MANAGEMENT • LONG-TERM INCENTIVE PLANS • VESTING • DEFINE VESTING SCHEDULES. You can also access the table directly with Transaction SM30 from Table view V_T71LTI08. Figure 3.38 shows vesting rule VE02 (Gradual vesting) with the breakdown of percentage by year (in 12-month intervals).

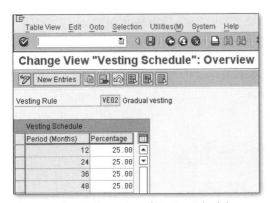

Figure 3.38 Configuration of Vesting Schedule

Next, let's look at exercise windows and exercise window rules.

3.5.3 Exercising

The exercise window rule lets you determine when employees can exercise their awards. You may need to send this information to your third-party stock administrator. Exercise window rules are configured within the IMG under the path: PERSONNEL MANAGEMENT • ENTERPRISE COMPENSATION MANAGEMENT • LONG-TERM INCENTIVE PLANS • EXERCISE WINDOW • DEFINE EXERCISE WINDOW RULES. You can also access the table directly with Transaction SM30 from Table view V_T71LTI09. Figure 3.39 shows Exercise Window Rule EX01 (Insider) as an example entry.

Figure 3.39 Configuration of Exercise Window Rules

Exercise windows define the time frame you allow your employees to exercise their awards in. Exercise windows are configured within the IMG under the path: PERSON-NEL MANAGEMENT • ENTERPRISE COMPENSATION MANAGEMENT • LONG-TERM INCENTIVE PLANS • EXERCISE WINDOW • DEFINE EXERCISE WINDOWS. You can also access the table directly with Transaction SM30 from Table view V_T71LTI10. Figure 3.40 shows Exercise Window EX01 (Insider) for employees who are considered insiders.

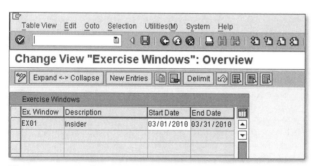

Figure 3.40 Configuration of Exercise Windows

3.5.4   LTI Plan Attributes

LTI plan attributes provide further definition of a compensation plan for LTIs. Each compensation plan identified as an LTI plan should have an entry in this table. The At Ex. indicator determines the exercise price per award on the exercise date (even though it is more common to set the exercise price as of the grant date). The Data

Evaluation Mode field specifies if (and how) the number of awards is sent during the transfer to the Accounting component. Available options include Per Personnel Number, Per Cost Center, Per Company Code, and No Data Evaluation. An exercise window can also be specified, if applicable.

LTI plan attributes are configured within the IMG under the path: Personnel Management • Enterprise Compensation Management • Long-Term Incentive Plans • LTI Plans • Assign LTI Plan Attributes. You can also access the table directly with Transaction SM30 from Table view V_T71LTI01. Figure 3.41 shows the plan attributes for two LTI plans, LTIE (Long-term Incentive Extra) and LTIR (Long-term Incentive).

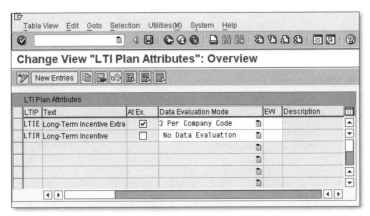

Figure 3.41 Configuration of LTI Plan Attributes

Time-dependent attributes determine the price of a security. The plan term defines the time between the grant date and the expiry date. A vesting rule is also (optionally) assigned to your LTI plan.

Within the stock information section, the pertinent stock unit is specified. If more than one stock unit is applicable (for example, due to a split), you must create a record for each stock unit. You can also specify the stock exchange and the price type of the security.

Time-dependent LTI attributes are configured within the IMG via path: Personnel Management • Enterprise Compensation Management • Long-Term Incentive Plans • LTI Plans • Assign Time-Dependent LTI Attributes. You can also access the table directly with Transaction SM30 from Table view V_T71LTI02. Figure 3.42 shows the time-dependent attributes for LTI plan LTIR (Long Term Incentive).

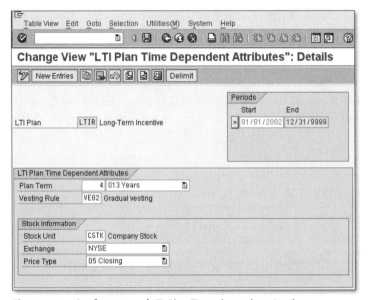

Figure 3.42 Configuration of LTI Plan Time-dependent Attributes

It is the stock unit specified here that drives the stock unit default in Infotype 0759. In the case of a stock split, the stock unit assigned to the compensation plan will change over time. Because the granting date of the employees processed during compensation planning can differ, the system must determine a unique stock unit to save against Infotype 0759. With BAdI HRECM00_STKUN (Determine Stock Unit for Compensation Review Item), you can define customer-specific logic to determine the reference stock unit of the award granted during the compensation planning process.

LTI plan pricing information allows you to default an exercise price for your plan. (The exercise price can also be overridden at the employee level on Infotype 0761.) LTI plan pricing information is configured within the IMG under the path: Person-nel Management • Enterprise Compensation Management • Long-Term Incentive Plans • LTI Plans • Set LTI Plan Pricing Information. You can also access the table directly with Transaction SM30 from Table view V_T71LTI03. Figure 3.43 shows the pricing information for LTI plan LTIR (Long-term Incentive).

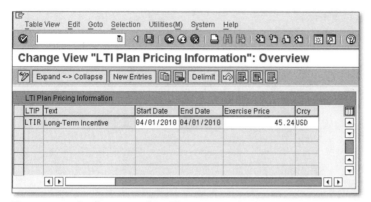

Figure 3.43 Configuration of LTI Plan Pricing Information

Payroll data for LTI plans are needed to store payroll-relevant attributes including wage types and an imputed income indicator. By setting the No Imputed Income indicator, SAP payroll (if used) will not calculate the imputed income associated with the security.

The following wage types are available in the standard system: Exercise Price LTI S (M550), Market Price Exercise (M554), Imputed Income LTI S (M551), and Withheld Amount (M557). The exercise price and the fair market value are for information purposes only, while the imputed income and the withheld amount are processed within the SAP payroll schema (if used). For more information on integration with payroll, see Chapter 11.

Finally, you can specify an LTI-specific off-cycle reason. This field can be recording against the employee's Infotype 0762 (LTI Exercising) for downstream payroll-processing logic.

LTI plan payroll data is configured within the IMG via path: PERSONNEL MANAGEMENT • ENTERPRISE COMPENSATION MANAGEMENT • LONG-TERM INCENTIVE PLANS • LTI PLANS • ASSIGN LTI PLAN PAYROLL DATA. You can also access the table directly with Transaction SM30 from Table view V_T71LTI04. Figure 3.44 shows the payroll data attributes for LTI plan LTIR (Long-term Incentive).

Next, we'll discuss life events in the context of LTI plans.

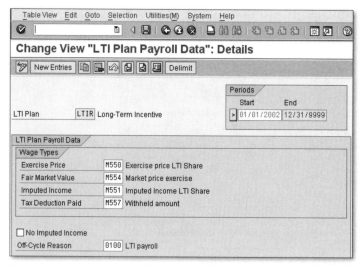

Figure 3.44 Configuration of LTI Plan Payroll Data

3.5.5 Life Events

Life events, such as marriage and termination, affect the administration of LTI plans and plan data — particularly with respect to the number of awards, the expiry date, and the manner in which vesting is handled.

Life events are configured within the IMG under the path: PERSONNEL MANAGEMENT • ENTERPRISE COMPENSATION MANAGEMENT • LONG-TERM INCENTIVE PLANS • LIFE EVENTS • DEFINE LIFE EVENTS. You can also access the table directly with Transaction SM30 from Table view V_T71LTI11. Figure 3.45 shows the example life events LE01 (Marriage) and LE02 (Employee termination).

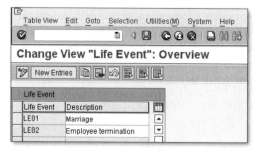

Figure 3.45 Configuration of Life Events for LTI Plans

Life event rules are established for handling vesting and forfeiture following an event. Each life event is configured per LTI plan with the appropriate defaults. Default values for life events are configured within the IMG under the path: PER-SONNEL MANAGEMENT • ENTERPRISE COMPENSATION MANAGEMENT • LONG-TERM INCENTIVE PLANS • LIFE EVENTS • SET DEFAULT VALUES FOR LIFE EVENTS. You can also access the table directly with Transaction SM30 from Table view V_T71LTI12. Figure 3.46 shows life event LE02 (Employee termination) defaults for LTI plan LTIR (Long-term Incentive).

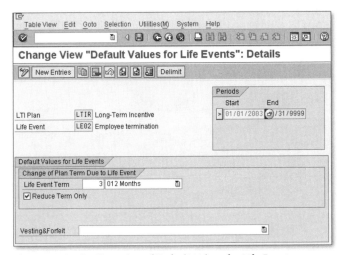

Figure 3.46 Configuration of Default Values for Life Events

In the Change of Plan Term Due to Life Event section, you can alter the expiry date of the grant based on your company's policy. You can also set the Reduce Term Only indicator to prevent the new term end date due to a life event from occurring later than the original term end date.

The available options for handling the vesting and forfeiture of awards include the following:

▶ **All remaining awards forfeit** — the system calculates the difference between granted and exercised awards and the result of the operation is forfeited.

▶ **All remaining unvested awards forfeit** — the system calculates the difference between granted and vested awards and the result of the operation is forfeited.

▶ **All remaining unvested awards vest immediately** — the remaining unvested awards vest.

3.6   LTI Infotypes

Once all LTI plan configuration is complete, LTI Infotypes 0761 (LTI Granting), 0762 (LTI Exercising), and 0763 (LTI Participant Data) can be used in conjunction with the compensation area, compensation plan, compensation review, and compensation review item configuration. Infotype 0759 is still used for LTI plans during compensation planning to record the number of awards granted for an employee. Infotype 0761 is created during an activation process, which is covered in detail in Chapter 5.

Figure 3.47 shows an Infotype 0761 record for an employee who has 500 awards under the LTI Plan Long-term Incentive. The grant date is 04/01/2010.

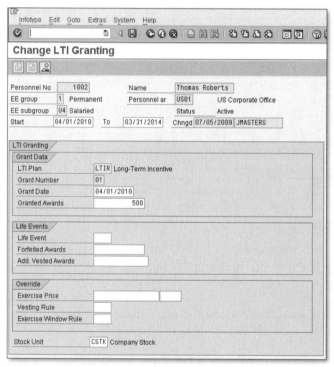

Figure 3.47   Infotype 0761 (LTI Granting)

If any life events are processed, the forfeited and additional vested awards are recorded as Life Events. These award amounts are updated by Transaction PECM_

PROCESS_EVENT (Process Event for LTI Plan Grants). The life event process is discussed further in Chapter 5.

Any override of exercise price, vesting rule, and exercise window rule at the employee level can also be specified on this infotype in the Override area.

The stock unit relevant to the grant is also stored on this record at the bottom of the screen.

Infotype 0762 is used to track exercised awards and sold shares. The data within this infotype is typically populated via an interface from your third-party stock plan administrator. Figure 3.48 shows an example Infotype 0762 record.

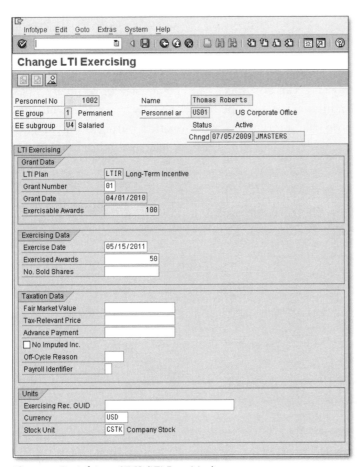

Figure 3.48 Infotype 0762 (LTI Exercising)

Each 0762 record containing exercised awards is tied back to the grant number (stored on Infotype 0761). The amount of exercisable awards is based on the grant date and the vesting rule for that LTI plan. In our example, 50 awards have been exercised by the employee, even though 100 are exercisable.

In addition to the exercising data (including exercise date, exercised awards, and number of sold shares), taxation data such as fair market value, tax-relevant price, and advance payment can be either populated by an interface or manually updated by an HR administrator. If you do not want SAP Payroll to generate an imputed income wage type during processes, select the No Imputed Inc. checkbox.

You can also specify an off-cycle reason. A payroll identifier is available if different off-cycle payroll runs are created on the same day.

The last specific infotype related to LTI we will discuss is Infotype 0763.

Infotype 0763 is used to specify whether or not an employee is an insider or a director of the company. You can also specify the percentage of company stock the employee owns (and thereby determine his voting power regardless of stock class). All information on this infotype is for information purposes only. Figure 3.49 shows this infotype with the Director checkbox selected, indicating that this employee is a director of the company.

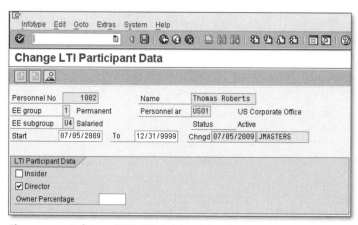

Figure 3.49 Infotype 0763 (LTI Paricipant Data)

This concludes our coverage of LTI plans and their configuration elements.

3.7 Summary

We reviewed the various parts of the ECM solution, including the important constructs and infotypes that drive the functionality. Building blocks such as compensation area, compensation plan, compensation review, and compensation review item are the foundation of the functionality. In addition, eligibility and guideline rules are established and linked to compensation plans to provide robust and extensible functionality.

We also looked at compensation from an LTI perspective. A review of the granting and exercising infotypes — and the configurations that support them — forms an essential part of the LTI functionality.

Next, we turn our focus to budgeting. Budgeting within compensation represents one of the most important concepts in any ECM implementation.

In today's economy, adhering to compensation budgets dictated by management has become especially important. Keeping to budgets for compensation matters is certainly easier said than done however, but by implementing the budgeting functionality available within SAP ERP HCM ECM you can achieve higher compliance. This chapter provides an overview of the budgeting functionality and how to use it. We will also explore some of the more popular budgeting topics including enhancements and Best Practices.

4 Compensation Budgeting

The topic of budgeting within ECM is one of the most important because compliance to a set budget is often mandated from a company's board or compensation committee. Adherence to budgets becomes a critical piece of financial viability for many companies, especially in harder economic times. This chapter provides a comprehensive review of the standard compensation budgeting functionality available in ECM. After providing an overview of the functionality, we will dive deep into the budgeting life cycle — the key steps from inception to closure — that are experienced when administering compensation management budgeting within the system. We will also explore some of the available enhancements for the functionality, and some Best Practices you can benefit from.

Let's start with an overview of what budgeting is and how it's used within ECM.

4.1 Budgeting Overview

Compensation budgeting functionality starts with a firm understanding of the organizational hierarchy in the Organizational Management (OM) component of SAP ERP HCM. This is because SAP manages compensation budgets based on *budget units* that form a hierarchy that directly mimics the organizational structure. The budget unit (object type BU) is an organizational management object that is created during the budgeting process. It is associated to an *organizational unit* via a standard OM relationship. The *budget hierarchy* itself (i.e., the roll-up of budget units) is formed based on the organizational structure. After creation, there is a one-to-one correlation between a budget unit and an organizational unit. Like organizational units, budget units report up to other budget units. This forms a hierarchy called the *budget structure*, which is why the official name for the budget unit object is actually *budget structure element*.

As with many concepts within OM, the concept of inheritance plays a key role in the functionality. Budget units contain and fund subordinate (lower-level) budget units. This way, budgets can be accounted for both from an individual and roll-up perspective. This makes reporting against these budget units more robust because a snapshot of a budget can be retrieved for the manager's own organizational unit and for that same manager's entire span of control (i.e., the manager's own organizational unit and all subordinate organizational units).

Budgets can be used to track both monetary funds and nonmonetary pools. Monetary budgets hold value and are currency dependent (e.g., dollars, Euros, etc.). Merit budgets, for example, would be considered a monetary budget because they are based on value (e.g., increases to base pay). A non–monetary budget, however, contains units and not value. Examples include restricted stock and stock options. Non–monetary budgets need to specify the relevant stock unit (i.e., stock ticker) applicable to the funding. However, only one stock type can be used within the budgets funding (i.e., you cannot mix options and shares together in one pool).

Each budget is tied to at least one compensation plan. Although two plans (such as a merit plan and lump-sum payment plan) can be tied to the same budget, typically there is a one-to-one mapping between a plan and a budget. The link is done at the compensation review item level on its attributes within the configuration. Linking budgets to compensation review items is explained in detail in Chapter 5, Process Administration.

The budgeting process itself can be represented in a sequential fashion, and can be implemented and managed in a systematized and methodical manner if the order of execution is known and prepped for. So let's discuss the budgeting life cycle and highlight the steps within the process in detail.

4.2   Life Cycle

The budgeting life cycle follows a four-step process from inception until closure. Managing your compensation budgeting process using the procedures specified within the life cycle will help arm your implementation team and compensation department with the knowledge needed to effectively complete the process. The four-step process includes the following steps:

▶ Preparation

▶ Initialization

▶ Maintenance

▶ Closure

Figure 4.1 shows the budgeting life cycle within SAP ERP HCM ECM.

Figure 4.1   Budgeting Life Cycle within SAP ERP HCM ECM

Let's discuss each step in this process beginning with the *preparation* step.

4.2.1   Preparation

Budget preparation involves the creation of the initial budget structure based on the organizational hierarchy. Before preparing the budget, an up-to-date organizational structure is critical. There are two ways to create the initial budget structure. In both ways, the budget structure is created without any funding. In other words, during the preparation step, only the budget structure is created but no budget is funded for any budget units. This comes in the next step of the process.

> **Note**
>
> It is a good idea to involve your Human Resources (HR) department in the timing of your budget structure creation. Before creating your budget structure, an attempt should be made at ensuring the organizational structure is as current as possible. This especially includes major reorganizations that could affect the creation of new organizational units or the reassignment of existing organizational units. Processing these updates before budget creation time provides a more accurate budget structure once planning starts. Careful consideration should be made to include any major restructuring during the planning process. We will cover the topic of on-cycle employee movement later in this chapter.

To create a "shell" budget structure, navigate to Transaction PECM_GENERATE_ BUDGET from the Easy Access page via the path: HUMAN RESOURCES • PERSONNEL MANAGEMENT • COMPENSATION MANAGEMENT • ENTERPRISE COMPENSATION MANAGEMENT • BUDGETING • GENERATE BUDGET FROM ORGANIZATIONAL HIERARCHY.

The use of Transaction PECM_GENERATE_BUDGET is a one-time event during the preparation step. Figure 4.2 shows the selection screen of the transaction with selection criteria Budget Type and Budget Period in the selection labelled Budget Selection. In this area, you provide both the budget type and budget period you want to create your budget structure against. Example values for Budget Types include Salary Increase, Bonus budget, and Long-term Incentive (LTI) budget. Example values for Budget periods include 2009, 2010, 2011, etc. The meanings behind budget type and budget period are described in detail in Section 4.5, Configuration.

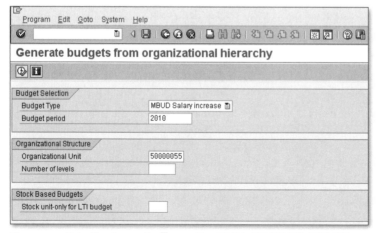

Figure 4.2 Selection Screen for Transaction PECM_GENERATE_BUDGET

The next section of the selection screen, Organizational Structure, requires specifying a top-node organizational unit. This is the organizational unit that represents the very top node for your budget, so it's important to select the correct one. For many companies, this organizational unit will be your root organizational unit (e.g., the top-most organizational unit in your organizational structure). The field, Number of Levels, determines how many levels of the organizational structure are referenced during the creation of the budget structure. The number entered in this field corresponds to the depth levels within a structure. In other words, a 1 represents the highest level, and all subsequent numbers represent lower levels. If you want to process the entire structure, just leave this field blank. Blank is also the default and is most typically used.

The last section on the selection screen contains a configurable dropdown called Stock Unit-Only for LTI Budget. This field contains a listing of stock units representing the elements associated to your company's non-monetary budgets. Again, this field is only required for LTI budgets because the stock unit is a dependency for all LTI budgets.

Note that there is no test run flag for this program. Once executed, the program creates the budget structure (see Figure 4.3).

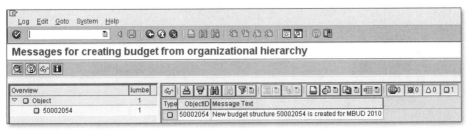

Figure 4.3 Confirmation Message About a Successful Budget Structure Creation

To view the newly created budget structure, go to Transaction PECM_DISPLAY_ BUDGETS or navigate the following path from the Easy Access page: HUMAN RESOURCES • PERSONNEL MANAGEMENT • COMPENSATION MANAGEMENT • ENTERPRISE COMPENSATION MANAGEMENT • BUDGETING • DISPLAY BUDGET.

On the selection screen of the Display Budget report (see Figure 4.4), select the relevant budget type and budget period. From the dropdown, select either the budget unit or organizational unit of the budget structure you want to display. If the Financing checkbox is checked, the accompanying organizational unit (for each budget unit) is displayed in the output. This is only for informational purposes because all organizational unit–level budget data is maintained and tracked to its associated budget unit.

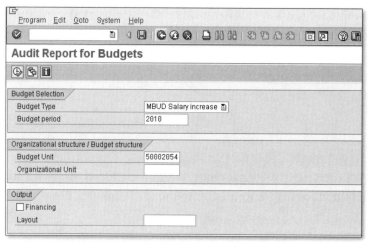

Figure 4.4 Selection Screen for the Display Budget Report

In addition, a standard layout option is available if you want to make any user-specific or system-wide defaults available.

The output of the program is shown in Figure 4.5. The budget structure is shown as a hierarchy. The following information is shown as a default from left to right in the hierarchy:

▸ **Budget Unit** — long description of the BU object

▸ **Object ID** — ID of the BU object

▸ **Total Budget** — total amount of funds available for allocation (from a roll-up perspective)

▸ **Total Spent** — total of funds spent (from a roll-up perspective)

▸ **Total Rest** — total remaining budget (from a roll-up perspective, i.e., Total Budget minus Total Spent Budget)

▸ **Distributable Budget** — total amount of funds available for allocation (from an individual organizational unit perspective)

▶ **Spent Budget** — total of funds spent (from an individual organizational unit perspective)

▶ **Own Rest** — total individual remaining budget (from an individual organizational unit perspective, i.e., Distributable Budget minus Spent Budget)

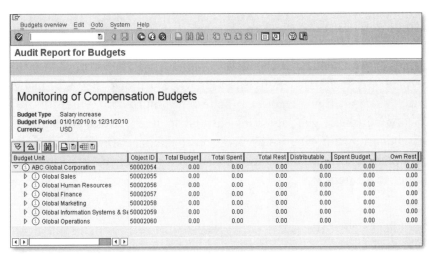

Figure 4.5 Output of the Program

The transaction is organized in two sections of three. The first section represents the budget view from a roll-up perspective (columns: Total Budget, Total Spent Budget, and Total Rest) whereas the second section represents the budget view from an individual organizational unit perspective (columns: Distributable Budget, Spent Budget, and Own Rest). The two views in total give you a holistic picture of how the organization is fairing once in the planning process. Obviously, after the preparation step, the budget structure is "hollow" (i.e., without any funding). We will return to this transaction later in the process to show the robustness of the information displayed.

> **Note**
>
> The new compensation functionality (application component PA-EM, ECM) actually uses the same budgeting functionality as the older compensation functionality (application component PA-CM, Compensation Management). This means that the previous transactions, programs, and user exits used to create or fund the budget structure can still be leveraged in the new ECM functionality. However, full regression testing should occur on any pre-existing programming targeted for use in the new functionality.

Transactions still available include:

HRCMP0015 — Change Budget (Administration)

HRCMP0014 — Display Budget (Administration)

HRCMP0011 — Create Budget Structure

HRCMP0012 — Display Budget Structure

HRCMP0013 — Change Budget Structure

There is another way to create and view your initial budget hierarchy. As of version Enterprise 4.7, Web-based Transaction PECM_START_BDG_BSP is available as an alternative for managing budgets. Despite being initiated from the SAP GUI, the transaction launches a web page using Business Server Pages (BSP) technology. This transaction, shown in Figure 4.6, gives you an alternate way of creating the budget within the Budget Maintenance link. (We'll discuss the other links as we work through those steps.)

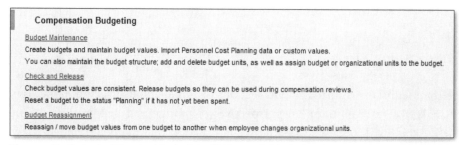

Figure 4.6 Output of Standard Budget Audit Report (with Budget Structure Not Funded Yet)

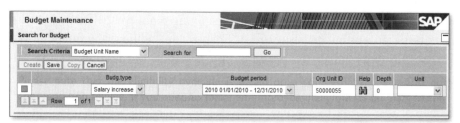

Figure 4.7 Create Budget Screen with Budget Type, Budget Period, Organizational Unit, and Depth Available

After selecting the Budget Maintenance link, click on the Create button. In this screen, select your Budget Type and Budget Period from the relevant dropdown selections (see Figure 4.7). In the Org Unit ID field, enter or search for the root organizational unit that you want to use as your top-node budget. For searching, click the Binoculars icon and select the appropriate organizational unit from the pop-up. Depth operates the same way as the functionality on the GUI version.

Note

Before using the budgeting BSP pages, you must work with your Basis team to activate all BSP applications starting with prefix hrecm_bdg_*. To do this, go to Transaction SICF (HTTP Service Hierarchy Maintenance). On the selection screen of the transaction, select Hierarchy Type "SERVICE." Activate the following BSP applications under path Default_Host • SAP • BC • BSP • SAP: hrecm_bdg_start (Overview), hrecm_bdg_srv02 (Budget Structure services), hrecm_bdg_srv (Budgeting Services), hrecm_bdg_ra_vl (Reassign Budget Value), hrecm_bdg_maint (Budget Maintenance), and hrecm_bdg_chkrl (Check and Release Budget).

Once you have selected (at least) Budg. Type, Budget Period, and Org Unit ID, click the Save button. This creates your budget hierarchy. Click Save again to save the budget. Figure 4.8 shows a newly created budget using this functionality. Like Transaction PECM_GENERATE_BUDGET, a new budget hierarchy is created with no funded budget units.

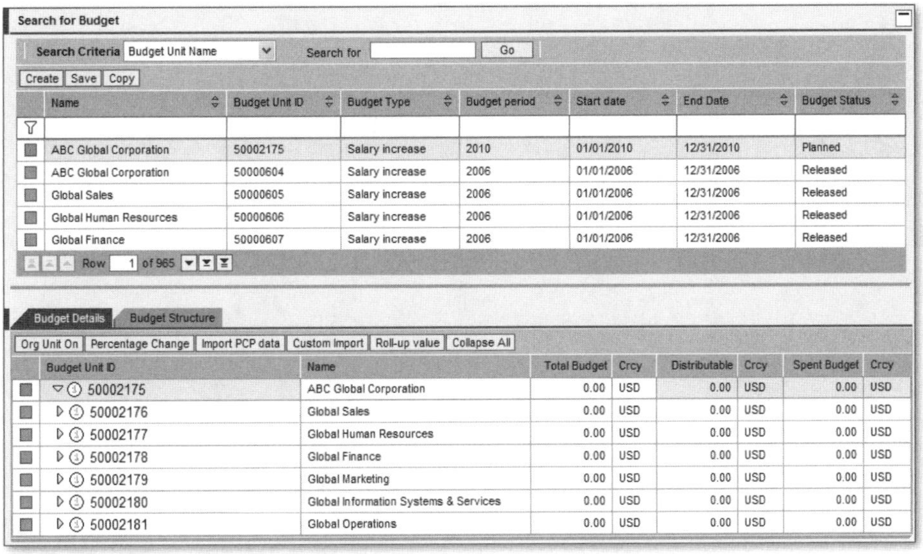

Figure 4.8 Newly Created Budget Structure Using Web-based Transaction PECM_START_BDG_BSP

You should note that all budgets are first created in status 1 (Planned). After creating these budgets during this preparation process, you may determine that a structure was either created in error or will no longer be used. In these cases, you can delete the budget hierarchy and all associated relationships via a standard program. To delete a budget in planned status, go to Transaction RE_RHRHDL00 or navigate the following path from the Easy Access page: HUMAN RESOURCES • ORGANIZATIONAL MANAGEMENT • TOOLS • DATABASE • DELETE DB RECORDS.

Warning

If you have been granted access to use this transaction in your production environment, be extremely careful using it.

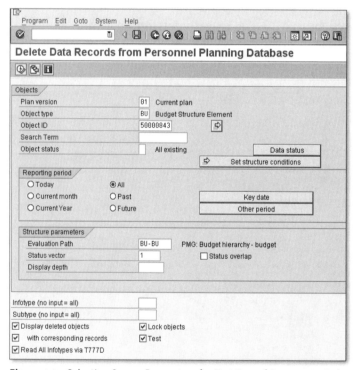

Figure 4.9 Selection Screen Parameters for Test Run of Program to Delete Budget Unit Hierarchy

You should always ensure the program is run in test mode first (the default has the Test flag checked) to verify the deletions from the database. In the selection screen (see Figure 4.9), specify the Plan Version as 01, Object Type as BU, Object ID (the top-node budget unit of the structure that you want to delete), and evaluation path BU-BU (PMG: Budget hierarchy — budget). You should leave the infotype and subtype fields blank, which tells the program to delete all relevant relationships for all objects selected in the evaluation path.

After running the program, a table of objects and relationships are listed with Plan Version, Object Type, Object ID, Infotype, Subtype, Planning Status, Start Date, End Date, and Object Abbreviation. Figure 4.10 shows this output. When performed in test mode, a message indicating Test Run Without DB Change confirms that no updates were made to the database. When the actual run is performed, no message appears.

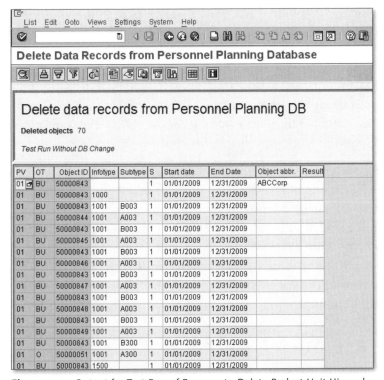

Figure 4.10 Output for Test Run of Program to Delete Budget Unit Hierarchy

Warning
Use extreme caution when using this program.

All program runs should first be performed in test mode before running for updates. It is also important to know what objects are being deleted, because inadvertently deleting other OM objects or relationships could be devastating and could require a system restore from a backup.

To review, step 1 of the process creates the "shell" of the budget hierarchy. After preparation, the budget structure is created but is still not funded. The funding of the budget occurs within the next step of the life cycle — *initialization*. So let's discuss the initialization step now.

4.2.2 Initialization

Budget initialization involves the funding, checking, and releasing of the budget structure. After the preparation step, the budget hierarchy is created but not funded. In this step, you fund and release the budget after performing a consistency check. A consistency check is used to ensure that all funds roll up properly and all data (objects, relationships between those objects, and infotypes) maintain integrity. It functions much like other consistency checks within the SAP system by indicating success messages (in green), warning messages (in yellow) and error messages (in red).

The actual budget structure can be funded either manually or automatically. How you fund your budget is one of the most important decisions you will make, if you're incorporating the standard budgeting functionality into your implementation. Regardless of the level of automation chosen, the funding of the budget structure populates Infotype 1520 (Original Budget) for each BU. Infotype 1520 holds both the individual and roll-up values — whether they are a value (e.g., dollars) or units (e.g., stock options). The values within Infotype 1520 cannot be maintained through a standard transaction.

If you decide to fund the budget manually, a few transactions can be used. Web-based Transaction PECM_START_BDG_BSP can be launched and used to initially fund the budget manually. After searching for and selecting your budget structure using one of the given selection options (e.g., budget unit name, organizational unit ID, etc.), the "total budget" amounts for each budget unit can be input. This way, you can manually establish your budget using either a "top-down" or "bottom-up" approach. In Figure 4.11, Budget Unit 50002183 (Sales, EMEA) is manually updated with US $35,000.00. This is the total amount that is allocated to employees within that budget structure. This amount then rolls up to Budget Unit 50002176 (Global Sales), which holds a total budget amount of US $840,000.00 — of which only US $160,000.00 has been distributed to its subordinate budget units: 50002182 (Sales, Americas), 50002183 (Sales, EMEA), and 50002184 (Sales, Asia Pacific / Australia). The Distributable column tells you how many funds are available to distribute to lower (child) organizations. The delta between Total Budget and Distributable is the amount allocated to employees within that budget unit itself.

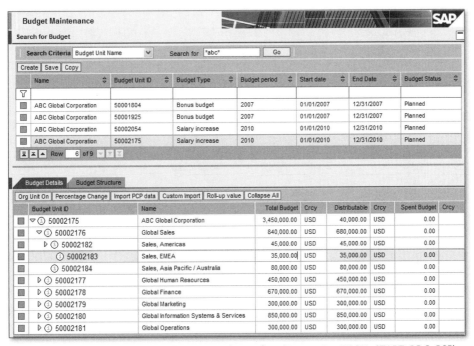

Figure 4.11 Manually Entering Budgets via Web Interface (Transaction PECM_START_BDG_BSP)

If you have a large organizational structure with complex budget calculations, this could be a difficult (if not impossible) feat to pull off. Most customers who manually fund their budget structure first calculate the budget numbers outside of the tool (using Excel or another familiar application) and then simply enter values in a top-down or bottom-up approach.

During a manual update, you can also apply mass percentage changes to one budget unit or a budget structure. Using this functionality, you can apply a percentage (either negative or positive) for one organizational unit (with the possibility to update superior budgets) or apply a "mass percentage change" that updates the entire node you are on and all of the subordinates (that budget unit and all budget units below). Another important option that is available while applying a percentage change is whether or not you want to update the superior budget values. By selecting the Update Superior Budget Values checkbox, the percentage change (whether applied individually or en masse) will roll up to the highest level of the budget structure. If left unchecked, the higher level budgets will remain unaffected. Figure 4.12 shows the options available for Percentage Change.

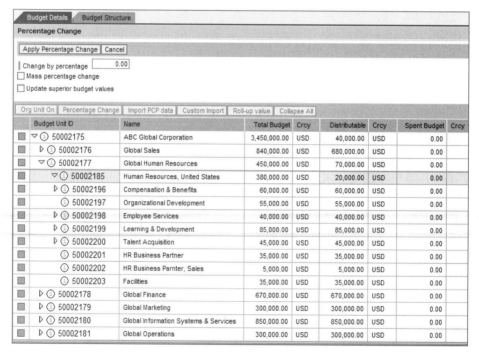

Figure 4.12 Applying Percentage Changes within Planned Budget Structure

Figure 4.13 shows 3% applied to Budget Unit 50002185 (Human Resources, United States) with both the Mass Percentage Change checkbox and the Update Superior Budget Values checkbox selected. This means a 3% budget increase is applied to the Total Budget values for the selected budget unit and all budget units below.

The increases also roll up to the highest level budget — Budget Unit 50002175 (ABC Global Corporation).

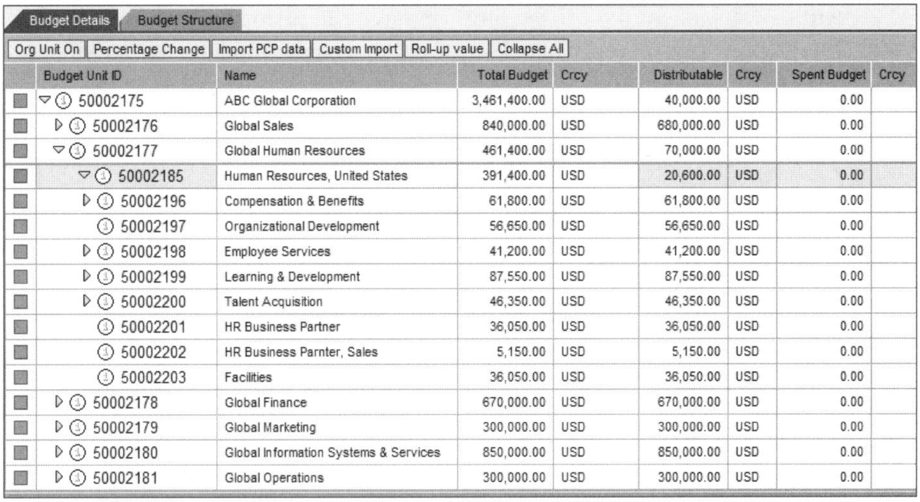

	Budget Unit ID	Name	Total Budget	Crcy	Distributable	Crcy	Spent Budget	Crcy
☐	▽ ⓘ 50002175	ABC Global Corporation	3,461,400.00	USD	40,000.00	USD	0.00	
☐	▷ ⓘ 50002176	Global Sales	840,000.00	USD	680,000.00	USD	0.00	
☐	▽ ⓘ 50002177	Global Human Resources	461,400.00	USD	70,000.00	USD	0.00	
☐	▽ ⓘ 50002185	Human Resources, United States	391,400.00	USD	20,600.00	USD	0.00	
☐	▷ ⓘ 50002196	Compensation & Benefits	61,800.00	USD	61,800.00	USD	0.00	
☐	ⓘ 50002197	Organizational Development	56,650.00	USD	56,650.00	USD	0.00	
☐	▷ ⓘ 50002198	Employee Services	41,200.00	USD	41,200.00	USD	0.00	
☐	▷ ⓘ 50002199	Learning & Development	87,550.00	USD	87,550.00	USD	0.00	
☐	▷ ⓘ 50002200	Talent Acquisition	46,350.00	USD	46,350.00	USD	0.00	
☐	ⓘ 50002201	HR Business Partner	36,050.00	USD	36,050.00	USD	0.00	
☐	ⓘ 50002202	HR Business Parnter, Sales	5,150.00	USD	5,150.00	USD	0.00	
☐	ⓘ 50002203	Facilities	36,050.00	USD	36,050.00	USD	0.00	
☐	▷ ⓘ 50002178	Global Finance	670,000.00	USD	670,000.00	USD	0.00	
☐	▷ ⓘ 50002179	Global Marketing	300,000.00	USD	300,000.00	USD	0.00	
☐	▷ ⓘ 50002180	Global Information Systems & Services	850,000.00	USD	850,000.00	USD	0.00	
☐	▷ ⓘ 50002181	Global Operations	300,000.00	USD	300,000.00	USD	0.00	

Figure 4.13 Three Percent Applied to Planned Budget Structure

Another available option is the Roll-up Value functionality. Using this functionality allows you to perform bottom-up budgeting. If you want to load budget values for individual budget units without considering superior budgets (bottom-up budgeting), it is possible to subsequently roll up budget values with this option. The Roll-up option automatically performs a roll-up of budget values such that both the roll-up and individual budget amounts are corrected. Let's say that budget unit C rolled up to budget unit B, and budget unit B rolled up to budget unit A. In the tool, we then gave all budget units US $1,000 for the total budget. If the Roll-up option was selected, then budget unit C would have US $1,000 as roll-up and individual amounts, budget unit B would have US $2,000 roll-up and US $1,000 individual amounts, and budget unit A would have US $3,000 roll-up and US $1,000 individual amounts.

As you can see, there are several options for assisting in a manual creation of the budget. The Mass Percentage and Roll-up Value functionality provide robust capabilities for speeding up an otherwise lengthy process. Despite these shortcuts, manual budget creation may still not be a viable alternative for your organization. If this is the case, you need to fund the budget automatically.

For most customers, automatic funding is the most popular method of budget allocation because it is more efficient and reduces the amount of errors caused by manual intervention. There are several ways to automate the funding of the budget structure. You can fund a budget unit hierarchy by using one of the methods listed in Table 4.1, which lists each option with a description and the technology used to implement it.

Funding Option	Description	Technology Used
Funding via values from the Personnel Cost Planning (PCP) component	Budget funded by importing a Personnel Cost Plan. Assumes budget values have already been created within the PCP component.	Standard Transaction PECM_INIT_BUDGET or through the Import PCP data button in the Web-based Transaction PECM_START_BDG_BSP.
Funding via SAP Business Add-In (BAdI) HRECM00_BDG0001	A BAdI (HRECM00_BDG0001) is provided from SAP that allows you to update the funding of the budget units.	Web-based Transaction PECM_START_BDG_BSP via the Custom import button calls the active implementation of BAdI HRECM00_BDG0001.
Funding via a custom program	A custom program can be written to fund a budget hierarchy.	Custom program (either purchased or built).

Table 4.1 Automated Funding Options for Budgets

With the first option, budgets can be created from personnel cost plans within the PCP component. The PCP component is used to calculate staff costs using cost items (e.g., salary wages, fringe benefits, and incentives) to create personnel cost plans. In Figure 4.14, an example of this type of cost plan has been created for the 2010 Merit Budget for the ABC Global Corporation.

By using PCP functionality, bottom-up budgeting can be performed. All budgets can be funded based on an employee-level calculation and can even incorporate guidelines based on current or previous performance management ratings. Within the PCP component, you would need to perform the necessary configuration to support the calculations, including cost items, cost plans, and planning scenarios. The calculations could incorporate a fixed percentage (e.g., 3% for all eligible employees) or guideline percentages based off the employee's own appraisal ratings. Using the latter approach would necessitate knowing that all (or at least most) of the appraisals for the eligible population are calibrated and completed.

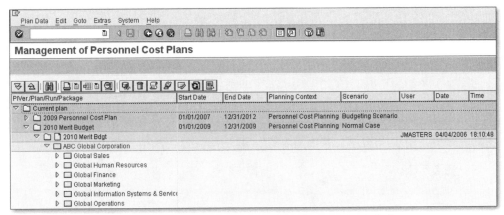

Figure 4.14 Example of a Personnel Cost Plan Established for the 2010 Merit Budget

---

Note

For more information on configuration steps for PCP, please refer to the SAP Help site at *http://help.sap.com/saphelp_erp60_sp/helpdata/en/e9/53c73c13b0ce5be10000000 a114084/frameset.htm.*

Specific help on the configuration of PCP for ECM budgeting can be found at: *http:// help.sap.com/saphelp_erp60_sp/helpdata/en/ef/56094043618f5ce10000000a155106 /frameset.htm.*

After a successful personnel cost plan run, the cost plan is ready for import into the compensation budget. The budget must always be in planned status during this import. Once released, the import utility can no longer be used. Figure 4.15 shows Transaction PECM_INIT_BUDGET and the pop-up dialog used to select the personnel cost plan. On the selection screen, the budget data must be selected under the Budget Attributes and Budget Unit sections. Budget Determination should be HCP1 (PCP). Clicking on the Parameters button displays a pop-up dialog. Here, specify 01 (Current Plan) as the plan version and the appropriate personnel cost plan created within PCP. If only some of the cost items should be included in (or excluded from) the budget, you can do this by using the cost item filter.

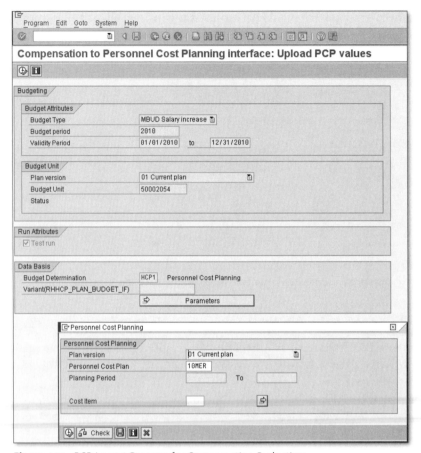

Figure 4.15 PCP Import Program for Compensation Budgeting

In addition to using Transaction PECM_INIT_BUDGET, PCP data can be imported using Web-based Transaction PECM_START_BDG_BSP. Within the Budget Maintenance section of the application, the Import PCP Data button can be used to import PCP plan data. Figure 4.16 shows the Web version. Fields Budget Determination, Personnel Cost Plan, and Cost Item(s) are available for use. Cost Item is optional, but if desired, more than one cost item can be specified to filter the import. Clicking on the Enter More Cost Items button allows you to enter additional cost items.

Both transactions serve the exact same purpose and achieve the same end state — the difference is more a matter of service delivery. If you are using the web interface for other budget matters (e.g., budget creation, budget reassignment, etc.), you may decide to use Web-based Transaction PECM_START_BDG_BSP. Otherwise, SAP GUI Transaction PECM_INIT_BUDGET is probably more practical.

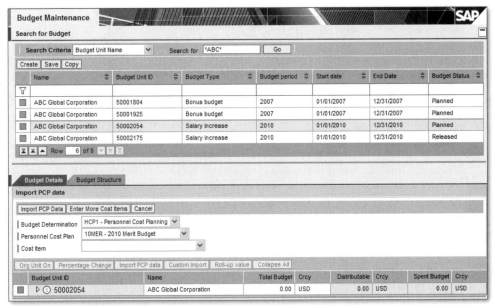

Figure 4.16 Importing PCP Data from Web Transaction PECM_START_BDG_BSP

There are two drawbacks to using the PCP approach for budget initiation. The first is that another PCP component must be configured (and tested) to leverage the functionality. Most SAP customers do not use PCP functionality within SAP ERP HCM, and those who do not would most likely also not implement the functionality to solely support the compensation budgeting process in ECM. The second drawback is that once the budget is released (and spent), it cannot be refreshed using this functionality. This is less of an issue if you plan on using a freeze date or period, but it makes the planning process unmanageable if you are trying to keep the budget allocation current based on employee movement.

Now let's take a look at a second approach for automating budget funds — using BAdI HRECM00_BDG0001 (Compensation Budgeting: User exit). This BAdI has one method — called DETERMINE_BUDGET_VALUES — which allows updates to the budget values stored within Infotype 1520. Figure 4.17 shows the method and interface of the BAdI.

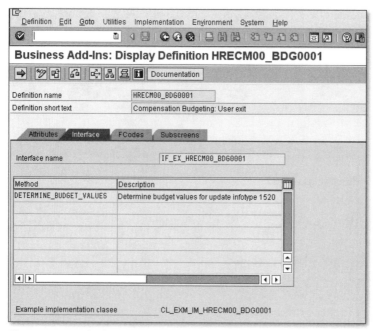

Figure 4.17 Method DETERMINE_BUDGET_VALUES for BAdI HRECM00_BDG0001

Within the Budget Maintenance section of the Web-based Transaction PECM_START_BDG_BSP, a Custom import button is available. Clicking on this button allows a budget (in planned status) to be recalculated based on the logic implemented within the active implementation of BAdI HRECM00_BDG0001. In addition, a custom program could call this BAdI implementation to apply specific logic to the budget funding.

The third approach is to use a custom program to fund budgets. As described earlier, this program may utilize BAdI HRECM00_BDG0001. However, logic can be written to update the budget structure based on your specific requirements — regardless of budget status (planned or released). That last point is extremely important because the standard functionality (via Web-based Transaction PECM_START_BDG_BSP) cannot automate mass refreshes.

Budget reassignment functionality is discussed in the next section, but another big win for using this approach is that you can use the same custom program to refresh the budgets (after budget release) as you do when initializing. Figure 4.18 shows an example of a Budget Allocation Program. In the selection screen, you are allowed to select a Budget Type, Compensation Review Item, Budget Period, Budget Unit, and Key Date to allocate the budget. In this design, the budget hierarchy with top Budget Unit (50000723) will be refreshed on Key Date 01/31/2007 based on the Budget Type, Compensation Review Item, and Budget Period.

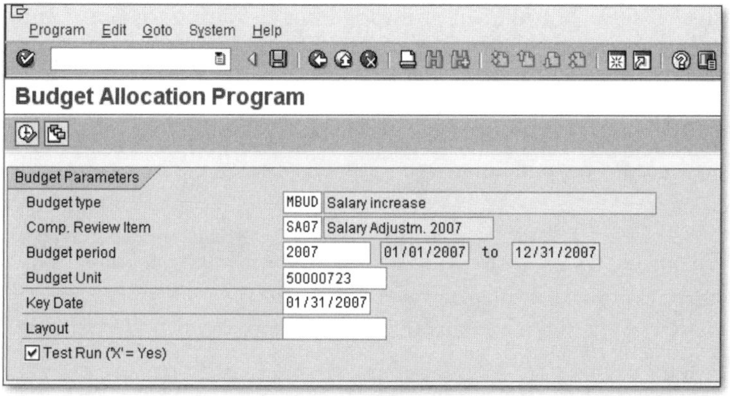

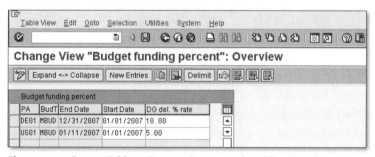

Figure 4.18 Custom Budget Allocation Program

The program can apply a fixed percentage (e.g., 3%) or can incorporate more complex logic. For example, in Figure 4.19, a custom table is shown that allows the storage of a percentage based on Personnel Area. In this scenario, employees in PA DE01 are budgeted at 10% while employees in PA US01 are budgeted at 5%. This is a simple scenario but more sophisticated logic can be implemented based on requirements and design considerations.

Figure 4.19 Custom Table to Support Custom Budget Allocation Program

You have now seen the differences between manually or automatically updating the budget hierarchy structure for its initialization. After initially funding the budget hierarchy, it's important that the budgets are checked for consistency before being released. Budgets must be programmatically changed from status 1 (Planned) to status 2 (Released) to be planned against in a productive environment. Figure 4.20 shows the Check and Release Budget section within Web-based Transaction PECM_START_BDG_BSP. While still in planned status, consistency can be checked by selecting the Check Values button. The message Budget Values are Consistent is displayed in the upper left corner of the screen when the budget has no issues. The budget check does a check to ensure budgets roll up consistency (i.e., superior budgets fund lower level budget units) and to review budget unit to organizational unit relationships to validate proper linkages.

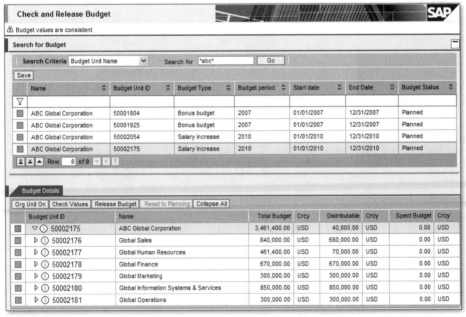

Figure 4.20 Check Budget for Consistency Using Web-based Transaction PECM_START_BDG_BSP

This same functionality is available from the SAP system via Transaction PECM_CHK_BUDGET (Check and Release Budget). Figure 4.21 shows Transaction PECM_CHK_BUDGET. On the selection screen, a Budget Type, Budget Period, and Budget Unit ID are specified. A Check Values radio button under the Processing Options section of the screen indicates that the consistency check should be performed.

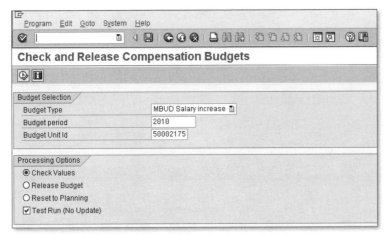

Figure 4.21 Selection Screen for Transaction PECM_CHK_BUDGET

After running Transaction PECM_CHK_BUDGET for consistency, an output screen is rendered with any issues listed. If the budget values are consistent, the message Budget Values are Consistent is prefixed with the Budget Unit ID (see Figure 4.22).

Figure 4.22 Successful Messages on Output for Budget Consistency Check

After a successful consistency check, the budget must be released. Like most of the budget functionality within ECM, the budget can be released in two ways — online or in the SAP GUI. If performed online, web-based Transaction PECM_START_BDG_BSP can be accessed for releasing the budget. Within the Check and Release Budget section, the Release Budget button is available (see Figure 4.23). To release the budget, you need to select the root object (top-level) budget. In other words, the budget hierarchy can only be released at its highest level.

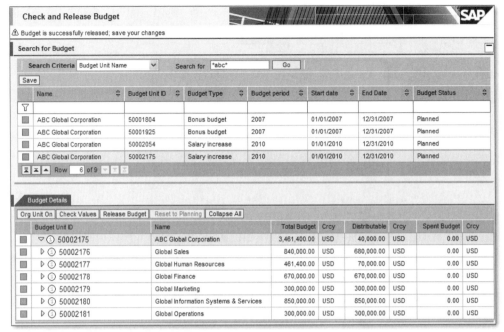

Figure 4.23 Release Budget before Save

After release, you will see the message Budget is Successfully Released; Save Your Changes. Be aware that the budget units will not be saved in released status until you actually select the Save button on the upper left section of the screen. Figure 4.24 shows a budget structure in released status. (Notice the Budget Status field on the top of the screen has been changed to Released).

The other option for budget release is via the standard SAP GUI Transaction PECM_CHK_BUDGET. On the selection screen, a Budget Type, Budget Period, and Budget Unit ID are specified (it is the same program as the consistency check). A Release Budget radio button under the Processing Options section of the screen indicates that the budget should be released. In Figure 4.25 you can see the output after budget release Message Text Budget 50002175 Status is Successfully Set to Released.

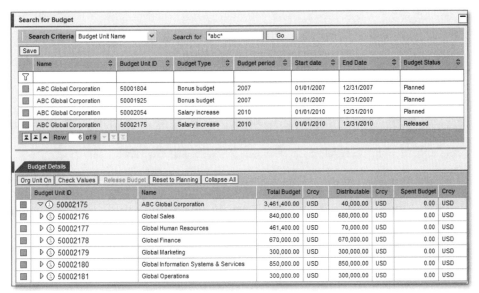

Figure 4.24 Saved Budget in Released Status

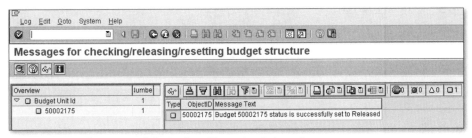

Figure 4.25 Budget Successfully Set from Planned to Released

Once a budget is released, you can only go back to the planning status if none of the budget has been spent. There are two ways to do this:

▶ The Reset to Planning Button on the Budget Details section of Check and Released from Web-based Transaction PECM_START_BDG_BSP

▶ Transaction PECM_CHK_BUDGET can be used to select Reset to Planning (see output in Figure 4.26)

Figure 4.26 Budget Successfully Set to Planned by Reset to Planning Functionality.

Once the budgets have been checked and released, you can begin compensation planning. This is usually the final step before giving access to the portal to your planning managers and HR professionals/specialists.

So, let's look at how to maintain the budget structure once you're in a production environment. The next step in the process — *maintenance* — enables the HR or Compensation department to update budget data even after release.

4.2.3 Maintenance

As of Enterprise 4.7, budgets can be maintained even after the budget has been released via the web-based Transaction PECM_START_BDG_BSP. The budget reallocation functionality is found in the Budget Reassignment section of the start page. Budgets can be manually reallocated using this functionality regardless of planned and released status.

The Budget Reassignment section within web-based Transaction PECM_START_BDG_BSP houses this functionality, which is composed of four steps:

- Choose Sending Org. Unit
- Choose Receiving Org. Unit
- Enter Values
- Review Results

In Figure 4.27, Organizational Unit 50000073 (Facilities) has been selected as the sending (losing) organizational unit. It is from this organizational unit (i.e., Budget Unit) that budget values are transferred.

Reassign Value | 1 Choose Sending Org. Unit | 2 Choose Receiving Org.Unit | 3 Enter Values | 4 Review Results

Next Step

Budget Unit ID	Org Unit ID	Name	Total Budget	Crcy	Distributable	Crcy	Spent Budget	Crcy
50002175		ABC Global Corporation	3,461,400.00	USD	40,000.00	USD	0.00	USD
	50000055	ABC Global Corporation	0.00		0.00		0.00	
50002176		Global Sales	840,000.00	USD	680,000.00	USD	0.00	USD
50002177		Global Human Resources	461,400.00	USD	70,000.00	USD	0.00	USD
	50000060	Global Human Resources	0.00		0.00		0.00	
50002185		Human Resources, United States	391,400.00	USD	20,600.00	USD	0.00	USD
	50000061	Human Resources, United States	0.00		0.00		0.00	
50002196		Compensation & Benefits	61,800.00	USD	61,800.00	USD	0.00	USD
50002197		Organizational Development	56,650.00	USD	56,650.00	USD	0.00	USD
50002198		Employee Services	41,200.00	USD	41,200.00	USD	2,500.00-	USD
50002199		Learning & Development	87,550.00	USD	87,550.00	USD	0.00	USD
50002200		Talent Acquisition	46,350.00	USD	46,350.00	USD	0.00	USD
50002201		HR Business Partner	36,050.00	USD	36,050.00	USD	0.00	USD
50002202		HR Business Parnter, Sales	5,150.00	USD	5,150.00	USD	0.00	USD
50002203		Facilities	36,050.00	USD	36,050.00	USD	2,500.00	USD
	50000073	Facilities	0.00		0.00		2,500.00	USD
50002178		Global Finance	670,000.00	USD	670,000.00	USD	0.00	USD
50002179		Global Marketing	300,000.00	USD	300,000.00	USD	0.00	USD
50002180		Global Information Systems & Services	850,000.00	USD	850,000.00	USD	0.00	USD
50002181		Global Operations	300,000.00	USD	300,000.00	USD	0.00	USD

Figure 4.27 Step 1 of Manually Reassigning Budget Values: Selecting Sending Org. Unit

In step 2, the receiving organizational unit is selected. Figure 4.28 shows Organizational Unit 50000074 (HR Business Partner) selected as the receiving organizational unit. It is from within this Organizational Unit (i.e., Budget Unit) that budget values are transferred.

Reassign Value | 1 Choose Sending Org. Unit | 2 Choose Receiving Org.Unit | 3 Enter Values | 4 Review Results

Previous Step | Next Step

Budget Unit ID	Org Unit ID	Name	Total Budget	Crcy	Distributable	Crcy	Spent Budget	Crcy
50002175		ABC Global Corporation	3,461,400.00	USD	40,000.00	USD	0.00	USD
	50000055	ABC Global Corporation	0.00		0.00		0.00	
50002176		Global Sales	840,000.00	USD	680,000.00	USD	0.00	USD
50002177		Global Human Resources	461,400.00	USD	70,000.00	USD	0.00	USD
	50000060	Global Human Resources	0.00		0.00		0.00	
50002185		Human Resources, United States	391,400.00	USD	20,600.00	USD	0.00	USD
	50000061	Human Resources, United States	0.00		0.00		0.00	
50002196		Compensation & Benefits	61,800.00	USD	61,800.00	USD	0.00	USD
50002197		Organizational Development	56,650.00	USD	56,650.00	USD	0.00	USD
50002198		Employee Services	41,200.00	USD	41,200.00	USD	2,500.00-	USD
50002199		Learning & Development	87,550.00	USD	87,550.00	USD	0.00	USD
50002200		Talent Acquisition	46,350.00	USD	46,350.00	USD	0.00	USD
50002201		HR Business Partner	36,050.00	USD	36,050.00	USD	0.00	USD
	50000074	HR Business Partner	0.00		0.00		0.00	
50002202		HR Business Parnter, Sales	5,150.00	USD	5,150.00	USD	0.00	USD
50002203		Facilities	36,050.00	USD	36,050.00	USD	2,500.00	USD
50002178		Global Finance	670,000.00	USD	670,000.00	USD	0.00	USD
50002179		Global Marketing	300,000.00	USD	300,000.00	USD	0.00	USD
50002180		Global Information Systems & Services	850,000.00	USD	850,000.00	USD	0.00	USD
50002181		Global Operations	300,000.00	USD	300,000.00	USD	0.00	USD

Figure 4.28 Step 2 of Manually Reassigning Budget Values: Selecting the Receiving Org. Unit

In step 3, the budget and spend values are specified (see Figure 4.29). The new values for Total Budget and Spent Budget are identified. After input, select the Reassign button. When you see the message Budget Has Been Successfully Transferred; Review and Save, this indicates that you can proceed in the process.

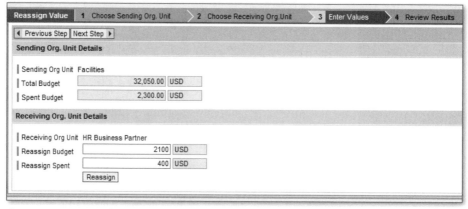

Figure 4.29 Step 3 of Manually Reassigning Budget Values: Enter Values

During the last step of the process, a review is done before any funds are transferred. For both the sending and receiving organizational units, the following information is displayed for final review (see Figure 4.30):

- Sending Org. Unit — Original Total Budget
- Sending Org. Unit — New Total Budget
- Sending Org. Unit — Original Spent Budget
- Sending Org. Unit — New Spent Budget
- Receiving Org. Unit — Original Total Budget
- Receiving Org. Unit — New Total Budget
- Receiving Org. Unit — Original Spent Budget
- Receiving Org. Unit — New Spent Budget

In addition, the new budget hierarchy is displayed with the new values within the structure. You can traverse through the structure to see how the proposed transfer affects the existing hierarchy, and to save the transfer of budget funds, you need to select the Save button.

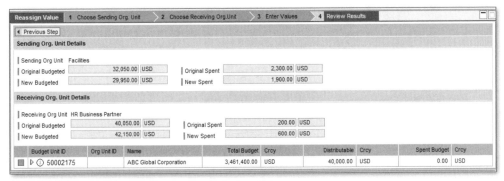

Figure 4.30 Step 4 of Manually Reassigning Budget Values

Although this manual process allows you to reallocate budget funds from one budget unit (or organizational unit) to another, it is not always sufficient due to the volume of employee changes that occur during planning time. For instance, employee movements (such as promotion and transfers) and employee terminations may account for hundreds (even thousands) of transactions.

You can, however, achieve a more automated means of keeping current with changing budget data using a custom program similar to the one describe during our initialization discussion. In fact, one program can be created to both initialize and continuously refresh the budgets units. This is the most popular means of refreshing the budget automatically.

> **Note**
>
> In versions of SAP before Enterprise 4.7, budgets could not be updated once in released status. The concept of manual or dynamic budget reassignment is regarded as one of the most critical pieces of the solution.

After the planning period ends, it is time for budget closure. Budget *closure* is the last step in the process.

4.2.4 Closure

Budget closure is the informal process that involves the final reconciliation between budgeted and spent funds from a roll-up perspective. Although there is no status for archiving the budget, the status is kept as "Released." Reports, such as PECM_DISPLAY_BUDGETS, can be run and given to management teams to validate adherence to the budget.

The four steps covered — Preparation, Initialization, Maintenance, and Closure — provide the storyboard for the budgeting process with ECM. Understanding the available options within each of these steps is important to your own implementation and maintenance.

4.3 Locking

Unfortunately, budget locking problems are quite common and can cause a lot of user frustration. Budget locking was actually built to maintain data integrity. When a user accesses the planning sheet on the SAP portal, the budget units associated with the employees being planned on become locked. A budget lock is intentionally placed on all BUs that are being processed to ensure that no other manager (or HR Professional) can decrease budget funds from those same budget units. This is a very good thing because it retains the integrity of the budget data being planned against.

However, when a manager does not exit out of the iView properly, the lock on a budget may not release. When that same manager tries to plan again (or if a higher-level manager attempts to plan) for employees in the affected budget units, a hard error message appears. Figure 4.31, for example, shows the error message Budget 50000773 is locked for user JMARTIN and Budget 50000774 is locked for user JMARTIN. The error message is repeated for all affected employees on the screen, which means that a line item appears on the portal worksheet for each case.

To manually release locks, you use Transaction SM12 (Select Lock Entries). Figure 4.32 shows the selection screen. You can easily determine budget unit locks for a particular user by providing the SAP username (e.g., JMARTIN) of the user and clicking on the List button.

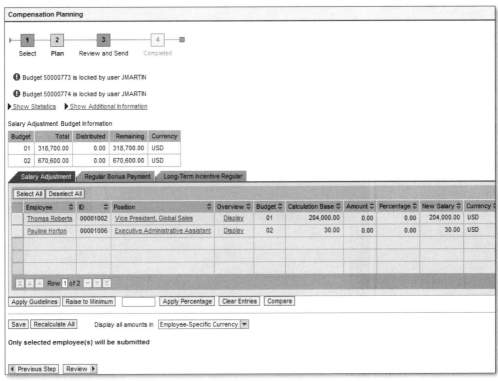

Figure 4.31 Budget Locking Error on Portal Compensation Worksheet

Figure 4.32 Selection Screen for Transaction SM12

Figure 4.33 shows the output of Transaction SM12. The lock entry list provides important information on the lock such as user name, time, mode, table, and lock argument. The lock argument specifies the exact budget unit being locked along with other technical information.

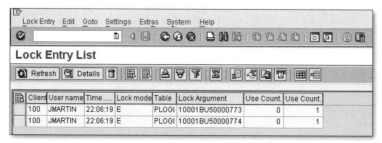

Figure 4.33 Output of Transaction SM12

Let's now discuss the infotypes integral to the budgeting process.

4.4   Infotypes

There are several infotypes that facilitate the budgeting functionality in SAP, so let's look at each in detail.

4.4.1   Infotype 1000 (Object)

Infotype 1000 (Object) holds the budget unit's short and long texts. The short and long texts are taken directly from the short and long texts of the organizational unit upon initial budget structure creation. You can change these manually via web-based Transaction PECM_START_BDG_BSP if you want.

4.4.2   Infotype 1001 (Relationships)

Infotype 1001 contains all of the relationships. In Table 4.2, the objects and relationships used within the budgeting process are listed.

Object	Object Type Text	Relationship Specification	Relationship	Relationship name	Related Object Type	Related Object Type Text
BU	Budget structure element	A	003	Belongs to	BU	Budget structure element
BU	Budget structure element	B	003	Incorporates	BU	Budget structure element
BU	Budget structure element	B	300	Finances...	O	Organizational unit
O	Organizational unit	A	300	Is financed by...	BU	Budget structure element

Table 4.2 Budget-related OM Objects and their Relationships to Other Objects

Relationship 003 is used to connect the budget structure with the organizational unit structure from an organizational structure hierarchy perspective, and relationship 300 is used to link a budget unit to an organizational unit from a financial (budget) perspective.

4.4.3 Infotype 1500 (BS Element Management)

Infotype 1500 provides important data on the budget unit such as budget type, status (planned versus released), whether the budget is allocable, and the financial year.

4.4.4 Infotype 1520 (Original Budget)

Infotype 1520 is where both the total roll-up and individual budget amount is stored.

Now let's discuss the configuration of the budgeting functionality. This configuration is required if you are budgeting within ECM.

4.5   Configuration

The configuration tasks supporting the budgeting functionality within ECM are relatively straightforward. All budgeting configurations are performed within the Implementation Guide (IMG) under the path: PERSONNEL MANAGEMENT • ENTERPRISE COMPENSATION MANAGEMENT • BUDGETING. The following components compose the configuration:

▸ Define Reference Currency for Budgeting

▸ Define Budget Types

▸ Define Budget Periods

▸ Set Budget Control Parameters

A link to display all implementations of BAdI HRECM00_BDG0001 is available under the path: PERSONNEL MANAGEMENT • ENTERPRISE COMPENSATION MANAGEMENT • BUDGETING • BUSINESS ADD-IN: INITIALIZE BUDGET VALUES.

In Figure 4.34, you can see the IMG activities to set up budgeting.

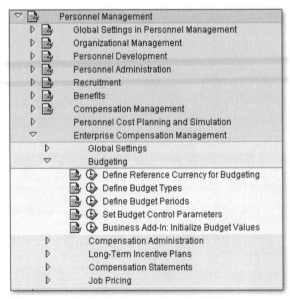

Figure 4.34 Budgeting Node within the IMG

The first configuration item is to Define the Reference Currency for Budgeting.

4.5.1 Defining Reference Currency

A reference currency is a key step within the process because all budgets must have one. And because all budgets must roll up to one and only one currency, a default (or reference) currency must be defined within the configuration. All other currencies are converted into the reference currency using the standard SAP currency conversion table (TCURR), which holds all of the exchange rates. Standard ECM uses exchange rate type M, which is defined within the system as the "standard translation at average rate."

The reference currency is configured within the IMG via the path: PERSONNEL MANAGEMENT • ENTERPRISE COMPENSATION MANAGEMENT • BUDGETING • DEFINE REFERENCE CURRENCY FOR BUDGETING. You can also access the reference currency directly from Transaction SM30 from Table view V_T7PM2_B.

In Figure 4.35 you can see that for Budget Type Group 02 (Compensation Management), USD (United States Dollar) has been defined as the reference currency.

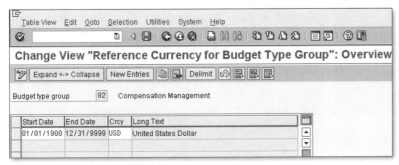

Figure 4.35 Reference Budget Currency within the IMG

Next, let's discuss the configuration of budget types.

4.5.2 Defining Budget Types

Budget types are set up to record the various budget "buckets" or "pools" within your organization. Budget types do not need to be created each year unless new compensation plans have been defined. For example, if some year in the future, you implement a new LTI plan, you will need to create a new budget type, assuming you have not been managing an LTI process in ECM previously.

Budget types are configured within the IMG via the path: PERSONNEL MANAGE-MENT • ENTERPRISE COMPENSATION MANAGEMENT • BUDGETING • DEFINE BUDGET TYPES. You can also access budget types directly from Transaction SM30 from Table view V_T7PM3_B. You can see this configuration table in Figure 4.36.

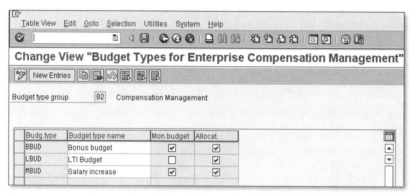

Figure 4.36 Budget Types Configuration within the IMG

Budget type is a four alphanumeric field and its name has a 20 character limit. Each budget type has two checkboxes. The first checkbox, Mon. Budget, is the indicator for monetary budget. If this checkbox is selected, it indicates to the system that the budget units associated with this budget type are managed in currency units. A budget for merit increases, for example, would be based on currency and the budget type would be selected as monetary. Most stock plans would not have this value selected because they are unit based, not currency based.

The last checkbox is an Allocat. flag. Budgets can only be allocated in the system when this flag is selected because it is equivalent to an active flag. Only when this flag is activated can budgets be distributed and operational. You could use this functionality if, for example, you retire a compensation plan within your system and want to be ensure that no future budgets use that particular budget type.

Now that we understand budget types, let's discuss what budget periods are and how they are used.

4.5.3 Define Budget Periods

A budget period defines the time frame in which you administer your budget. The timeline (start and end date) should include the effective date of the compensation element (i.e., Infotype 0759 record). For example, if the effective date of your merit adjustment is 04/01/2009, then your budget period should contain this date within its range. Examples of budget periods include 04/02/2008 - 04/01/2009, 01/01/2008 - 04/02/2009, and even 04/01/2009 - 04/01/2009 in this scenario.

The key date is the day on which the currency conversion takes place during the budget creation process (if any conversion is needed). If left blank, the system uses the system date as its conversion date when creating the budget unit.

To configure your budget periods within the IMG you follow the path: PERSONNEL MANAGEMENT • ENTERPRISE COMPENSATION MANAGEMENT • BUDGETING • DEFINE BUDGET PERIODS. You can also access budget periods directly from Transaction SM30 from Table view V_T7PM9_B. Figure 4.37 shows this configuration table view.

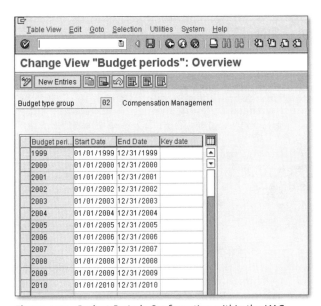

Figure 4.37 Budget Periods Configuration within the IMG

After configuring budget periods, control parameters can be set within the configuration. This is performed in the next IMG activity, which we will explain next.

4.5.4 Set Budget Control Parameters

By setting certain control parameters within the configuration, you can influence the behavior of some important budgeting functionality. The first control parameter determines if the reassignment of a budget is permitted after (at least) some of it has already been spent (i.e., allocated) on an employee. The second is related to the budget allocation of the planning manager. Based on this flag, the system either funds the manager's own organizational unit or the organizational unit above the organizational unit where the manager sits.

You can set budget control parameters within the IMG under the path: Personnel Management • Enterprise Compensation Management • Budgeting • Set Budget Control Parameters. You can also access these control parameters directly from Transaction OOECM_BD.

Figure 4.38 shows the two control parameters. If this view looks familiar, it's because both values are stored in Table T77S0.

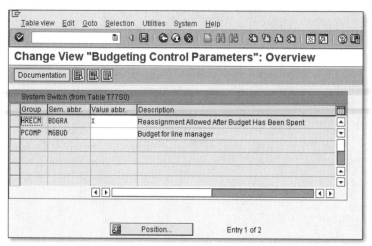

Figure 4.38 Budgeting Control Parameters Configuration within the IMG

This transaction simply isolates these two compensation budget-relevant values. In Table 4.3, each value is described in detail with comments.

This concludes the configuration review of budgeting functionality within ECM. As you can see, several important constructs including budget types, budget periods, and other specifics — such as reference currency and control parameters — need to be configured to utilize the budget functionality within ECM.

Group	Semantic Abbreviation	Value Abbreviation (default)	Description	Comments
HRECM	BDGRA	X	Reassignment allowed after budget has been spent	X = you can reassign this budget, even if part of it has already been spent. If blank, the system checks if any part of this budget has already been spent. If so, you cannot reassign this budget.
PCOMP	MGBUD		Budget for line manager	If X, the budget of the next highest organizational unit (for which a budget is available) is used. In other words, the line manager of an organizational unit is paid from a different budget than the other employees in the organizational unit.

Table 4.3 Budget-related OM Objects and Their Relationships to Other Objects

4.6 Summary

As you learned in this chapter, compensation budgets constitute a critical piece of the process. Frequently, Key Performance Indicators (KPIs) and metrics are reported out against how well a functional area, division, subsidiary — and eventually — company have done in keeping to budget. Managing the life cycle — from preparation, initialization, maintenance, and closure — will enable a smooth process from start to finish.

In the next chapter, we will discuss the compensation planning and approval process, and one of the key activities within ECM — activation.

Administering compensation processes efficiently is a challenge for any company. The process steps — from system preparation to manager planning to activation — require a lot of coordination to complete successfully. In this chapter, we will review the major process events that occur during the annual compensation cycle and highlight the key system transactions that are needed for a successful result.

5   Process Administration

This chapter provides an in-depth review of the process steps for the annual compensation planning cycle. The topics focus on the annual compensation process — including how and when it is managed and by whom. (The handling of off-cycle increases is discussed in Chapter 8, Advanced Topics and Additional Enhancements). We will review system transaction functionality and place it in context with the process, and we will pay special attention to lessons learned from past implementations.

Let's start with an overview of the annual process.

5.1   Process Overview

The annual compensation process is divided into the following four steps:

- Prepare
- Plan and Review
- Calibrate`
- Activate and Communicate

Figure 5.1 shows a graphic of these four steps. Next to each step is a short explanation of the more important activities occurring during that stage of the process.

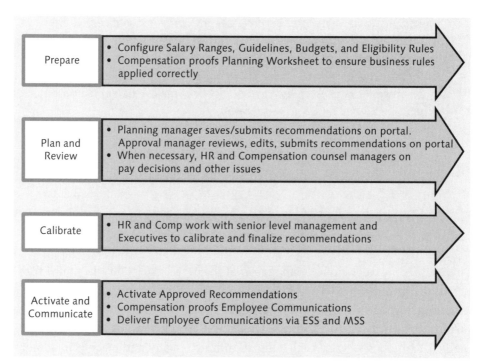

Figure 5.1 Four Key Steps During the Annual Compensation Planning Cycle

Within each of these steps, important work is performed —by the Compensation department, Human Resources (HR), Information Technology (IT), managers, proxies, or employees — so that the entire process executes efficiently.

It is helpful for you to have a solid process definition (broken down to at least a level-4 decomposition) so that all parties involved in the process know what is expected of them and when it is expected. A process definition document (PDD) should be created to detail the system and manual activities involved and note who is responsible for which activities in the process. Popular "swimlane" process flows are an excellent way to visually lay out the flow between the process activities mapped against the roles. In Figure 5.2 you can see an example of a flow for the annual merit process. Each role within the process is listed in a unique "swimlane." Common roles for the annual compensation process include employee, manager, one-up manager, compensation department, HR, and IT.

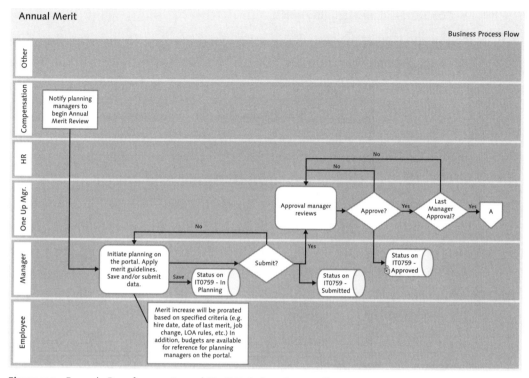

Figure 5.2 Example Page from an Annual Merit Swimlane Process Flow

Once your process definition is in place, tool design (including configuration and development) becomes a much easier task. Working from a solid blueprint, the solution becomes easier to implement because the business requirements and system flow are known and agreed upon by the stakeholders.

Let's discuss the first step in the process, preparation, next.

5.2   Prepare

Preparing your organization for an upcoming planning cycle should be a routine procedure (regardless of which tool or manual process is performed). And you should prepare a checklist that is maintained and refined each year during the preparation process.

The main activities within the preparation step include:

- Configuration of eligibility rules
- Configuration of budgets
- Configuration of salary ranges
- Configuration of guidelines
- Compensation worksheet proofing

The last item on the list — compensation worksheet proofing — provides an opportunity for the compensation department or HR to check the planning worksheet ahead of others to ensure business rules (such as eligibility, guidelines, etc.) are applied correctly.

So let's discuss the first activity — eligibility rules.

5.2.1 Eligibility Rules

In order for employees to be eligible for a compensation plan, they must pass both the macro- and micro-eligibility requirements. (Macro- and micro-eligibility are discussed in Chapter 3, Baseline Configuration and Infotypes). Macro-eligibility is based on values stored in Infotype 0758 (Compensation Program). Infotype 0758 stores the compensation area, the first compensation program grouping, and the second compensation program grouping.

As part of ECM project cutover, all employees receive at least one Infotype 0758 record. Standard Transaction PECM_CREATE_0758 (Create Compensation Program Records) should be run for mass creation of this infotype. Figure 5.3 shows the selection screen for the Create Compensation Program Records program.

On the selection screen, you should leave the Compensation Area, 1st Program Grouping and 2nd Program Grouping fields blank because these values should default based on the feature configuration. (This selection is here only if you want to force values to the infotype.)

For Earliest Begin Date, you can select the Hire Date, Date Type, and Fixed Date options. If the latter is selected, you must specify a date in the Fixed Date field. The earliest begin date sets the start date of the Infotype 0758 record based on the selection made here. If the fixed date is before the employee's hire date, the begin date uses the hire date instead.

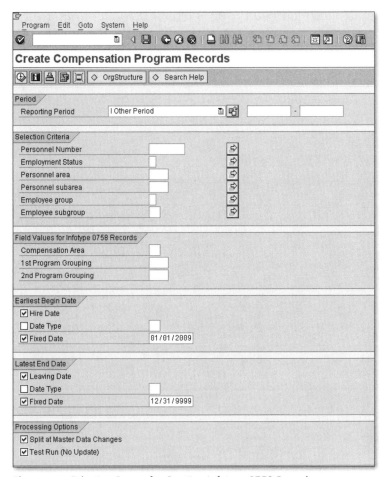

Figure 5.3 Selection Screen for Creating Infotype 0758 Records

Similar logic is used for the latest end date. The end date cannot be later than the leaving date, the date assigned to the date type, or the fixed date you have specified. If more than one indicator is set, the system reads the earliest end date and uses that for the end date of the Infotype 0758 record.

Within the processing options at the bottom of the screen, the Split at Master Data Changes checkbox is available. If selected, Infotype 0758 records are created (and split) to reflect any changes on Infotypes 0001 (Organizational Assignment) and 0008 (Basic Pay) during the span of creation. If this selection is marked, expect some employees to have multiple Infotype 0758 records (due to changes to their master data). We recommend that you select this indicator so as to ensure all macro-eligiblity changes are detected during the time the infotype is created.

The output of the program lists all success, warning, and hard error messages. Figure 5.4 shows an example output.

Figure 5.4 Output for the Mass Infotype 0758 Program

Please note that this program should only be used for processing Infotype 0758 as a one-time event. Once live, it is expected that Infotype 0758 be part of the various infogroups for actions such as hiring, rehiring, transferring, and changes in position and pay.

You may need to execute this program again if the company is merging or buying another company (assuming you need to create Infotype 0758 records in bulk for a select population). You might also need to run the program if you want to create additional compensation program records to support another process (e.g., a new global equity plan).

Now that we have addressed eligibility, let's briefly discuss budgets.

5.2.2 Budgets

Chapter 4, Compensation Budgeting, covered budgeting preparation in detail so you can refer to the preparation and maintenance steps for budgeting discussed there.

But it is important to note that how you decide to incorporate budgets into the solution dictates the level of effort involved in this task. Whether or not you decide to use the standard budgeting functionality, expect to spend a significant amount of time ensuring that the budgeting feature is working per specification.

Next, we'll review the activities needed to ensure that salary ranges are up to date.

5.2.3 Salary Ranges

Salary ranges stored in Table T710 need updating on an annual basis (at minimum) to support the compensation function. Table T710 holds pay grades with their respective pay ranges based on a pay structure. A *pay structure* is a combination of pay grade type, pay grade area, pay grade group, and pay grade level.

Another important pay structure Table, T510, may also need updating depending on where your configuration resides. T510 was the original pay structure table but now functions mostly as the table to hold employees on step progressions or indirectly valuated pay.

You can configure Table T710 via Transaction SM34 by using the cluster Table view V_T710CL. You can also access this table view cluster within the IMG under the

following path: PERSONNEL MANAGEMENT • ENTERPRISE COMPENSATION MANAGE-
MENT • JOB PRICING • PAY GRADES AND LEVELS • CHECK PAY GRADES AND LEVELS.

Salary structures and their ranges represent one of the most significant elements
of compensation design. Structures and ranges drive compa-ratios, percentage
in range, and other compensation concepts. For most companies, Table T710 is
already updated on an annual basis. With ECM, content is more available because
range information can be accessed by more people (managers, employees, etc.).

Figure 5.5 Mass Increase Update Functionality

If mass adjustments to reference salaries within Table T710 are required, you can
use the Change Amounts button. Figure 5.5 shows the pop-up box used to collect

the necessary information needed to increase (or decrease) the salary range components, and rounding rules can also be specified. But in all cases, the key date is required and dictates the effective date of the change.

If you are implementing the job pricing module, you can also use the salary structure adjustment functionality to import planned salary structure proposals to the pay structure, which is discussed in Chapter 10, Job Pricing.

In addition to salary ranges, guidelines also need to be configured, so let's discuss those.

5.2.4 Guidelines

We talked about guidelines in detail in Chapter 3, Section 3.3, so here we will be talking about the configuration that is performed during the preparation step.

Depending on the process defined in your company, you may need to pre-populate guideline values into the employees' Amount and Percentage fields before the worksheet opens for compensation planning. This means that a manager accessing his worksheet for the first time would already see "recommended" adjustments for his employees.

You can do pre-populating recommendations based on guidelines using standard Transaction PECM_CREATE_COMP_PRO (Create Compensation Process Records). Figure 5.6 shows the selection screen for this program. Both Compensation Plan and Compensation Review are required fields, and under the Function Selection section, the Apply Guidelines option is selected by default.

> **Note**
>
> Using Transaction PECM_CREATE_COMP_PRO, you can also bring an employee's salary to the minimum of their salary range. For example, if an employee is earning US $50,000 and the minimum for their salary range is US $45,000, a compensation review item of US $5,000 would be created by the program automatically.

This program was built for mass processing, so if you execute the program against a large number of employees, we recommend that you run it in the background via the menu path: PROGRAM • EXECUTE • BACKGROUND and select the desired batch processing options.

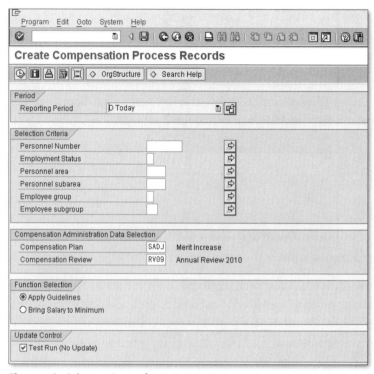

Figure 5.6 Selection Screen for Create Compensation Process Records

An example output of the program is displayed in Figure 5.7, and the following list contains some of the messages that the program returns:

▶ Whether an employee is missing an appraisal document

▶ Whether the new salary has placed an employee over the maximum of their salary range

▶ Whether the budget for a budget unit has been exceeded

▶ Whether the infotype record has been successfully created or not (in real or test mode)

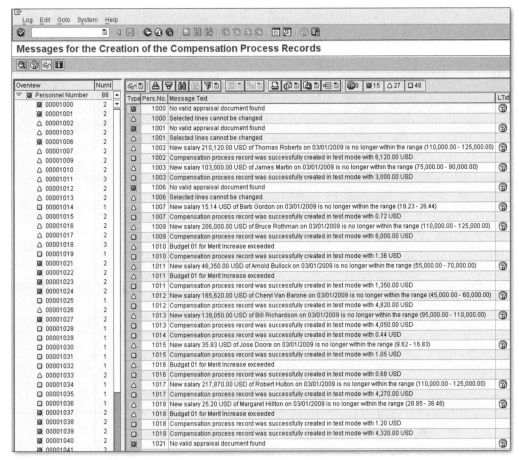

Figure 5.7 Output of the Create Compensation Process Records Report

Once guideline configuration is complete, you can coordinate with the compensation department to proof the worksheet.

5.2.5 Compensation Worksheet Proofing

The proofing process is something that the compensation department should already be familiar with. Ensuring that the guidelines, eligibility, budget, and back-end data is current, accurate, and working per specification is an important step to ensure the process executes smoothly. The proofing is performed against production — it is important that those assisting with the process understand this.

You have to work with your SAP portal team to figure out how best to achieve this because you need to expose the application to a small set of users (e.g., compensation department) before managers can get access to the application. There are several ways to provide this access, but it depends on how your user administration and portal roles are set up in the system. Proofing typically begins anywhere from two weeks to two days before the launching of the portal to managers. The amount of time permitted for proofing is really based on your scope and the support team's ability to react quickly if something is incorrect.

Now let's discuss some specific items for customers using the multilevel approval process (only available with SAP ERP 6.0, enhancement pack 4).

5.2.6 Prerequisites for Multilevel Approvals

The following two programs – Preparing Organizational Units for Planning and Notifying Managers — are only available with SAP ERP 6.0, enhancement package 4 to support the new multilevel approval process. The only time you will use these programs is if you are using the multilevel approval scenario. The first program is used to initialize the organizational structure.

Prepare Organizational Units for Compensation Planning

The Prepare Organizational Units for Compensation Planning program locates organizational units within the organizational structure to which no eligible employees are assigned for the selected compensation review. We recommend that you run this report just before planning begins to incorporate the latest eligibility rules.

This information is used within the Review Planning iView to suppress irrelevant information from being displayed, for example, compensation reviews for which a manager is not responsible for, or organizational units that have no eligible employees for a specific review.

The program determines all subordinate organizational units that lie below the selected organizational unit that have eligible employees. An entry is logged in Table T71ADM_PROCESS (Process History) for the selected organizational unit (and each organizational unit below it).

The Prepare Organizational Units for Compensation Planning program is available from the SAP Easy Menu screen via the following path: HUMAN RESOURCES • PERSONNEL MANAGEMENT • COMPENSATION MANAGEMENT • ENTERPRISE COMPENSATION MANAGEMENT • COMPENSATION PLANNING • PREPARATION • PREPARE ORG. UNITS FOR COMP. PLNG. Figure 5.8 shows both the selection screen and output example in test mode.

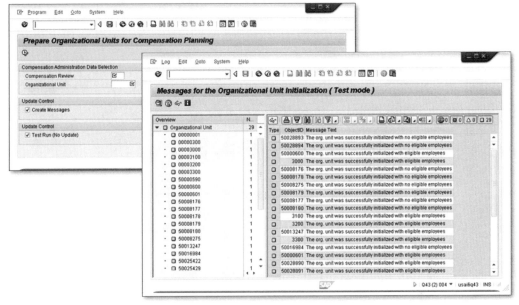

Figure 5.8 Prepare Organizational Units for Compensation Planning Program

Another program, Notify Managers, is available in SAP ERP 6.0, enhancement package 4 for sending notifications to all planning managers at the beginning of the process.

Notify Managers

The Notify Managers program informs planning managers that the compensation planning cycle has begun. Once notifications have been sent to the planning managers, the system records in Table T71ADM_PROCESS (Process History) that the notification took place.

Notifications may only be sent to the planning manager of a selected organizational unit once during a given compensation review. Subsequent attempts to execute the program will not result in repeated notification.

You can access the Notify Managers program from the SAP Easy Menu screen via the following path: HUMAN RESOURCES • PERSONNEL MANAGEMENT • COMPENSATION MANAGEMENT • ENTERPRISE COMPENSATION MANAGEMENT • COMPENSATION PLANNING • PREPARATION • NOTIFY MANAGERS. Figure 5.9 shows both the selection screen and output example in test mode.

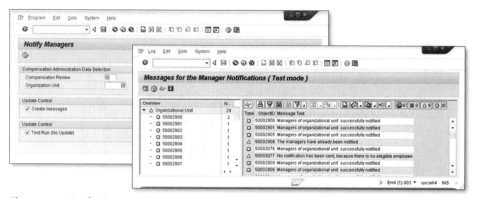

Figure 5.9 Notify Managers Program

This concludes the activities involved in the preparation step. Now let's look at the Plan and Review step.

5.3 Plan and Review

During the Plan and Review step, planning managers save and submit their recommendations on the portal. Approval managers review, edit, and submit recommendations. When necessary, Compensation managers and HR advise managers on pay decisions and any other issues that arise during the planning process. If delegation is implemented, proxies can access the planning worksheet to act on behalf of the manager they are supporting.

The entire planning process from a self-service perspective is covered in Chapter 6, Self-Service. An in-depth review of the functionality available in the compensation planning iView (and the latest Review Planning iView available in SAP ERP 6.0, enhancement package 4) is covered.

At any time during the planning process, compensation managers and HR can update Infotype 0759 (Compensation Process) manually in the backend via Transaction PA30. The amount of updates performed in the backend should be kept to a minimum. However, changes via Transaction PA30 are sometimes necessary. For example, if mandatory increases need to be applied to a group of employees or if an employee needs a seniority increase, backend updates may be warranted. Depending on the scope and complexity of the update, an employee's Infotype 0759 or 0008 record(s) may be updated individually via Transaction PA30 or en masse via a batch process.

After the planning and approval activities conclude on the portal, the next step in the process is calibration.

5.4   Calibrate

During calibration, compensation managers and HR work closely with senior management to review and finalize the recommendations approved by the line management. This process varies depending on the organization. Options for handling calibration are discussed in detail in Chapter 14, Lessons Learned.

Typically, at a minimum, several custom reports are built to provide the data needed to support the calibration review meetings. Before each calibration session with the management team, the compensation department executes key reports to extract information needed for the meeting.

In Figure 5.10 you can see an example custom report that could be executed in the SAP backend by the compensation department to provide analytic information for management, including pie charts, bar charts, and scatter plots.

Any necessary mass adjustments can be performed via Transaction RHECM_ADJUST_0759 (Adjust Compensation Process Records), available for those with

SAP ERP 6.0, enhancement package 4. This program updates Infotype 0759 records based on either applying guidelines, adjusting by a percentage, or deletion. This program can actually be used at any time during the planning process, as long as the Infotype 0759 record is not activated.

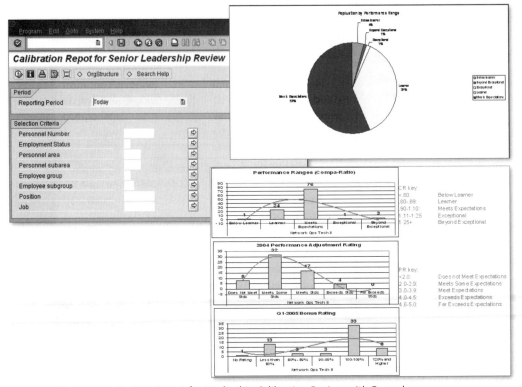

Figure 5.10 Custom Report for Leadership Calibration Review with Example

The Adjust Compensation Process Records program is available from the SAP Easy Menu screen via the following path: HUMAN RESOURCES • PERSONNEL MANAGE-MENT • COMPENSATION MANAGEMENT • ENTERPRISE COMPENSATION MANAGEMENT • COMPENSATION PLANNING • FOLLOW-UP • ADJUST COMPENSATION PROCESS RECORDS. A screenshot of the selection screen and the output is provided in Figure 5.11.

When calibration is complete, it is time to activate the recommendations and communicate to employees.

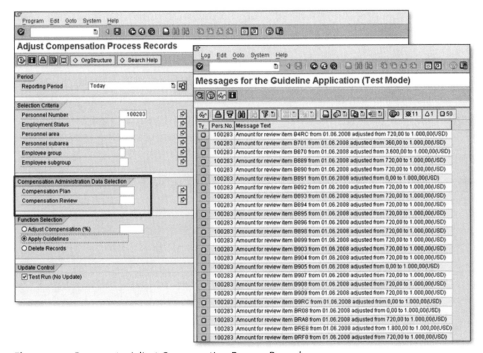

Figure 5.11 Program to Adjust Compensation Process Records

5.5 Activate and Communicate

The Activate and Communicate step represents one of the most important series of events during the process, because the accuracy of increases and bonuses is now reflected on payroll-relevant infotypes and communicated to employees via a compensation review statement. Perhaps no other process is so critical in terms of precision and consistency of calculations.

To activate approved recommendations, Transaction PECM_CHANGE_STATUS (Change Compensation Process Status) is used. The activation routine is triggered when the status is changed from Approved (status 3) to Active (status 5). In Figure 5.12 you can see an activation of compensation plan SADJ within compensation review RV09. Because no other selection criteria are entered, the change in status affects all eligible employees within that compensation review and eligible for that compensation plan. If implemented, BAdI HRECM00_ACTIVATION (Activation) is called during the processing. You can find more information on this BAdI in Chapter 7, BAdIs.

You can access the Change Compensation Process Status program from the SAP Easy Menu screen via the following path: HUMAN RESOURCES • PERSONNEL MANAGE-MENT • COMPENSATION MANAGEMENT • ENTERPRISE COMPENSATION MANAGEMENT • COMPENSATION ADMINISTRATION • CHANGE COMPENSATION PROCESS STATUS.

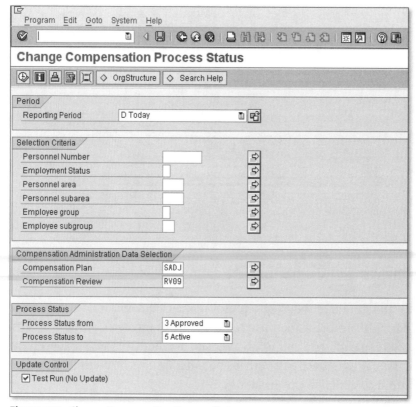

Figure 5.12 Change Compensation Process Status

Once activation is performed, the next activity you need to do within this step is to prepare the employee communications. The compensation department can use Transaction PECM_PRINT_CRS (Print Compensation Review Statement) to print the compensation statements for one or more employees. The selection screen for this program is shown in Figure 5.13. Most companies, however, let managers print an employee's compensation review statement from the portal. This way, the manager can have full control over when and where he discusses the review with the employee. A lot of companies are now giving this capability to the employees online because some managers are late with their reviews. We will talk about online compensation statements in Chapter 8, Advanced Topics.

You will find the Print Compensation Review Statement program via the SAP Easy Menu path: HUMAN RESOURCES • PERSONNEL MANAGEMENT • COMPENSATION MANAGEMENT • ENTERPRISE COMPENSATION MANAGEMENT • COMPENSATION ADMINISTRATION • PRINT COMPENSATION REVIEW STATEMENT.

Some compensation groups like to proof employee communications before allowing managers or employees access to them, which can be done in the backend via Transaction PECM_PRINT_CRS.

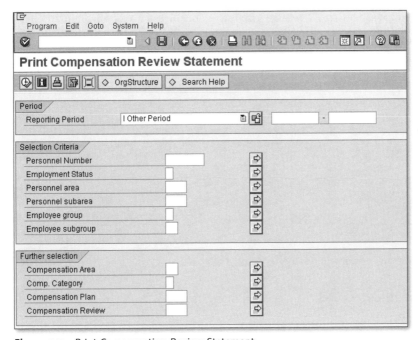

Figure 5.13 Print Compensation Review Statement

After the compensation review is complete, there is some cleanup activity needed if you use SAP ERP 6.0, enhancement package 4, functionality. Transaction RHECM_DELETE_HISTORY_DATA (Delete Comp. Planning History Data) is available to delete planning history for a specific compensation review, so once a compensation review has been completed and its planning history data is no longer needed, you can use this program to delete storage data used within the multilevel approval process. Figure 5.14 shows the selection screen and output in test mode.

The Delete Comp. Planning History Data program is available from the SAP Easy Menu screen via the following path: HUMAN RESOURCES • PERSONNEL MANAGEMENT • COMPENSATION MANAGEMENT • ENTERPRISE COMPENSATION MANAGEMENT • COMPENSATION PLANNING • FOLLOW-UP • DELETE COMP. PLANNING HISTORY DATA.

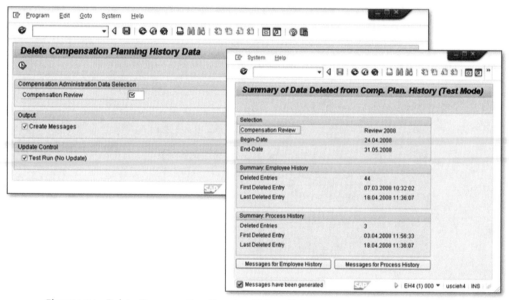

Figure 5.14 Delete Compensation Planning History Data

The program deletes entries from the following Tables:

▶ T71ADM_EE_HIST (Employee History)

▶ T71ADM_PROCESS (Process History)

- T71ADM_EE_NOTE (Employee Notes)

- T71ADM_PROC_NOTE (Compensation Review Notes)

- T71ADM_SPENT_AMT (Spent Amounts)

Although this program is optional, it is important in cases where data from completed compensation reviews start to adversely affect storage capacity within the database. Because the five history tables store actual data that is associated with the compensation approval process, SAP recommends that you exercise caution before executing the program, because any data stored in these tables for the selected compensation review is irrevocably deleted once this program is executed. SAP recommends that you execute the program once every two to three years.

This concludes the Activate and Communicate step. Now let's look at specific transactions pertinent to Long Term Incentives (LTIs) next.

5.6   LTI-Specific Processes

In this section, we provide an overview of the some of the LTI-specific transactions available in the standard system.

Transaction PECM_EVALUATE_GRANT (Evaluate LTI Grants) lets you view the following LTI information for those employees who have received grants in the system: grant number, grant date, expiry date, number of granted awards, number of forfeited awards, number of vested awards, number of unvested awards, number of outstanding awards, number of exercised awards, number of exercisable awards, and gross gain on exercising. The information in this report is sourced from Infotype 0761 (LTI Granting).

You can access the Evaluate LTI Grants program from the SAP Easy Menu screen via the following path: HUMAN RESOURCES • PERSONNEL MANAGEMENT • COMPENSATION MANAGEMENT • ENTERPRISE COMPENSATION MANAGEMENT • LONG-TERM INCENTIVES • EVALUATE LTI GRANTS. Figure 5.15 shows the selection screen of the program with LTI Plan as LTIR.

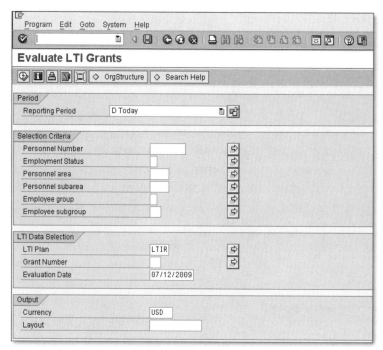

Figure 5.15 Evaluate LTI Grants

Now let's discuss how to process LTI-related life events.

5.6.1 Process Life Events

Transaction PECM_PROCESS_EVENT (Process Event for LTI Grants) processes LTI-related life events and updates Infotype 0761 according to configured business rules. The following options are available:

▸ Cancel All — cancels all awards

▸ Cancel Unvested — cancels all unvested awards

▸ Process Life Event — processes the selected life event based on configuration

▸ Vest Pct. of Granted — vests a percentage of the granted awards

▸ Vest Pct. of Unvested — vests a percentage of the unvested awards

▸ Override Vest. Rule — uses vesting rule other than the one you have specified in the configuration

The Process Event for LTI Plan Grants program is available from the SAP Easy Menu screen via the following path: HUMAN RESOURCES • PERSONNEL MANAGEMENT • COMPENSATION MANAGEMENT • ENTERPRISE COMPENSATION MANAGEMENT • LONG-TERM INCENTIVES • PROCESS EVENT FOR LTI GRANTS. Figure 5.16 shows the selection screen of the program with LTI Plan as LTIR and processing life event LE01 on 03/01/2010.

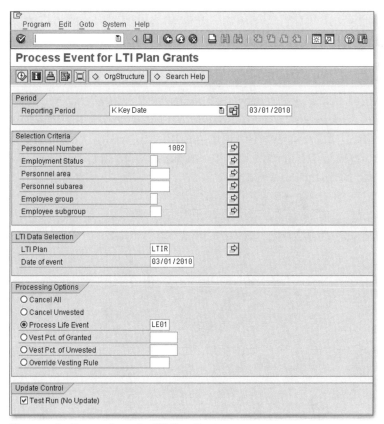

Figure 5.16 Process Event for LTI Plan Grants

Next, we'll discuss how stock splits are handled in the system.

5.6.2 Handling Stock Splits

SAP also offers the capability of handling stock splits within ECM for LTI plans. Two programs are available to assist during a stock split situation — one for converting budget stock units (BUs) and one for converting LTI grants.

Transaction PECM_CONV_BDG_STKUN (Convert Budget Stock Unit) converts data of an existing budget structure from one stock unit to another. This program converts all data on budget Infotype 1520 that belongs to a specific budget type and budget period.

You will find the Convert Budget Stock Unit program from the SAP Easy Menu screen via the following path: HUMAN RESOURCES • PERSONNEL MANAGEMENT • COMPENSATION MANAGEMENT • ENTERPRISE COMPENSATION MANAGEMENT • BUDGETTING • CONVERT BUDGET STOCK UNIT. In Figure 5.17 you can see the selection screen of the program with budget type LBUD (LTI Budget), budget period 2006, and budget unit 50002230. Under Stock Unit Selection, the old stock unit is specified as SP98 and the new stock unit as CSTK.

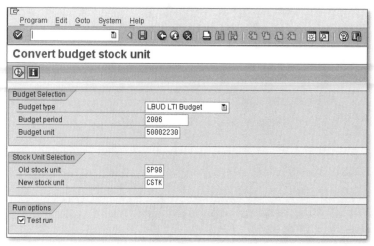

Figure 5.17 Convert Budget Stock Unit

In addition to the budget, the grant data must also be converted during a stock split situation. Transaction PECM_CONV_LTI_STKUN (Convert LTI Grant Stock Unit) is available to perform stock splits and reflect pre-split and post-split situations. Depending on the validity period of the records, the LTI data stored on Infotype 0761 is either converted (if the validity start date of the record is equal to or later than the split date) or delimited on the split date (if the validity start date of the record is earlier than the split date). In the latter case, the new records are created containing the updated numbers of granted, additionally vested, and forfeited awards, and the new exercise price and stock unit.

You can access the Convert LTI Grant Stock Unit program from the SAP Easy Menu screen via the following path: HUMAN RESOURCES • PERSONNEL MANAGEMENT • COMPENSATION MANAGEMENT • ENTERPRISE COMPENSATION MANAGEMENT • LONG-TERM INCENTIVES • CONVERT LTI GRANT STOCK UNIT. In Figure 5.18 you can see the selection screen of the program with LTI Plan as LTIE and stock split date as 01/01/2010.

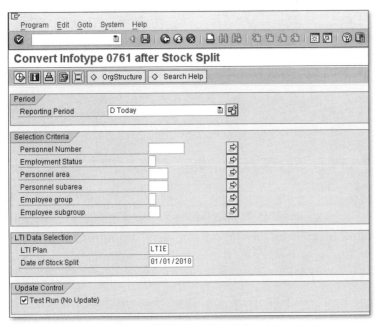

Figure 5.18 Convert Infotype 0761 After Stock Split

This wraps up our review of LTI-related transactions.

5.7 Summary

In this chapter, we reviewed the four main process steps within the annual compensation cycle — prepare, plan and review, calibrate, and activate and communicate. Within each step, standard transactions provide the necessary functionality to enable the efficient movement of the process from start to finish. We also reviewed some important transactions needed for the processing of LTI plans.

In the next chapter, we discuss the self-service offerings within ECM including those for employee, manager, and HR.

The evolution of Manager Self-Service (MSS) has greatly reduced the administrative burden in preparing and delivering worksheets, along with the necessary indicative data, that enable managers to effectively plan and administer compensation. In this chapter, we explore the online components available within Enterprise Compensation Management (ECM) including those supporting the annual compensation process and year-round views.

6   Self-Service

In this chapter, we will explore the applications that enable self-service functionality for managers and employees. Self-service functionality is delivered through a series of iViews on the SAP NetWeaver Portal. The packaging of these iViews into various "business packages" is an essential step to the delivery and administration of compensation throughout the organization.

The iViews that enable self-service can be categorized as informational and transactional. Informational iViews provide managers with access to employee compensation data. These iViews display information such as salary grades, salary ranges, and compa-ratios. Transactional iViews, on the other hand, are designed to enable the planning and review of compensation (such as the annual cycle), which may or may not trigger workflow.

Most of the functionality outlined in this chapter is provided by SAP within MSS. The iViews described in this chapter can be sourced from MSS and are arranged to provide an intuitive experience for managers planning for compensation. Some of the functionality can be used anytime to make effective decisions on how to reward and retain key employees. Working with your SAP portal team, you can lay out the online experience for employees, managers, and other portal users.

Note

Additional information on self-service and its business packages can be found in the SAP PRESS book, *Implementing Employee and Manager Self-Services in SAP ERP HCM*, by Jeremy Masters and Christos Kotsakis.

6.1   Delivered Compensation iViews

The MSS component delivers a suite of iViews that enable the annual compensation planning activities and compensation data visibility. The following iViews can be included within your own portal environment to provide managers with robust, online compensation functionality for their organization:

- Compensation Planning
- Compensation Approval
- Compensation Planning Overview
- Salary Development
- Salary Data
- Long-Term Incentives (LTIs)
- Compensation Eligibility
- Compensation Guidelines
- Compensation Adjustments
- Salary Survey Data

Using these iViews, you can create a comprehensive view that provides managers with a dedicated area to both review key compensation information about employees and conduct compensation planning activities during specific times of the year.

We will also cover the Total Compensation Statement (TCS), which is available for employees within Employee Self-Service (ESS) business package.

Let's begin with a review of the functionality provided by each MSS iView and see how it can be incorporated as part of the overall solution.

6.1.1 Compensation Planning

The Compensation Planning iView is the central component of the planning process for managers. The iView provides a comprehensive view of employee data in the form of a worksheet that lets managers perform salary planning and allocate bonuses and stock for eligible employees within their span of control. This planning iView replaces the Excel worksheets many companies currently use to support their manual process.

The Compensation Planning iView follows a simple process for planning compensation. The iView allows managers to first select which employees they will plan for. This is done by letting the manager select a specific level within their organization and then selecting the employees within that level. For example, a manager can determine that he wants to plan for all of his directly reporting employees. This selection lists all of the employees that are reporting directly to that manager. Other views are also available including direct/indirect by organizational structure and direct/indirect by organizational list. There is also an option to conduct a search for an employee based on key employee attributes such as position, job, employee group, and personnel area. These views are based on the Object and Data Provider (OADP) framework.

> **Note**
>
> Additional information on the OADP framework can be found on the SAP Help site at: *http://help.sap.com/erp2005_ehp_04/helpdata/en/e7/947e40ec66ce62e10000000a1 55106/frameset.htm*.

Upon selecting the employees to plan for, the manager is presented with the planning worksheet. Each compensation plan is represented on a tab that combines planning data and employee data to assist the manager in making decisions about how to effectively plan compensation adjustments. Each tab represents a compensation plan. The tab order (left to right) is based on the alphanumeric code of the compensation plan. For example, a compensation plan naming convention such as 1MER (for the merit plan), 2BNS (for the bonus plan), and 3STK (for the stock plan) guarantees the tab order as merit, bonus, and stock from left to right. We are not necessarily recommending that you code your plans this way, but want to caution you on how the standard logic applies to the tab order.

You can see a screenshot of the initial step in the process in Figure 6.1. You can configure this to be skipped if you do not want the manager to have to select the compensation review and employees to plan for. Skipping this screen selects all of the employees defined by a given view (identified in the iView properties) and brings the manager directly to the worksheet.

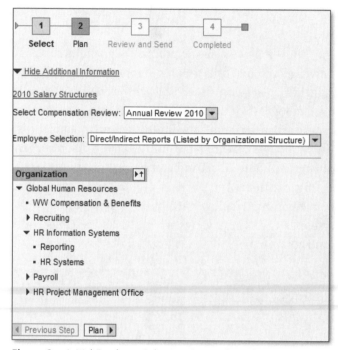

Figure 6.1 Initial Employee Selection Option from the Compensation Planning Worksheet

Once the manager has selected an organization, he is presented with the screenshot shown in Figure 6.2, prompting for a selection of employees the manager wants to plan for. Once the manager has selected the employees to plan for, he is presented with the planning worksheet.

One of the most powerful capabilities of ECM is the framework to customize and enhance the compensation worksheet. Depending on your organization and your previous process for administering compensation, you may want to provide managers with a rich set of indicative employee data that will enable them to make effective compensation recommendations. Enhancing the worksheet is accomplished by adding columns that represent data about the employee. For example, in Figure 6.3, the screenshot shows additional columns such as Compa Ratio and Salary Range. If you are using SAP Performance Management, you can also add information about the employee's performance in the form of an appraisal rating.

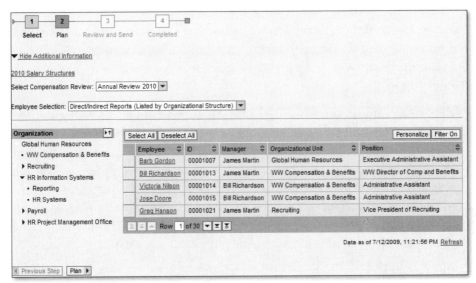

Figure 6.2 Employee Selection Results from the Compensation Planning Worksheet

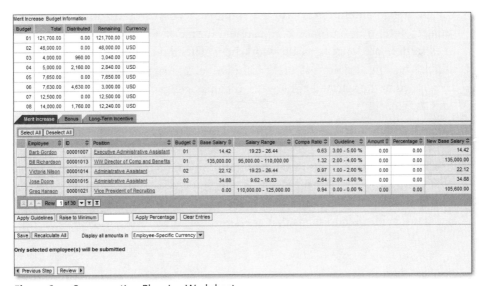

Figure 6.3 Compensation Planning Worksheet

As of SAP ERP 6.0, enhancement package 4, a standard column allows managers access to the appraisal document directly from the worksheet.

Compensation Planning Functionality

The planning worksheet incorporates functionality that makes the compensation process more intuitive and simplifies the administration of compensation recommendations. The following is a list of the functionalities available to managers on the worksheet:

▸ **Apply Percentage:** The worksheet provides a text field at the bottom of the worksheet that accepts a default percentage to apply against selected employees. To use this functionality, the manager selects one or more employees in the worksheet, provides a percentage value in the text field, and then clicks the Apply Percentage button. The worksheet then applies the percentage adjustment entered to each of the selected employees. If any of the employees generate warnings (for example, the selected employee exceeds his salary range), the iView displays a warning message highlighting this information.

▸ **Apply Guidelines:** The worksheet also provides a button that enables guidelines to be applied based on the rules within the configuration. Guidelines can be configured to provide a proposed adjustment based on several dimensions. For example, guidelines can use the employee's compa-ratio and performance rating to determine a proposed adjustment for merit. Clicking the Apply Guidelines button pre-populates the worksheet with guideline recommendations, thereby making the process more intuitive for managers. After the guidelines are applied to the selected employees, the manager can make adjustments manually as needed.

▸ **Raise to Minimum:** Another feature available to managers is the raise to minimum functionality. Managers can quickly determine which employees need to be adjusted to the minimum salary within the configured salary range. This is useful as it provides managers with a simple way to adjust employees to the minimum salary. This feature is only relevant with merit compensation plans and is not applicable to plans that are dedicated to bonuses or LTIs.

▸ **Currency Conversion:** The planning worksheet offers a powerful feature that lets managers convert all of the employee-specific currencies to a base currency. This is especially useful for managers that manage a global team. The functionality is exposed on the worksheet through a dropdown that enables the manager to select a base currency or return to the employee-specific currency.

▸ **Clearing Entries:** The planning worksheet has several of the functions previously described. Some of these functions (e.g., applying guidelines) propose values by completing entries on the worksheet. After making mass edits on the worksheet, the manager may realize that they would prefer to start over, especially if they are being prompted with warning messages or are not meeting their budget. Managers can select employees and then press the Clear Entries button to clear out all entries and return to the default values.

With any of the previously mentioned functionalities, managers must be careful to not unintentionally overwrite existing planning data from managers below them. If the planned compensation review items are still in the In Planning stage, then any manager that has access to this record can update it. In most ECM implementations, we have either removed some (or all) of the options because of this fact.

Compensation Planning iView Configuration

The Compensation Planning iView provides a set of properties that can be configured to change its behavior and show (or remove) functionality. Table 6.1 lists the properties.

Property	Description	Type of Entry	Configuration Options
ACTIONS_ BONOFF	Determines what options are available for the off-cycle bonus plan. The actions are tied to the functionality described earlier, for example, GDL enables the Apply Guidelines option.	Required	GDL, PCT, CLR, CMP, CUR

Table 6.1 Properties for the Compensation Planning iView

Property	Description	Type of Entry	Configuration Options
ACTIONS_ BONREG	Determines what options are available for the regular bonus plan. The actions are tied to the functionality described earlier, for example, CUR enables the Display All Amounts in Specific Currency option.	Required	GDL, PCT, CLR, CMP, CUR
ACTIONS_LTI	Determines what options are available for the LTI plan.	Required	GDL, CLR, CMP
ACTIONS_SAL	Determines what options are available for the salary adjustment plan.	Required	GDL, PCT, CLR, MIN, CMP, CUR
ADDITIONAL_ LINKS	Allows you to configure a key value that will provide a set of additional links for the manager. These links can be both internal portal links and external links to your intranet.	Required	Key from SAP Table T7XSSSERRES. Default entry = MSS_HCM_ECM_ ADDLINK_SAMPLE
CREVI	This property determines if the user needs to select the compensation review. This property can be used in conjunction with the Skip Object option. Pre–defining CREVI and setting the Skip Object option immediately redirects users to the planning worksheet.	Optional	Key from SAP Table T71ADM08

Table 6.1 Properties for the Compensation Planning iView (Cont.)

Property	Description	Type of Entry	Configuration Options
CURRENCY	This property allows you to set the base currencies that can be used to convert amounts on the worksheet. It is very important to confirm that the currency is maintained in the SAP system and that the values can be correctly translated from one currency to the another.	Optional	use the currency key from SAP. Example entries: USD, EUR, CAD, GBP
DATAVW_ COMPLETED_ ADD	Data View for a specific plan: Confirmation page	Required	Key from SAP Table TWPC_DATA_VW
DATAVW_ COMPLETED_ BONOFF	Data View for off-cycle bonus: Confirmation page	Required	Key from SAP Table TWPC_DATA_VW. Default entry = MSS_ ECM_REV_BON
DATAVW_ COMPLETED_ BONREG	Data View for regular bonus: Confirmation page	Required	Key from SAP Table TWPC_DATA_VW. Default entry = MSS_ ECM_REV_BON
DATAVW_ COMPLETED_ LTI	Data View for LTI: Confirmation page	Required	Key from SAP Table TWPC_DATA_VW. Default entry = MSS_ ECM_REV_LTI
DATAVW_ COMPLETED_ SALADJ	Data View for salary adjustment: Confirmation page	Required	Key from SAP Table TWPC_DATA_VW. Default entry = MSS_ ECM_REV_SAL
DATAVW_ PLAN_ADD	Data View for a specific plan	Required	Key from SAP Table TWPC_DATA_VW
DATAVW_ PLAN_BONOFF	Data View for off-cycle bonus	Required	Key from SAP Table TWPC_DATA_VW. Default entry = MSS_ ECM_PLA_BON

Table 6.1 Properties for the Compensation Planning iView (Cont.)

Property	Description	Type of Entry	Configuration Options
DATAVW_ PLAN_BONREG	Data View for regular bonus	Required	Key from SAP Table TWPC_DATA_VW. Default entry = MSS_ ECM_PLA_BON
DATAVW_ PLAN_LTI	Data View for LTI	Required	Key from SAP Table TWPC_DATA_VW. Default entry = MSS_ ECM_PLA_LTI
DATAVW_ PLAN_SALADJ	Data View for salary adjustment	Required	Key from SAP Table TWPC_DATA_VW. Default entry = MSS_ ECM_PLA_SAL
DATAVW_ REVIEW_ADD	Data View for a specific plan: Review page	Required	Key from SAP Table TWPC_DATA_VW
DATAVW_ REVIEW_ BONOFF	Data View for off-cycle bonus: Review page	Required	Key from SAP Table TWPC_DATA_VW. Default entry = MSS_ ECM_REV_BON
DATAVW_ REVIEW_ BONREG	Data View for regular bonus: Review page	Required	Key from SAP Table TWPC_DATA_VW. Default entry = MSS_ ECM_REV_BON
DATAVW_ REVIEW_LTI	Data View for LTI: Review page	Required	Key from SAP Table TWPC_DATA_VW. Default entry = MSS_ ECM_REV_LTI
DATAVW_ REVIEW_ SALADJ	Data View for salary adjustment: Review page	Required	Key from SAP Table TWPC_DATA_VW. Default entry = MSS_ ECM_REV_SAL
DEFAULT_ ORGVW_ SELECT	Default OADP Organizational View for object selection	Required	Key from SAP Table TWPC_ORG_VW
DISABLE_ APPREJ_ COLUMN	Disable the Approve/ Reject column	Required	Possible values are TRUE or FALSE. Default entry = FALSE

Table 6.1 Properties for the Compensation Planning iView (Cont.)

Property	Description	Type of Entry	Configuration Options
HIDE_SUBMIT_ BUTTON	Disable Submit functionality of the application	Required	Possible values are TRUE or FALSE. Default entry = FALSE
INITIAL_ SORTING_ COLUMN	This property enables you to set the preferred sorting value when the worksheet is first shown to the user. This applies to both the planning worksheet and the approval worksheet.	Optional	Use the column key from SAP Table TWPC_COL. Default value is to sort based on last name so the property is configured to CP_NAME.
OADP_ EENAME_ COLUMN	OADP column ID in which employee names are used for reference	Required	Default entry = ECM_ EENAME. If you want to change the default value, but still want to use this column to launch the employee's compensation profile, you need to maintain the service key in View V_TWPC_COL_ERP.
ORGVW_ SELECT_UI_ VISTYPE	Definition of how each of the Organization Views are to be displayed in the selection perspective: Tree structure or table view	Required	Default entry = MSS_ECM_SEL_ LIS=TABLE or MSS_ ECM_SEL_LIS=TREE. Note that if the Org. View is set to use a Tree structure, in the backend the Object Selection Rule used by this Org. View has to leave the Delete Duplicates checkbox open. If the Org. View is set to use a Table structure, in the backend, the Object Selection Rule used by this Org. View has to check this checkbox.

Table 6.1 Properties for the Compensation Planning iView (Cont.)

179

Property	Description	Type of Entry	Configuration Options
ORGVWGRP_ SELECT	OADP Organization View Group for object selection	Required	Key from SAP Table TWPC_ORG_VWGRP. Default value = MSS_ ECM_SEL
OTYPE	Object type	Required	Key from SAP Table T778O. Default entry = P
PLVAR	Plan version	Required	Key from SAP Table T778P. Default entry = 01
SHOW_ BUDGET_ TOTALS	This property determines if you want to have all budgets totaled at the bottom of the table on the worksheet. If you set this property to TRUE, it will insert a total line at the bottom of the budget table and provide the totals.	Required	Possible values are TRUE or FALSE. Default value = FALSE
SKIP_OBJECT_ SELECTION	This property can be used in conjuntion with the CREVI property to avoid the initial selection screen. SKIP_OBJECT_ SELECTION can be set to TRUE to remove the administion choice from the manager.	Required	Possible values are TRUE or FALSE. Default value = FALSE
SKIP_REVIEW_ PAGE	This property determines if the review screen will be part of the process. The review screen is typically used as a confirmation step for users.	Required	Possible values are TRUE or FALSE. Default value = FALSE. This property works together with the FPM Application configuration. To skip the review page, set this property to TRUE and set the FPM application to Skip review page.

Table 6.1 Properties for the Compensation Planning iView (Cont.)

6.1.2   Compensation Approval

The Compensation Approval iView lets higher-level managers approve compensation recommendations made for employees within their span of control. Once a subordinate manager has completed making recommendations using the Compensation Planning iView, they are submitted for review and approval by a higher-level manager.

Higher-level managers can then log in and use the Compensation Approval iView to review and approve the recommendations. If the submitted recommendation is approved by a higher-level manager (not necessarily the one-up manager!), the Infotype 0759 record is set to Approved status. Once approved, the record can no longer be changed on the portal by any user. Any higher-level manager wanting to change the recommendation would have to call for support. The record would have to be manually reset to In Planning status via Transaction PA30 by an administrator. Then the planning manager could resubmit the recommendation using the Compensation Planning iView. If the higher-level manager rejects the recommendation, the status in the Infotype 0759 record becomes Rejected. This then permits the planning manager to resubmit the recommendation using the Compensation Planning iView.

A notes column provides a place for written communication between the planning and approval managers. This should not replace the dialog that should occur between the managers during their collaboration, but does provide a place to record their reasons for approval or denial.

Figure 6.4 shows the Compensation Approval iView, which lists the proposed compensation recommendations for selected employees.

The iView can be configured to provide the same employee information as the Compensation Planning iView (i.e., the same columns). This approach provides the higher-level manager with the same information that the submitting manager used to make his decisions regarding compensation.

The Compensation Approval iView works much like the Compensation Planning iView with the exception of the Approval and Reject columns and the Approve All and Reject All buttons on the worksheet.

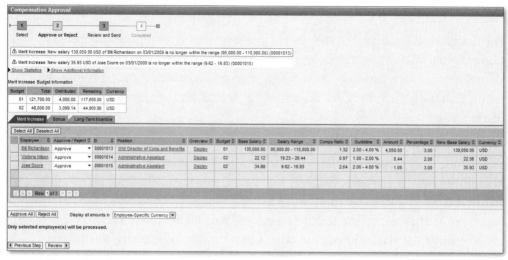

Figure 6.4 Compensation Approval iView

Compensation Approval iView Configuration

The Compensation Approval iView provides a set of properties that can be configured to change its behavior and expose (or remove) functionality. The properties mirror the ones that are available in the Compensation Planning iView and can be set with the same settings (see Table 6.1).

6.1.3 Compensation Review iView in Enhancement Package 4

SAP has provided some powerful capabilities with the release of SAP ERP 6.0, enhancement package 4. The enhancement package introduced a new approval process allowing for multilevel approval and an additional iView that supports this enhanced approval process. In this process, approval is managed at an organizational unit level and not at an individual employee level. The iView is based on the Web Dynpro for ABAP technology and integrates with the Compensation Planning iView. If the Compensation Review iView is used, the Compensation Approval iView is not needed in the process.

Figure 6.5 shows a screenshot of the Compensation Review iView for manger George Harvey. In this view, the manager can see his organizational hierarchy on the left and associated budgeting information on the right based on compensation review selection.

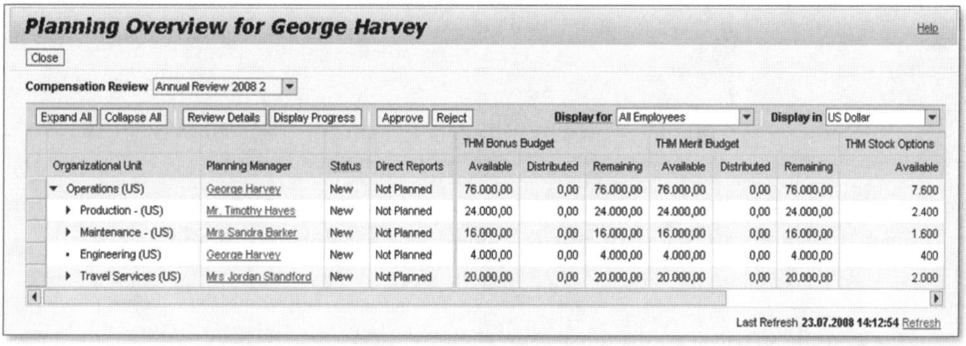

Figure 6.5 Compensation Review iView

Unlike the Compensation Approval iView, the manager can approve or reject a whole organizational unit using the Approve or Reject buttons at the top of the screen. At any time within the cycle, managers can track the progress of any subordinate planning manager. A new feature is available via the Display Progress button that lets you view the action history of an organizational unit. Figure 6.6 shows the Travel Planning organizational unit and the associated progress of the planning.

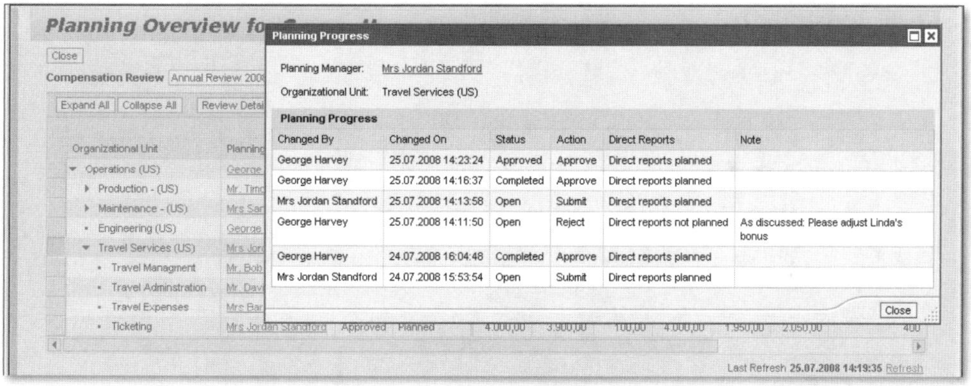

Figure 6.6 Planning Progress from Planning Overview iView

Details on the planning manager (including contact information) are available when selecting the manager's name in the hierarchy.

The Compensation Review iView is configured within the IMG under the following path: PERSONNEL MANAGEMENT • ENTERPRISE COMPENSATION MANAGEMENT • COMPENSATION ADMINISTRATION • USER INTERFACE SETTINGS • DEFINE ATTRIBUTES FOR PLANNING OVERVIEW. Figure 6.7 shows the Planning Overview configuration for this iView.

The configuration peformed within this step is by compensation review. There are three main sections within this configuration activity: the approval process, the attributes for the planning overview, and the planning detail access for higher-level managers. You can consult the standard SAP documentation for details on each of these items.

Next, we'll discuss some additional iViews that can help support a manager throughout the year.

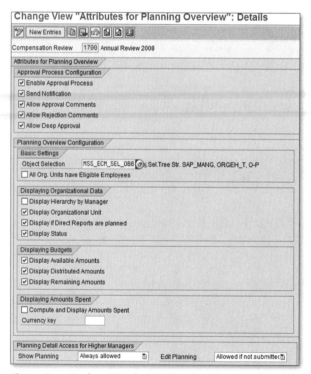

Figure 6.7 Configuration for the Planning Overview iView

6.1.4 Salary Development

The Salary Development iView lets managers display changes in salary for employees within their span of control. The Salary Development iView works with the Employee Search iView to link employee salary data. Managers can see the salary data by searching for and then selecting an employee from the Employee Search iView.

Depending on your requirements, the Salary Development iView can read data directly from SAP Payroll or from Infotypes 0008 (Basic Pay), 0014 (Recurring Payments and Deductions), and 0015 (Additional Payments). The iView can determine annual salary values from each source and can be configured to display a certain number of years.

The screenshot in Figure 6.8 is an example of the Salary Development iView displaying salary information that is sourced from infotypes.

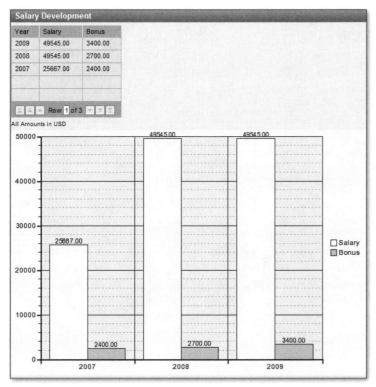

Figure 6.8 Salary Development iView

Salary Development iView Configuration

The Salary Development iView provides a set of properties that can be configured to change its behavior and show (or remove) functionality. Table 6.2 lists the properties.

Property	Description	Maintained By	Settings
YearsPast	Number of years that the iView will display.	Administrator, but personalized by user	Accepts a number value for the number of years to display. Default = 5.
SalaryBackend	This property lets you determine the source of the payroll infomration. You can have it calculated directly from infotypes or use the Payroll results.	Administrator	Accepts an integer value of either 1 or 2. One tells the iView to get the data from the Payroll cluster and 2 tells it to get it from the infotypes. Default = 1.
SalaryApplication	This property is a required field and tells the iView which wage types to use. It does that by using wage type configuration in table view VC_596A_C.	Administrator	The default value is MSSH and can be changed to another corresponding key.
YearColumn	This property determines the format for the dates. You can configure the iView to display the year or the start and end dates.	Administrator, but personalized by user	Accepts an integer value of either 1 or 2. One shows the year and 2 shows the start and end date. Default value = 1.

Table 6.2 Salary Development iView Properties

Property	Description	Maintained By	Settings
DisplayChart	The property lets you display a chart of the data making it easier for the user to visualize the progression of salary changes.	Administrator, but personalized by user	Accepts a TRUE or FALSE value with the default setting set to TRUE.
DisplayChart Values	If the chart is displayed, you can use this property to display the values, too.	Administrator, but personalized by user	Accepts a TRUE or FALSE value with the default setting set to TRUE.
ChartType	This property lets you select the chart type that is best suited for the data being displayed.	Administrator, but personalized by user	Accepts two values: Columns and Stacked_ columns.

Table 6.2 Salary Development iView Properties (Cont.)

6.1.5 Salary Data

The Salary Data iView lets managers display each employee's current salary compared to elements of the employee's pay structure. The manager can quickly evaluate where the employee's current salary falls within the salary range and get additional data such as current salary, grade level, and compa-ratio. Managers can only use this iView after selecting an employee from the Employee Search iView.

Data is displayed both numerically and graphically allowing the manager to better visualize the difference between the employee's salary and the reference salary.

The screenshot in Figure 6.9 shows the Salary Data iView with reference information and also shows a representation of the data in chart format.

Salary Data iView Configuration

The Salary Data iView provides a set of properties that can be configured to change its behavior and expose functionality. Table 6.3 lists the properties.

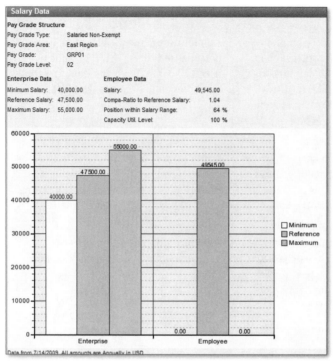

Figure 6.9 Salary Data iView

Property	Description	Maintained By	Allowed Entries
Currency	This property determines which currency to display amounts in. This propery is required.	Administrator	Three-character currency abbreviation from SAP Table TCURC. For example, USD, EUR, GBP, etc.
Frequency	This property determines the time unit for displaying amounts.	Administrator	01 = Monthly; 02 = Semimonthly; 03 = Weekly; 04 = Bi-weekly; 05 = Every four weeks; 06 = Annually; 07 = Quarterly; 08 = Half-yearly; 99 = Hourly

Table 6.3 Salary Data iView Properties

Property	Description	Maintained By	Allowed Entries
DisplayCompaRatio	This property determines if the compa-ratio comparison to reference salary is displayed.	Administrator	Accepts a TRUE or FALSE value. Default = TRUE.
DisplayPercentInRange	This property determines if the position within the salary range is displayed. Setting this to TRUE lets managers see how much an employee earns as a percentage of the salary range.	Administrator	Accepts a TRUE or FALSE value. Default = TRUE.
DisplayChart	Display chart	Administrator, but personalized by user	Accepts a TRUE or FALSE value. Default = TRUE.
DisplayChartValues	Display values in chart	Administrator, but personalized by user	Accepts a TRUE or FALSE value. Default = TRUE.

Table 6.3 Salary Data iView Properties (Cont.)

6.1.6 Long Terms Incentives

The LTIs iView lets managers display the current status of LTI information for all employees within their span of control. Managers can only use this iView after selecting an employee from the Employee Search iView. The LTIs iView displays data from the LTI-specific Infotypes 0761 (LTI Granting) and 0762 (LTI Exercising).

Figure 6.10 shows an example of the LTIs iView, showing LTI-specific data including grant number, exercised number, and vesting and expiry dates.

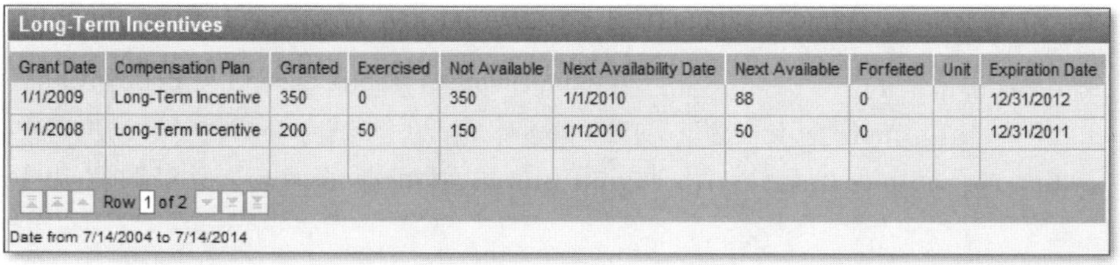

Long-Term Incentives

Grant Date	Compensation Plan	Granted	Exercised	Not Available	Next Availability Date	Next Available	Forfeited	Unit	Expiration Date
1/1/2009	Long-Term Incentive	350	0	350	1/1/2010	88	0		12/31/2012
1/1/2008	Long-Term Incentive	200	50	150	1/1/2010	50	0		12/31/2011

Row 1 of 2

Date from 7/14/2004 to 7/14/2014

Figure 6.10 LTIs iView

Long Term Incentives iView Configuration

The LTIs iView provides a set of properties that can be configured to change its behavior and show (or remove) functionality. Table 6.4 lists the properties.

Property	Description	Maintained By	Allowed Entries
FutureYears	This property determines the number of years data will be displayed.	Administrator, but personalized by user	Accepts an integer number representing the number of years. Default = 5.
PastYears	This property determines the number of years past that data will be displayed.	Administrator, but personalized by user	Accepts an integer number representing the number of years past. Default = 5.

Table 6.4 LTIs iView Properties

6.1.7 Compensation Eligibility

The Compensation Eligibility iView displays an employee's eligibility for a compensation plan and the eligibility criteria used. For each eligibility criterion, the iView displays whether the employee is eligible based on the required value compared with the employee's actual value. The iView can also be called directly from the worksheet to provide detailed information on employee eligibility for a compensation plan.

Figure 6.11 shows a screenshot of the Compensation Eligibility iView showing the results for compensation plans merit, bonus, and LTIs.

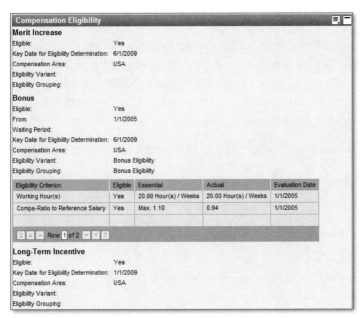

Figure 6.11   Compensation Eligibility iView

Compensation Eligibility iView Configuration

The Compensation Eligibility iView provides a set of properties that can be configured to change its behavior and show (or remove) functionality. Table 6.5 lists the properties.

Property	Description	Maintained By	Allowed Entries
Display Compensation Area	Displays the Compensation Area	Administrator	Optional
Display Eligibility Key Date	Displays the Eligibility Key Date	Administrator	Optional
Display Eligibility Variant	Displays the Eligibility Variant	Administrator	Optional
Display Eligibility Grouping	Displays the Eligibility Grouping	Administrator	Optional
Display Eligibility Criteria	Displays the Eligibility Criteria	Administrator	Optional

Table 6.5   Compensation Eligibility iView Properties

6.1.8   Compensation Guidelines

The Compensation Guidelines iView can be a powerful source of guideline information for managers. Managers can view the guidelines for an employee for a related compensation plan. The information can include default values or minimum and maximum limits. This iView is used to provide managers with information that can assist in their decision-making process.

Figure 6.12 shows the Compensation Guidelines iView with salary, bonus, and LTI guideline criteria.

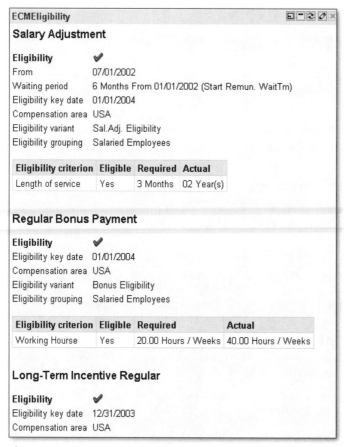

Figure 6.12   Compensation Guidelines iView

Compensation Guidelines iView Configuration

The Compensation Guidelines iView provides a set of properties that can be configured to change its behavior and show (or remove) functionality. Table 6.6 lists the properties.

Property	Description	Maintained By	Allowed Entries
DisplayCompensationArea	This property determines if the Compensation Area is displayed.	Administrator	TRUE or FALSE. Default = TRUE
DisplayGuidelineKeyDate	This property determines if the Guideline Key Date is displayed.	Administrator	TRUE or FALSE. Default = TRUE
DisplayGuidelineVariant	Displays the Guideline Variant.	Administrator	TRUE or FALSE. Default = TRUE
DisplayGuidelineGrouping	Displays the Guideline Grouping.	Administrator	TRUE or FALSE. Default = TRUE
DisplayGuidelineCriteria	Displays the Guideline Criteria.	Administrator	TRUE or FALSE. Default = TRUE

Table 6.6 Compensation Guidelines iView Properties

6.1.9 Compensation Adjustments

The Compensation Adjustments iView lets managers view all of the compensation adjustments for an employee for a given period. Managers can configure the period and display data from Infotype 0759 for all employees within their span of control using the personalization options. The data that is shown is for all Infotype 0759 records, including LTIs.

Figure 6.13 shows a screenshot of the Compensation Adjustments iView. In addition to the Base, Amount, %, and No. of Stocks column, the Status column is also shown.

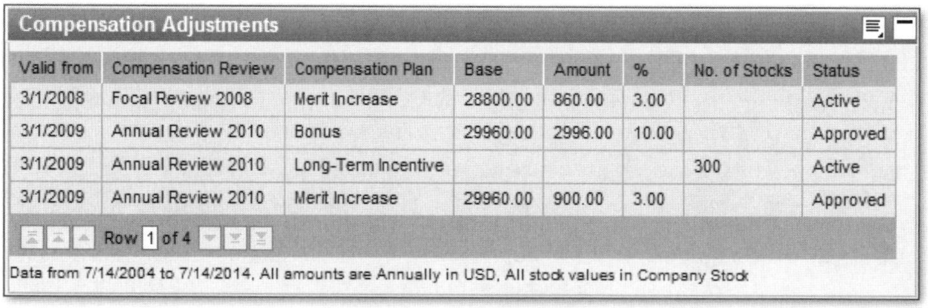

Compensation Adjustments

Valid from	Compensation Review	Compensation Plan	Base	Amount	%	No. of Stocks	Status
3/1/2008	Focal Review 2008	Merit Increase	28800.00	860.00	3.00		Active
3/1/2009	Annual Review 2010	Bonus	29960.00	2996.00	10.00		Approved
3/1/2009	Annual Review 2010	Long-Term Incentive				300	Active
3/1/2009	Annual Review 2010	Merit Increase	29960.00	900.00	3.00		Approved

Row 1 of 4

Data from 7/14/2004 to 7/14/2014, All amounts are Annually in USD, All stock values in Company Stock

Figure 6.13 Compensation Adjustments iView

Compensation Adjustments iView Configuration

The Compensation Adjustments iView provides a set of properties that can be configured to change its behavior and show (or remove) functionality. Table 6.7 lists the properties.

Property	Description	Maintained By	Allowed Entries
FutureYears	This property determines the number of years that data will be displayed.	Administrator, but personalized by user	Accepts an integer number representing the number of years. Default = 5.
PastYears	This property determines the number of years past data will be displayed.	Administrator, but personalized by user	Accepts an integer number representing the number of years past. Default = 5.

Table 6.7 Compensation Adjustments iView Properties

6.1.10 Salary Survey Data

The Salary Survey Data iView provides managers with information related to the composite results built from salary surveys collected by the compensation team. Managers are presented with a graphical view of employee's salary compared against the percentile survey data (10th percentile, 25th percentile, etc.). In addition to comparing the employee's salary to a composite, the manager can also compare against various pay categories (e.g., Base Salary, Total Bonus, etc.). To use this iView, you need to implement Job Pricing and store the results of salary surveys in SAP. For more information on the job pricing functionality in SAP, see Chapter 10, Job Pricing.

The administrator has some flexibility on what data is displayed to the manager. The administrator can set up which percentile should be displayed for the salary and survey data and whether average values should be displayed. The administrator can also specify whether the percentage and absolute difference between the survey result and the employee salary data should be displayed.

Figure 6.14 shows an example screenshot of the Salary Survey Data iView. In this example, an employee's base salary is being compared against the stored composite salary for Human Resources – VP.

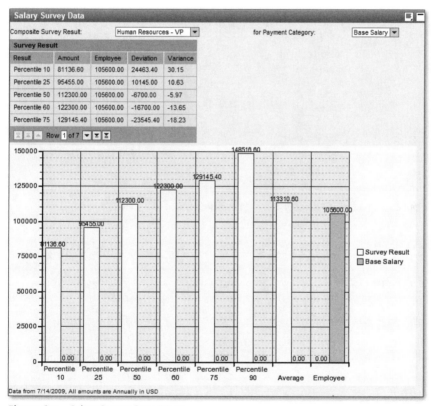

Figure 6.14 Salary Survey Data iView

Salary Survey Data iView Configuration

The Salary Survey Data iView provides you with a set of properties that can be configured to change its behavior and show (or remove) functionality. Table 6.8 lists the properties.

Property	Description	Maintained By	Allowed Entries
Currency	This property determines the currency used to display amounts.	Administrator	Three-character currency abbreviation from Table TCURC. For example, USD, EUR, or GBP.
Frequency	This property determines which time unit will be used for displaying amounts.	Administrator	01 = Monthly; 02 = Semimonthly; 03 = Weekly; 04 = Bi-weekly; 05 = Every four weeks; 06 = Annually; 07 = Quarterly; 08 = Half-yearly; 99 = Hourly
PayCategories	This property determines the permitted payment category.	Administrator	TRUE (Default) or FALSE
DisplayPercentile10	10th display percentile	Administrator	TRUE (Default) or FALSE
DisplayPercentile25	25th display percentile	Administrator	TRUE (Default) or FALSE
DisplayPercentile50	50th display percentile	Administrator	TRUE (Default) or FALSE
DisplayPercentile60	60th display percentile	Administrator	TRUE (Default) or FALSE
DisplayPercentile75	75th display percentile	Administrator	TRUE (Default) or FALSE
90. Display percentile	90th display percentile	Administrator	TRUE (Default) or FALSE

Table 6.8 Compensation Adjustments iView Properties

Property	Description	Maintained By	Allowed Entries
DisplayAverage	This property determines if the average is displayed.	Administrator	TRUE (Default) or FALSE
DisplayDelta	Displays the difference between employee and survey results.	User	TRUE (Default) or FALSE
DisplayChart	Displays the chart	User	TRUE (Default) or FALSE
DisplayChartValues	Displays the values in the charts	User	TRUE (Default) or FALSE

Table 6.8 Compensation Adjustments iView Properties (Cont.)

This concludes our review of the available MSS components for compensation support, so now let's discuss the Total Compensation Statement (TCS).

6.1.11 TCS

The TCS is a self-service application that is provided for employees (versus managers) in the SAP NetWeaver Portal. The TCS is delivered within the SAP Portal via an Adobe PDF document that the employee can print and retain for their records. It is usually available periodically (at least on an annual basis) and regarded by most compensation managers and HR professionals as an effective tool for motivating employees.

Figure 6.15 shows a screenshot of the TCS iView. Please note that the embedded PDF statement has not been customized. Depending on the complexity of your requirements, you may need to make a sizeable amount of enhancements to the form. The form is customized based on SMARTFORM technology.

The iView lets employees enter a Begin and End date. This functionality allows employees to query compensation data as of a given date or time span.

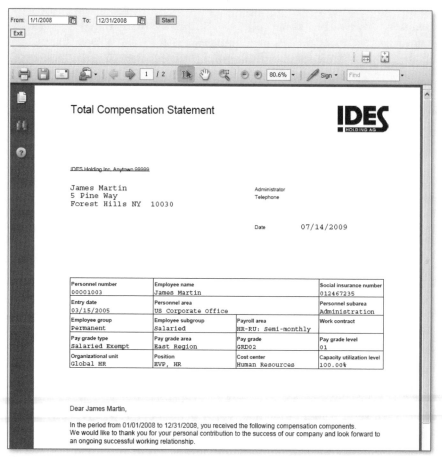

Figure 6.15 TCS

The TCS usually contains several sections including salary, benefits, other compensation (such as LTIs and bonuses), and investments in personal development such as training. All information contained in the statement is designed to give employees a more holistic view of compensation — showing their total rewards with the company. Most employees never realize what the company truly invests in them and are surprised when they see that their total compensation is far greater than their base salary (which they most often consider as compensation).

6.2 Summary

This chapter provided a summary of the main self-service iViews used to review compensation data and perform compensation planning for eligible employees. The information provided you with details regarding the functionality of the iViews and the associated configuration required to show (or remove) the functionality to users.

As described earlier, SAP provides a powerful set of iViews through self-service business packages. Many of the iViews can be consolidated into a single view or can be incorporated into smaller, more targeted views, allowing managers to access key employee compensation data without having to navigate the portal or ask for a report from HR or the Compensation department. We recommend that you experiment with the iViews and provide managers with quick access to relevant information about compensation information so that they can more effectively reward and retain key employees.

In the next chapter, we will discuss the Business-Add Ins (BAdIs) available in ECM and their relevance to the compensation process.

Business Add-Ins (BAdIs) provide a robust way of enhancing Enterprise Compensation Management (ECM) functionality by allowing you to implement customer-specific rules according to your business requirements. SAP provides over 25 of these user exits. Without these BAdIs, ECM would not be nearly as extensible. In this chapter, we will explore the available BAdIs along with typical usage scenarios.

7   Business Add-Ins (BAdIs)

One of the most robust aspects of the ECM functionality is the abundance of available BAdIs. *BAdIs* are user exits available for SAP customers to implement. BAdIs provide a means of enhancing the system to meet your unique business requirements. Put another way, BAdIs and their implementations provide "the hook" needed for organizations to implement their unique customer-specific requirements in their system.

Because a BAdI is programmed and not configured, you need to work with an ABAP-knowledgeable resource to enhance an existing BAdI implementation (if one exists) or create a new implementation. Once a BAdI implementation is activated, the logic coded within it affects system functionality.

Most BAdIs within the core ECM functionality start with the prefix HRECM00*. Other BAdIs not prefixed as such provide additional functionality within the compensation management space, such as the Total Compensation Statement (TCS) or pay scale reclassifications.

In this chapter, we explore each BAdI within the ECM functionality. Each BAdI is reviewed with delivered implementations (if any exist), method(s), and examples of usage.

7.1 BAdI Overview

As of SAP ERP 6.0, SAP delivers over 25 BAdIs as part of its ECM functionality. These BAdIs allow enhancements in several areas of ECM including compensation planning, compensation administration, long-term incentives (LTIs), job pricing, statements, and other areas.

SAP delivers many core ECM BAdIs. By "core," we mean BAdIs that enhance the core capability within the ECM functionality such as eligibility, guidelines, calculation bases, and activation.

Table 7.1 lists the core ECM BAdIs, their description, and their release availability. Those few BAdIs identified as "discontinued" are no longer supported by SAP and are discussed in more detail later in the chapter.

BAdI	Description	Availability
HRECM00_ACTIVATION	Enhance activation	As of Enterprise 4.7 Extension Set 2.0
HRECM00_AGEDATA	Age survey market data	As of Enterprise 4.7 Extension Set 2.0
HRECM00_BDG0001	Initialize budget values	As of Enterprise 4.7 Extension Set 2.0
HRECM00_CALCBASE	Determine calculation base	As of Enterprise 4.7 Extension Set 2.0
HRECM00_CARGP	Default compensation area	As of Enterprise 4.7 Extension Set 2.0
HRECM00_CONSISTENCY	Provide additional online validation	As of Enterprise 4.7 Extension Set 2.0
HRECM00_CP1GP	Default first program grouping	As of Enterprise 4.7 Extension Set 2.0
HRECM00_CP2GP	Default second program grouping	As of Enterprise 4.7 Extension Set 2.0
HRECM00_CRS	Extract compensation data for compensation review statement	As of Enterprise 4.7 Extension Set 2.0
HRECM00_EE_CURRENCY	Determine employee currency	As of SAP ERP 6.0, Enhancement Pack 4

Table 7.1 BAdIs for Core ECM with Their Release Availability

BAdI	Description	Availability
HRECM00_EFFDATE	Determine effective date	As of Enterprise 4.7 Extension Set 2.0
HRECM00_ELIGIBILITY	Determine micro–eligibility	As of Enterprise 4.7 Extension Set 2.0
HRECM00_ELIGP	Determine eligibility grouping	As of Enterprise 4.7 Extension Set 2.0
HRECM00_EXERCISE	Accept inbound processing for exercise confirmation iDoc	Discontinued
HRECM00_GDEGP	Determine guideline grouping	As of Enterprise 4.7 Extension Set 2.0
HRECM00_GRANT_INFO	Extract LTI pan grant information for outbound iDoc	Discontinued
HRECM00_GUIDELINE	Determine guidelines	As of Enterprise 4.7 Extension Set 2.0
HRECM00_MATRIX_SEGM	Method for matrix dimensions	As of Enterprise 4.7 Extension Set 2.0
HRECM00_PARTICIPANT	Extract participant info for outbound iDoc	Discontinued
HRECM00_SALARY	Enhance salary, compa-ratio, and percentage-in-range calculations	As of Enterprise 4.7 Extension Set 2.0
HRECM00_STATSTYPE	Get value for a statistical pay group of an employee	As of Enterprise 4.7 Extension Set 2.0
HRECM00_STKUN	Determine stock unit for review item	As of Enterprise 4.7 Extension Set 2.0

Table 7.1 BAdIs for Core ECM with Their Release Availability (Cont.)

In addition to the BAdIs supporting core ECM functionality, there are ten BAdIs specific to the TCS. These BAdIs are important to extend the delivered functionality of the TCS, because the standard configuration may not capture all data needed for display on the statement. Table 7.2 lists the BAdIs available for the TCS.

BAdI	Description	Availability
HRCMP00TCS0001	Read TCS data for SAP-defined subcategory (PAY)	As of Enterprise 4.7 Extension Set 2.0
HRCMP00TCS0002	Read TCS data for customer-defined subcategory (PAY)	As of Enterprise 4.7 Extension Set 2.0
HRCMP00TCS0003	Read TCS data for SAP-defined subcategory (CMP)	As of Enterprise 4.7 Extension Set 2.0
HRCMP00TCS0004	Read TCS data for customer-defined subcategory (CMP)	As of Enterprise 4.7 Extension Set 2.0
HRCMP00TCS0005	Read Person's TCS data for customer-defined category	As of Enterprise 4.7 Extension Set 2.0
HRCMP00TCS0006	Authorization check for TCS	As of Enterprise 4.7 Extension Set 2.0
HRPDV00TCS0001	Read data on subcategory defined by SAP (Personnel Development)	As of Enterprise 4.7 Extension Set 2.0
HRPDV00TCS0002	Read data on customer-defined subcategory (Personnel Development)	As of Enterprise 4.7 Extension Set 2.0
HRBEN00PAY0013	Read data on subcategory defined by SAP (Benefits)	As of Enterprise 4.7 Extension Set 2.0
HRBEN00TCS0001	Read data on customer-defined subcategory (Benefits)	As of Enterprise 4.7 Extension Set 2.0

Table 7.2 BAdIs for TCS with Their Release Availability

There are also a few general compensation-related BAdIs, available since Release 4.6C. Although not essential to ECM or relevant to the TCS, these BAdIs are available for use.

BAdI	Description	Availability
HRCMP00_PS_RECL	Pay scale reclassification	As of Release 4.6C
HRCMP00COMPA_RATIO	Reference salary for calculation of compa-ratio	As of Release 4.6C
HRCMP00SAL0001	Revise employee salary data for salary survey	As of Release 4.6C

Table 7.3 General Compensation-Relevant BAdIs with Their Release Availability

Figure 7.1 shows a list of ECM BAdIs from Transaction SE18. Transaction SE18 provides a full inventory of BAdIs. As opposed to the BAdIs available in SAP's Performance Management component, only a few ECM BAdIs have standard implementations delivered from SAP. This is mostly due to the fact that each company's compensation practices vary so much. BAdI HRECM00_MATRIX_SEGM is an example of a BAdI that has standard delivered implementations. Although SAP provides six standard implementations for this BAdI, you can also create a custom one if none of the standard implementations suit your business requirements. To do this, you create a copy from an existing BAdI implementation via Transaction SE19. Your ABAP resource can help you with BAdIs and any implementations that need to be created or extended.

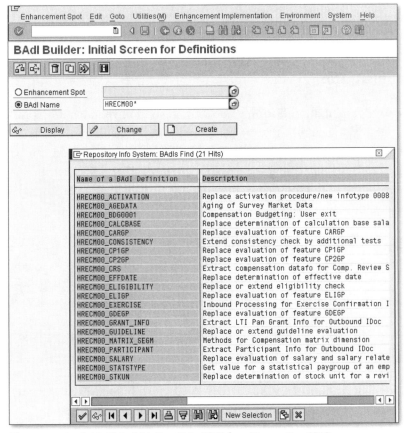

Figure 7.1 Available List of BAdIs within ECM from Transaction SE18

In an effort to logically group the vast functionality available in these user exits, we have grouped the BAdIs into several "BAdI groups." The following list represents the BAdI groups available within ECM:

- Compensation Planning and Administration
- LTIs
- Job Pricing
- Statements
- Other

In this chapter, we will cover each BAdI, available BAdI implementations, and their typical usage. Let's first look at the BAdI group Compensation Planning and Administration.

7.2   BAdI Group: Compensation Planning and Administration

The BAdI group Compensation Planning and Administration contains BAdIs relevant to the planning and administration components of compensation. Processes such as merit planning, bonus administration, and equity administration can be enhanced using functionality contained within these BAdIs. The BAdIs within this group represent some of the most core functionality available within SAP's compensation management functionality.

Tip
Throughout the chapter, the availability of each BAdI and BAdI implementation is listed with release availability (e.g., Release 4.7, SAP ERP 6.0, etc.). It should be noted that: ▶ Any BAdI implementation available as of Enterprise Extension 4.7 Set 2.0 is also available in SAP ERP 5.0 and SAP ERP 6.0. ▶ Any BAdI implementation available as of SAP ERP 5.0 is also available in SAP ERP 6.0.

Let's look at the first BAdI, HRECM00_GUIDELINE, which influences how guidelines are calculated during the planning and administration of compensation.

7.2.1 HRECM00_GUIDELINE (Determine Guidelines)

BAdI HRECM00_GUIDELINE enables you to enhance your plan's guidelines or replace them completely. Through standard configuration, guidelines are established based on defined matrices. These matrices (consisting of up to three dimensions) are used to derive guidelines for merit increases, bonus awards, or equity grants. By implementing logic within this BAdI, guidelines can be adjusted based on specific plan business rules.

You can access this BAdI through Transaction SE18 or via the Implementation Guide (IMG) path: PERSONNEL MANAGEMENT • ENTERPRISE COMPENSATION MANAGEMENT • COMPENSATION ADMINISTRATION • GUIDELINES • BUSINESS ADD-IN: DETERMINE GUIDELINE.

Table 7.4 lists the standard methods for BAdI HRECM00_GUIDELINE and their release availability.

BAdI	Method	Method Description	Availability
HRECM00_ GUIDELINE	EVALUATE_ GUIDELINE	Replace complete guideline evaluation	As of Enterprise 4.7 Extension Set 2.0
HRECM00_ GUIDELINE	EVALUATE_GDL_ CONTRIB	Manipulate guideline contribution result	As of Enterprise 4.7 Extension Set 2.0

Table 7.4 BAdI Methods for HRECM00_GUIDELINE and Their Release Availability

A typical usage scenario for this BAdI is when complex proration rules are needed against guidelines. The method EVALUATE_GDL_CONTRIB is frequently used to implement proration logic against the guidelines — something that cannot be handled through the standard configuration.

Standard guideline proration is handled within the configuration via the IMG path: PERSONNEL MANAGEMENT • ENTERPRISE COMPENSATION MANAGEMENT • COMPENSATION ADMINISTRATION • GUIDELINES • DEFINE GUIDELINE PRORATION RULES. As we explained in Chapter 3, Baseline Configuration and Infotypes, the standard proration functionality allows proration based on days or months. However, if standard proration does not satisfy your business requirements, you can apply your own custom logic for proration using method EVALUATE_GDL_CONTRIB. For example, proration of guidelines may be dependent on a certain action or action/ reason combination. A custom table, for example, could be maintained to determine which actions or action/reasons are suitable to count for proration purposes (e.g., leaves of absence).

> **Note**
>
> Several BAdIs for ECM can replace the complete logic of a corresponding component, if you implement the BAdIs. However, customers may want to use the standard logic and just add changes on top of the function. For several BAdIs, there is an import option "SKIP_BADI." Using this flag, an ABAP programmer can more effectively use standard functionality in addition to custom logic. This applies to BAdIs HRECM00_CALCBASE, HRECM00_ACTIVATION, BAdI HRECM00_EFFDATE, BAdI HRECM00_ELIGIBILITY, and BAdI HRECM00_GUIDELINE.
>
> For more information, see SAP Note 878336 (ECM Function modules: parameter to ease BAdI implementations).

The next BAdI, HRECM00_GDEGP, enhances logic for configured guideline groupings.

7.2.2 HRECM00_GDEGP (Determines Guideline Grouping)

BAdI HRECM00_GDEGP replaces logic in Feature CGDGP (Compensation Guideline Grouping). Guideline groupings group employees for guideline purposes and were described in Chapter 3. By implementing this BAdI, guideline groupings are determined via the BAdI's custom programming rather than via the standard Feature CGDGP (Compensation Guideline Grouping).

Table 7.5 lists the standard method for BAdI HRECM00_GDEGP and its release availability.

BAdI	Method	Method Description	Availability
HRECM00_ GDEGP	READ_FEATURE_ GDEGP	Determine guideline grouping	As of Enterprise 4.7 Extension Set 2.0

Table 7.5 Method for BAdI HRECM00_GDEGP and Its Release Availability

You can access this BAdI through Transaction SE18 or via the IMG path: Personnel Management • Enterprise Compensation Management • Compensation Administration • Guidelines • Business Add-In: Determine Guideline Grouping.

You can implement this BAdI if, for example, you need to group employees based on a custom infotype.

The next BAdI, HRECM00_MATRIX_SEGM, allows you to create a custom matrix dimension method. Matrix dimension methods are used within guideline configurations to determine data needed in the overall calculation of guidelines.

7.2.3 HRECM00_MATRIX_SEGM (Method for Matrix Dimensions)

BAdI HRECM00_MATRIX_SEGM allows you to create alternative matrix dimensions to incorporate into your guideline decision making. A guideline is composed of matrices based on matrix dimensions. By implementing this BAdI, a new matrix dimension is available for use within your configuration.

You can access this BAdI through Transaction SE18 or via the IMG path: PERSONNEL MANAGEMENT • ENTERPRISE COMPENSATION MANAGEMENT • COMPENSATION ADMINISTRATION • GUIDELINES • MATRIX • BUSINESS ADD-IN: METHODS FOR MATRIX DIMENSIONS

> **Note**
>
> Please note that enhancement MBOA is for the newer Performance Management component (i.e., Object Setting and Appraisals) versus enhancement APPR, which is for the older version (i.e., Performance Appraisals).

Table 7.6 lists the standard implementations for BAdI HRECM00_MATRIX_SEGM and their release availability.

Enhancement Name	BAdI Implementation	BAdI Implementation Description	Availability
AGE	HRECM00_MATR_AGE	Matrix dimension method: Age	As of Enterprise 4.7 Extension Set 2.0
APPR	HRECM00_MATR_APPR	Matrix dimension method: Appraisal	As of Enterprise 4.7 Extension Set 2.0
CRAT	HRECM00_MATR_CRATIO	Matrix dimension method: Compa-ratio	As of Enterprise 4.7 Extension Set 2.0

Table 7.6 Standard BAdI Implementations for HRECM00_MATRIX_SEGM and Their Release Availability

Enhancement Name	BAdI Implementation	BAdI Implementation Description	Availability
MBOA	HRECM00_MATR_MBOAPPR	Matrix dimension method: MBO Appraisal	As of Enterprise 4.7 Extension Set 2.0
PIR	HRECM00_MATR_PIRANGE	Matrix dimension method: Percent in salary range	As of Enterprise 4.7 Extension Set 2.0
SERV	HRECM00_MATR_SERVICE	Matrix dimension method: Length of service	As of Enterprise 4.7 Extension Set 2.0

Table 7.6 Standard BAdI Implementations for HRECM00_MATRIX_SEGM and Their Release Availability (Cont.)

Commonly used implementations include MBOA and CRAT. Using these dimensions allows you to build a guideline matrix that considers both performance appraisal rating and compa-ratio.

BAdI HRECM00_MATRIX_SEGM has five methods to support its implementation (see Table 7.7). Method CALCULATE_SEGMENT_VALUE provides the primary logic for the calculation. In this method, the segment value is obtained. In implementation MBOA, for example, a call within this method is made to standard SAP function HRHAP_PA_ECM_PERFORMANCE_GET to retrieve the appraisal rating.

BAdI	Method	Method Description	Availability
HRECM00_MATRIX_SEGM	CALCULATE_SEGMENT_VALUE	Calculate value of the method for an employee	As of Enterprise 4.7 Extension Set 2.0
HRECM00_MATRIX_SEGM	EVALUATE_GDL_CONTRIB	Value check for the generic dimension parameter	As of Enterprise 4.7 Extension Set 2.0
HRECM00_MATRIX_SEGM	F4_HELP_FOR_PARAMETER	F4 help for the generic dimension parameter	As of Enterprise 4.7 Extension Set 2.0

Table 7.7 BAdI Methods for HRECM00_MATRIX_SEGM and Their Release Availability

BAdI	Method	Method Description	Availability
HRECM00_MATRIX_SEGM	CHECK_UNIT	Value check for the dimension unit	As of Enterprise 4.7 Extension Set 2.0
HRECM00_MATRIX_SEGM	F4_HELP_FOR_UNIT	F4 help for the dimension unit	As of Enterprise 4.7 Extension Set 2.0

Table 7.7 BAdI Methods for HRECM00_MATRIX_SEGM and Their Release Availability (Cont.)

The next set of BAdIs is relevant for eligibility. SAP provides BAdIs that assist with enhancing both macro- and microeligibility, including:

- HRECM00_CARGP, for defaulting Compensation Area
- HRECM00_CP1GP, for defaulting First Program Grouping
- HRECM00_CP2GP, for defaulting Second Program Grouping
- HRECM00_ELIGIBILITY, for determining microeligibility
- HRECM00_ELIGP, for determining eligibility groupings

The first three BAdIs provide enhancement to the defaults within Infotype 0758. The standard Features (CARGP, CP1GP, and CP2GP) within the configuration can be replaced with logic from these three BAdIs, if implemented. So let's take a look at these.

7.2.4 HRECM00_CARGP (Default Compensation Area)

Feature CARGP can be replaced by logic within BAdI HRECM00_CARGP, which provides the ability to default the compensation area in Infotype 0758 based on customer-specific criteria.

You can access this BAdI through Transaction SE18 or via the IMG path: Personnel Management • Enterprise Compensation Management • Compensation Administration • Business Add-In: Determine Compensation Area.

Table 7.8 lists the method for BAdI HRECM00_CARGP and its release availability.

BAdI	Method	Method Description	Availability
HRECM00_CARGP	READ_FEATURE_CARGP	Determine compensation area	As of Enterprise 4.7 Extension Set 2.0

Table 7.8 Standard BAdI Method for HRECM00_CARGP and Its Release Availability

Please note that although this functionality determines the defaulting on Infotype 0758, you can always override the compensation area from the selections in the dropdown. As with other infotypes within Personnel Administration, this default will occur during a create infotype operation within an action or directly from Transaction PA30.

The next BAdI, HRECM00_CP1GP, performs a similar operation for the first program grouping field in Infotype 0758.

7.2.5 HRECM00_CP1GP (Default First Program Grouping)

Feature CP1GP can be replaced by logic within BAdI HRECM00_CP1GP, which provides the ability to default to the first program grouping in Infotype 0758 based on customer-specific criteria.

You can access this BAdI through Transaction SE18 or via the IMG path: PERSONNEL MANAGEMENT • ENTERPRISE COMPENSATION MANAGEMENT • COMPENSATION ADMINISTRATION • COMPENSATION PROGRAMS • BUSINESS ADD-IN: DETERMINE FIRST COMPENSATION PROGRAM GROUPING.

Table 7.9 lists the standard method for BAdI HRECM00_CP1GP and its release availability.

BAdI	Method	Method Description	Availability
HRECM00_CP1GP	READ_FEATURE_CP1GP	Determine first compensation program grouping	As of Enterprise 4.7 Extension Set 2.0

Table 7.9 Method for BAdI HRECM00_CP1GP and Its Release Availability

The next BAdI, HRECM00_CP2GP, performs a similar operation for the second program grouping field in Infotype 0758.

7.2.6 HRECM00_CP2GP (Default Second Program Grouping)

Feature CP2GP can be replaced by logic within BAdI HRECM00_CP2GP, which provides the ability to default the second program grouping on Infotype 0758 based on customer-specific criteria.

You can access this BAdI through Transaction SE18 or via the IMG path: PERSONNEL MANAGEMENT • ENTERPRISE COMPENSATION MANAGEMENT • COMPENSATION ADMINISTRATION • COMPENSATION PROGRAMS • BUSINESS ADD-IN: DETERMINE SECOND COMPENSATION PROGRAM GROUPING.

Table 7.10 lists the standard method for BAdI HRECM00_CP2GP and its release availability.

BAdI	Method	Method Description	Availability
HRECM00_CP2GP	READ_FEATURE_CP2GP	Determine second compensation program grouping	As of Enterprise 4.7 Extension Set 2.0

Table 7.10 Method for BAdI HRECM00_CP2GP and Its Release Availability

The preceding three BAdIs influence the defaulting in Infotype 0758 if the features cannot satisfy your requirements. There are also two BAdIs that can influence microeligibility: HRECM00_ELIGIBILITY and HRECM00_ELIGP. Let's discuss HRECM00_ELIGIBILITY first.

7.2.7 HRECM00_ELIGIBILITY (Determine Micro–eligibility)

BAdI HRECM00_ELIGIBILITY can partially or fully replace micro–eligibility logic. Using this BAdI, complex eligibility rules can be implemented to your employee population.

Table 7.11 lists the standard methods for BAdI HRECM00_ELIGIBILITY and their release availability.

BAdI	Method	Method Description	Availability
HRECM00_ELIGIBILITY	CHECK_ELIGIBILITY	Replace complete eligibility check	As of Enterprise 4.7 Extension Set 2.0
HRECM00_ELIGIBILITY	GET_PROGRAM_PERIOD	Replace evaluation of program period	As of Enterprise 4.7 Extension Set 2.0
HRECM00_ELIGIBILITY	CHECK_MICRO_ELIGIBILITY	Define additional eligibility criteria, change end of waiting period	As of Enterprise 4.7 Extension Set 2.0

Table 7.11 Methods for BAdI HRECM00_ELIGIBILITY and Their Release Availability

This BAdI is commonly implemented because many organizations have unique requirements for eligibility. For example, eligibility for bonus or equity plans may be more complex for retired employees or those involuntarily terminated on severance. In cases like this, method CHECK_ELIGIBILITY could be used to read the employee's employment status, customer status, or actions/action reasons.

Eligibility could also be influenced by other factors. For example, an employee placed on probation may not be eligible for one or more compensation programs. In this case, an employee's ineligibility could be determined based on his "good standing."

You can access this BAdI through Transaction SE18 or via the IMG path: Personnel Management • Enterprise Compensation Management • Compensation Administration • Eligibility • Business Add-In: Determine Eligibility.

The next BAdI, HRECM00_ELIGP, can be implemented to determine eligibility groupings via customer-specific requirements not achievable through standard feature configuration.

7.2.8 HRECM00_ ELIGP (Determine Eligibility Grouping)

BAdI replaces logic in Feature CELGP (Compensation Eligibility Grouping). By implementing this BAdI, eligibility groupings are determined via the BAdI's custom programming rather than via the standard Feature CELGP (Compensation Eligibility Grouping).

Table 7.12 lists the standard method for BAdI HRECM00_ELIGP and its release availability.

BAdI	Method	Method Description	Availability
HRECM00_ELIGP	READ_FEATURE_ELIGP	Determine eligibility grouping	As of Enterprise 4.7 Extension Set 2.0

Table 7.12 Method for BAdI HRECM00_ELIGP and Its Release Availability

You can access this BAdI through Transaction SE18 or via the IMG path: PERSONNEL MANAGEMENT • ENTERPRISE COMPENSATION MANAGEMENT • COMPENSATION ADMINISTRATION • ELIGIBILITY • BUSINESS ADD-IN: DETERMINE ELIGIBILITY GROUPING.

The next set of BAdIs influence some of the most important aspects of compensation administration — enhancements to calculation base, activation, salary, and effective date, among others, and it's very likely that you will implement one or more of these BAdIs. BAdIs for calculation base and activation are two of the most commonly implemented BAdIs within ECM projects and will surely end up on your project's development object list. Let's first review the calculation base BAdI, HRECM00_CALCBASE.

7.2.9 HRECM00_CALCBASE (Determine Calculation Base)

A calculation base, defined per plan within the configuration, allows the basis for a compensation adjustment (e.g., meritable base pay for merit planning). As mentioned in Chapter 3, a cumulative wage type (i.e., a group of wage types specified in Table T539J) is configured as the calculation base via the IMG path: PERSONNEL MANAGEMENT • ENTERPRISE COMPENSATION MANAGEMENT • COMPENSATION ADMINISTRATION • PLAN ATTRIBUTES • ASSIGN COMPENSATION PLAN PAYROLL DATA. In this step, a calculation base wage type is specified for each country grouping/compensation area combination. Per compensation review item, a key date can also be implemented to determine on what date the system should evaluate those wages. (If left blank, the current system date is used.) If this BAdI is implemented, the standard configuration is overridden with logic included in the BAdI.

You can access this BAdI through Transaction SE18 or via the IMG path: PERSONNEL MANAGEMENT • ENTERPRISE COMPENSATION MANAGEMENT • COMPENSATION ADMINISTRATION • PLAN ATTRIBUTES • BUSINESS ADD-IN: DETERMINE CALCULATION BASE.

Table 7.13 lists the standard method for BAdI HRECM00_CALCBASE and its release availability.

BAdI	Method	Method Description	Availability
HRECM00_ CALCBASE	GET_ CALCULATION_ BASE	Evaluate the calculation base salary	As of Enterprise 4.7 Extension Set 2.0

Table 7.13 Method for BAdI HRECM00_CALCBASE and Its Release Availability

The calculation base BAdI is frequently implemented in many ECM implementations. It is especially useful in Infotype 0008 for countries with multiple wages. For example, an employee may have one or more wages (e.g., food allowance, vacation premium, etc.) on their Infotype 0008 record that — although contributing to their annual salary — should not be included in their meritable base.

The calculation base BAdI can also be used to annualize the salary of an hourly worker if that employee is planned on in an annual basis. (If this is true, you must ensure that you "de–annualize" the new annual salary back to their hourly rate during activation using the activation BAdI.)

Finally, the calculation base BAdI can annualize any part-timer's salary if the employee's salary is stored as an actual figure. To annualize the salary, the employee's employment percentage (in Infotype 0007) or their capital utilization percentage (in Infotype 0008) must correctly reflect their full-time equivalency (FTE). By knowing the employee's FTE percentage and their actual salary, an annualized salary can easily be determined using the calculation base BAdI.

The next BAdI is important if you need to use an alternate effective date in lieu of the configured one.

7.2.10 HRECM00_EFFDATE (Determine Effective Date)

The HRECM00_EFFDATE BAdI allows you to determine the default effective date of a compensation review item (i.e., Infotype 0759 (Compensation Process) record)

when using the compensation planning iView within Manager Self-Service (MSS). This default overrides the logic configured within the IMG for a particular compensation review item.

You can access this BAdI through Transaction SE18 or via the IMG path: Personnel Management • Enterprise Compensation Management • Compensation Administration • Compensation Plans and Reviews • Business Add-In: Determine Effective Date.

Table 7.14 lists the standard method for BAdI HRECM00_EFFDATE and its release availability.

BAdI	Method	Method Description	Availability
HRECM00_ EFFDATE	GET_DEFAULT_ EFF_DATE	Determination of default effective date	As of Enterprise 4.7 Extension Set 2.0

Table 7.14 Method for BAdI HRECM00_EFFDATE and Its Release Availability

You may want to implement this BAdI if, for example, all elements of a compensation plan are similar except for the effective date of a particular group (perhaps due to payroll requirements). In this case, the group of employees (e.g., an hourly population that gets paid weekly) could still share the same compensation review item with other employees, but when their recommendations are saved on the portal, the effective dates of their Infotype 0759 records are created using an effective not-configured date within the compensation review item.

The next BAdI, HRECM00_SALARY, controls the calculation of an employee's salary and the salary-related concepts compa-ratio and percentage in range.

7.2.11 HRECM00_SALARY (Determine Salary, Compa-Ratio, and Percent in Range)

BAdI HRECM00_SALARY allows customer-specific programming to influence the calculation of an employee's salary, compa-ratio, and percent in range. There are three methods:

- ▸ CALCULATE_SALARY

- ▸ CALC_COMPA_RATIO

- ▸ CALC_PERCENT_IN_RANGE

Using the method CALCULATE_SALARY, you can replace the standard routine for evaluating an employee's base salary with customer-specific logic. For example, you may only want certain wage types within Infotype 0008 to contribute to an employee's base salary.

In addition, using the method CALC_COMPA_RATIO, you can replace the standard routine for evaluating an employee's compa-ratio. The compa-ratio is normally evaluated as the ratio of the employee's salary against the reference salary of the range (of the employee's grade). You can also use customer-specific code to determine a compa-ratio. For example, store ranges at the job level (and not grade) on a custom infotype and determined compa-ratio using an employee's salary against the reference salary on this custom infotype.

You can use method CALC_PERCENT_IN_RANGE to replace the standard routine for evaluating the percent in range. In the standard system, the percent in range is evaluated according to the formula: (actual salary - min) / (max - min) * 100, where min and max are the minimum and maximum salaries as defined for the employee's salary range. As with compa-ratio, customer-specific logic can be written to derive the percent in range based on a maximum or minimum not stored on standard tables.

You can access this BAdI through Transaction SE18 or via the IMG path: PERSONNEL MANAGEMENT • ENTERPRISE COMPENSATION MANAGEMENT • COMPENSATION ADMINISTRATION • OTHER SETTINGS • BUSINESS ADD-IN: CALCULATE EMPLOYEE SALARY DATA.

Table 7.15 lists the standard methods for BAdI HRECM00_SALARY and their release availability.

BAdI	Method	Method Description	Availability
HRECM00_ SALARY	CALCULATE_ SALARY	Calculate employee salary	As of Enterprise 4.7 Extension Set 2.0

Table 7.15 Methods for BAdI HRECM00_SALARY and Their Release Availability

BAdI	Method	Method Description	Availability
HRECM00_SALARY	CALC_COMPA_RATIO	Calculate compa-ratio	As of Enterprise 4.7 Extension Set 2.0
HRECM00_SALARY	CALC_PERCENT_IN_RANGE	Calculate percent in range	As of Enterprise 4.7 Extension Set 2.0

Table 7.15 Methods for BAdI HRECM00_SALARY and Their Release Availability (Cont.)

There is another critical BAdI that enhances the activation routine once compensation adjustments are approved and activated. The activation BAdI represents one of the most important pieces to the solution, because it allows for flexibility on how the activated recommendations update employees' payroll-relevant infotype records.

7.2.12 HRECM00_ACTIVATION (Enhance Activation Routine)

BAdI HRECM00_ACTIVATION is a foundational component of any ECM implementation. Most companies need the enhanced activation routine to support their business requirements. Two methods are available — ACTIVATE_PROCESS and CALC_SAL_ADJUSTMENT.

Using the ACTIVATE_PROCESS method you can revise or create a secondary infotype during activation, for example, by updating a customer-specific infotype. During the activation process, the system not only changes the status of the Infotype 0759 record from Approved to Active in the standard coding, but also creates or updates a record of a secondary infotype.

> **Example**
>
> A global customer maintained a custom infotype for all of their Italian employees. This infotype had to be updated after each pay increase. Activation logic was needed to implement the updates.

Using the CALC_SAL_ADJUSTMENT method you can define an alternative algorithm for evaluating an employee's new Infotype 0008 record. During the activation of a salary adjustment, the system determines the new Infotype 0008 record on the basis of the compensation process data and the old Infotype 0008 record. This method is especially critical for countries that have a set distribution of wages in Infotype 0008. Some countries (most notably India, Spain, Italy, Mexico, and Colombia) frequently have complex wage-type models with multiple wage types in Infotype 0008. When merit increases are activated, the wage types should be updated based on a set distribution of wages. For example, in Spain, wage *plus convenio* is calculated at a maximum of 35% of the monthly base salary (according to some industry general agreements). Using this method within BAdI HRECM00_ ACTIVATION enables the proper recalculation of this (and other) wage types in Infotype 0008 during the activation routine.

You can access this BAdI through Transaction SE18 or via the IMG path: PERSONNEL MANAGEMENT • ENTERPRISE COMPENSATION MANAGEMENT • COMPENSATION ADMIN-ISTRATION • OTHER SETTINGS • BUSINESS ADD-IN: REPLACE ACTIVATION ROUTINES.

Table 7.16 lists the standard mthods for BAdI HRECM00_ACTIVATION and their release availability.

BAdI	Method	Method Description	Availability
HRECM00_ ACTIVATION	ACTIVATE_ PROCESS	Replace creation and/or update of a secondary infotype	As of Enterprise 4.7 Extension Set 2.0
HRECM00_ ACTIVATION	CALC_SAL_ ADJUSTMENT	Replace calculation of a new Infotype 0008 record	As of Enterprise 4.7 Extension Set 2.0

Table 7.16 Methods for BAdI HRECM00_ ACTIVATION and Their Release Availability

The next BAdI, HRECM00_CONSISTENCY, provides additional validation on the compensation planning iView for the manager performing the planning.

7.2.13 HRECM00_CONSISTENCY (Provides Additional Online Validation)

BAdI HRECM00_CONSISTENCY provides additional customer-specific consistency checks when managers perform actions within the compensation planning iView in MSS. Although the standard routine already includes several checks, including guideline and budget, additional checks can be built to reject data records and generate error messages, for example. Online portal validation can be enhanced if this BAdI is implemented.

You can access this BAdI through Transaction SE18 or via the IMG path: PERSON-NEL MANAGEMENT • ENTERPRISE COMPENSATION MANAGEMENT • COMPENSATION ADMINISTRATION • OTHER SETTINGS • BUSINESS ADD-IN: DEFINE ADDITIONAL CHECK CRITERIA.

Table 7.17 lists the standard methods for BAdI HRECM00_CONSISTENCY and their release availability.

BAdI	Method	Method Description	Availability
HRECM00_CONSISTENC	CHECK_CONSISTENCY	Define additional tests for consistency check	As of Enterprise 4.7 Extension Set 2.0

Table 7.17 Method for BAdI HRECM00_CONSISTENCY and Its Release Availability

The next BAdI is one of the newest in ECM. BAdI HRECM00_EE_CURRENCY allows you to determine an employee's currency based on customer-specific logic.

7.2.14 HRECM00_EE_CURRENCY (Determine Employee Currency)

BAdI HRECM00_EE_CURRENCY is used to determine an employee's default currency within Infotype 0759 records based on customer-specific logic. By default, the currency of an employee is based on the country of the employee's Infotype 0001 (Organizational Assignment) record. Logic can be implemented to change this.

You can access this BAdI through Transaction SE18 or via the IMG path: PERSONNEL MANAGEMENT • ENTERPRISE COMPENSATION MANAGEMENT • COMPENSATION ADMIN-ISTRATION • OTHER SETTINGS • BUSINESS ADD-IN: DETERMINE EMPLOYEE CURRENCY.

Table 7.18 lists the standard method for BAdI HRECM00_EE_CURRENCY and its release availability.

BAdI	Method	Method Description	Availability
HRECM00_EE_CURRENCY	GET_CURRENCY	Determine employee currency	As of ECC 6.0, Enhancement Package 4

Table 7.18 Method for BAdI HRECM00_EE_CURRENCY and Its Release Availability

Table 7.19 lists the standard implementation for BAdI HRECM00_EE_CURRENCY and its release availability. Using the BASICPAY enhancement, an employee's currency can be determined from Infotype 0008, instead of through Infotype 0001.

Enhancement Name	BAdI Implementation	BAdI Implementation Description	Availability
BASICPAY	HRECM00_EE_CURR_BASICPAY	Determine currency from Basic Pay of employee	As of ECC 6.0, Enhancement Package 4

Table 7.19 Standard BAdI implementation for HRECM00_EE_CURRENCY and Its Release Availability

From a budgeting perspective, BAdI HRECM00_BDG0001 allows you to import budget values into budget units. Let's discuss this BAdI next.

7.2.15 HRECM00_BDG0001 (Initialize Budget Values)

BAdI HRECM00_BDG0001, previously discussed in Chapter 4, Compensation Budgeting, can be implemented to upload initial budget values from another source (for example, a spreadsheet or flat file), into the budget values of Infotype 1520. The values can be amounts for monetary budgets (e.g., merit) or numbers for equity-based pools (e.g., stock options).

You can access this BAdI through Transaction SE18 or via the IMG path: Personnel Management • Enterprise Compensation Management • Budgeting • Business Add-In: Initialize Budget Values.

Table 7.20 lists the standard method for BAdI HRECM00_BDG0001 and its release availability.

BAdI	Method	Method Description	Availability
HRECM00_BDG0001	DETERMINE_BUDGET_VALUES	Determine budget values for update Infotype 1520	As of Enterprise 4.7 Extension Set 2.0

Table 7.20 Method for BAdI HRECM00_BDG0001 and Its Release Availability

This concludes our list of core ECM BAdIs. The BAdIs we covered up to this point focused on the core components of the solution including eligibility, guidelines, calculation bases, and activation. Now let's focus on some of the BAdIs specifically for LTI plans.

7.3   BAdI Group: LTIs

The BAdI group LTIs allows enhancements on equity-based compensation processes. Although some have recently been discontinued by SAP, the following BAdIs extend the functionality by offering user exits for extracting and accepting LTI information from your third-party stock administrator.

7.3.1   HRECM00_GRANT_INFO (Extract LTI Pan Grant Information for Outbound iDoc)

Program RHECM_GRANT_IDOC_OUT (Export LTI Grant Data) was created to generate an iDOC with grant information to send to a third-party stock administrator. By using BAdI HRECM00_GRANT_INFO, the extract of LTI Plan information from Infotype 0761 (LTI Granting) can be enhanced.

> **Note**
>
> SAP is no longer supporting this interface due to a technology shift and lack of demand. (See SAP Note 889056 for more information.)

Table 7.21 lists the standard method for BAdI HRECM00_GRANT_INFO and its release availability.

BAdI	Method	Method Description	Availability
HRECM00_GRANT_INFO	GET_LTI_GRANT_INFO	Get all relevant LTI grants information	Discontinued

Table 7.21 Method for BAdI HRECM00_GRANT_INFO and Its Release Availability

7.3.2 HRECM00_EXERCISE (Accept Inbound Processing for Exercise Confirmation iDoc)

Program RHECM_EXERCISE_IDOC_IN (Import LTI Exercise Data) was created to accept iDOC information sent from a third-party stock administrator. By using BAdI HRECM00_EXERCISE, exercised stock information can be manipulated before an update to Infotype 0762 (LTI Exercising).

> **Note**
>
> SAP is no longer supporting this interface due to a technology shift and lack of demand. (See SAP Note 889056 for more information.)

Table 7.22 lists the standard methods for BAdI HRECM00_EXERCISE and their release availability.

BAdI	Method	Method Description	Availability
HRECM00_ EXERCISE	PROCESS_ IDOC	User-defined inbound processing; can replace the standard	Discontinued
HRECM00_ EXERCISE	SET_EXPORT_ PARAMETERS	Set output parameters for FM HRECM00_PROCESS_ EXERCISE_IDOC	Discontinued
HRECM00_ EXERCISE	IDOC_STATUS_ PROCESS	Work through list of status records	Discontinued

Table 7.22 Methods for BAdI for HRECM00_EXERCISE and Their Release Availability

The next BAdI, HRECM00_STKUN, can be used during equity granting on the portal to default an alternate stock unit for a compensation review item.

7.3.3 HRECM00_STKUN (Determine Stock Unit for Review Item)

BAdI HRECM00_STKUN can be used to determine a different stock unit for an employee based on specific business rules.

Table 7.23 lists the standard methods for BAdIHRECM00_STKUN and its release availability.

BAdI	Method	Method Description	Availability
HRECM00_STKUN	GET_CITEM_STKUN	Determine stock unit for review item	As of Enterprise 4.7 Extension Set 2.0

Table 7.23 Method for BAdI HRECM00_STKUN and Its Release Availability

Now that we've covered the BAdIs available for the LTI functionality within ECM, let's move on to the useful BAdIs in the job pricing functionality.

7.4 BAdI Group: Job Pricing

As with the previous BAdI groups, the Job Pricing BAdI group is full of functionality that makes the ECM functionality more robust.

7.4.1 HRECM00_PARTICIPANT (Extract Participant Info for Outbound iDoc)

Although BAdI HRECM00_PARTICIPANT supports Program RHECM_PARTICIPANT_IDOC_OUT, the program itself has been discontinued by SAP.

> **Note**
>
> As with the LTI interfaces, SAP is no longer supporting this interface due to a technology shift and lack of demand. (See SAP Note 889056 for more information.)

Table 7.24 lists the standard methods for BAdI HRECM00_PARTICIPANT and their release availability.

BAdI	Method	Method Description	Availability
HRECM00_PARTICIPANT	GET_EMPLOYEE_NAME_INFO	Get all information about the name of the employee	Discontinued
HRECM00_PARTICIPANT	GET_EMPLOYEE_CONTACT_INFO	Get contact information about the employee	Discontinued

Table 7.24 Methods for BAdI HRECM00_PARTICIPANT and Their Release Availability

BAdI	Method	Method Description	Availability
HRECM00_PARTICIPANT	GET_EMPLOYEE_POSTAL_ADDRESS	Get all information about post address of the employee	Discontinued
HRECM00_PARTICIPANT	GET_EMPLOYEE_ADDITIONAL_INFO	Get additional information about the employee	Discontinued
HRECM00_PARTICIPANT	GET_EMPLOYEE_TAX_INFO	Get all relevant tax information about the employee	Discontinued

Table 7.24 Methods for BAdI HRECM00_PARTICIPANT and Their Release Availability (Cont.)

The next BAdI enhances the job pricing functionality with respect to market data analysis. Chapter 10, Job Pricing, explores this functionality in more detail.

7.4.2 HRECM00_AGEDATA (Aging of Survey Market Data)

BAdI HRECM00_AGEDATA allows you to age market data based on company-specific criteria. Using standard aging functionality, the calculation of market data is based on a straight percentage entered by the user. Using this BAdI, customer-specific logic can be introduced to alter that calculation.

You can access this BAdI through Transaction SE18 or via the IMG path: PERSONNEL MANAGEMENT • ENTERPRISE COMPENSATION MANAGEMENT • JOB PRICING • SALARY SURVEYS • BUSINESS ADD-IN: AGE MARKET DATA.

Table 7.25 lists the standard method for BAdI HRECM00_AGEDATA and its release availability.

BAdI	Method	Method Description	Availability
HRECM00_AGEDATA	AGE_MARKET_DATA	Aging survey market data	As of Enterprise 4.7 Extension Set 2.0

Table 7.25 Method for BAdI HRECM00_EXERCISE and Its Release Availability

The next BAdI allows manipulation of the pay groups for survey data imported into the system.

7.4.3 HRECM00_STATSTYPE
(Get Value for a Statistical Pay Group of an Employee)

BAdI HRECM00_STATSTYPE allows you to calculate the value for an employee's pay category. If you have defined your own pay categories, and if no wage type groups have been specified, you can implement this BAdI to obtain values for the employee. Examples of pay categories could be "Total Compensation" and "Total Base."

Table 7.26 lists the standard methods for BAdI HRECM00_STATSTYPE and their release availability.

BAdI	Method	Method Description	Availability
HRECM00_ STATSTYPE	GET_VALUE_ HANDLER	Who (customer or standard) handles the value determination	As of Enterprise 4.7 Extension Set 2.0
HRECM00_ STATSTYPE	GET_VALUE_FOR_ STATSTYPE	Calculates the value for a statistical pay group	As of Enterprise 4.7 Extension Set 2.0

Table 7.26 Methods for BAdI HRECM00_EXERCISE and Their Release Availability

This concludes the job pricing BAdIs available within ECM. Let's look at compensation statements and BAdI enhancements next.

7.5   BAdI Group: Compensation Statements

The BAdI Compensation Statements group covers two types of statements. The first — Compensation Review Statement — is typically delivered after administering a compensation process (e.g., annual merit planning). Examples of compensation review statements include merit letters, bonus statements, and equity grant statements. These statements are frequently delivered by a manager to an employee in a formal or informal setting to discuss performance ratings, pay increases, or bonus and equity awards.

A second type of statement is the TCS. The TCS is typically available throughout the year via Employee Self-Service (ESS) for employees and can represent a snapshot (e.g., point-in-time), the year-to-date, or a rolling 21 months of that employee's total compensation. Let's look at the BAdIs for these statements.

7.5.1 HRECM00_CRS (Extract Compensation Data for Compensation Review Statement)

BAdI HRECM00_CRS can be used to enhance the data extracted for the Compensation Review Statement.

You can access this BAdI through Transaction SE18 or via the IMG path: Personnel Management • Enterprise Compensation Management • Compensation Statements • Business Add-In: Get Data for Compensation Review Statement.

Table 7.27 lists the standard method for BAdI HRECM00_CRS and its release availability.

BAdI	Method	Method Description	Availability
HRECM00_CRS	GET_CRS_DATA	Get all relevant Compensation Review Statement data	As of Enterprise 4.7 Extension Set 2.0

Table 7.27 Standard Method for BAdI HRECM00_CRS and Its Release Availability

The following BAdIs are relevant to the TCS. There are ten BAdIs in all, representing all of the major areas of the standard statement.

7.5.2 HRCMP00TCS0001 (Read TCS Data for SAP-Defined Subcategory (PAY))

BAdI HRCMP00TCS0001 enables you to define how the system determines the data for the subcategories of the Payment (PAY) category on the TCS.

You can access this BAdI through Transaction SE18 or via the IMG path: Personnel Management • Enterprise Compensation Management • Compensation Statements • Country Specific Enhancements • Read Data on Subcategory Defined by SAP (PAY).

Table 7.28 lists the standard method for BAdI HRCMP00TCS0001 and its release availability.

BAdI	Method	Method Description	Availability
HRCMP00TCS0001	TCS_DATA_READ	Determine TCS data for person for SAP-defined subcategory	As of Enterprise 4.7 Extension Set 2.0

Table 7.28 Standard Method for BAdI HRCMP00TCS0001 and Its Release Availability

7.5.3 HRCMP00TCS0002 (Read TCS Data for Customer-Defined Subcategory (PAY))

BAdI HRCMP00TCS0002 enables you to define how the system determines the data for the customer-defined subcategories of the Payment (PAY) category on the TCS.

You can access this BAdI through Transaction SE18 or via the IMG path: PERSONNEL MANAGEMENT • ENTERPRISE COMPENSATION MANAGEMENT • COMPENSATION STATEMENTS • COUNTRY SPECIFIC ENHANCEMENTS • READ DATA ON CUSTOMER-DEFINED SUBCATEGORY (PAY).

Table 7.29 lists the standard method for BAdI HRCMP00TCS0002 and its release availability.

BAdI	Method	Method Description	Availability
HRCMP00TCS0002	TCS_DATA_READ	Determine TCS data of person for customer-defined subcategory	As of Enterprise 4.7 Extension Set 2.0

Table 7.29 Standard Method for BAdI HRCMP00TCS0002 and Its Release Availability

7.5.4 HRCMP00TCS0003 (Read TCS Data for SAP-Defined Subcategory (CMP))

BAdI HRCMP00TCS0003 enables you to define how the system determines the data for the subcategories of the Other Compensation category (CMP) on the TCS.

You can access this BAdI through Transaction SE18 or via the IMG path: PERSONNEL MANAGEMENT • ENTERPRISE COMPENSATION MANAGEMENT • COMPENSATION STATE-

MENTS • COUNTRY SPECIFIC ENHANCEMENTS • READ DATA ON SUBCATEGORY DEFINED BY SAP (OTHER COMPENSATION).

Table 7.30 lists the standard method for BAdI HRCMP00TCS0003 and its release availability:

BAdI	Method	Method Description	Availability
HRCMP00TCS0003	TCS_DATA_READ	Determine TCS data for person for SAP-defined subcategory	As of Enterprise 4.7 Extension Set 2.0

Table 7.30 Standard Method for BAdI HRCMP00TCS0003 and Its Release Availability

7.5.5 HRCMP00TCS0004 (Read TCS Data for Customer-Defined Subcategory (CMP))

BAdI HRCMP00TCS0004 enables you to define how the system determines the data for the customer-defined subcategories of the Other Compensation (CMP) category on the TCS.

You can access this BAdI through Transaction SE18 or via the IMG path: PERSONNEL MANAGEMENT • ENTERPRISE COMPENSATION MANAGEMENT • COMPENSATION STATEMENTS • COUNTRY SPECIFIC ENHANCEMENTS • READ DATA ON CUSTOMER-DEFINED SUBCATEGORY (OTHER COMPENSATION).

Table 7.31 lists the standard method for BAdI HRCMP00TCS0004 and its release availability.

BAdI	Method	Method Description	Availability
HRCMP00TCS0004	TCS_DATA_READ	Determine TCS data of person for customer-defined subcategory	As of Enterprise 4.7 Extension Set 2.0

Table 7.31 Standard Method for BAdI HRCMP00TCS0004 and Its Release Availability

7.5.6 HRCMP00TCS0005 (Read Person's TCS Data for Customer-Defined Category)

BAdI HRCMP00TCS0005 enables you to determine which data the system uses for customer-specific categories on the TCS.

You can access this BAdI through Transaction SE18 or via the IMG path: PERSONNEL MANAGEMENT • ENTERPRISE COMPENSATION MANAGEMENT • COMPENSATION STATEMENTS • COUNTRY SPECIFIC ENHANCEMENTS • READ DATA ON CUSTOMER-DEFINED CATEGORY.

Table 7.32 lists the standard method for BAdI HRCMP00TCS0005 and its release availability.

BAdI	Method	Method Description	Availability
HRCMP00TCS0005	TCS_DATA_READ	Determine TCS data of person for customer-defined category	As of Enterprise 4.7 Extension Set 2.0

Table 7.32 Standard Method for BAdI HRCMP00TCS0005 and Its Release Availability

7.5.7 HRCMP00TCS0006 (Authorization Checks for TCS)

BAdI HRCMP00TCS0006 enables you to perform an additional authorization check on the TCS.

You can access this BAdI through Transaction SE18 or via the IMG path: PERSONNEL MANAGEMENT • ENTERPRISE COMPENSATION MANAGEMENT • COMPENSATION STATEMENTS • BUSINESS ADD-IN: AUTHORIZATION CHECK FOR TOTAL COMPENSATION STATEMENT.

Table 7.33 lists the standard method for BAdI HRCMP00TCS0006 and its release availability.

BAdI	Method	Method Description	Availability
HRCMP00TCS0006	TCS_AUTH_CHECK	TCS authority check	As of Enterprise 4.7 Extension Set 2.0

Table 7.33 Standard Method for BAdI HRCMP00TCS0006 and Its Release Availability

7.5.8 HRPDV00TCS0001 (Read Data for SAP Subcategory (PDV))

BAdI HRPDV00TCS0001 enables you to define how the system should determine data on the subcategories defined for the Personnel Development (PDV) category on the TCS.

You can access this BAdI through Transaction SE18 or via the IMG path: Personnel Management • Enterprise Compensation Management • Compensation Statements • Country Specific Enhancements • Read Data on Subcategory Defined by SAP (Personnel Development).

Table 7.34 lists the standard method for BAdI HRPDV00TCS0001 and its release availability.

BAdI	Method	Method Description	Availability
HRPDV00TCS0001	TCS_DATA_READ	Determine TCS data for person for SAP-defined subcategory	As of Enterprise 4.7 Extension Set 2.0

Table 7.34 Standard Method for BAdI HRPDV00TCS0001 and Its Release Availability

7.5.9   HRPDV00TCS0002 (Read Data for Customer-Specific Subcategory (PD))

BAdI HRPDV00TCS0002 enables you to define how the system should determine data on the customer-specific subcategories of the Personnel Development (PDV) category on the TCS.

You can access this BAdI through Transaction SE18 or via the IMG path: Personnel Management • Enterprise Compensation Management • Compensation Statements • Country Specific Enhancements • Read Data on Customer-Defined Subcategory (Personnel Development).

Table 7.35 lists the standard method for BAdI HRPDV00TCS0002 and its release availability.

BAdI	Method	Method Description	Availability
HRPDV00TCS0002	TCS_DATA_READ	Determine TCS data for person for SAP-defined subcategory	As of Enterprise 4.7 Extension Set 2.0

Table 7.35 Standard Method for BAdI HRPDV00TCS0002 and its Release Availability

7.5.10 HRBEN00PAY0013
(Read Data on Subcategory Defined by SAP (Benefits))

BAdI HRBEN00PAY0013 enables you to define costs and contributions in benefits plans according to the Benefits (BEN) category and show the appropriate data on the TCS.

You can access this BAdI through Transaction SE18 or via the IMG path: PERSONNEL MANAGEMENT • ENTERPRISE COMPENSATION MANAGEMENT • COMPENSATION STATEMENTS • COUNTRY SPECIFIC ENHANCEMENTS • READ DATA ON SUBCATEGORY DEFINED BY SAP (BENEFITS).

Table 7.36 lists the standard method for BAdI HRBEN00PAY0013 and its release availability.

BAdI	Method	Method Description	Availability
HRBEN00PAY0013	READ_CUMUL_RESULTS	Read cumulated payroll results for Compensation Management	As of Enterprise 4.7 Extension Set 2.0

Table 7.36 Standard Method for BAdI HRBEN00PAY0013 and Its Release Availability

7.5.11 HRBEN00TCS0001
(Read Data on Customer-Defined Subcategory (Benefits))

BAdI HRBEN00TCS0001 enables you to define how the system determines data for customer-defined subcategories of the Benefits (BEN) category on the TCS.

You can access this BAdI through Transaction SE18 or via the IMG path: PERSONNEL MANAGEMENT • ENTERPRISE COMPENSATION MANAGEMENT • COMPENSATION STATEMENTS • COUNTRY SPECIFIC ENHANCEMENTS • READ DATA ON SUBCATEGORY DEFINED BY SAP (BENEFITS).

Table 7.37 lists the standard method for BAdI HRBEN00TCS0001 and its release availability.

BAdI	Method	Method Description	Availability
HRBEN00TCS0001	BEN_TCS_DATA_READ	Read customer-specific benefits data	As of Enterprise 4.7 Extension Set 2.0

Table 7.37 Standard Method for BAdI HRBEN00TCS0001 and Its Release Availability

This concludes our discussion of the BAdIs available to enhance the Compensation Review Statements and the TCS. The next BAdI group lists all other compensation-relevant BAdIs.

7.6   BAdI Group: Other

Within the BAdI group Other, only HRCMP00_PS_RECL is covered here, because BAdIs HRCMP00COMPA_RATIO and HRCMP00SAL0001 are more relevant for older (Release 4.6c) functionality. BAdI HRCMP00SAL0001 is available for adjusting an employee's salary data for salary survey participation. However, this functionality is better implemented using BAdI HRECM00_SALARY, method CALCULATE_SALARY. Likewise, BAdI HRCMP00COMPA_RATIO is available to retrieve the compa-ratio from the employee's salary and reference point of their grade, but this information is better implemented using BAdI HRECM00_SALARY, method CALC_COMPA_RATIO.

BAdI HRCMP00_PS_RECL enables you to make customer-specific adjustments to employees' pay scale reclassifications when performing Infotype 0008 updates using the pay scale reclassification program (RPIPSR00). You can use this BAdI to influence how the system determines the records of Infotype 0008 that are generated by the pay scale reclassification program.

You can access this BAdI through Transaction SE18 or via the IMG path: PERSONNEL MANAGEMENT • PAYROLL DATA • BASIC PAY • PAY SCALE CHANGES • PAY SCALE RECLASSIFICATION • BUSINESS ADD-IN FOR PAY SCALE RECLASSIFICATION.

Table 7.38 lists the standard methods for BAdI HRCMP00_PS_RECL and their release availability:

BAdI	Method	Method Description	Availability
HRCMP00_PS_RECL	AFTER_RECLASSIFICATION	Process after reclassification	As of Release 4.6c
HRCMP00_PS_RECL	CHANGE_RECLASSIFICATION_DATE	Process after determination of reclassification date	As of Release 4.6c
HRCMP00_PS_RECL	CHOOSE_RECLASSIFICATION_TYPES	Process for selecting reclassification Types	As of Release 4.6c
HRCMP00_PS_RECL	DO_RECLASSIFICATION	Process Instead of Standard Reclassification	As of Release 4.6c
HRCMP00_PS_RECL	CHANGE_BATCH_INPUT_DATA	Make Changes to Batch Input Session	As of Release 4.6c
HRCMP00_PS_RECL	APPEND_ALV_OUTPUT_DATA	Complete list of displayed Data (ALV)	As of Release 4.6c

Table 7.38 Standard Methods for BAdI HRCMP00_PS_RECL and Their Release Availability

The standard system contains several standard implementations for BAdI HRCMP00_PS_RECL. For example, implementations relevant for pay scale reclassifications in Germany, Norway, and Great Britain are offered within the standard system.

This concludes our coverage of the BAdIs within the Other grouping and of all BAdIs in general.

7.7   Summary

In this chapter, we looked at the available BAdIs within the ECM functionality, including their release availability. Although most BAdIs in ECM do not contain standard implementations that can be used "off-the-shelf," many contain robust capabilities to extend the system's compensation functionality. We also discussed, enhancing logic concerning eligibility, guidelines, calculation basis, and activation greatly enhances the core system's capabilities.

In the next chapter, we will review several advanced topics within ECM including the handling of promotions, workflow/approvals, and off-cycle increases.

*The consistent marker for a successful Enterprise Compensation Manage-
ment (ECM) project is how the project team addresses the inherent critical challenges within the compensation processes and the technology that
supports them. In this chapter, we will address some of the more advanced
topics that tackle the difficult challenges experienced with any ECM implementation. And we will review some proven accelerators that improve the
usability and adoption of ECM tools.*

8   Advanced Topics and Additional Enhancements

Some of the more advanced topics we will cover regarding compensation projects involve the challenges specific to the tools within ECM, while others do
not involve tools at all. The focus and care that goes into addressing these issues
directly impacts a tool's adoption and the overall success of a project, so the more
attention you give to these topics, the higher the likelihood that your project will
be successful.

We will begin with some "hot topics" regarding compensation management. For
each hot topic, we will discuss the business requirement, the dilemma most companies face when trying to address it, and some options to mitigate or resolve the
dilemma. Most of the business requirements listed are common within the marketplace and become a source of many pain points when not addressed properly.

After addressing these topics, we will review some of the ways customers are
enhancing the experience for employees, managers, Human Resources (HR), and
Compensation professionals. The enhancements covered in this section offer
advanced techniques for satisfying some of the most urgent requests we have
heard from customers.

8.1   Hot Topics

Let's first review some of the more complex challenges facing companies implementing ECM. These topics are listed by common business requirement, the dilemma faced, and the options for mitigation/resolution. The first topic is handling promotions during the planning cycle.

8.1.1   Handling Growth and Organizational Promotions During Planning

Common Business Requirement

Growth and organizational promotions that occur during the planning process may involve a change to an employee's position or job. This means a change to the employee's Infotype 0001 (Organizational Assignments), Infotype 0000 (Actions), and a potential change in pay structure (i.e., grade). In most organizations, HR must still process promotions and other employee information during the planning process while the business operates "as usual."

Dilemma

The planning worksheet accepts monetary (or nonmonetary) amounts (or numbers) but does not have the ability to request a change to a position or job for an employee. Although the planning worksheet can be configured to always retrieve the most current salary, the difficulty is that (depending on the company) a growth or organizational promotion could necessitate a change to the employee's position or job. This would inevitably impact the processing of the promotion and the merit increase — especially if their effective dates coincide.

Options

1. *Discourage (or disallow) coincident growth and organizational promotions during the annual planning process.* Through proper communication, ensure that manage-

ment understands that promotions cannot be requested or processed during planning time. Implement a change management plan to educate managers through the process. Ensure that HR is on board and supports the decision.

2. *Advise managers to use the Notes functionality (or an online template) to request the promotion.* Information such as the details of the new position and new salary grade must be provided. After review and approval by the Compensation department, the adjustment can be processed by an HR administrator.

3. *Build custom functionality on top of the planning worksheet to select a new salary grade or position/job.* You can choose to only allow promotions not affecting job and position assignments (i.e., grade-changing promotions only) to be processed within the planning worksheet. All planned promotions are reviewed and validated by the Compensation department before approval and activation. During activation, the employee's Infotype 0008 (Basic Pay) is updated with the merit or promotion increases and the grade (if approved for change).

You can also allow the capability to search for and select the new position/job via a link from the planning sheet. A separate approval path is needed for this recommendation, but all requests for merit and promotion are initiated within the planning tool.

4. *Use Adobe Interactive Forms to submit and track the position, job and salary grade changes.* Using the latest HCM Processes and Forms functionality, promotions and processes involving employee movement can be routed based on business rules. The timing and coordination between the completion of this request and the completion of the annual compensation cycle is crucial for aligning the two processes.

Another factor in the viability of this option regards the handling of the budget. If the promotion increase must deduct from the merit budget, you must ensure that this is accounted for within ECM. This typically means creating the promotion as its own Infotype 0759 (Compensation Process). It becomes challenging to coordinate and synchronize both planned compensation records (Infotype 0759) and change request forms (HCM Processes and Forms). Unless driven by a strong business need, try to avoid the complexities inherent with this option.

8.1.2 Higher-Level Manager Planning

Common Business Requirement

All levels of management — including upper-level management — need the ability to plan and approve compensation adjustments on the portal in a fast and efficient manner.

Dilemma

The planning worksheet operates at an employee level. Managers can plan and adjust recommendations for individual employees using the online compensation tool, but oftentimes, performance (latency) issues arise due to the large size of the manager's span of control. Depending on the number of columns being retrieved, the planning sheet's performance can be adversely affected. And, unfortunately, too often, the planning worksheet comes under scrutiny from senior-level management who become disenchanted with the speed and agility of the tool.

Options

1. *Do not grant access to the tool for senior management.* Instead, hold targeted calibration sessions using Excel reports and other tools to facilitate these meetings. The tools used must have a way to quickly recalculate budget and other pertinent metrics during the meetings. After the meeting, the compensation or HR teams can update the system based on the feedback provided by the leadership team.

2. *Train managers to plan and approve recommendations by area or business unit on the portal rather than by their full span of control.* Having managers review and calibrate employees as separate groups reduces the chance of performance issues on the portal.

3. *Utilize SAP's Planning Overview component (available as of SAP ERP 6.0 Enhancement Package 4).* Using this tool, a more holistic view of planning is available throughout the entire planning process. Figure 8.1 shows a screenshot of the new iView. The manager can view aggregate information at an organizational unit level including budget roll-ups and the status of their direct reports' planning.

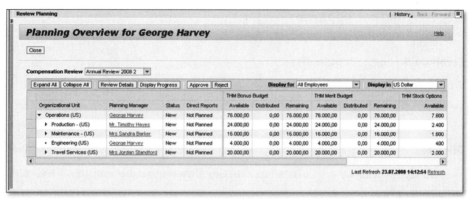

Figure 8.1 Planning Overview iView for Managers

Within this iView, a manager can drilldown to review/edit the recommendations from any lower-level manager. Keeping the initial view at the organizational unit level provides faster response times.

> **Tip**
>
> Caching can greatly improve the performance of the compensation planning worksheet. The following tips are available for your Advanced Business Application Programming (ABAP) team to improve performance on the planning worksheet.
>
> 1. When possible, read cached data from the global memory of the planning worksheet. Function module HR_ECM_READ_GLOBAL_COMP_DATA can be used to read the information stored within the planning sheet's global memory and return it back to the screen faster than getting the data from the SAP backend again.
>
> 2. Function module HRWPC_RFC_OADP_EVAL_DATAVIEW can be enhanced to use parameter CACHEMAXAGE. By setting the parameter at the beginning of the function to, for example, the value 1, the data is read once and kept in the cache for one day. To do this, you must implement an enhancement spot using the new Enhancement Framework. Please be careful with this, however, because the data is cached for one full day and can only be reset with function module HRWPC_OADP_DELETE_DATA-VWCACHE.
>
> 3. Use the ABAP statements EXPORT TO MEMORY variables... and IMPORT FROM MEMORY variables... for planning sheet data that you want to set in session memory from the employee selection screen to the worksheet.
>
> 4. Write all function modules for the planning sheet columns as lean as possible. For example, the standard function to retrieve the appraisal result (Function module HR_ECM_UI_DISP_APPRAISAL) returns the entire appraisal document (and writes to the Performance Management action log!) when, in reality, all that needs to be retuned is the ratings on the appraisal document.

8.1.3 Workflow Approvals

Common Business Requirement

Workflow approvals or notifications are needed at various points in the compensation planning process.

Dilemma

No standard workflow or notification functionality is available until SAP ERP 6.0, enhancement package 4.

Options

1. *Handle approvals and communication through manual mediums and offline mechanisms (e.g., emails, portal content, desk drops, etc.).* Typically, companies allow 2 - 3 weeks for managers to plan their recommendations. During this condensed timeframe, the Compensation department can send targeted emails to managers before close-out.

2. *Create your own custom workflows or notifications.* SAP Note 802992 (Standard workflow not available for ECM) provides direction from SAP on how to modify SAP standard function HR_ECM_HANDLE_PROCESS_DATA (after the call of form SUBMIT_ALL_RECS). Even though SAP provides this information, it is not a recommendation or consulting advice. SAP prefers customers choose the next option.

3. *Implement workflow and notification functionality, available as of SAP ERP 6.0 enhancement package 4.* There are several workflow/notification functionalities available with the new functionality. The program RHECM_NOTIFY_MANAGERS notifies planning managers that the compensation planning cycle has started. To use this report, the multilevel approval process (discussed in Chapter 5, Process Administration) needs to be activated and part of the process. Notifications are received only by planning managers that have eligible employees reporting to them.

   Throughout the process, as managers submit, approve, and reject recommendations, appropriate parties (e.g., managers, HR, Compensation, etc.) can be notified by enhancing the SAP-provided workflows. The workflow notification can be sent via the SAP portal inbox (Univeral Worklist (UWL)) or via corporate email. Either way, a link can be provided within the notification to bring the manager directly to the planning worksheet for follow-up.

8.1.4   Initialization and Reallocation of Budget Funds

Common Business Requirement

Budgeting functionality needs to be dynamic during the compensation planning cycle to account for employee movement (transfers, promotions, etc.) and employee separations.

Dilemma

Standard SAP budgeting functionality is not dynamic. Once funded, budget unit funds do not (automatically) get redistributed during employee movement and separations. Although a transaction exists to transfer funds from one budget unit to another, this manual effort is not an efficient way to keep the budget hierarchy current.

Options

1. *Institute a "freeze" date and manage to a static budget.* If instituting a freeze date for your implementation is an option, the budgeting issue can be easily resolved because no refresh is needed. The only conceivable refresh would only occur if a correction to an employee's pay was performed before the budget cutoff date. In this case, Transaction PECM_START_BDG_BSP can be used to update the appropriate budget unit.

2. *Use standard Transaction PECM_START_BDG_BSP to manage budgets manually.* Depending on how much movement occurs during the planning process, you can implement a manual procedure for identifying movement and process fund transfers between the appropriate budgets units based on business rules. This would only work for companies where the movement was not too frequent and that have the bandwidth to keep current.

3. *Create or purchase a custom budget program that can automatically initialize and reallocate funds based on events.* Many companies rely on automated programs to recalculate budget unit allocations based on certain predefined criteria. For

example, you can use country grouping, personnel area, and personnel subarea to derive merit budgets (essentially, merit budget by country). During a nightly process, the program runs in batch and reallocates the budget funds based on business logic. This way, no manual intervention is needed by the Compensation department or an HR administrator. This option assumes you use the standard SAP budgeting concept.

4. *Create budgets "on the fly" using a custom solution to drive the calculations.* If standard SAP budgeting is not used, a custom solution can be established to determine budgets based on the employees selected or the manager's span of control. Budgets can be based at an employee level (via a custom infotype in Personnel Administration) versus an organizational unit level. This way, any program, report, iView, etc., can display the summation of the budget information based on this data.

For example, you can choose to not store the budget "allocated" and "remaining" buckets in SAP, but instead use backend configuration to drive the derivation of the budget pool at runtime. This means that no budget housekeeping is needed during the planning process as everything is calculated in real time based on backend configuration.

8.1.5 Lack of Migration Path Available from Old to New Compensation Functionality

Common Business Requirement

Porting compensation management data from Infotype 0380 (Compensation Adjustment) to ECM is needed.

Dilemma

No standard tools within SAP exist to assist in the migration/conversion effort from Infotype 0380 to Infotype 0759.

Options

1. *Do not migrate/convert any data — leave all master data in the old module for reference.* Depending on the requirements, programs and enhancements may be

needed to report from the old compensation infotypes before a certain key date and from the new compensation infotypes starting on or after the key date.

2. *Create/purchase a migration/conversion program.* An LSMW program can be used to upload the data. Field mapping needs to be done so that the conversion can be created.

3. If Business Warehouse (BW) is available, store both old and new infotypes within your data warehouse cubes and merge the two infotypes so reporting is transparent. Using this approach, you may not be able to satisfy all reporting requirements, because this "merged" view is only available for reports based off Business Intelligence (BI) content.

8.1.6   Clean Master Data

Common Business Requirement

ECM uses real-time master data to more accurately represent the employee's compensation circumstances. Real-time data from the employee, including Infotype 0001, Infotype 0002 (Personal Data), Infotype 0041 (Date Specifications), Infotype 0007 (Planned Working Time), and Infotype 0008 must be kept current and up to date throughout the process to have a successful cycle.

Dilemma

Employees' master data may not be as clean as it should be within your production environment. Conduct audit checks before, during, and after the process to ensure that master data changes are accurate. Data such as salary grade, annual salary, and salary structures may be out of date.

Options

There is really only one option here: clean up your data! Making a formal process for data validation/clean-up is a smart thing to do and should be part of the cutover plan.

8.1.7 Handling Off-Cycle Increases

Common Business Requirement

Off-cycle increases — such as promotions, adjustments, and mandated/general increases — are needed in addition to on-cycle planning.

Dilemma

Although compensation review planning on the portal can be flagged as "anytime," this process may not lend itself to ECM functionality. Batch programs, for example, may be needed for mass increases (workers' populations) or due to government-mandated increases.

Options

1. *Use Infotype 0759 to process off-cycle changes.* You may or may not use the portal for these adjustments.

2. *Do not use Infotype 0759 for off-cycle changes.* Either directly update Infotype 0008 or use an Adobe Interactive Form to update it after the appropriate approvals.

This concludes our "hot topics" review. As you can see, many complex challenges are in store for companies as they implement ECM, so the manner in which you provide resolution for these challenges directly influences the project's success.

Now let's turn our focus onto some additional enhancements many companies look at when implementing ECM.

8.2 Additional Enhancements

Additional enhancements to extend the capabilities of ECM can be built or purchased from third-party vendors, such as Worklogix®. With the exception of the SAP program discussed first, all enhancements are delivered as iViews via the SAP NetWeaver Portal. Incorporating additional, robust software components into the process allows deeper leverage of the underlying data and SAP functionality.

Let's look at the following enhancements:

▶ Budget Reallocation Program

- Budget Analyzer
- Enhanced Compensation Planning User Interface
- Compensation Scorecards
- Compensation Statements
- Compensation Proxy Manager

Let's begin with the budget reallocation program.

8.2.1 Budget Reallocation Program

The custom reallocation program, previously mentioned in Chapter 4, Compensation Budgeting, and earlier in this chapter, allows for automatic refreshing of budgets. Figure 8.2 shows the selection screen of the program which — given a top-level budget unit —traverses the hierarchy and reallocate budget unit funding based on configured business rules.

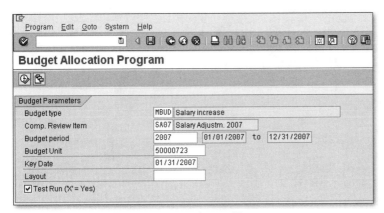

Figure 8.2 Budget Allocation Program by Worklogix

For more information on the budget reallocation program, you can review its use and fit within the overall budgeting process in Chapter 4.

8.2.2 Budget Analyzer

The budget analyzer allows managers to view or print individual and budget roll-up amounts. Modeled off standard Transaction PECM_DISPLAY_BUDGETS (Audit Report for Budgets), this iView gives managers a look at the budget hierarchy from an individual organizational unit (i.e., budget unit) and an overall/roll-up perspective.

In Figure 8.3, the manager for the Global Human Resources organizational unit can look at both the total budget (roll-up) on the left side (budget = US $245,700) and his individual budget unit total on the right side (budget = US $121,700). The manager can also view pie charts for a more visual picture of the budget's status. Also, a budget report is available for the manager in Adobe PDF format.

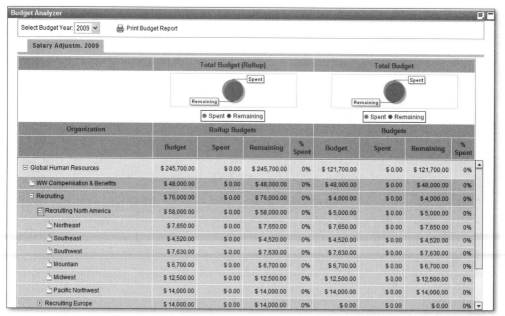

Figure 8.3 Budget Analyzer by Worklogix

8.2.3   Enhanced Compensation Planning User Interface

For those companies seeking a more intuitive front end for manager planning, an alternate front end for compensation planning can be created/re-written based on SAP NetWeaver. Figure 8.4 shows a screen mock-up of the enhanced compensation planning iView.

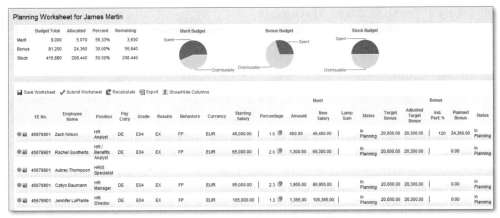

Figure 8.4 Enhanced Front End for Compensation Planning by Worklogix

8.2.4 Compensation Scorecards

Compensation scorecards can be created or purchased from a vendor. These score-cards provide managers, HR, and Compensation with Key Performance Indicators (KPIs), such as statistics and status. Metrics around guideline variance, compliance to budget, and planning status are all important for managers to evaluate during their decision-making process. Figure 8.5 shows two example scorecards.

Compensation Statistics

Select Organization Depth: Direct Reports

Planning Area		Planning Status				Adjustments		
Compensation Plan	Organization Unit	In Planning	Submitted	Approval	Active	Min Adj.	Mid Adj.	Max Adj.
Merit Review 2007	ABC Corporation	70%	10%	10%	10%	1.2%	3.0%	4.1%
Bonus Review 2007	ABC Corporation	70%	10%	10%	10%	1.2%	3.0%	4.1%
LTI Quarterly Review 2007	ABC Corporation	70%	10%	10%	10%	1.2%	3.0%	4.1%

Compensation Status

Select Organization Depth: Direct Reports

Planning Area		Budget			Guidlines		
Compensation Plan	Organization Unit	Planned Budget Units	Actual Budget Units	Variance	Planned Guideline	Actual Guideline	Variance
Merit Review 2007	ABC Corporation	2,500,000	1,900,000	600,000	3.0%	3.6%	0.6%
Bonus Review 2007	ABC Corporation	2,500,000	1,900,000	600,000	3.0%	3.6%	0.6%
LTI Quarterly Review 2007	ABC Corporation	14,000	3000	11,000	1000	800	200

Figure 8.5 Compensation Scorecards by Worklogix

8.2.5 Compensation Statements

One of the most important outputs of the compensation process is the compensation statements for employees. The compensation statement iView provides managers (and employees) the ability to view or print compensation review statements. Typically, the manager obtains access to the statements iView a few weeks before the employee does. This way, the manager can print the statement and sit with the employee for their pay/performance review. Figure 8.6 shows a compensation statements iView.

More information on compensation statements can be found back in Chapter 5, Process Administration.

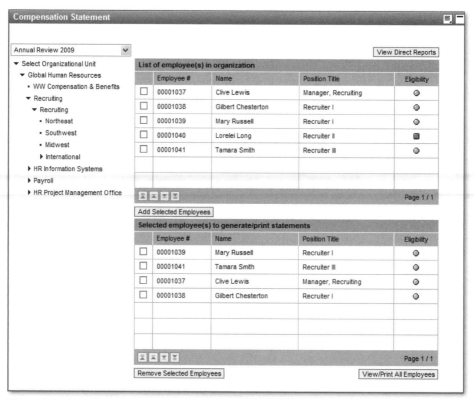

Figure 8.6 Compensation Statements (for Managers) by Worklogix

8.2.6 Compensation Proxy Manager

The Compensation Proxy Manager iView allows managers to search and select an employee to perform proxy duties on his behalf. Although not as common as other Manager Self-Service (MSS) areas (such as personnel change requests), there are many companies that require compensation proxy privileges. Proxies are typically given a life span (e.g., six months). Depending on business requirements, all employees could be a proxy or, for example, only employees below a certain grade level. The request process could include workflow (the request would route to the requesting manager's manager for approval and the proxy for acceptance). You can see the proxy manager in Figure 8.7.

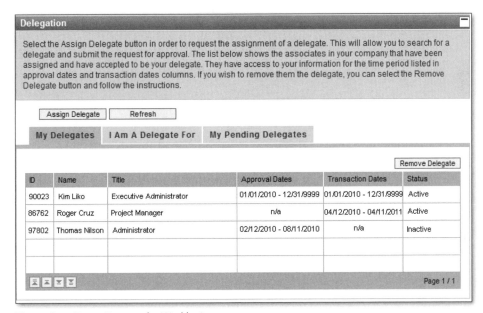

Figure 8.7 Proxy Manager by Worklogix

More information on the use of compensation proxy within the compensation process can be found in Chapter 5.

8.3 Summary

In this chapter, we reviewed some of the most challenging concepts faced when implementing compensation management within SAP. We offered some options for mitigating or resolving the issues presented. In addition, we discussed some of the customizations typically built (or purchased) to enhance the functionality and usability of ECM.

In the next chapter, we will explore the authorization aspects of ECM, including backend security, structural authorizations, standard-delivered roles, and data privacy.

When dealing with sensitive employee data, such as salary and bonus information, no topic is more important than security. Authorization management within Enterprise Compensation Management (ECM) offers enhanced capabilities for restricting access based on standard and structural authorizations. In this chapter, we will discuss security and how it is most effectively used within ECM. The concept of data privacy is also covered, because the protection of employee data is integral to any Human Resources (HR) process.

9 Authorization Management

Authorization management plays a crucial role within ECM functionality. Without fostering a secure environment, administering compensation processes is impossible for an organization to support. Sensitive employee compensation data such as salary, bonuses, and stock data is personal and confidential. A leak of compensation-related data into an organization can be devastating. Project teams, now more than ever, seek solutions that offer the most robust set of controls when implementing ECM.

SAP leverages its standard HCM security concepts to deliver robust authorization management to ECM. Existing authorization objects PLOG, P_ORGIN, and P_PERNR all continue to play a crucial role in securing employee compensation data. New authorization objects S_RFC and S_SERVICE offer enhanced security necessary to restrict access from the portal side. In addition, structural authorizations are available for enhanced structure-based security.

We will also discuss the standard-delivered backend roles that are provided by SAP for compensation management activities. As with other standard roles, you should make copies of these to your customer namespace and edit based on requirements. And, we will inventory each role and highlight its usage.

It is imperative that you work with your security and portal resources when designing the authorizations needed for your implementation. Many of the authorization objects will be familiar to your security resource, but special attention should be paid to the nuances when delivering ECM.

Finally, we will cover data privacy and its implication on your project. The most successful projects consider data privacy and access control issues from the start, especially if the project has global scope. Over the past few years, data privacy has become more and more critical as compensation data becomes more accessible online and to more interested parties.

For a more comprehensive look at security in the HCM component, please refer to the SAP Press book *Authorizations in SAP ERP HCM*, by Martin Esch and Anja Junold.

9.1 Important Authorizations Used within ECM

We recommend that a security resource familiar with HCM authorizations spend ample time architecting the security design to support the implementation. This is especially true if your organization has implemented (or is planning to implement) structural authorizations. Structural authorizations offer a way to apply additional security via Organizational Management (OM) objects, relationships, and structures. Before discussing the benefits and challenges associated with integrating structural authorizations with your overall security model, we will first cover an overview of the standard authorization objects. All core HR authorization objects, including P_PERNR, P_ORGIN, and PLOG, are needed to implement ECM.

Let's first start with one of the most important authorization objects — P_PERNR.

9.1.1 P_PERNR

Authorization object P_PERNR is used to control access to a user's (i.e., employee's) own HR data. P_PERNR restricts access based on infotype and subtype. If you have already implemented some type of Employee Self-Service (ESS), this authorization object is likely part of your existing ESS role. Based on what kind of compensation functionality you are rolling out via ESS, this authorization object may need updating. Also, backend compensation users (from Compensation and HR) may need changes to this authorization in their roles.

The following authorization fields comprise the P_PERNR authorization object. Each field is described separately and highlighted with important information on usage.

▶ **Authorization Level (AUTHC)**
Determines what level of authorization a user has. The following values are permissible: M (read with entry helps), R (read), S (write-locked record; unlock if the last person to change the record is not the current user), E (write-locked record), D (change lock indicator), W (write data records), and * (all operations).

▶ **Infotype (INFTY)**
Determines which infotypes a user has access to. Some common compensation-related Infotypes are 0008, 0758, 0759, 0761, and 0762. Only infotypes from Personnel Administration are available within this authorization field. Infotypes available for inclusion within this field include 0000 to 0999 (for employee master data), Infotypes 2000 - 2999 (for time management data), and Infotypes 9000 - 9999 (for customer-specific data, if applicable).

▶ **Intepretation of Assigned Personnel Number (PSIGN)**
This field defines how the user logged in should be interpreted when authorization checks of HR infotypes are performed (i.e., whether to include or exclude). Only values I and E are permissible: the value I means that authorizations for the assigned personnel number are included within the authorization while the value E means that authorizations for the assigned personnel number are excluded. If both authorizations I and E are entered, authorization E is given preference. Please note that the value * is not allowed in this field.

▶ **Subtype (SUBTY)**
Determines which subtypes a user has access to. Values for subtypes go hand-in-hand with those infotypes identified in your infotype authorization field (INFOTYP). For example, inclusion of subtype 10MT for Infotype 0759 could allow an employee to access his own merit increase record for the plan year 2010.

Let's look at another example. The following authorization indicates that the employee has read (and search) access for Infotype 0008 data.

▶ Authorization level: M, R

▶ Infotype: 0008

▶ Interpretation of assigned personnel number: I

▶ Subtype: *

In Figure 9.1, this authorization is depicted, but in this example, only one authorization is expanded.

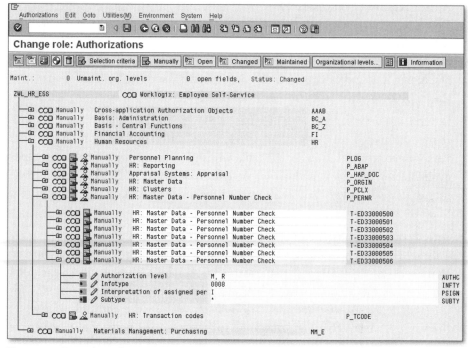

Figure 9.1 Example Authorization Using Authorization Object P_PERNR within Single Custom Role ZWL_HR_ESS

Authorization object P_PERNR represents a foundational element within your security design. Without it, employees cannot view or update any of their own HR data. Be sure to spend sufficient time and energy on designing P_PERNR authorizations, because this is your entire employee population.

Next, we discuss another important authorization object, PLOG, which allows us to control components within the OM and personnel development (PD) areas.

9.1.2   PLOG

For most ECM implementations, updates are needed for authorizations provided by authorization object PLOG. Authorization object PLOG provides access to OM and PD objects, infotypes, and relationships. Any transaction in SAP or iView within Manager Self-Service (MSS) and ESS that reads or writes data to OM or PD objects, such as position (object type S), organizational unit (object type O), and budget unit (object type BU) need to incorporate authorizations within the PLOG authorization object.

The following authorization fields comprise the PLOG authorization object. Each field is described separately and highlighted with important information on usage.

▶ **Infotype (INFOTYP)**
Determines which infotypes a user has access to. The group of Infotypes 1000 (Object), 1001 (Relationships), 1002 (Description) contain the core infotypes of any OM or PD object. Without read authorization to these infotypes, no OM and PD information can be read from SAP. Infotypes sepcified in PLOG only refer to those within OM and PD (but not Personnel Administration). Other relevant infotypes commonly used in compensation management include 5050 (Compensation Job Attributes), 1271 (Composite Survery Result), 1050 (Job Evaluation Results), and 1051 (Survey Results) on the job object; 1005 (Planned Compensation) on the position level (typically as an override); 1500 (BS element management) and 1520 (Original Budget) on the budget unit object (BU).

▶ **Planning Status (ISTAT)**
Determines which planning statuses a user has access to. The vast majority of objects are set in staus 1 (Active).

▶ **Object Type (OTYPE)**
Determines which object types a user has access to. Objects commonly found in authorizations for ECM roles include P (employee), S (position), O (organizational unit), C (job), and BU (Budget Unit). If you are integrating with performance management, you also need to include objects VA (appraisal template), VB (criteria groups), and VC (criteria).

▶ **Plan Version (PLVAR)**
Determines which plan versions a user has access to. Plan version 01 (Active plan) is the default plan version for most objects and should be the only plan version used. Using other plan versions should be avoided. Plan versions ** and .: should never be used.

▶ **Function Code (PPFCODE)**
Determines what permissions the user has — read, write, delete, and so on — for the object. Most likely, you will use one or more of the following function codes in your implementation: AEND (Change), DEL (Delete), DISP (Display), and INSE (Insert).

▶ **Subtype (SUBTYP)**
Determines which subtypes a user has access to. Values for subtypes go hand-in-hand with those infotypes identified in your infotype authorization field (INFOTYP), discussed earlier. Subtypes in PLOG only refer to subtypes within OM and PD (but not Personnel Administration).

As shown in Figure 9.2, you can view all relationships (subtypes) of objects job (C), organizational unit (O), employee (P), qualification (Q), and position (S) in the active plan version (01) and in planning status 1 (Active) with the PLOG authorization.

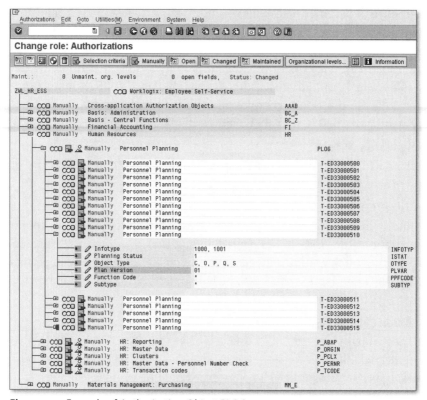

Figure 9.2 Example of Authorization Object PLOG

Now, let's turn our focus to another important authorization, P_ORGIN.

9.1.3   P_ORGIN/P_ORGINCON

P_ORGIN and P_ORGINCON are important authorization objects because they permit users to access HR data on other employees. Both provide a similar function within SAP backend security but differ in one important way: P_ORGINCON includes an authorization profile. For those clients seeking a context-sensitive security solution, P_ORGINCON enables the use of structural authorizations in the overall profile. We'll discuss the use of context-sensitive structural authorizations later in this chapter.

Both authorization objects provide a way to restrict access based on infotype, subtype, personnel area, personnel subarea, and organizational key. The following authorization fields comprise the P_ORGIN and P_ORGINCON authorization object.

▸ **Authorization Level (AUTHC)**
Determines the access level a user is granted. Available options are M (search help), R (read record), S (write-locked record; unlock if the last person to change the record is not the current user), E (write-locked record), D (change lock indicator), W (write record), and * (all operations).

Within ECM, additional authorization levels are needed to allow users to create or change records in Infotype 0759. Authorization levels P (for planning and submitting compensation process records) and A (for approving or rejecting compensation process records) have been added to authorization object P_ORGIN. The standard authorization levels R (read) and W (write) are required for line and higher-level managers involved in the online planning process. The authorization levels P and A are checked in the SAP portal on the compensation planning iViews and in program RHECM_CREATE_COMP_PROCESS (Create Compensation Process Records). However, these authorization levels are not checked within the standard Transactions PA30 and PA20 (Maintain and Display HR Master Data).

▸ **Infotype (INFTY)**
Determines which infotypes a user has access to. This is the infotype in question. Infotypes 0000 to 0999 are used for employee master data, Infotypes 2000 to 2999 for time data, Infotypes 4000 to 4999 for applicant data, and Infotypes 9000 to 9999 are customer specific.

▶ **Personnel Area (PERSA)**
Determines which personnel areas a user has access to. This is the personnel area (field PERSA) that is located on an employee's Infotype 0001 (Organizational Assignment) record.

▶ **Employee Group (PERSG)**
Determines which employee groups a user has access to. This is the employee group (field PERSG) that is located on an employee's Infotype 0001 record.

▶ **Employee Subgroup (PERSK)**
Determines which employee subgroups a user has access to. This is the employee subgroup (field PERSK) that is located on an employee's Infotype 0001 record.

▶ **Organizational Key (VDSK1)**
Determines which organizational keys a user has access to. This is the organizational key (field VDSK1) that is located on an employee's Infotype 0001 record.

In addition, P_ORGINCON also includes one other important field:

▶ **Authorization Profile (PROFL)**
Identifies the authorization profile to be used. If structural authorizations are used in your organization, you can integrate an authorization profile directly in P_ORGINCON through this authorization field. Any profile defined in Table T77PR can be used. Authorization profiles are built and maintained in Transaction OOSB.

Figure 9.3 shows an example of authorization P_ORGIN, which provides the user with read and matchcode (or search) access to Infotypes 0000 (Actions), 0001, and 0002 (Personal Data). No restrictions are placed on personnel area, employee group, employee subgroup, or organizational key. This user has expansive access to view employee HR information around actions, organizational, personnel and enterprise structure, and personal data.

Next, we discuss a new authorization object used exclusively within the Performance Management component (Objective Setting and Appraisals). Many clients implement Performance Management and Compensation Management together due to their tight integration. If you are not implementing (or integrating with) SAP's Performance Management component, this section is not pertinent for you.

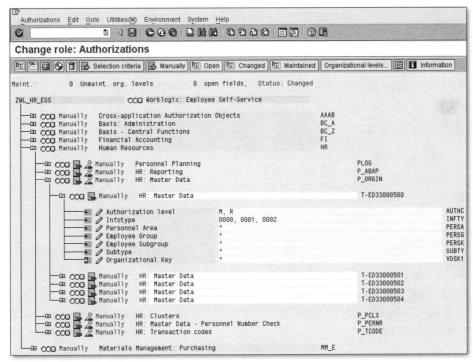

Figure 9.3 Example P_ORGIN Authorization with Read and Search Access to Infotypes 0000, 0001, and 0002

9.1.4 P_HAP_DOC

P_HAP_DOC is a new authorization object within the objective setting and appraisals functionality (i.e., ECM). P_HAP_DOC is a mandatory authorization for implementing appraisals and must be used in conjunction with P_PERNR, PLOG, and P_ORGIN or P_ORGINCON. Figure 9.4 shows an example implementation of authorization object P_HAP_DOC.

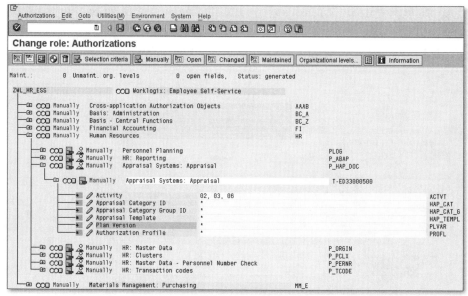

Figure 9.4 Authorization Object P_HAP_DOC Used Within Performance Management

The following authorization fields comprise the P_HAP_DOC authorization object:

▶ **Activity (ACTV)**
Determines what operations (or activities) a user can perform on an appraisal form. The options are 02 (Change), 03 (Display), and 06 (Delete). There is no Create activity. Without change authorization, an appraisee or appraiser is unable to create an appraisal.

▶ **Appraisal Category ID (HAP_CAT)**
Determines which catalog ID a user has access to. The appraisal category ID is the eight-digit ID category defined in your configuration. In addition to Transaction PHAP_CATALOG, you can also view your categories via Transaction OOHAP_CATEGORY.

▶ **Appraisal Category Group ID (HAP_CAT_G)**
Determines which catalog group ID a user has access to. The appraisal category group ID is the eight-digit ID category group defined in your configuration. In addition to Transaction PHAP_CATALOG, you can also view your category groups via Transaction OOHAP_CAT_GROUP. Standard SAP delivers category groups 1 (Personnel Appraisals), 10 (Learning Solution), and 100 (E-Recruiting).

▶ **Appraisal Template ID (HAP_TEMPL)**

Determines which appraisal template ID a user has access to. The appraisal template is the eight-digit ID defined in your configuration. The appraisal template ID is the same as the VA object ID of the form.

▶ **Plan Version (PLVAR)**

Determines which plan versions a user has access to. Plan version 01 (Active plan) is the default plan version and should be the only plan version used in your process. Using other plan versions should be avoided. Again, plan versions ** and .: should never be used under any circumstances.

▶ **Authorization Profile (PROFL)**

Identifies the authorization profile to be used (this is optional). If structural authorizations are used in your organization, you can integrate an authorization profile directly in P_HAP_DOC through this authorization field. Any profile defined in Table T77PR can be used. Structural profiles are built and maintained in Transaction OOSB.

> **Note**
>
> More information on authorizations within employee performance management can be found in the SAP Press book *SAP ERP HCM Performance Management* by Jeremy Masters and Christos Kotsakis.

Several new authorization objects are available to further control access within self-service transactions on the portal. These include S_SERVICE, S_RFC, and P_HAP_DOC. Nearly all functionality on the portal calls the same backend authorizations used throughout HCM. This is because the same infotypes are being updated in HCM — just through a different medium. For example, Infotype 0006 (Address) information is updated regardless of whether an HR administrator updates the employee's address in Transaction PA30 or whether this update is performed by the employee himself on the SAP Portal

Let's discuss authorization object S_SERVICE first.

9.1.5   S_SERVICE

Authorization object S_SERVICE is needed to authorize access to external services, including Web Dynpro applications. When Web Dynpro applications are started, the authorization S_SERVICE is called. Only if authorization has been granted to the service will the Web Dynpro application start. Much like authorization objects

S_TCODE and P_TCODE grant access to transaction codes, authorization object S_SERVICE grants access to external services such as Web Dynpro applications.

The following authorization fields comprise the S_SERVICE authorization object. Each field is described separately and highlighted with important information on usage.

▶ **Service Program, Transaction, or Function (SRV_NAME)**
Determines what external service is available to start.

▶ **Type of Check Flag and Authority (SRV_TYPE)**
Determines the type of external service

Figure 9.5 shows the detail behind these two authorization fields. Each external service is defined with a 30-character string (e.g., 445CEEE82008415A65CAE2EF-9EC10A) along with its more popular name (e.g., Service WEBDYNPRO *sap.com/mss~ecm/EcmPlanningApp*). Also, the service type dropdown identifies the external service type as Web Dynpro.

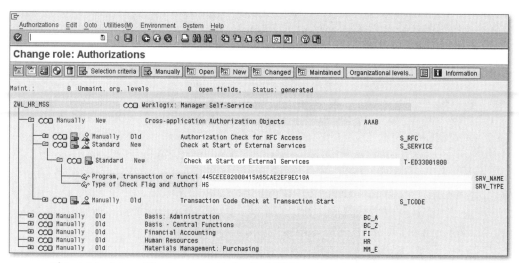

Figure 9.5 External Services Available for Start Within a Sample Authorization using the S_SERVICE Authorization Object

If you enter value * for the authorization object S_SERVICE, you will grant users with the authorization to start all external applications, including Web Dynpro. Some customers that do this think the portal will do all of the security "naturally."

This is because portal roles can be constructed in such a way as to limit which Web Dynpro services a user can access based on portal page and iView design. Although this approach is viable, we recommend that you assign authorizations explicitly for the external services you introduce into your profiles.

> **Note**
>
> For more information on setting up Web Dynpro services for self-service iViews within your SAP portal, reference the SAP PRESS book *Implementing Employee and Manager Self-Services in SAP ERP HCM*, by Jeremy Masters and Christos Kotsakis.

As of Release SAP ERP 6.0, the following compensation-related Web Dynpro applications are available:

- sap.com/mss~ecm/EcmPlanningApp
- sap.com/mss~ecm/EcmApprovalApp
- sap.com/mss~ppro~compensation/CompensationApp
- sap.com/mss~eepro~compensationprofiles/CompensationProfiles_Config
- sap.com/mss~eepro/CompensationInformation

You probably won't use all of these Web Dynpro applications, so it's imperative that the security and portal teams work together in defining these authorizations.

Next, let's discuss authorization object S_RFC — another critical authorization object for self-service functionality.

9.1.6   S_RFC

Without providing access to the backend ABAP functions, data cannot be viewed or saved in SAP from the Web Dynpro applications on the portal. Using authorization object S_RFC, access to program components (via function groups) can be granted. The following authorization fields comprise the S_RFC authorization object. Each field is described separately and highlighted with important information on usage.

- **Activity (ACTVT)**
  Determines the activity level the user has access to. In the standard delivery, the only value is 16 (Execute).

▶ **Name of the Remote Function Call (RFC) to be protected (RFC_NAME)**
Contains the names of function groups granted access to. This authorization
field can have a maximum of 18 characters. For example, function group HREC-
M00UI includes specific compensation planning function modules such as HR_
ECM_UI_GET_POSS_COMP_REVS, HR_ECM_UI_GET_PROC_PREP_DATA, and
HR_ECM_UI_SET_SELECTED_CPLAN.

▶ **Type of RFC object to be protected (RFC_TYPE)**
Contains the type of RFC to be checked. In the standard system, only function
group (type FUGR) is available.

Figure 9.6 shows an example of an SAP role containing the values of an authorization using authorization object S_RFC. SAP delivers over 50 compensation-
related function groups beginning with HRECM*. All areas within compensation —
including job pricing, budgeting, and Long-Term Incentives (LTIs) — have function
groups. However, only those called from the portal that check this S_RFC authorization need to be identified. Work with your security team to understand which
function groups need to be included within your authorizations.

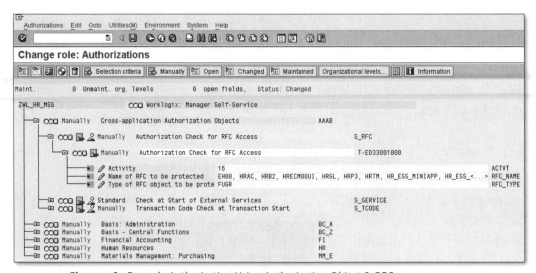

Figure 9.6 Example Authorization Using Authorization Object S_RFC

This concludes our detailed review of the most common authorizations used
within ECM. Let's step back a moment to review.

9.1.7 Summary of Main Authorization Objects Used in ECM

Table 9.1 contains a list of the most important authorization objects used within ECM. Each authorization object is listed with its primary use. Most of these objects will not be new to your organization as they form the basis of any HR authorization security design.

Authorization Object(s)	Use
P_PERNR	Used to control access to the user's own HR employee data such as Infotype 0008 and Infotype 0759.
PLOG	Used to control access to OM objects, such O (organizational unit), S (position), C (job), and BU (budget unit) and performance management objects including VA (appraisal template), VB (criteria group), and VC (criterion).
P_ORGIN / P_ORGINCON	Used to control access to other employee's infotype data, including Infotype 0008, Infotype 0758, and Infotype 759. Can also include authorization profiles (using structural authorizations) if P_ORGINCON is used.
P_HAP_DOC	Used within Performance Management only. Used to control access to appraisal documents.
S_SERVICE	Used to check whether an external service (such as a Web Dynpro application) can be started by the user.
S_RFC	Used to specify if the user has access to RFCs (i.e., function groups). For example, S_RFC with a value of HRECM00UI would allow user access to the functions used within the Compensation Planning service.

Table 9.1 Common Authorization Objects Used Within ECM

There are a few other authorization objects that are used within a compensation management context. Adobe Interactive Forms and Personnel Change Requests (PCRs) that handle off-cycle increases such as promotions and changes in pay have specific authorizations. Table 9.2 lists some of these important authorization objects. Besides off-cycle increases, reporting, and access to payroll clusters are often needed within compensation-relevant activities.

Authorization Object(s)	Use
P_ABAP	Used to allow access to HR reports, including compensation-related reports.
P_PCLX	Used to determine access to PCLx cluster tables, including payroll data per country.
P_PCR	Used to determine access to payroll control records, based on payroll area.
B_NOTIF, I_QMEL, S_USER_GRP, S_BDS_DS	Used for supporting the PCR functionality — B_NOTIF for controls notifications, I_QMEL for notification types, S_USER_GRP for user groups, and S_BDS_DS for access to documents.
P_ASRCONT	Used within HCM Process and Forms. Controls whether the user can start, approve, reject, or process a form. Any off-cycle increase forms executed using this functionality require this authorization.

Table 9.2 Authorization Objects and Their Intended Use

As we already discussed, security within ECM leverage standard HCM authorizations. Working with your security team, you have a full suite of authorizations available to secure sensitive compensation-related data.

Let's now review the authorization activation switches in system Table T77S0.

9.1.8 Activation Switches in T77S0

To activate authorization objects P_PERNR, P_ORGIN, and P_ORGINCON for use in your system, you must ensure that the proper switches have been activated in system Table T77S0. Please note that these switches may have already been configured, as they are paramount to the basic design of HCM authorizations.

> **Warning**
>
> Changing this configuration has major implications for the security design, so do not change this configuration without first discussing it with your security resource!

For P_PERNR, switch AUTSW/PERNR needs value 1 to activate; for P_ORGIN, switch AUTSW/ORGIN needs value 1 to activate; and for P_ORGINCON, switch AUTSW/INCON needs value 1 to activate. Figure 9.7 shows authorization objects P_PERNR and P_ORGIN being used, but not P_ORGINCON.

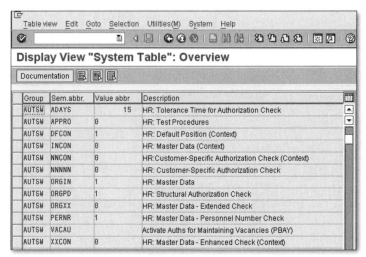

Figure 9.7 Authorization Switches Within System Table T77S0, Group AUTSW

Now that you know about all of the relevant standard authorizations within ECM, let's move on to the out-of-the-box backend roles provided by SAP.

9.2 Standard Roles in ECM

In the standard system, SAP delivers several backend security roles for ECM that can be copied to your customer namespace and altered according to your specific security requirements via Transaction PFCG (Role Maintenance). Depending on your own security practices you may or may not use composite roles within your functionality. Table 9.3 lists the standard SAP-delivered roles related to ECM and a short description of each. Only the first two roles (SAP_EP_HR_HRECM and SAP_HR_ECM_COMP_SPECIALIST) are specific to ECM. The other five roles are based on the older compensation functionality (application PA-CM), but can be leveraged and adapted for your ECM implementation, if needed.

SAP Standard Role	Description
SAP_EP_HR_HRECM	HR ECM. Specialist role for Compensation Management, assuming use of ECM (application component PA-EC).
SAP_HR_ECM_COMP_SPECIALIST	Compensation Specialist. Another specialist role for Compensation Management, assuming use of ECM (application component PA-EC).
SAP_HR_CM_BEN-COMP-MANAGER	Benefits and Compensation Manager (Compensation Management). Relevant for older versions of Compensation Managemenent (PA-CM).
SAP_HR_CM_HR-ADMINISTRATOR	HR Administrator Compensation Management (Compensation Management). Relevant for older versions of Compensation Managemenent (PA-CM).
SAP_HR_CM_HR-MANAGER	HR Manager (Compensation Management). Relevant for older versions of Compensation Managemenent (PA-CM).
SAP_HR_CM_MANAGER	Manager Generic Compensation Management (Compensation Management). Relevant for older versions of Compensation Managemenent (PA-CM).
SAP_HR_CM_SPECIALIST	System Specialist Compensation Management (Compensation Management). Relevant for older versions of Compensation Managemenent (PA-CM).

Table 9.3 SAP Standard–Delivered Roles for ECM (PA-EC) and Older Versions of Compensation Management (PA-CM)

Although all roles starting with prefix SAP_HR_CM* were created for older versions of compensation management (application component PA-CM), you can leverage them if needed, as certain items — such as the budgeting functionality — have remained the same. Just be sure to substitute Infotype 0380 (Compensation Adjustment) with Infotype 0759 and include other ECM-relevant infotypes such as

Infotype 0758, Infotype 0760 (Compensation Eligibility Override), Infotype 0761, and Infotype 0762 where relevant.

Now that we discussed the available standard roles, let's cover structural authorizations in more detail to learn their place within the ECM functionality.

9.3 Using Structural Authorizations with ECM

This section addresses implementing structural authorization security in addition to the standard authorization for your ECM implementation. Implementing structural authorization is not a requirement for the deployment of ECM, but instead, serves as an additional means of securing data. In this section, we review structural authorizations — including an overview, its place within ECM, and some Best Practices for implementation.

9.3.1 Overview

Structural authorization allows you to restrict authorizations based on underlying structures (organizational structures, business event hierarchies, qualification catalogs, etc.). Structural authorization access — in the form of authorization profiles — is granted at the position or user level. Access to organizational objects (organizational units, budget units, positions, jobs, etc., from SAP OM) is granted based on this access. A root object (e.g., organizational unit) is sometimes explicitly specified along with an evaluation path (e.g., SBESX (Staffing Assignments Along Organizational Structure)) to return all objects in a given time period (e.g., day, month, or year). Other times objects can be determined dynamically based on a function module identified in the authorization profile.

SAP delivers two standard function modules: RH_GET_MANAGER_ASSIGNMENT (which determines all organizational units for which the user is the chief manager) and RH_GET_ORG_ASSIGNMENT (which determines the organizational unit the user is assigned to). From any root node that is returned from these functions, an evaluation path (such as SBESX) can be used to retrieve all objects (organizational units, positions, and employees) underneath that user's span of control. You use these returned objects in conjunction with your standard authorizations to present a complete authorization check from both the standard authorization side (that uses authorization objects P_ORGIN, PLOG, P_PERNR, etc.) and from the structural authorization side (using the structures hierarchy previously mentioned). The intersection of these authorization checks provides SAP customers with added security.

Although structural authorizations provide an additional level of security, some customers decide against using structural authorizations in their design. Many of these customers have full HCM functionality but do quite well without implementing structural authorizations. But we recommend that you establish a sound business plan if you want to use structural authorizations.

Let's get into more detail by first looking at function module RH_GET_MANAGER_ASSIGNMENT and learn how it can be used within an ECM context.

9.3.2 Function Module RH_GET_MANAGER_ASSIGNMENT

As part of the manager's structural authorization profile, standard function module RH_GET_MANAGER_ASSIGNMENT (or a customized version of it) is typically used. As previously mentioned, this function retrieves all organizational units for which the user is the chief manager. If the manager is a chief of multiple organizational units, all organizational units will be returned as root nodes. The manager can sit anywhere in the organizational structure; it's the Infotype 0012 (Manages) relationship on his position to an organizational unit that drives the identification of organizational units managed. Within this function module, standard evaluation path MANASS is used to retrieve the organizational units.

Once the root node (or nodes) is retrieved, an evaluation path is used to identify all underlying objects that should be available for the user's authorization. Figure 9.8 shows an example authorization profile Z_MANAGER with evaluation path SBESX. The following parameters are used to fully define the authorization profile.

- ► Authorization Profile: Z_MANAGER
- ► No.: (sequence number of your choice)
- ► Plan Version: 01
- ► Object Type: O
- ► Object ID: (leave blank)
- ► Maintenance Flag: (unchecked)
- ► Evaluation Path: SBESX

- Status Vector: 12 (where 1=Active and 2=Planned)
- Depth: (blank, meaning no restriction in depth)
- Sign: (blank, meaning process objects "top down" and not "bottom up")
- Period: (blank, meaning no time period restriction)
- Function Module: RH_GET_MANAGER_ASSIGNMENT

Additional authorization profiles can be built and assigned to users in a similar fashion.

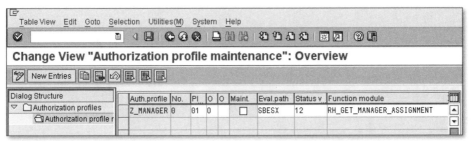

Figure 9.8 Authorization Profile Z_MANAGER Within Table T77PR Containing Function Module RH_GET_MANAGER_ASSIGNMENT

According to authorization profile Z_MANAGER, a manager can view his full span of control, including organizational units, positions, and employees. This profile — together with the authorizations from his standard authorization — forms the total picture of backend security for the user.

In some cases, a combination of standard and structural authorizations is not enough to satisfy complex business requirements. Some customers need to implement context-sensitive authorizations to handle these cases. Context-sensitive authorizations are discussed next.

9.3.3 Context-Sensitive Authorizations

A context-sensitive solution is required when you need to associate individual standard and structural authorization profiles together within the same context. A classic example is that of a payroll manager. The payroll manager has certain responsibilities for the organization in his role as a manager of corporate payroll and certain responsibilities for his direct and indirect reports in his role as a people manager (i.e., "chief"). This segregation of duties is typically seen most within the

HR function but could exist elsewhere. Other examples include compensation managers, HR generalists, and HR administrators. To handle this complexity, you can either issue two separate user IDs for this employee or implement context-sensitive authorizations.

In Figure 9.9, authorization P_ORGINCON contains read and search access to Infotypes 0000, 0001, 0002, and 0008 but only for the objects (e.g., employees) available within structural authorization profile Z_MANAGER. Another P_ORGINCON authorization could give this user access to update Infotype 0759 for a different contextual scenario (e.g., to save and submit salary recommendations).

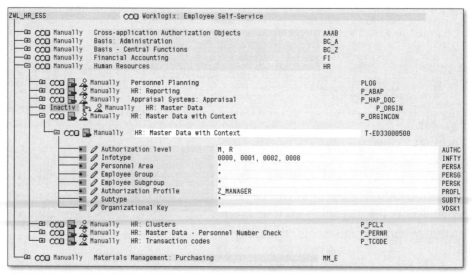

Figure 9.9 Example of Context-sensitive Authorization Using P_ORGINCON

We have seen how context-sensitive authorizations can provide a segregation of duties without the need for creating duplicate user IDs. By maintaining context-sensitive authorizations, you can more tightly integrate standard and structural authorizations together. This may be more pertinent to your implementation if the same manager using MSS functionality will also be using backend HR transactions (e.g., payroll or compensation manager).

It's clear that structural authorizations can provide a more robust way to handle complex security requirements. If structural authorizations are used for your implementation, give yourself additional testing time for unexpected challenges to surface. We caution you, though, to only implement structural authorizations if there is a clear business need to do so. Implementing structural authorizations is a major shift in the backend security approach and you should expect additional maintenance to support it.

That about covers everything for standard and structural authorizations, so let's shift focus and discuss data privacy and its importance within ECM.

9.4   Data Privacy

Data privacy considerations are quickly becoming an important part of ECM projects today — especially with global implementations. Many firms that are headquartered or have subsidiaries in Europe or Asia may need to consider local regulatory or legal requirements. Work councils, unions, bargaining units, and other groups of "represented" employees may influence what data can be made available for employees and managers to view or update and what data can cross international borders. This is especially challenging when a particular function like supply chain, legal, or information technology is global in nature. There may be challenges, for example, if a manager in the United States manages employees in Ireland, China, or South Africa. Data privacy statutes, local laws, or bargaining unit rules may place certain restrictions on what employee data can be seen by whom and from where. You will need to work with your local works councils (e.g., in France and Germany) or unions (e.g., United States and United Kingdom) in the pertinent countries.

Personally identifiable information (PII) — such as national identification, private address, credit card data and sensitive HR data — must be protected. Some countries, like the United States, regard information on date of birth and race with extreme sensitivity compared to other countries. European countries, in contrast, are frequently concerned with data privacy directives for those parts of the European Union. These directives concern important rights regarding sensitive data, including:

- a right of access to that data;
- a right to know where the data originated (if such information is available);
- a right to have inaccurate data rectified;

► a right of recourse in the event of unlawful processing; and

► a right to withhold permission to use data in certain circumstances.

Based on our experience implementing global projects, we have established some Best Practices with regard to data privacy and access control, including the following:

► Ensuring proper guidelines are in place with cross-border data transfers to ensure compliance with directives from regulatory or legal laws;

► Applying data masking of sensitive data wherever possible and whenever appropriate;

► Ensuring appropriate segregation of duties with online processes (such as performance and compensation management) and auditing regularly;

► Ensuring data privacy is maintained when communicating sensitive information to third-party vendors; and

► Limiting, authorizing, and tracking electronic and physical exchange of sensitive data, such as compensation data.

In addition, it is best to categorize data on its level of sensitivity. The three categories (confidential, internal, and public) are defined as follows:

► **Confidential** — Information that is highly sensitive and critical to the operation of the organization. Information of this type is for use only within the organization or a department within an organization. Examples of this information include sealed bids from vendors, software code, or sensitive employee information such as base salary and bonus data.

► **Internal** — Information that is used within the organization but which is of a less sensitive nature. Information of this type, while not publicly exposed, would not create a significant loss if it were to become exposed. Examples of this information include employee phone directories and organizational charts.

► **Public** — Information that has a negligible level of sensitivity. Information that has no potential for causing harm to the organization and can be distributed freely internally or externally. Examples of this information include mission statements and product lines.

With these levels in mind, it is important to work with the information technology (IT) Security, legal, and compliance teams within your organization to ensure that proper attention is given to the data being used within compensation processes. PII must be kept secure and private, and data privacy provisions must be respected and complied with so that you can stay compliant with regulatory laws.

9.5   Summary

We covered a wide range of authorization, security, and data privacy topics in this chapter. And hopefully we armed you with the information you need to ensure that proper system controls are implemented to support your ECM implementation. Regardless of scope, implementing security for ECM is complex because of the various layers involved, including standard and structural backend authorizations, and portal access. In addition, data privacy and access control requirements may mean that additional controls are necessary to secure your employee's HR data based on local practices or regulatory mandates.

In the next chapter, we will discuss one of the most strategic processes within compensation — job pricing. We will discuss all components of the process — from salary survey participation to market data analysis to salary structure adjustments.

Competitive pay is one of the key factors behind employee retention. To remunerate employees fairly and reward key talent, market analysis must be performed with outside survey data. In this chapter, we discuss SAP's job pricing functionality.

10   Job Pricing

Paying and rewarding employees competitively is one of the most fundamental principles of compensation management. It is also one of the main outcomes from the job pricing process discussed in this chapter. If executed successfully, the market analysis performed with job pricing enables an organization to reward and retain key resources and attract outside talent. Perhaps no other concept within compensation is more strategic — if a company does not compensate its employees fairly and reward talent appropriately, staff will become disinterested, and key employees will leave the company. Without human capital, a business cannot function and prosper.

As of SAP Enterprise 4.7 Extension Set 2.0, the job pricing functionality is available in Enterprise Compensation Management (ECM). Participating in salary surveys and conducting market analysis are the two main activities supporting job pricing. Within job pricing, job composites are created from market data and are matched against internal jobs, positions, and employees to obtain a clearer view of how well the company is compensating employees versus the market. At the end of this analysis, composite information can be aggregated and your company's salary structures can be updated.

In this chapter, we highlight the job pricing configuration, step through the market pricing process, and discuss salary survey participation. Best Practices are also reviewed.

Let's first discuss the preliminary steps for using job pricing.

10.1 Getting Started

Configuring the job pricing functionality within ECM is not a laborious task. The functionality, which is tightly organized and bound to the backend data, does not contain a lot of configuration steps; instead most of your time is spent familiarizing yourself with how to most effectively import and work with the data received from outside survey vendors. The functionality is entirely data driven — based on survey jobs and survey market data.

Let's discuss two configuration elements: pay categories and compensation job groups.

10.1.1 Pay Categories

Pay categories are important as they help you group market data into similar buckets for comparison purposes. For example, you may want to split your categories into the following groupings:

- Base Salary
- Total Cash
- Total Bonus
- Long-Term Incentive (LTI)
- Total Direct Compensation

Organizing your pay categories lets you import market data (such as the 10th, 25th, 50th, 60th, 75th, and 90th percentile data points) into separate groups for comparison. As an example, you could view Base Salary 50th percentile, Total Cash 50th percentile, Total Bonus 50th percentile, etc. The same goes with any percentile. Later in the chapter, you will see how the combination of percentile and pay categories forms a unique key during data upload and manipulation.

Pay categories are configured within the IMG under the following path: PERSONNEL MANAGEMENT • ENTERPRISE COMPENSATION MANAGEMENT • JOB PRICING • SALARY SURVEYS • DEFINE ADDITIONAL PAY CATEGORIES. You can also access the table directly with Transaction SM30 from Table view V_T71JPR23, and you can see the listing of standard pay categories in Figure 10.1.

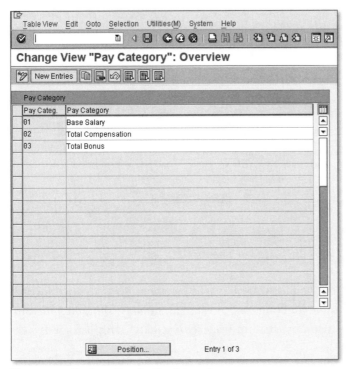

Figure 10.1 Configuration for Pay Categories

For every pay category, key attributes describe the wages. The category's attributes define the technical wage types that comprise the data collected for that category. This is important when doing comparisons between internal and external pay data; for example, when comparing a market data composite to an employee's current base pay. The latter is calculated based on the wage types specified.

You configure pay category attributes within the IMG under the following path: PERSONNEL MANAGEMENT • ENTERPRISE COMPENSATION MANAGEMENT • JOB PRICING • SALARY SURVEYS • DEFINE PAY CATEGORY ATTRIBUTES. You can also access the table directly with Transaction SM30 from Table view V_T71JPR29. Figure 10.2 shows the listing of base wage types for Pay Category 01 (Base Salary).

Pay categories are defined by country grouping. For each country grouping, a base valuation wage type (defined in Table T539J) is specified along with a method begin date and a method end date.

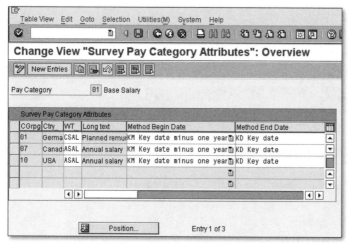

Figure 10.2 Configuration for Pay Categories Attributes

The base wage type should be linked to all wages pertinent for that pay category. For example, you might link all bonus wages (annual, holiday, spot, etc.) in your system to a base wage type (say, custom wage type ZBON). This linkage is performed in View V_T539J.

The Method Begin Date and the Method End Date tell the system when to evaluate the wages based on a Key date. The Key date is always a system date. SAP provides seven possible entries for the Method Begin Date and the Method End Date, including:

- Key date
- Start of calendar year of key date
- End of calendar year of key date
- Start of calendar year prior to key date
- End of calendar year prior to key date
- Key date plus one year
- Key date minus one year

This means, for example, that you could calculate a rolling 12-month lag for a pay category if your Method Begin Date was set at Key date minus one year and your Method End Date was set at Key date. Different pay categories may require a different date scenario. A pay category for base pay, for example, could have both the

Method Begin Date and Method End Date as the Key date because you may want to return to the employee's current base pay for comparison purposes.

Only one base wage type can be entered per country grouping and pay category. If you cannot obtain all of the necessary wages using this configuration (or if you require a customer-specific calculation of doing so), Business Add-In (BadI) HRECM00_STATSTYPE (Get Value of Pay Category for Employee) can be implemented to provide the values. Method GET_VALUE_FOR_STATSTYPE returns a value for an employee based on a specific pay category.

10.1.2 Compensation Job Groupings

Compensation job groupings provide a way of categorizing jobs within job pricing for (mostly) job matching purposes. Some Compensation Professionals might want to think of a compensation job grouping like job family. The compensation job grouping is stored against the job object within Organizational Management (OM) on Infotype 5050 (Compensation Job Attributes). Possible values for compenstion job groupings include the following:

▶ Administrative

▶ Customer Support

▶ Executive Management

▶ Finance

▶ Human Resources (HR)

▶ Information Systems

▶ Legal

▶ Operations

▶ Research and Development

▶ Sales and Marketing

The groupings should represent a logical family of jobs. You can also get more granular with the values, if needed. For example, instead of just having HR as a job grouping, you could use the following:

▶ HR — Business Partner

▶ HR — Compensation

▶ HR — Benefits

► HR – Organizational Development

► HR – Recruiting

► HR – Learning

► HR – HRIS

These are just some examples. The values you put here should be meaningful to your Compensation department because this information is only used by them.

Compensation job groupings are configured within the IMG under the following path: PERSONNEL MANAGEMENT • ENTERPRISE COMPENSATION MANAGEMENT • JOB PRICING • SALARY SURVEYS • DEFINE COMPENSATION JOB GROUPS. You can also access the table directly with Transaction SM30 from Table view V_T71JPR28. Figure 10.3 shows a listing of sample compensation job groupings.

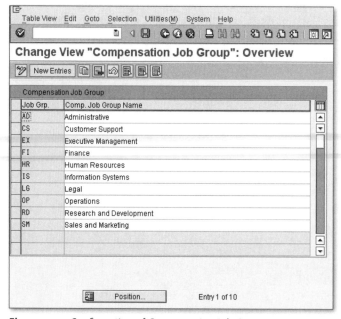

Figure 10.3 Configuration of Compensation Job Groups

After performing this configuration, you can define a compensation job grouping for each job in your organization in Infotype 5050 via Transaction PP01 or PO03.

Figure 10.4 shows the Finance (FI) compensation job group recorded against a job called Analyst, Financial.

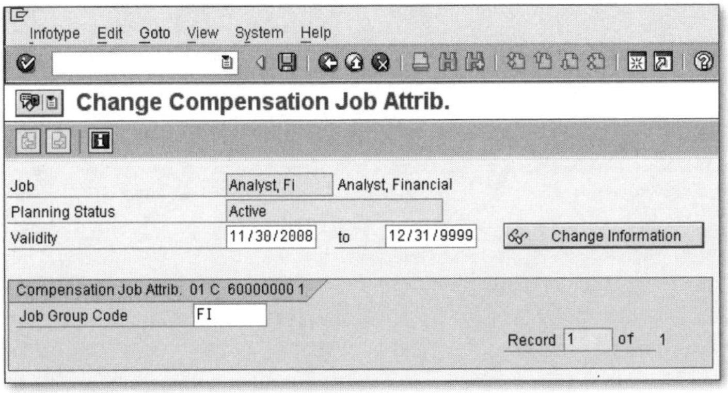

Figure 10.4 Infotype 5050 on the Job

The preparation steps mentioned previously should be performed before any job matching is done. Despite its use, the compensation job grouping is an optional data element — it is neither required for the market analysis nor the survey participation.

Let's move on to discuss the market analyis process.

10.2 Market Analysis

The job pricing functionality is provided via a web-based tool. Business Server Pages (BSP) form the basis of the web experience for the compensation user. To access these pages, use Transaction PECM_START_JPR_BSP. This transaction launches a web browser. If you are prompted for a username and password, enter your SAP username and password (the same one you used to log into the SAP GUI with). The main start screen for job pricing (seen in Figure 10.5) will appear and have the following links:

▸ Provider Data

▸ Import Data

▸ Job Matching

▸ Aging

- Composite Result by Internal Job
- Create Mass Composite Result
- Salary Structure Adjustment

Job Pricing

Provider Data
Create salary survey providers and maintain survey provider information. Display and change provider job catalog and job descriptions. View market results and individual salary surveys.

Import Data
Import survey provider data, including salary survey results, job catalogs and job descriptions.

Job Matching
Match internal benchmark jobs with salary survey jobs that have been imported from salary survey provider(s).

Aging
Age market data that has been imported from salary survey providers by job or by survey.

Composite Result by Internal Job
Create market composite results by internal job, and compare to internal payment at the employee, job or position level.

Create Mass Composite Result
Create mass composite results.

Salary Structure Adjustment
Compare internal salary structure to market salary structure, based on a market composite result.
Create one or more planned salary structures and adapt them to the market.

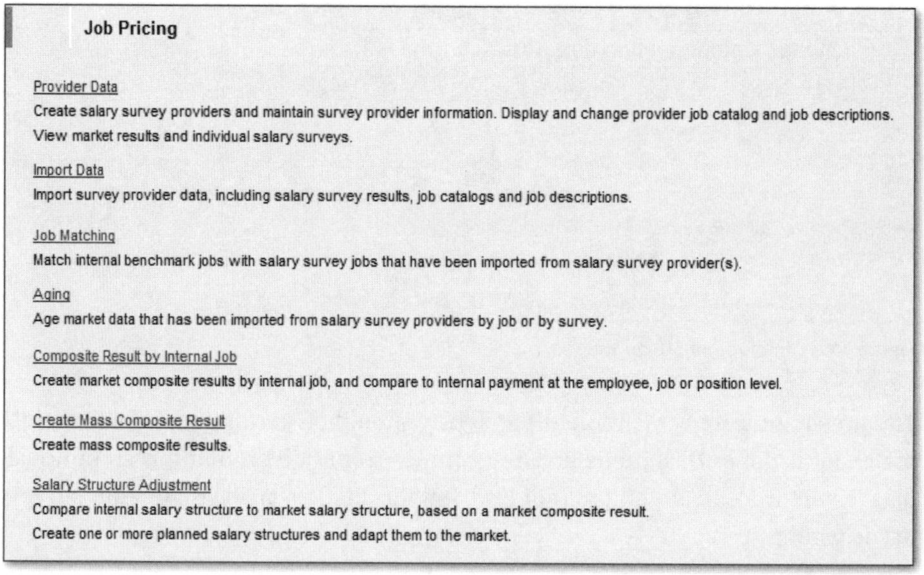

Figure 10.5 Job Pricing Start Screen

Each of these links launches its own web page. The first link (and first step in the process) is to create a vendor, which we will discuss next.

10.2.1 Vendor Setup

Your salary survey vendors (which SAP calls providers) need to be set up in the system before any surveys or analysis can be done. To create a vendor in the system, you must click the Provider Data link from the main start screen. You can create providers by clicking the Create Provider button (Figure 10.6). You can also delete a provider.

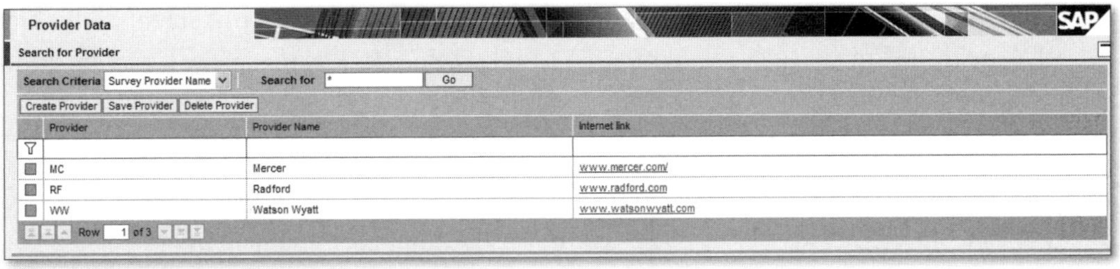

Figure 10.6 List of Salary Survey Providers

Each provider is given a two-character provider ID. For example, a provider ID for Mercer could be MC and for Watson Wyatt could be WW. In addition, you can optionally specify a link to the provider's website, if needed.

Clicking on the row of a provider returns that vendor's survey job catalog, the surveys, and market criteria (by tab) that have been loaded into the tool. Figure 10.7 shows a list of survey jobs for a vendor. Each job is listed with job grade, job level, survey job name, job family (compensation job grouping), job family name, grade low, and grade high. Obviously, you only see data for vendors whose survey jobs have been loaded.

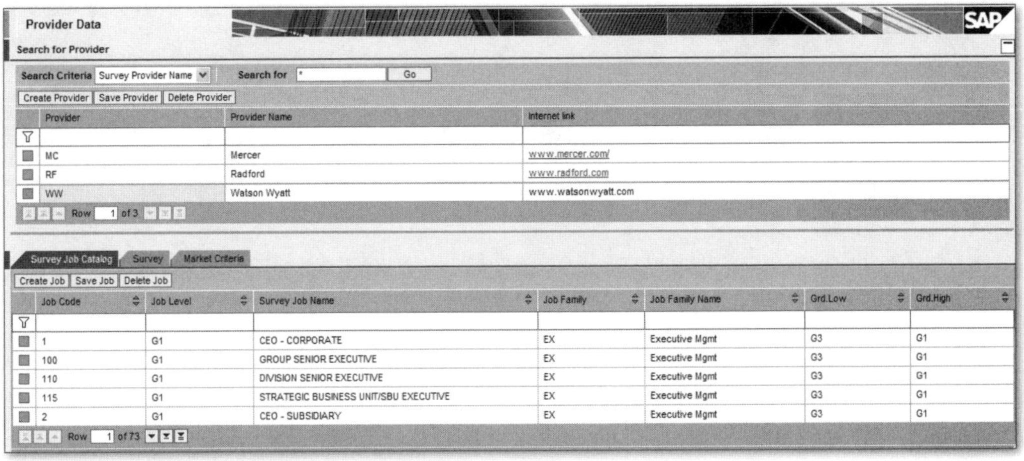

Figure 10.7 Survey Job Catalog for a Provider

You can also manually add, change, or delete a survey job on this screen. Editable fields include Survey Job name, Job Family, Job Family Name, Grd. Low, and Grd. High. Job code, and Job Level cannot be changed.

Selecting a survey job returns that survey job's market data, aged market data (if relevant), and job desciption. Figure 10.8 shows you the selection of survey job FACILITIES/REAL ESTATE EXECUTIVE. You cannot change the market data or aged market data of a survey job, but you can update the job description, line of reporting, and experience under the Job Description tab.

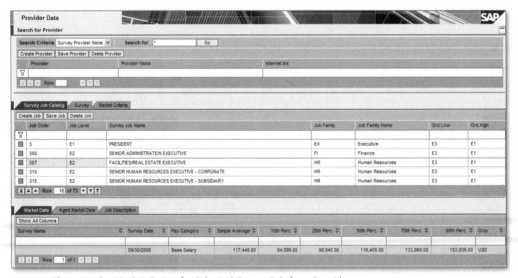

Figure 10.8 Market Data of a Selected Survey Job for a Provider

The Survey tab stores all of the providers' surveys, by survey date. Each survey and survey date combination is stored here. Only the survey name can be changed after uploading a survey. You can also delete a survey using the functionality provided.

Finally, the text behind the uploaded market criteria be changed after upload. Market criteria such as industry, region, revenue size, company size, company type, and length of service can be changed and translated.

The import of survey job and market data is an important part of the functionaity. This is discussed next.

10.2.2 Data Import

You can access the data import utility of job pricing by clicking the Import Data link on the main screen. After searching for and selecting one of your providers, a screen for data transfer is displayed.

There are three steps to data import: specifying the import parameters and the location of the file for upload, mapping the survey fields to the SAP fields, and importing and saving the data. These steps must be performed sequentially.

Three files are needed to upload into the system — one for the survey job catalog, one for the survey job descriptions, and another for the survey data. The input source files must be in .txt (Tab delimited) ASCII format to be imported. You can create .txt from Excel using the Save as option.

In Figure 10.9 you can see an upload of a survey job file from a vendor. In this example, the Data Type specified in the dropdown is Survey Job Catalog. Depending on whether or not the file you are working with has header lines will determine the value for No. of Header Lines. You can also select the language.

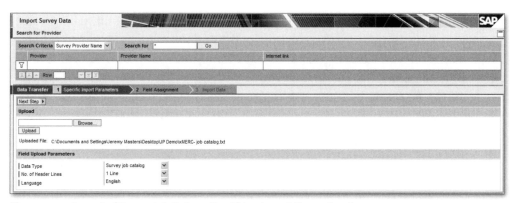

Figure 10.9 Import of Survey Job Data — Specifying Import Parameters for Survey Job Catalog Data

The Field Assignment tab (step 2) lets you map the provider fields to the SAP fields for a particular salary survey. The system remembers the mapping for later uploads of the same survey. You do not have to remap the fields every year unless the file column layout changes. SAP keeps track of the mapping based on the position of the columns within the file. When mapping is complete, click the Save

Field Matching button. If you click the Next Step button, the mapping is saved automatically.

Figure 10.10 shows an example mapping of a survey. Please note that not all mapping is required — only job code and job level are required.

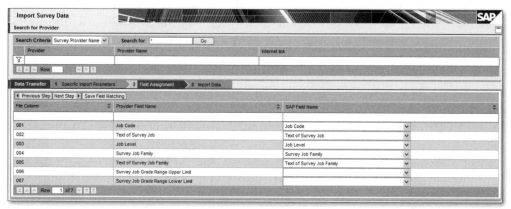

Figure 10.10 Import of Survey Job Data – Field Assignment

Figure 10.11 shows you the last step in the import process. In this tab, users can review the imported data associated with the survey jobs. Additional columns can be shown by clicking the Show All Columns button. If you want to save the imported data, click the Save Imported Data button. Any of the columns in the list can be sorted by ascending or descending order by clicking on the column name.

The second file to upload is for the survey job descriptions. The import process is the same as the first procedure, but the fields are different. You can see the data fields of this import including Job Description, Experience, and Reporting To in Figure 10.12.

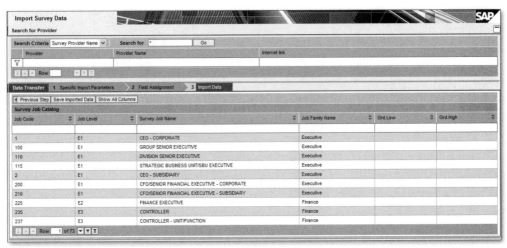

Figure 10.11 Import of Survey Job Data — Import Data

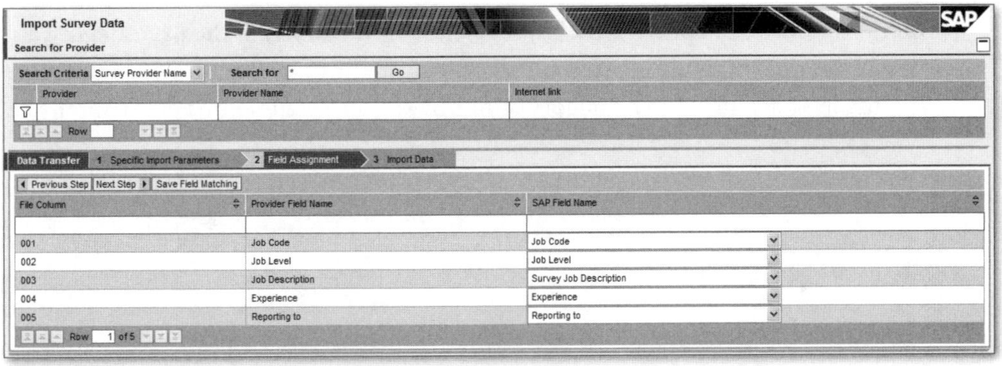

Figure 10.12 Import of Survey Job Data — Field Assignment

The third file is by far the largest. It contains all of the survey market data that your vendor has provided. Notice that when you select the Survey market data selection under File Upload Parameters, the Survey section becomes available. In this section, you can identify the survey name, the survey date, and the currency key. Figure 10.13 displays this selection.

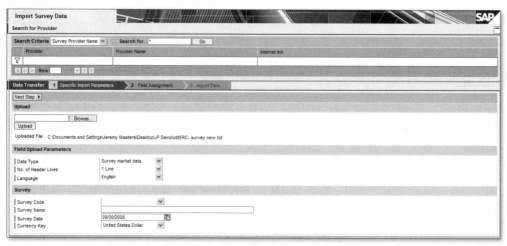

Figure 10.13 Import of Survey Job Data — Specifying Import Parameters for Survey Market Data

Within the Field Assignment tab, you need to account for the pay category for each of the SAP fields mapped to the survey field. The values from the pay category are based on the configuration discussed previously. Any amount-based value must be mapped against a pay category. You can see an example of field mapping in Figure 10.14.

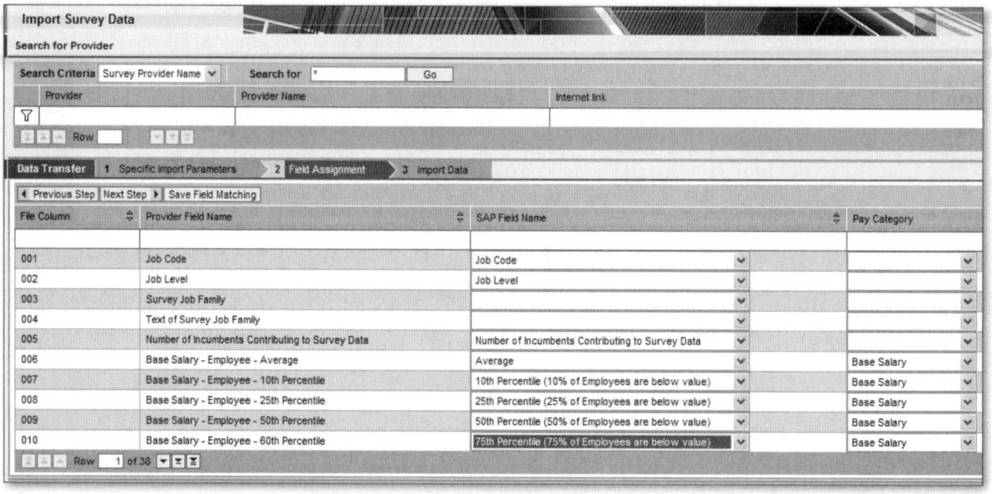

Figure 10.14 Import of Salary Survey Data — Field Assignment

Some key items to keep in mind during file preparation including the following:

- ▶ Remove all commas from numbers
- ▶ Enter all currency and salary survey amounts in full-dollar-amount format (Example: 81000 and not 81)
- ▶ Remove all currency symbols
- ▶ Never use percent signs in a percent field. Fifteen percent is 15 not 15% or .15. SAP sees .15 as .15%
- ▶ When working with international surveys, be sure to select the correct currency during import
- ▶ Beware of leading zeros in survey jobs and other fields used to match data. SAP does not see 0056 the same as 56

Table 10.1 shows the fields available in SAP to map the data import processes discussed. The field name, data type, and field length are displayed, along with a definition and examples. (This data contains all fields from the three files.)

Field Name	Data Type	Field Length	Definition/Example
10th Percentile (10% of employees are below value)	CURR	15	Note: You can use these percentile fields to map to a different percentile of your choice. However, the name of the field must remain unchanged.
25th Percentile (25% of employees are below value)	CURR	15	Self-explanatory
50th Percentile (50% of employees are below value)	CURR	15	Self-explanatory
60th Percentile (60% of employees are below value)	CURR	15	Self-explanatory

Table 10.1 Standard SAP Mapping Fields within Job Pricing

Field Name	Data Type	Field Length	Definition/Example
75th Percentile (75% of employees are below value)	CURR	15	Self-explanatory
90th Percentile (90% of employees are below value)	CURR	15	Self-explanatory
Aging factor %	DEC	5	Aging factor as a percentage used at the survey level.
Average of Salary Weighted by Incumbents	CURR	15	Self-explanatory
Average of Salary Weighted by Companies	CURR	15	Self-explanatory
Average Salary/ Actual Bonus Expressed as Percentage of Base Salary	DEC	5	Self-explanatory
International Organization for Standardization (ISO) Country Code	CHAR	2	Two-digit ISO code.
Experience	STRING		Description of the work experience for this survey job.
Job Match indicator	CHAR	1	Indicates the degree of job match from the survey provider. Typically, the values for the indicator are '-,' '=,' or '+.'
Lower Limit of Survey Job Grade Range	CHAR	8	This field is used to store the lower end of the grade range for the job, as determined by the survey provider. Sometimes the provider indicates its job evaluation with this field.

Table 10.1 Standard SAP Mapping Fields within Job Pricing (Cont.)

Field Name	Data Type	Field Length	Definition/Example
Number of Companies Contributing to Survey Job Data	DEC	7	Self-explanatory
Number of Incumbents Contributing to Survey Job Data	DEC	7	Self-explanatory
Other Adjustment Factor %	DEC	5	Self-explanatory
Pay Category	CHAR	2	Type of market statistics (Base, Total Cash Compensation, Bonus). Values are based on your own configuration. SAP standard includes the following: 01 (Base Salary), 02 (Total Cash Compensation), and 03 (Total Bonus). This field is required.
Percentage of Employees Eligible for Short-term Incentives	DEC	5	Self-explanatory
Percentage of Employees receiving Short-term Incentives	DEC	5	Self-explanatory
Reporting to	STRING		Line of reporting for the survey job.
Short-term Incentive Actual Percentage of Base	DEC	5	Self-explanatory
Short-term Incentive Percentage of eligible employees	DEC	5	Self-explanatory

Table 10.1 Standard SAP Mapping Fields within Job Pricing (Cont.)

Field Name	Data Type	Field Length	Definition/Example
Short-term Incentive Target Percentage of Base	DEC	5	Self-explanatory
Simple Average of Salary	CURR	15	Self-explanatory
Company Size Text	CHAR	60	Market data criteria
Survey Date	DATS	8	Effective date of the survey in the YYYYMMDD format.
Industry Text	CHAR	60	Market data criteria
Job code	CHAR	8	The job code as supplied by the survey provider.
Job Description	STRING		Description of the survey job and its responsibilities.
Job Family	CHAR	8	A group of jobs having the same nature of work (e.g., FI) but requiring different levels of skill, effort, responsibility, or working conditions (e.g., entry-level vs. advanced).
Job Level	CHAR	2	Some survey providers divide jobs into levels within the survey. You can use the level to indicate the level of skill.
Job Matching Percent	DEC	5	This field is used to indicate the confidence level of the survey provider regarding their job match, displayed as a percentage.
Job Status according to Fair Labor Standards Act (FLSA) Indicator	CHAR	1	This indicator field is used to store the exempt/nonexempt job indicator from the survey provider, according to FLSA. This is a local field relevant to the United States only.
Job Weight Factor	DEC	4	The weighting factor to be applied at the job level to adjust the market data.
Length of Service Text	CHAR	60	Market data criteria.

Table 10.1 Standard SAP Mapping Fields within Job Pricing (Cont.)

Field Name	Data Type	Field Length	Definition/Example
Region Text	CHAR	60	Market data criteria
Revenue Size Text	CHAR	60	Market data criteria
Salary Range Maximum	CURR	15	Self-explanatory
Salary Range Midpoint	CURR	15	Self-explanatory
Salary Range Maximum	CURR	15	Self-explanatory
Target Bonus Expressed as Percentage of Base Salary	DEC	5	Self-explanatory
Text of Survey Job	CHAR	60	Job title
Text of Survey Job Family	CHAR	60	Job family name (if only this field is used, Survey Job Family is generated).
Unit of Time	NUMC	2	Unit of time for which the amounts are valid. Yearly values are the default if this field is not matched: 01 = monthly, 02 = semimonthly, 03 = weekly, 04 = 2 weekly, 05 = 4 weekly, 06 = yearly, 07 = quarterly, 08 = half yearly
Upper Limit of Survey Job Grade Range	CHAR	8	This field is used to store the upper end of the grade range for the job, as determined by the survey provider. Sometimes the provider indicates its own job evaluation with this field.

Table 10.1 Standard SAP Mapping Fields within Job Pricing (Cont.)

The fields in Table 10.1 represent all of the SAP fields available. There is no standard way to add additional fields to map to. If additional fields are needed, an SAP modification would be necessary (meaning you would need to request object keys for each object needing updating).

Now that the data has been imported, let's discuss how to match internal jobs to survey jobs.

10.2.3 Job Matching

Job matching is one of the most analytical parts of the job pricing process. This is where the knowledge and experience of a Compensation professional comes into play.

You can access the job matching functionality within job pricing by selecting the Job Matching link from the main screen. A screen appears with two tables — one for internal jobs (on the left) and the other for survey jobs (on the right).

On the left side, the selection for internal jobs is available. Each job is listed with the job grouping (from Infotype 5050) and the end date (end date on the job's Infotype 1000 (Object) record). Each internal job text is hyperlinked. If selected, a pop-up window appears and contains the following information: job ID, job name, start date, end date, job grouping ID, job grouping name, and job description (from Infotype 1002 (Description), subtype 0001 (General)).

On the right side is the selection for survey jobs. Each survey job is listed with the provider name, job level, and job family. Each survey job is hyperlinked. If selected, a pop-up window appears and contains the following information: survey provider ID, survey provider name, survey job code, survey job name, survey job level, experience, line of reporting, and job description.

Matches are then made between the internal job (on the left) and one or more survey jobs (on the right). The matches appear beneath the tables. A Compensation professional must determine how closely a survey job matches an internal job. This is done by adding the matching percentage and the weighting factor in the appropriate fields. Please note that the matching percentage and the weighting percentage are simply for information purposes only. The weighting factor is a key field used to calculate the market composite result (discussed later in this chapter). Changing the weighting factor changes the weighting percentage automatically.

Figure 10.15 displays an example match for a Senior Vice President, Human Resources internal job mapped to two survey jobs. Each survey job has its own weighting factor and matching percentage.

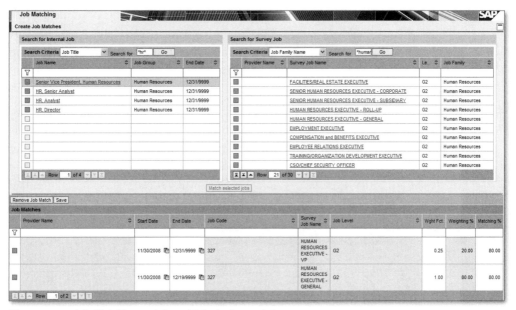

Figure 10.15 Job Matching — Internal Jobs to Survey Jobs

That concludes the coverage of job matching, so let's talk about aging survey data.

10.2.4 Aging

You can age your survey data to reflect ongoing changes in the market. Aging survey data is useful if a survey is several months old and you wish to apply a certain percentage factor against it to age it to a different time frame. Some companies do not receive survey data every year from their vendors, so this functionality is important so you can extrapolate market data from older surveys.

You can access the aging functionality within job pricing by selecting the Aging link from the main screen. To age your data, you must first search for and select the survey you want to age. Once you have selected the survey, you have the flexibility to either select some or all of the survey jobs to age within that survey.

Once you have selected the jobs you want to age, you can enter either a market movement rate or an age factor for aging data in the Aging Parameters section. (You can either age the data by a market movement rate or an age factor.) Some key differences are highlighted here:

▶ The market movement rate is an annual percentage rate that is prorated according to the specified age date. The actual age factor is calculated from the survey date, the age date, and the market movement rate. Using this method, the age date — and length of time from the survey date — are factored into the calculation.

▶ The age factor is applied to the data without any date considerations. The aging date is still required for identification purposes later in the process. Using this approach, the calculation is based on a straight percentage. Unlike the market movement rate, the length of time from the survey date is not factored into the calculation. BAdI HRECM00_AGEDATA (Age Market Data) lets you manipulate the aging calculation based on your customer-specific logic.

> **Note**
>
> Regardless of whether you choose to age your survey data based on a market movement rate or an aging factor, you should always enter an age date as it is a key date stored in the system and used for reference purposes.

You can also use the market criteria (sometimes referred to as "scope") to filter certain data within a survey. The market criteria available to you depends on what type of scope data you provided during the import of the survey data. The standard market criteria categories include:

▶ Country

▶ Industry

▶ Region

▶ Revenue Size

▶ Company Size

▶ Company Type

▶ Length of Service

If other scope categories are needed, the only option is to use an existing category (if not already used). Although this is certainly not Best Practice, it does provide a workaround to incorporate one-off categories (such as Average Age of Incumbent) that are not provided by SAP. As an example, the standard market criteria category Length of Service could be utilized for the Average Age of Incumbent scope.

In Figure 10.16 you can see an example of market data aging from a selected survey. In this scenario, the survey was aged based on an age factor of 1.25% with an age data of July 1, 2010.

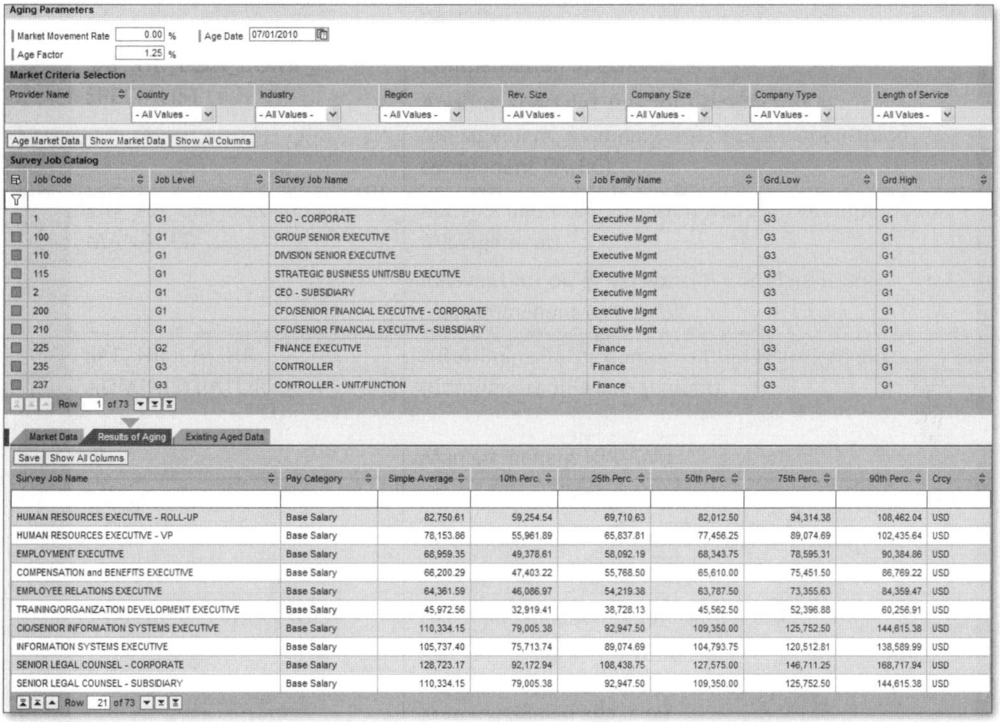

Figure 10.16 Aging Survey Data

The three tabs at the bottom of the screen (from left to right) show the original survey data (from import), the results of the current aging activity, and the previously aged data (if applicable). Clicking the Show All Columns button shows all of the survey fields (not just the percentile data points).

Whether or not you have aged your data, the next step in the process is to create job composites.

10.2.5 Job Composite Creation (By Individual Job)

Creating and comparing job composites to internal jobs, positions, and employees provides a significant analytical capability for Compensation professionals. By creating hybrid jobs, robust comparisons to internal data can be achieved. The analysis available during this step provides one of the most robust aspects of the job pricing solution because the Compensation department can compare how well they are compensating employees against the market.

You can access the individual job composite creation functionality by selecting the Composite Result by Internal Job link from the main screen. After searching for and selecting an internal job, the results of your job matching are displayed in the middle of the screen. You can also use a cut of this data via the market criteria selection, which includes survey, survey date, and age data per provider. In addition, another opportunity to age the data further is by using a market movement rate.

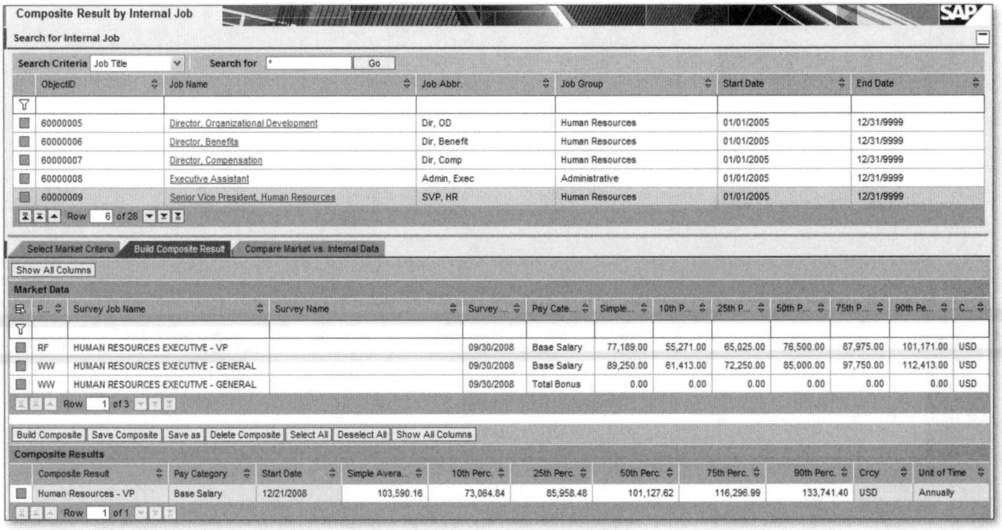

Figure 10.17 Composite Result — Build Composite Result

After selecting the appropriate market data on the first tab, the second tab displays the chosen cut of data. On this tab, you can save your job composite. If you want to save a composite, you must select one or more survey jobs and provide a name. After selecting the appropriate market data you want to incorporate into your composite, click the Build Composite button to generate the composite results based on pay category. You can show more columns via the Show All button. To save the composite, click the Save as button. For any new composite, leave the Composite Result dropdown blank and provide the composite name, start date, and country grouping. All three fields are very important as they form a key for future data records. In Figure 10.17, composite result Human Resources – VP is shown with one pay category —Base Salary. Composites can be updated by selecting the suitable market data and the composite from the Composite Result selection.

On the third tab, a composite result can be compared to an internal employee, job, or position. Additional comparison parameters include the following:

▶ Percentile (10th, 25th, 50th, 60th, 75th, 90th, and All Values)

▶ Frequency (Annually, Bi-weekly, Every four weeks, Half-yearly, Monthly, Quarterly, Semi-monthly, and Weekly)

▶ Pay category (based on your configured values)

▶ Currency

Clicking the Compare Values button performs the analysis of internal versus external data based on the selection options chosen. Based on the object being compared, one or more internal jobs, positions, or employees will be shown in the result set. Comparisons to jobs and positions can only be performed if Infotype 1005 (Planned Compensation) is maintained on those objects. Most companies do not maintain this infotype on both objects (with the exception being for override scenarios where the infotype is maintained at the position level instead of or in addition to the job). This way, only one of the objects will be available for comparison against the market data.

The employee comparison is available based on the wage types configured by pay category. For each pay category, the wages are evaluated based on the method begin date and method end date specified in the configuration (Table T539J). Options are available to show more data columns and to display a graphical representation of the output.

Figure 10.18 shows a job composite Human Resources — VP compared against two employees, James Martin and Greg Hanson, based on their Base Salary 50th percentile data point. The results show the interval value (based on their employee data in the system), the market value, and the differences in amount and percentage. You can view amounts in any currency as long as you have maintained the exchanged rates (exchange rate type M) in Table TCURR. You should discuss maintaining this table with your Finance department.

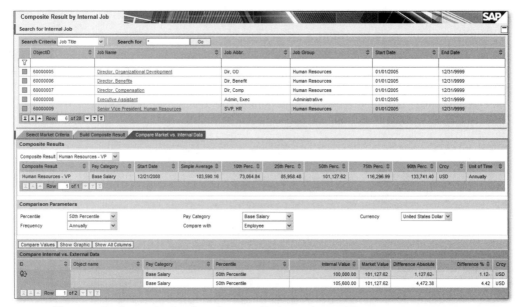

Figure 10.18 Composite Result — Compare Market vs. Internal Data

We have now seen how job composites can be created via an individual job selection. Job composites can also be created en masse. Let's look at this option next.

10.2.6 Job Composite Creation (En Masse)

Composites can also be created en masse. This allows for a more streamlined way of creating job composites. You can access the mass job composite creation functionality within job pricing by clicking the Create Mass Composite Result link from the main screen. You can search for and select one or more internal jobs to incorporate into a composite. Clicking the Get Market Criteria Selection from Job Selection button retrieves the appropriate market criteria (by provider) based on the job matches created earlier against those jobs. Clicking the Get Market Data button then retrieves the survey data based on the selection. After selecting the appropriate cut of data, you can save your composite as described previously.

Figure 10.19 shows an example of mass composite creation.

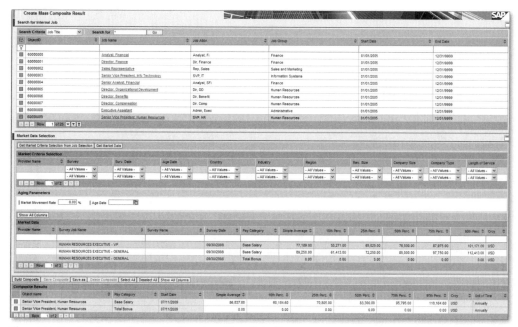

Figure 10.19 Creating a Composite Based on Mass Selection

Unlike the previous scenario, you do not have the ability to compare the composite against an employee, position, or job. To do this, you have to use the Composite Result by Internal Job link after creating the composite.

Whether you have saved a composite through individual selection or through the en masse option, composite data is stored in Infotype 1271 (Composite Survey Result) against the job object. Pictured in Figure 10.20, Infotype 1271 is a new infotype for job pricing that stores the following data per composite/pay category:

► Composite Result

► Pay Category

► Currency

► Unit of Time

► Simple Average

- Average % of Base
- Target % of Base
- Actual % of Base
- 10th Percentile
- 25th Percentile
- 50th Percentile
- 60th Percentile
- 75th Percentile
- 90th Percentile

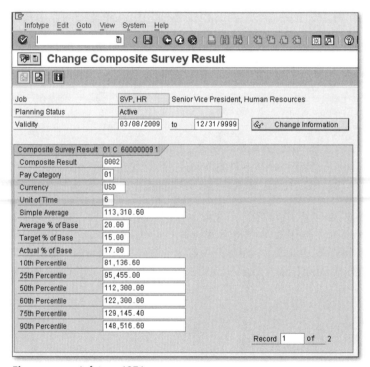

Figure 10.20 Infotype 1271

Once you have built your composites, you may want to consider how to update your company's pay structures. Adjustments to salary structures are discussed next.

10.2.7 Salary Structure Adjustment

Adjusting your salary structures based on composite information is an optional task. Many companies prefer to leave this activity as part of their annual maintenance process (though not through this tool). However, for those that want to leverage the functionality, you can both compare your company's salary structure to the market based on composite results and create one or more planned salary structures to adapt more competitively to the market.

You can access the salary structure adjustment functionality within job pricing by clicking the Salary Structure Adjustment link from the main screen. You can find a given salary structure by searching country grouping, salary type (i.e., pay grade type), or salary area (i.e., salary area). These values all come from Table T710. (This functionality does not have the ability to update Table T510).

By selecting a combination of country grouping, salary type, and salary area, the salary structure (i.e., including the pay grade group and the pay grade level with their minimum, reference, and maximum salaries) is displayed on the first tab. This table also has valuable information such as the number of jobs and the number of positions holding that structure in Infotype 1005.

On the second tab, composite results can be compared against the salary structure. Results can be aggregated in three ways: by pay grade, by pay grade and job group, and by pay grade and pay level. Variables such as pay category, percentile, time unit, and currency can also be selected.

On the third tab, you can either select an existing (previously created) planned salary structure proposal or create a new planned proposal for the salary structure. The latter is accomplished by clicking the Create from Market Data button. Market data for all survey jobs matched to jobs holding that salary structure are sourced for the proposal. You can overwrite the values of the planned structure by changing the proposed values directly or by changing the difference percentage columns and selecting the Recalculate button. The percentage can be either positive or negative depending on how you want to adjust the salary structure. The current and planned minimum, maximum, and reference salaries are available for comparison purposes.

When the proposed salary structure is finalized, click the Save as button to save as an adjustment version with the start date. The adjustment version is the technical name of the proposed change in salary adjustment. Figure 10.21 shows the planned structure Salary_Structure_All_SalaryExempt_Grades 01/01/2010.

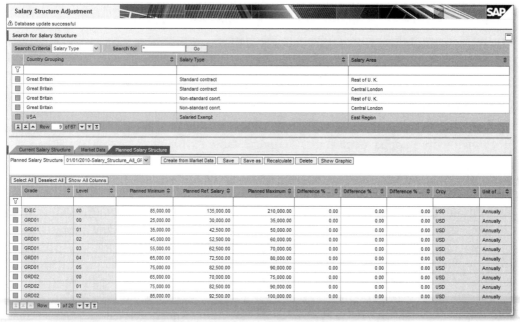

Figure 10.21 Example Proposal for Planned Salary Structure Adjustment

The salary structure adjustment proposal created during the composite process can be actualized against the salary structure table (Table T710) based on program RHECM_ADJ_SALARY_STRUC. You can also reach this program with Transaction PECM_ADJ_SAL_STRU or within the IMG under the following path: PERSONNEL MANAGEMENT • ENTERPRISE COMPENSATION MANAGEMENT • JOB PRICING • PAY GRADES AND LEVELS • UPDATE PAY GRADE AMOUNTS FROM MARKET DATA. Figure 10.22 shows the selection screen for this transaction.

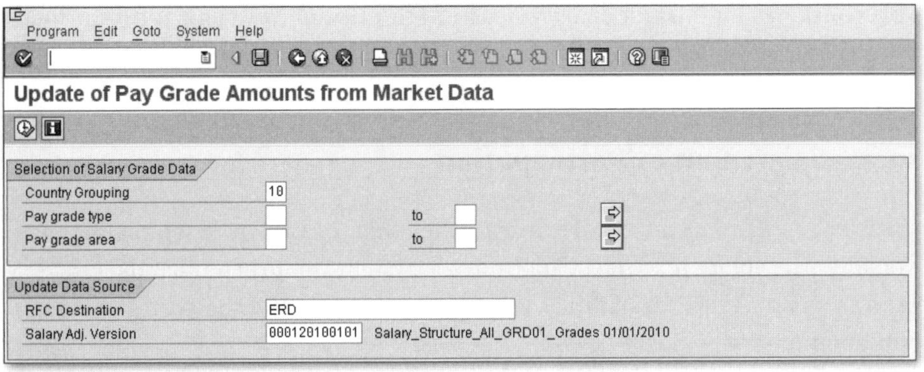

Figure 10.22 Selection Screen for Transaction PECM_ADJ_SAL_STRU

Using Transaction PECM_ADJ_SAL_STRU, you can update the proposed salary adjustment to Table T710 by saving the changes to a transport. By choosing the Remote Function Call (RFC) Desination as your production system, you can pull in the proposed salary adjustments (performed in production) to the development tables. You should always run this report in your development system. You may need additional security because you need to use an RFC call to your production system to retrieve the modeling performed there.

Figure 10.23 shows the transport request prompt after clicking the Perform Update button. This is available only after executing the report.

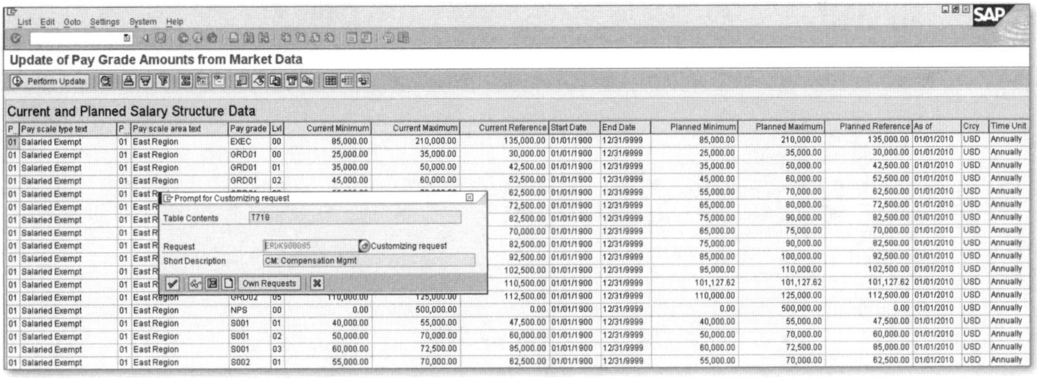

Figure 10.23 Saving Salary Structure Changes to a Transport

This concludes the market analysis part of job pricing. Now let's turn our focus onto salary survey participation.

10.3 Salary Survey Participation

Participation in salary surveys represents the other major part of job pricing functionality. The ability to extract data from the system and to send that data to your external vendors in a format they are expecting is an important part of this compensation process.

Transaction PECM_QUERY_SURVEY (seen in Figure 10.24) is a standard query that can extract data based on provider code, benchmark job indicator, or the compensation job grouping. This query — along with other reports identified in Chapter 13, Reporting, — can provide a mechanism to output data based on the survey vendors' needs. Depending on the type of data you need to extract (and the logic that is needed to extract it), you may or may not be able to use the SAP Query tool. For more complex data extraction, a custom ABAP program may be a better option.

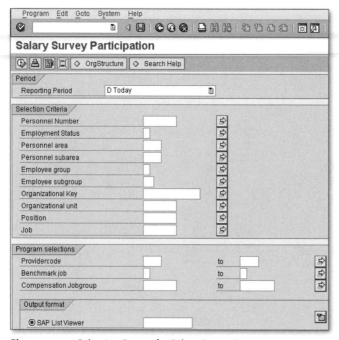

Figure 10.24 Selection Screen for Salary Survey Participation

For global organizations that contribute to both local and global surveys, the solution may differ depending on the approach taken. A lot of companies create one large custom ABAP report with output that can be used to contribute to the majority of their surveys (including international, if needed). This means that members of the Compensation department need to manipulate the Excel files produced from the report before sending them to the vendor (e.g., removing columns not needed for a survey, adding columns for data not housed in SAP, etc.). For other salary participation reports, see Chapter 13.

Now let's discuss the application support for job pricing.

10.4   Application Support

The application is supported under the application area PA-EC-JP (Job Pricing) within SAP's Service Marketplace. At the time of this book's writing, the following SAP Notes were available:

- ▶ 1224387 — Selection in BSP Application HRECM_JPR_CMAS
- ▶ 1243242 — Importing market data, currency type without decimal places
- ▶ 1268574 — Job Pricing: No further development
- ▶ 989940   — Search for Internal Job by Job Title >12 chars fails
- ▶ 990544   — Result of aging empty if last job catalog has no Market Data
- ▶ 883955   — Time unit error handling
- ▶ 886465   — Survey Data upload does not store the 60th percentile
- ▶ 921064   — Runtime error when removing job match
- ▶ 923034   — Data Import: Key fields saved with lowercase
- ▶ 1034384 — Parts of job pricing without language dependency
- ▶ 979082   — Search for Survey Job by Survey Code with no result
- ▶ 861869   — Transaction PECM_START_BDG_BSP: Error when closing
- ▶ 774498   — Field attribute control in datasource 0EC_CJOB_ATTR
- ▶ 702448   — BSP User Interface for Job Pricing
- ▶ 759026   — Job Matching: Session for Job Descriptions stays open
- ▶ 720143   — Corrections of Job Pricing and Budgeting UI

- ▶ 724390 — Enterprise Compensation Management - job pricing
- ▶ 730941 — Correction of BSP Interface Texts
- ▶ 741054 — PA-EC-JPR Invalid info object 0EC_CJOB_ATTR
- ▶ 654858 — Correction Job Pricing Business Logic

The most effective SAP Note related to job pricing is 1268574 (Job Pricing: No further development). In this note (issued in October 2008), SAP states that, "as of release ERP 6.0, this functionality will not be enhanced anymore, i.e., no further development will take place." SAP also confirms that the "…job pricing functionality remains in the system and can still be implemented and used, however, no further development will be done." Whether you are considering implementing job pricing for the first time or looking to add incremental changes on existing functionality, this means that although SAP still supports the application, there are currently no plans to extend its functionality. This is not necessarily news to be alarmed by, but rather an important point for consideration as you work through the functionality.

10.5 Summary

In this chapter, we reviewed the job pricing functionality available in ECM. We learned how to create provider data, import survey job and market data, match internal jobs to survey jobs, age data, create composites, and create and update a new salary structure (based on the market data). We have learned how to address salary survey participation. Finally, we documented important SAP Notes to help address known defects.

In the next chapter, we'll focus on solution integration — from a module, platform and vendor perspective.

Integration is one of SAP's hallmarks. Key touch points across components and platforms allow data and processes to harmonize and become more efficient. SAP provides critical areas for integrating functionalities — such as performance management — into the compensation management solution. In this chapter we will explore the integration components relevant to Enterprise Compensation Management (ECM) and highlight areas specifically for making compensation processes more robust.

11 Integration Components

Tight integration is one of SAP's most powerful features. Within ECM, a vast number of key integration opportunities are available for leverage. Integration within ECM allows compensation processes to become better synchronized and data to be better utilized for employees, managers, Human Resources (HR) and Compensation department. Efficiency is gained and Return on Investment (ROI) is increased.

In this chapter, we will discuss integration on three levels. The first level is at a component level. ECM integrates with other SAP HCM modules including Personnel Administration (PA), Organizational Management (OM), and Payroll (PY). The second level of integration is at a platform level. Delivery platforms such as Employee Self-Service (ESS), Manager Self-Service (MSS), and Business Warehouse (BW) offer enhanced capabilities to increase employee and manager efficiency. The SAP NetWeaver Portal, for example, provides the key delivery platform for annual compensation planning via standard MSS iViews. The third level is at a vendor level. Vendor integration (e.g., with payroll, survey provides, banks/brokerages) is a critical piece for compensation processes to work seamlessly.

11.1 Overview

Figure 11.1 shows a diagram depicting the various integration modules for ECM. In the center of the diagram, the connectedness of ECM with other SAP HCM components is illustrated. The following SAP ERP HCM modules are available for integration with ECM:

- Personnel Administration (PA)
- Organizational Management (OM)
- Performance Management (also referred to as Object Settings and Appraisals)
- Payroll (PY)
- Personnel Cost Planning and Simulation (PCP)

In addition, elements of SAP Finance are available for integration.

The following delivery channels are also supported:

- Employee and Manager Self Service via the SAP NetWeaver Portal
- Business Intelligence via the SAP NetWeaver Business Warehouse

These platforms are represented left to right in Figure 11.1.

Vendor integration is also a key part of the solution. Vendors providing services for payroll, salary surveys, and banking/brokeraging are often critical success factors during and after implementation.

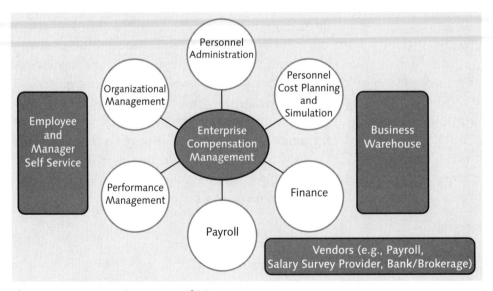

Figure 11.1 Integration Components of ECM

In the next section, we will review each integration point and highlight key touch points. We will also talk about common integration pain points and "gotchas," along with the appropriate mitigation steps you can take to alleviate any impact to implementation and operational support.

11.2   Module Integration

The first two modules we will review — Personnel Administration (PA) and Organizational Management (OM) — are prerequisites for ECM. The other modules we will look at are optional (such as Performance Management and Payroll (PY)) but common.

Let's first discuss integration between ECM and PA.

11.2.1   Integration with Personnel Administration (PA)

PA is one of the core modules within SAP ERP HCM. PA provides all of the employee master data such as name, action and organizational history, planned working time, and basic pay data. Having at least a "mini-master" within PA is a prerequisite for ECM. By mini-master, we mean having a core set of PA infotypes for employees that can provide a baseline for ECM functionality. These core infotypes include:

- Infotype 0000 (Actions)
- Infotype 0001 (Organizational Assignment)
- Infotype 0002 (Personal Data)
- Infotype 0007 (Planned Working Time)
- Infotype 0008 (Basic Pay)

In addition, other common infotypes used in compensation process include:

- Infotype 0015 (One-time Payments)
- Infotype 0267 (Off-cycle One-time Payments)
- Infotype 0041 (Date Specifications)
- Infotype 0006 (Address)

ECM uses infotypes within PA to deliver its functionality. The following infotypes collectively comprise the set of data within ECM:

- Infotype 0758 (Compensation Program)
- Infotype 0759 (Compensation Process)
- Infotype 0760 (Compensation Eligibility Override)
- Infotype 0761 (Long-term Incentive (LTI) Granting)
- Infotype 0762 (LTI Exercising)
- Infotype 0763 (LTI Participant Data)

> **Tip**
>
> ECM does not use any of the older compensation infotypes from Compensation Management module (application component CM) such as Infotype 0380 (Compensation Adjustment) and Infotype 0381 (Compensation Eligibility). For more information on a migration path from the old to new compensation module, see Chapter 8, Advanced Topics and Additional Enhancements.

Let's turn our focus to the other vital module for ECM — Organizational Management (OM).

11.2.2 Integration with Organizational Management (OM)

OM is the other required module for ECM. Without OM, online compensation reviews cannot occur because the organizational structure provides the backbone for manager planning and approval. Organizational units, positions, and jobs are all housed within this component. The relationships between these objects and the hierarchies established from them form a critical part of ECM. In addition, the budget hierarchy uses OM objects and relationships to track allocation and spend throughout the planning process. The budget hierarchy is mirrored off the organizational unit hierarchy to provide its functionality for tracking budgets, including roll-up amounts.

The pay structure stored in Infotype 1005 (Planned Compensation) is critical for compensation processes because grade and range information is stored on the job (and on the position for override scenarios). These pay structures default to the employee's Infotype 00008 record during employee events such as hire, rehire, promotion, and transfer. Infotype 1005 is one of the most critical parts of compensation (whether ECM is implemented or not) and is (unfortunately) often misunderstood.

It is also common to store custom values or flags within OM at the job, position, or organizational unit level to support compensation processes. For example, you can tie bonus targets to a job via a custom infotype or object. (This often works well for customers because the designs of bonus plans are usually unique to each organization.) The position could store a flag indicating management level for outgoing interfaces (such as for third-party stock systems). The organizational unit (or a linked business unit) could store a performance modifier or achievement result necessary to calculate the bonus basis or payout. The enhancement possibilities are endless for OM to support compensation processes. And the extensibility within SAP's OM framework to create and maintain these custom objects, relationships, and infotypes offers you tremendous flexibility for supporting compensation practices for any organization.

The Job Pricing sub-module uses two new OM infotypes — Infotype 5050 (Compensation Job Attributes) and Infotype 1271 (Composite Survey Result) — to support its functionality. Both are linked to the job object, and were discussed in detail in Chapter 10, Job Pricing.

The following OM objects are used within ECM:

▶ Organizational Unit (O)

▶ Position (S)

▶ Job (C)

▶ Budget Unit (BU)

The following OM infotypes are used within ECM:

▶ Infotype 1000 (Object)

▶ Infotype 1001 (Relationships)

▶ Infotype 1002 (Description)

▶ Infotype 1005 (Planned Compensation)

▶ Infotype 1271 (Composite Survey Result)

▶ Infotype 1500 (BS Element Management)

▶ Infotype 1520 (Original Budget)

▶ Infotype 5050 (Compensation Job Attributes)

Depending on how much functionality you implement, you may or may not use all of these infotypes. Now that we have covered the PA and OM modules, let's review integration with Performance Management.

11.2.3 Integration with Performance Management (PM)

One of the most popular integration scenarios within all of SAP ERP HCM is the linkage between Performance Management and Compensation Management. The correlation between "performance" and "pay" supports the decades' old philosophy that links high performance with fair and rewarding pay. With the new Performance Management application (Object Setting and Appraisals), you now have the opportunity to link Performance Management and Compensation Management.

Within the configuration, ECM allows you to pull ratings information from the Performance Management database. The ratings for the new Performance Management system are stored in Table HRHAP_FINAL. This table is not captured in PA (i.e., it cannot be found on an infotype record). This differs from the previous Performance Management module in which appraisal ratings were stored in Infotype 0025 (Appraisals). Regardless of whether you use the old or new Performance Management module, you can integrate the ratings into the ECM application.

Tip

For more information on SAP Performance Management, please refer to the SAP PRESS book *SAP ERP HCM Performance Management*, by Jeremy Masters and Christos Kotsakis.

You can integrate with Performance Management to retrieve ratings through BAdI HRECM00_MATRIX_SEGM (Methods for Matrix Dimensions). Standard Implementation BAdI HRECM00_MATR_APPR (Matrix Dimension Method: Appraisal) retrieves the rating from Infotype 0025 while standard Implementation BAdI HRECM00_MATR_MBOAPPR (Matrix Dimension Method: MBO Appraisal) retrieves the rating from Table HRHAP_FINAL. If your ratings are stored in another location (such as a custom infotype), then you can create a custom BAdI implementation to retrieve this information. After defining the relevant method for the matrix dimension, the guideline matrix and guideline values (for that matrix) can be established within the configuration.

Besides guidelines, you can base eligibility on Performance Management compliance. In other words, an employee's eligibility can be based (in part) on the completeness of their appraisal form, and appraisal rules can be configured within the Implementation Guide (IMG) to incorporate this business logic.

Now let's discuss payroll and its integration with compensation.

11.2.4 Integration with Payroll (PY)

The level of payroll integration depends on your payroll set up and process. If you are running SAP Payroll, infotypes within ECM — when activated — create payroll-relevant infotypes that will be processed during the next payroll run. If you are running interfaces to a third-party payroll vendor you will have similar — though somewhat more indirect — impacts. (Third-party payroll integration is discussed later in this chapter.) Because ECM infotypes provide a real-time pull from payroll-relevant infotypes (i.e., from Infotype 0008) for calculation bases and a real-time update (to Infotypes 0008, 0015, and 0267) during activation, understanding integration with SAP Payroll is critical because there are payment and stock implications.

The following payroll-relevant infotypes are integrated into the solution:

▸ Infotype 0007

▸ Infotype 0008

▸ Infotype 0015

▸ Infotype 0267

Wage types are integral throughout the compensation process — from the calculation of merit and bonus bases to the activation process. As described in Chapter 3, Baseline Configuration and Infotypes, a valuated wage type (e.g., CSAL) is configured to represent the calculation basis for merit increases or bonuses. This wage type must be configured within wage type Tables T511 (Wage Type Characteristics) and T539J (Base Wage Type Valuation). Configuration of IMG activity Assign Compensation Plan Payroll Data provides the logic for the system to build the various calculation bases for each compensation component (merit and bonus). Each component does not need to use the same valuated wage for its basis. For example, merit could use CSAL (the SAP-provided Compensation Management Salary) whereas bonus could use ZSAL (a custom version of CSAL). In Figure 11.2

you can see the configuration of Table view V_T539J where wage types (e.g., 9001, 9003) are associated with the relevant merit or bonus basis (e.g., CSAL).

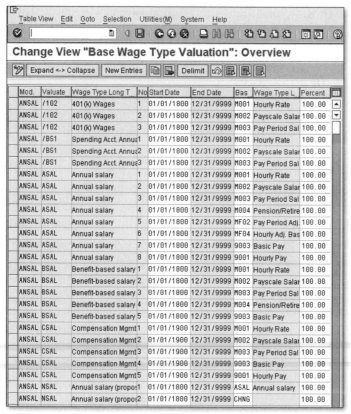

Figure 11.2 Table View V_T539J from Transaction SM30

During the activation routine, amounts or numbers stored in Infotype 0759 systematically update Infotype 0008, Infotype 0015, Infotype 0267, and Infotype 0761 records. For all non-LTI plans, a wage type can be stored in the Compensation Component field within the configuration. If you leave this blank, the activation program will assume updating of the wage type in the first position on Infotype 0008. The Compensation Component field is required for bonus plans, but it is optional for salary adjustments, and cannot be used for LTI plans.

In both the calculation basis and activation, a BAdI is available for providing logic that cannot be achieved via standard configuration. BAdIs for calculation base

(HRECM00_CALCBASE) and activation (HRECM00_ACTIVATION) are available for implementation. Both are discussed in Chapter 7, BAdIs, in detail.

Incorporating Infotype 0007 into the compensation processes is critical for the calculation of merit increases and bonuses. Infotype 0007 stores — among other things — the employee's work schedule rule, part-time indicator, and employment percentage. In Figure 11.3 you can see an example Infotype 0007 record for an employee. The employment percentage in Infotype 0007 may or may not influence the Working Hours/Period and Capacity Utilization Percentage fields in Infotype 0008, because this is controlled via configuration through entry PCOMP/BPDF1 in Table T77S0. The configuration value in this switch (along with Feature DFINF) allows you to control whether the working time data in Infotype 0007 is always transferred to fields BSGRD (Capacity Utilization Level) and DIVGV (Working Hours Period) in Infotype 0008 when updates are made.

Employment percentage and work schedule rules are usually extremely important to compensation processes, because eligibility, guidelines, and proration can all be affected. For example, the bonus calculation base for an employee may be determined from their December 31 salary multiplied by their capacity utilization percentage (in Infotype 0008) during that particular segment. As segments are collected and calculated throughout the plan year, the bonus program needs to know how to reduce the basis based on these important indicators.

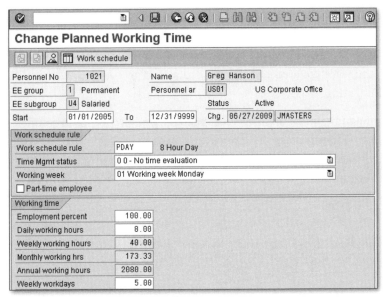

Figure 11.3 Example Record for Infotype 0007

Payroll integration is also relevant if you want to use SAP Payroll to write the imputed income (from exercising stock) to certain wage types for taxation purposes. This functionality is currently only available for the United States and Germany. In the standard system, the module is not available in the schema (i.e., you must manually add it to schemas U000 or U00C for the United States).

> **Tip**
>
> For more information, please refer to SAP Note 624019 (U.S. Payroll Schema Changes for Compensation Management).

To store the exercise price, the fair market value, the imputed income, and the tax advance for the United States, the following model wage types are available: Exercise price LTI S (M550), Market price exercise (M554), Imputed Income LTI S (M551), and Withheld amount (M557). The exercise price and the fair market value are for information purposes only, while the imputed income and the withheld amount are processed within the schema.

That covers the SAP Payroll aspects of ECM integration. Now let's discuss integration with the Personnel Cost Planning (PCP) and Simulation module.

11.2.5 Integration with Personnel Cost Planning (PCP) and Simulation

The PCP and Simulation (PCP) module is available for integration with ECM in a budgeting context. You can use PCP to allocate budget hierarchies based on bottom-up calculations. And after creating personnel cost plans within the PCP module, costs can be imported into the budgeting hierarchy and released for planning worksheet use. (We covered this process from start to finish in Chapter 4, Compensation Budgeting.)

With PCP and Simulation, budgets can also be created based on proposed compensation guidelines, a set percentage, or any other means via BAdI HRHCP00_DC_EMPLOYEE. Results are stored in cluster tables (cluster PCL5) and then uploaded via a standard program (Transaction PECM_INIT_BUDGET) based on data saved for that personnel cost plan. Costs can be filtered by "cost items" during import to further refine the upload amounts.

Now that we have covered all of the HCM-relevant module integration, let's review how ECM and SAP ERP Financials are connected.

11.2.6 Integration with SAP ERP Financials

There are several items linking ECM with SAP ERP Financials. The following integration areas are seen as being the most critical:

- *G/L accounts* (which are linked via symbolic accounts) to wage types.
- *Currency* definition (configured in Table TCURC). Currencies are defined in Finance and leveraged in HR. If HR and Finance are on separate SAP instances, Application Link Enabling (ALE) can be established to pull in currency dates via a batch process.
- *Exchange rates* (configured in Table TCURR). Exchange rate (type M) is used within the space. If HR and Finance are on separate SAP instances, ALE can be established to pull in currency dates via a batch process.
- *Accruals* from exercised LTI awards can be sent to the SAP Finance Accruals Engine. Two programs are available to assist in this process: Transfer of Granting of Awards from HR System (report name: ACE_SOP_HR_DATA_TRANSFER) and Calculate and Post Provisions for Award Grants (report name: ACE_SOP_PERIODIC_POSTING)

This concludes our review of the integration for ECM. So now let's discuss integration from a platform perspective.

11.3 Platform Integration

Understanding how the ECM is implemented across delivery environments is an integral part of success. In Figure 11.4 you can see an illustrative, architectural diagram that combines several perspectives of integration to show the high level of interdependencies across and within platforms.

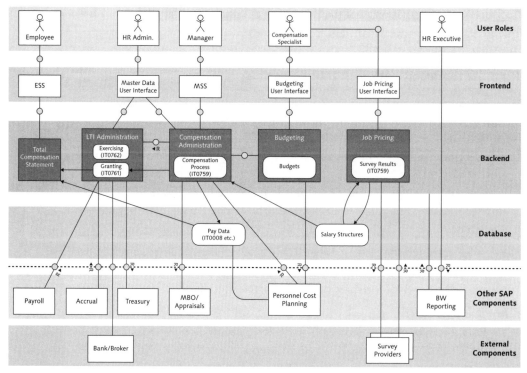

Figure 11.4 Integration Architecture Diagram of SAP ECM

The first area of platform integration we will discuss is ESS and MSS.

11.3.1 ESS and MSS

As you probably know, ESS and MSS provide the service delivery channel for employees and managers (and proxies) to participate in compensation processes via the SAP NetWeaver Portal. (Self-services specific to ECM were discussed in detail in Chapter 6, Self-Service) ESS and MSS provide end users with the tools necessary to complete the online compensation processes more efficiently. Whether it is the planning worksheet (to support the annual compensation process) or an Adobe Interactive Form (to support an off-cycle increase such as a promotion or change in pay), SAP's self-service platform provides you with the necessary solution.

Note

For more information on SAP ESS and MSS, please refer to the SAP PRESS book *Implementing Employee and Manager Self-Services in SAP ERP HCM*, by Jeremy Masters and Christos Kotsakis.

Let's now turn to the integration considerations for using SAP NetWeaver BW.

11.3.2 SAP NetWeaver BW

The functionality available within SAP NetWeaver BW can provide robust analytical capabilities for Compensation and HR professionals, managers, and executives. By providing a data mart for stakeholders, compensation data can be used in a more powerful manner — as tough pay decisions are extremely strategic for all organizations.

The available BI content provides dashboards and metrics for end users within the SAP NetWeaver Portal.

And finally, let's look at vendor-level integration.

11.4 Vendor Integration

The ability to integrate with third-party vendors such as payroll processors, salary survey providers, and banks/brokerages provides you another opportunity for harmonization. The relationship to and management of these vendors is regarded as a critical success factor to the implementation because the success of the project is dependent on the competence of the vendor(s) engaged. The following is a partial list of the vendor types you can integrate with:

- Payroll Providers
- Salary Survey Providers
- Banks/Brokerages

Although other vendors (such as those handling recognition or service awards) are important players in compensation processes, these three types of vendors are the most common.

11.4.1 Payroll

For those customers not using SAP Payroll, integration with your payroll provider is a necessary part of your implementation. It takes a lot of coordination to make the necessary changes and test them, so for those customers running SAP Payroll, full payroll regression testing must be planned and executed.

11.4.2 Salary Surveys

Salary survey providers — such as Mercer, Watson Wyatt, Hewitt, and Towers Perrin — provide survey jobs, survey job descriptions, and salary survey market data for upload to the Job Pricing functionality. You can elect to participate in vendor surveys and pay for market data results in the form of salary surveys. This data is critical for the market analysis done via the Job Pricing module.

11.4.3 Banks and Brokerages

In addition, banks and brokerages — such as Morgan Stanley Smith Barney, E*Trade, and Merrill Lynch — can integrate with SAP for stock granting (outbound from SAP) and exercising (inbound to SAP). These companies typically accept employee demographic and grant file information from SAP. All stock administration is performed in the vendor's systems, so financial reporting, including Financial Accounting Standards (FAS), is performed within the vendor's tool because it is the system of record for stock administration purposes. Daily, weekly, or monthly interfaces are established based on the functionality being deployed. For example, those companies granting stock awards typically look to interface approved grants (and demographic employee data) to the vendor for automatic processing. After formal approval is secured and activation is performed, grant data in Infotype 0761 can be interfaced to the third party. Also, data on the employee in Infotype 0763 (LTI Participant Data) indicates whether the employee is an insider or director and how much percentage of ownership they have (if any).

This concludes our review of the integration points for ECM.

11.5 Summary

Throughout this chapter we reviewed the integration components of ECM. We reviewed the types of integration — application, module, platform, and vendor. In all cases, we talked covered highlights and identified key issues.

In the next chapter, we review some of the key considerations when implementing ECM globally.

Implementing Enterprise Compensation Management (ECM) globally?
This chapter explores the various challenges you will likely experience while
doing so. Topics such as global employment, currency, budgeting, language,
and data privacy are discussed.

12 Global Considerations

Companies administering compensation processes globally share many common challenges during and after implementation. In this chapter, we will explore some of the more common issues companies face when implementing ECM on a global scale. Some of these issues are quite complex and require a great deal of technical know-how and out-of-the-box innovation to address or mitigate. Still others are not technical issues but rather legal requirements or cultural practices that need to be addressed through change management.

After first discussing project team composition, we will review key global issues such as the handling of global employees, currency, and language requirements, and important localization topics such as government-mandated and general increases.

Let's first begin our discussion by addressing the importance of the project team.

12.1 Project Team

Gathering the right team is fundamental for any successful project. Without strong leadership and skilled resources, a project will not be successful. Implementing ECM is no different — especially for a global deployment. In the next section, we discuss how to form the right team and make your project a success.

12.1.1 Regional and Country Representation

Without regional or country representation on the project team, local regulatory requirements and cultural practices cannot be efficiently gathered, documented, and incorporated into the blueprint. Often, global team members fail to fully understand the nuances of local pay practices, especially if they have not been through a global project. Concepts such as mandatory increases and global employment are frequently misunderstood and sometimes mishandled. Data privacy and open disclosure are often not given the time and importance needed.

Having regional or country project team members stationed and (better yet) native from each area of the project is ideal because local requirements can be gathered and verified closer to the source. Local resources (including hired business partners) know their country requirements better than any other because they have either lived through them or have experienced implementing them.

12.1.2 Regional Leadership

Appointing regional leaders in strategic posts on the project ensures that local requirements can be stewarded and incorporated into the global design. Let's take an example of a Fortune 100 global company based in the United States. The project team may be split into the four regions: North America; Latin America (LATAM); Europe, Middle East, and Africa (EMEA); and Asia Pacific (AsiaPac). If the global team is based in North America, you should ensure that you're LATAM, EMEA, and AsiaPac teams have regional leadership influence on the project.

12.1.3 Communication

Although project documentation and language will most likely be English, it is important to allow the countries to talk in their native language when discussing critical project issues. Often, requirements are misunderstood because the local resources did not get a fair chance at understanding their impact to the global design. If project resources are able to conduct meetings on site at each locale or hub, follow-up meetings with the global team can be a more productive way of collective and validating local business requirements.

As you can see, implementing ECM without the right project team or approach can create roadblocks to success. Let's now turn our focus to some of the challenges that project teams commonly experience when implementing ECM globally.

12.2 Global Challenges

In this section, some of the most challenging global design questions are represented. For each topic, we review key issues and address the associated implementation risks. By no means is this an exhaustive list, but it does provide us with good background on some of the more common challenges you might face.

Our first topic concerns global employment.

12.2.1 Global Employment

Global employees are often part of complex business scenarios and sometimes an even more complex technology solution. Because of the varied manner in which companies have set up their global workforce in the system, global employees may or may not be a real issue for your organization. The following global employee types are common in many global companies:

- Expatriates
- Inpatriates
- Transpatriates
- Third-country Nationals
- International Rotation Programees
- Secondees

You may refer to these employees with different terminology but their place within the organization is clear. From a compensation perspective, administrating global employees may be a problem because special rules commonly apply. This population frequently has exceptions (on eligibility, guidelines, payment, etc.).

The complexities inherent in their processing may in fact prevent them from being a part of certain compensation processes. This depends partially on how the global employee is set up in your system. Many companies embrace the Central Person (object type CP) to establish the linkage between the home and host personnel numbers. Depending on their employment status (active versus inactive) and whether they are attached to valid positions within the organizational structure, the handling of these employees may need to be manual.

Without a doubt, global employment is a complex scenario that must be firmly designed into the overall compensation processes. Let's now discuss currency and exchange rate.

12.2.2 Currency and Exchange Rate

Within the standard compensation planning worksheet (as seen in Figure 12.1), managers can plan on either an employee's local (i.e., employee-specific) currency or another currency (based on their screen selection) for comparison. The currency that is saved back to the employee's Infotype 0759 (Compensation Record) record depends on the configuration behind switch HRECM/XEECU in Table T77S0.

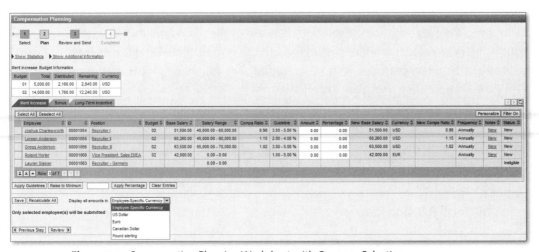

Figure 12.1 Compensation Planning Worksheet with Currency Selection

If the switch is set as blank, the amounts are saved on Infotype 0759 in the display currency. For example, if a manager in France has one direct report in the United States, he could plan on that employee in Euros. The amount (in Euros) would be saved to that employee's Infotype 0759 record. During activation, however, the amount would be converted to the employee's actual currency (in this example, USD).

If the switch is set to "X," however, the amounts are saved on Infotype 0759 in the local (i.e., employee-specific) currency and *not* the display currency. The display currency is used only for managers at the time of planning for comparison purposes. Revisiting the previous example, the manager in France could still plan on the U.S. employee in Euros, but the amount saved back on the Infotype 0759 record would be in USD. In this case, there would be no conversion needed during activation because it was already saved in the employee's local currency.

The default for the switch is blank. You can access the switch in Table T77S0 through Transaction SM30 or via the Implementation Guide (IMG) path: PERSONNEL MANAGEMENT • ENTERPRISE COMPENSATION MANAGEMENT • COMPENSATION ADMINISTRATION • SET COMPENSATION ADMINISTRATION CONTROL PARAMETERS. Please reference SAP Note 901896 (Compensation Planning (ECM): currency handling), which describes this switch in greater detail.

> **Note**
>
> New functionality in SAP ERP 6.0, enhancement package 4 allows you to determine currency for an employee based on Infotype 0001 (Organizational Assignment), 0008 (Basic Pay), or a custom Infotype. BAdI HRECM00_EE_CURRENCY (Determine Employee Currency) allows you to manipulate the standard currency logic. The default logic uses the employee's country (from the employee's Personnel Area on Infotype 0001) to retrieve the currency. To override this logic, you can use SAP's provided implementation or create your own with the help of an ABAP professional.

The exchange rate is another important area used within compensation calculations. Table TCURR (Exchange Rates) holds the currency exchange rates within the system. Exchange rate type "M" is used throughout the standard ECM functions (e.g within function module HR_ECM_CONVERT_CURRENCY). Many customers maintain this table on the Finance side. The exchange rates in this table can be pushed from the Finance system to the Human Resources (HR) system (if the two are decoupled) via Application Link Enabling (ALE). It is important that you discuss the upkeep of this table with Finance. This table is often "owned" by the Finance team and not the HR team. The exchange rate table is displayed in Figure 12.2.

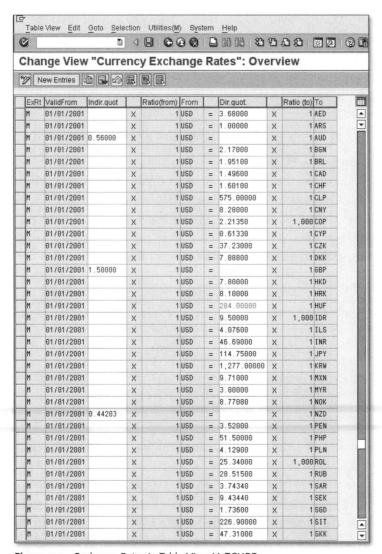

Figure 12.2 Exchange Rates in Table View V_TCURR

Now that we have seen how currency and exchange rates impact compensation processes, let's discuss the topic of language.

12.2.3 Language

Language is critical for global processes. Let's first look at the portal experience for the manager. The compensation planning worksheet is multilingual. Based on the manager's web browser language settings and portal language personalization settings, the labels, headers, and buttons within the iView are language dependent. In Figure 12.3, a manager in France is viewing his compensation planning worksheet. As you can see, it is in French. Please note that the master data is *not* in French because it is stored in English.

> **Note**
>
> If you want to force the planning worksheet to be in English only, work with your SAP Portal team to implement this iView. In some deployments, companies have opted to always ensure that the manager's planning worksheet was in English. Whether you do this or not depends on how fluent your managers are in English.

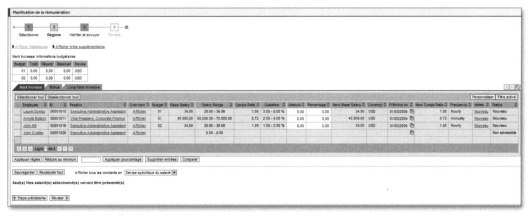

Figure 12.3 Compensation Planning Worksheet in French

From an employee perspective, compensation statements — both the total compensation statement and the compensation review statement — add tremendous value. Without these communication vehicles, recognizing employee achievement would not be as standardized and formalized. The challenge with compensation statements lies in its broad scope. For organizations with operations in only four or five countries, deploying multi-language statements is certainly achievable. Organizations that have employees in over 100 countries can be quite another thing. These countries represent employees who speak (let's say) some 15 - 20 languages. Managing templates for this many languages can be overwhelming unless some strict governance is applied to the template's standards.

For those up to the challenge of providing language-specific compensation statements to their employee population, the question becomes: *How do I know what language to render the form in for a particular employee?* You cannot always assume a language from the employee's country (or country grouping). For example, in Canada, there are laws regarding the use of French in lieu of English in Quebec but not anywhere else. Another challenge is with respect to global employees. Depending on how you have set up your global employees in the system, you might have an active personnel record for (let's say) a U.S. employee in Thailand. It would be unrealistic (and probably wrong) to assume that the expatriate in Thailand wants to see their statement in Thai.

One possibility is to drive language preference from the employee's Infotype 0002 (Personal Data) Field SPRSL (Communication Language). Figure 12.4 shows an example of the Language field for an employee. This information can be referenced during the creation of the statement. In scenarios where this field is not maintained in an employee's Infotype 0002, a default language can be used instead (stored in the form or in a custom table by country).

Now that we have covered some challenges with respect to language, let's review budgeting from a global perspective.

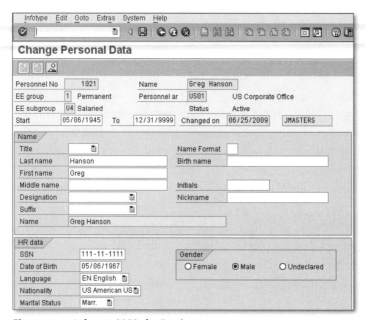

Figure 12.4 Infotype 0002 for Employee

12.2.4 Budgeting

Chapter 4, Compensation Budgeting, covered the budgeting process in detail, providing insight on how the budget hierarchy is established and maintained throughout the compensation planning process. The budget structure — which directly mimics the organizational structure — provides budget allocation and spend both from an individual budget unit and roll-up perspective.

The challenge for companies regarding budgeting from a global perspective comes when trying to manage highly matrixed organizations or global functions. For relationships and hierarchies that cross countries, establishing and tracking budget allocation and spend is a challenging task because budgets are typically set at the country level. If your company has one or more global functions (e.g., Supply Chain, Information Technology (IT), or Legal), managing the overall budget becomes difficult because an organizational hierarchy supporting a global function is set along functional lines and not along country lines.

In addition to tracking the overall budget with these complexities, the reference currency for the budget can only be established in one currency in ECM. This means that planning managers can only view the budget roll-up and budget unit totals based on this reference currency. This might pose a challenge in countries where the reference currency is not as well understood. Enhancements to display the local currency are possible, but not without development.

In addition to currency issues, you also need to consider proration rules.

12.2.5 Proration

Proration rules typically vary based on compensation plans. Proration of bonus and merit, for example, may or may not follow the same business rules. In certain countries, special treatment — sometimes governmentally mandated — applies to employees who are on certain leaves of absence. The definitions of unpaid and paid leaves of absence are not global. Assuming that proration logic can be applied globally based on employee actions (and action reasons) is not realistic. In some countries, absence types can also drive proration (influencing the reduction rules for a bonus plan, for example).

Another global issue that varies from country to country is the handling of mandated and general increases.

12.2.6   Mandated and General Increases

In several countries, mandated increases are required by the government annually (or more frequent). General increases are also compulsory in some countries based on agreements with employees belonging to collective bargaining units or unions. Mandated increases can be remunerated in either a percentage or amount depending on the increase type and contract stipulation. Increases can also be applied retrospectively or prospectively based on contract agreements.

The following countries commonly have employee populations requiring mandated or general increases. This is not a complete list, but represents some of the more common countries.

▸ Italy

▸ Spain

▸ Belgium

▸ France

▸ Germany

▸ Austria

▸ Brazil

▸ Chile

▸ Uruguay

In situations where the mandated or general increase is applied coincident to the merit increase, the overall budget must consider how to apply the mandated increase (in addition to the merit portion). How you incorporate the mandated increase percentage or amount into the overall budget depends (in part) on the date used for retrieving the calculation base (current or another date) and whether or not the mandated or general increase has already been applied to the base.

Now let's discuss another heavily localized topic — data privacy.

12.2.7   Data Privacy

Data privacy — discussed in Chapter 9, Authorization Management — is another hot topic with global implications. Data privacy concerns exist wherever Personally Identifiable Information (PII) is collected and stored.

The right to data privacy is heavily regulated and rigidly enforced in Europe. The European Union, for example, has a directive on the protection of personal data. The Data Protection Directive (officially named *Directive 95/46/EC*) regulates the processing of personal data within the European Union. Although the U.S. Department of Commerce created the *Safe Harbor* certification program in response to the E.U. Data Protection Directive, data privacy is not highly regulated in the United States.

When implementing compensation processes globally, be sure to involve the proper authorities. In Europe, the works councils are most important to involve. A works council is an organization representing workers that complements national labor negotiations. Works councils exsist with different names in a number of European countries, including:

- Germany and Austria — *Betriebsrat*
- Luxembourg — *Comité Mixte*
- The Netherlands and Flanders in Belgium — *Ondernemingsraad*
- Wallonia in Belgium — *Conseil d'Entreprise*
- France — *Comité d'Entreprise*
- Spain — *Comité de empresa*

There is also a European Works Council that applies to companies operating at the European Union level with at least 1,000 employees within the E.U. and at least 150 employees in each of at least two member states.

12.3 Summary

In this chapter, we reviewed some of the most important issues facing companies as they implement and support ECM on a global scale. From global employment to currency issues to data privacy concerns, the topics reviewed in this chapter uncovered and addressed some of the key challenges you will likely experience.

In the next chapter, we will discuss the robust reporting capabilities within ECM including backend reports, queries, and BW content.

Compensation data and its metrics are key components for effectively administering any compensation process. Having critical pay-related information at the fingertips of administrators and end users is one of the critical success factors for any implementation. In this chapter, we will review the key reporting capabilities of Enterprise Compensation Management (ECM) that are available for Human Resources (HR) and Compensation managers.

13 Reporting

Access to a robust reporting framework is paramount to any successful compensation department. Whether it's a manager, HR professional, or compensation specialist, all compensation users need to analyze and interpret data to support their critical decision making, such as annual compensation planning, which is vital to an organization's ability to "pay for performance." Without strong reporting capabilities, process efficiencies are exacerbated and pay practices inevitably suffer.

SAP provides reporting capabilities in several areas of compensation. First, a suite of backend reports is available for HR and compensation teams to execute, review, and support key processes such as compensation planning/approval, pay scale reclassifications, salary survey participation, and pay structure design. Second, standard SAP query functionality is available within ECM. In addition to the standard queries that are provided, you can also create queries by a functional resource via the query builder. Third, standard Business Intelligence (BI) content is available within the SAP NetWeaver Business Warehouse (BW); however, this last piece is only available to those customers who have purchased the BW platform.

> **Note**
>
> For more information on reporting capabilities within ECM (and HCM in general), refer to the SAP PRESS book, *HR Reporting with SAP*, by Hans-Jürgen Figaj, Richard Haßmann, and Anja Junold.

In this chapter, we will only cover the reporting tools provided by SAP within ECM, beginning with standard Advanced Business Application Programming (ABAP) reporting and then moving on to review the ad hoc query and BW capabilities.

13.1 ABAP Reports

In this section, we'll look at the standard ABAP reports within ECM. In Table 13.1, each of the standard reports is listed with a short description and release availability.

Report / Name	Description	Area	Release Availability
Audit Report for Budgets (RHECM_ BUDGET_RPT)	Displays the budget structure, including roll-up, based on budget type and budget period	Budgeting	Enterprise 4.7, Extension Set 2.0
Display Compensation Planning Progress (RHECM_DISPLAY_ PROGRESS)	Provides detail status during the compensation planning process at the organizational unit level (based on new functionality)	Planning	ERP 6.0, EhP 4
Display Compensation Planning Changes (RHECM_DISPLAY_ CHANGES)	Provides an audit on all Infotype 0759 (Compensation Process) record changes	Planning	ERP 6.0, EhP 4
Summarize Compensation Planning Changes (RHECM_ SUMMARIZE_ CHANGES)	Provides a summary of changes performed on Infotype 0759, including how current recommendations compare against first planned recommendations and against guidelines (based on new functionality)	Planning	ERP 6.0, EhP 4

Table 13.1 Compensation Planning Reports with Description and Release Availability

Report / Name	Description	Area	Release Availability
Salary Survey Participation (Transaction PECM_QUERY_SURVEY)	Provides output for salary survey vendors based on standard selection criteria, provider code, benchmark job indicator, and compensation job groupings	Job Pricing	Enterprise 4.7, Extension Set 2.0
Data Extraction for Salary Survey Participation (Transaction S_PH9_46000228)	Provides output of key compensation information for external salary survey providers	Job Pricing	Release 4.6C
Hay PayNet: Data Extraction for Salary Survey Participation (Transaction S_PH9_46000227)	Provides output of key compensation information for salary surveys from Hay	Job Pricing	Release 4.6C
Defaults for Pay Scale Reclassification (RPLTRF10)	Displays the next standard pay scale reclassification for employees	Pay Scale Reclassification	Release 4.6C
Time Spent in each Pay Scale type/area/group/level (RPLTRF00)	Displays the pay scale classification and the duration of an assignment to a pay scale or level for employees	Pay Scale Reclassification	Release 4.6C
Compa-Ratio Analysis (RHCMPCR0)	Calculates the compa-ratio	Compa-ratio	Release 4.6C

Table 13.1 Compensation Planning Reports with Description and Release Availability (Cont.)

Report / Name	Description	Area	Release Availability
Compare Actual Base Salary to Planned Compensation (RHCMPCOMPARE_ACTUAL_PLANNED)	Compare the current Infotype 0008 (Basic Pay) that an employee receives against the planned compensation assigned to the job or position in the Infotype 1005 (Planned Compensation) record	Planned Compensation	Release 4.6C
Pay Grade Structure for Jobs (RHCMPJOBPLCOMP)	Displays the salary structure for jobs based on a selected organizational unit(s) or job(s)	Pay Structure	Release 4.6C
Display Pay Grade Structure (RPLCMP01)	Displays the pay grades and levels, according to Table T710	Pay Structure	Release 4.6C
Display Pay Scale Structure (RHPAYSC0)	Displays the pay scales and levels, according to Table T510	Pay Structure	Release 4.6C
Planned Labor Costs (RHXSOLO0)	Calculates the planned compensation per position for one or more organizational units	Pay Structure	Release 4.6C

Table 13.1 Compensation Planning Reports with Description and Release Availability (Cont.)

These programs represent the inventory of ABAP-based reports to support ECM and compensation-related processes. In the next section, you'll find an overview of each program and its use along with its program name and transaction code.

The first program is useful from a budgeting perspective, so let's discuss it now.

13.1.1 Audit Report for Budgets

The Audit Report for Budgets report is a standard budget program that shows the total budget allocation and spend — both at an individual organizational unit and roll-up perspective. Figure 13.1 shows the budget unit hierarchy with columns to support the distributed and spent budget amounts (or numbers). For more information on this report, please see Chapter 4, Compensation Budgeting.

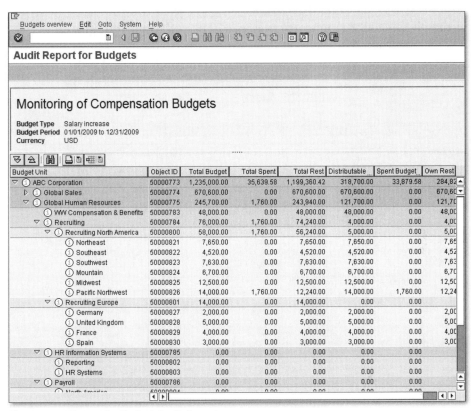

Figure 13.1 Output for Budget Audit Report

Its program name is RHECM_BUDGET_RPT. The Transaction code is PECM_DISPLAY_BUDGETS and can be accessed via the SAP Easy Access menu by following the path HUMAN RESOURCES • PERSONNEL MANAGEMENT • COMPENSATION MANAGEMENT • ENTERPRISE COMPENSATION MANAGEMENT • BUDGETING • DISPLAY BUDGET.

As part of SAP ERP 6.0 enhancement package 4, three reports are delivered that provide enhanced visibility to the compensation planning process. To use these reports, you must use the new multilevel approval process (discussed in Chapter 5, Process Administration). Let's look at each of these reports.

13.1.2 Display Compensation Planning Progress

The Display Compensation Planning Progress report provides detailed status information for the compensation planning process by analyzing the progress of the planning at the organizational level (but not at the employee's Infotype 0759 record level). This report displays the contents of the process history Table (T71ADM_PROCESS) for the selected organizational unit(s) during that compensation review. This report is only relevant if you use the new multilevel approval process.

Its program name is RHECM_DISPLAY_PROGRESS and can be accessed via the SAP Easy Access menu by following the path HUMAN RESOURCES • PERSONNEL MANAGEMENT • COMPENSATION MANAGEMENT • ENTERPRISE COMPENSATION MANAGEMENT • COMPENSATION PLANNING • MONITORING • DISPLAY COMP. PLANNING PROGRESS. Figure 13.2 shows the output of the report.

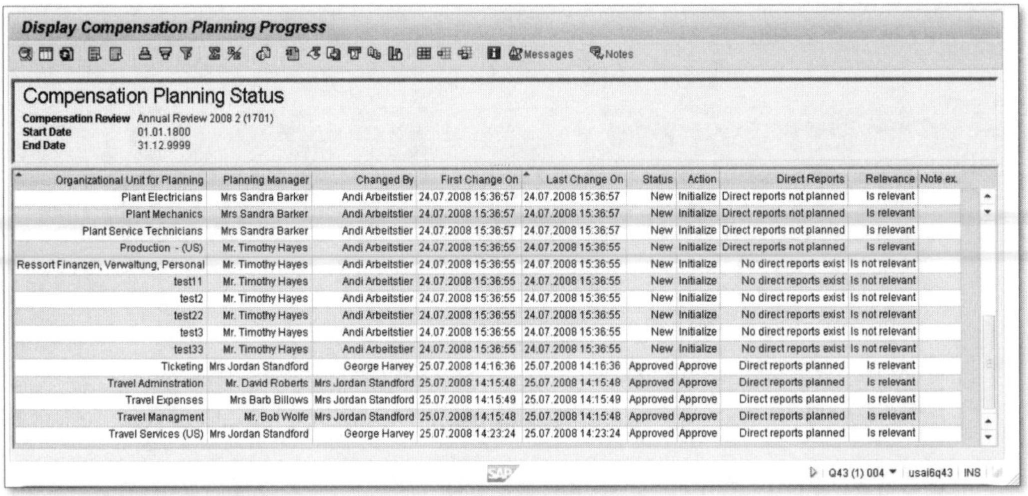

Organizational Unit for Planning	Planning Manager	Changed By	First Change On	Last Change On	Status	Action	Direct Reports	Relevance	Note ex.
Plant Electricians	Mrs Sandra Barker	Andi Arbeitstier	24.07.2008 15:36:57	24.07.2008 15:36:57	New	Initialize	Direct reports not planned	Is relevant	
Plant Mechanics	Mrs Sandra Barker	Andi Arbeitstier	24.07.2008 15:36:57	24.07.2008 15:36:57	New	Initialize	Direct reports not planned	Is relevant	
Plant Service Technicians	Mrs Sandra Barker	Andi Arbeitstier	24.07.2008 15:36:57	24.07.2008 15:36:57	New	Initialize	Direct reports not planned	Is relevant	
Production - (US)	Mr. Timothy Hayes	Andi Arbeitstier	24.07.2008 15:36:55	24.07.2008 15:36:55	New	Initialize	Direct reports not planned	Is relevant	
Ressort Finanzen, Verwaltung, Personal	Mr. Timothy Hayes	Andi Arbeitstier	24.07.2008 15:36:55	24.07.2008 15:36:55	New	Initialize	No direct reports exist	Is not relevant	
test11	Mr. Timothy Hayes	Andi Arbeitstier	24.07.2008 15:36:55	24.07.2008 15:36:55	New	Initialize	No direct reports exist	Is not relevant	
test2	Mr. Timothy Hayes	Andi Arbeitstier	24.07.2008 15:36:55	24.07.2008 15:36:55	New	Initialize	No direct reports exist	Is not relevant	
test22	Mr. Timothy Hayes	Andi Arbeitstier	24.07.2008 15:36:55	24.07.2008 15:36:55	New	Initialize	No direct reports exist	Is not relevant	
test3	Mr. Timothy Hayes	Andi Arbeitstier	24.07.2008 15:36:55	24.07.2008 15:36:55	New	Initialize	No direct reports exist	Is not relevant	
test33	Mr. Timothy Hayes	Andi Arbeitstier	24.07.2008 15:36:55	24.07.2008 15:36:55	New	Initialize	No direct reports exist	Is not relevant	
Ticketing	Mrs Jordan Standford	George Harvey	25.07.2008 14:16:36	25.07.2008 14:16:36	Approved	Approve	Direct reports planned	Is relevant	
Travel Adminstration	Mr. David Roberts	Mrs Jordan Standford	25.07.2008 14:15:48	25.07.2008 14:15:48	Approved	Approve	Direct reports planned	Is relevant	
Travel Expenses	Mrs Barb Billows	Mrs Jordan Standford	25.07.2008 14:15:49	25.07.2008 14:15:49	Approved	Approve	Direct reports planned	Is relevant	
Travel Managment	Mr. Bob Wolfe	Mrs Jordan Standford	25.07.2008 14:15:48	25.07.2008 14:15:48	Approved	Approve	Direct reports planned	Is relevant	
Travel Services (US)	Mrs Jordan Standford	George Harvey	25.07.2008 14:23:24	25.07.2008 14:23:24	Approved	Approve	Direct reports planned	Is relevant	

Figure 13.2 Output for Compensation Planning Status Report

13.1.3 Display Compensation Planning Changes

The Display Compensation Planning Changes report provides detailed tracking data for all changes performed on employees' Infotype 0759 records. This report displays the contents of the employee history Table (T71ADM_EE_HIST) for the selected employees, compensation plans, and compensation reviews. This report is only relevant if you use the new multilevel approval process.

Its program name is RHECM_DISPLAY_CHANGES and you can access it via the SAP Easy Access menu by following the path Human Resources • Personnel Management • Compensation Management • Enterprise Compensation Management • Compensation Planning • Monitoring • Display Comp. Planning Changes. You can see the output of the report in Figure 13.3.

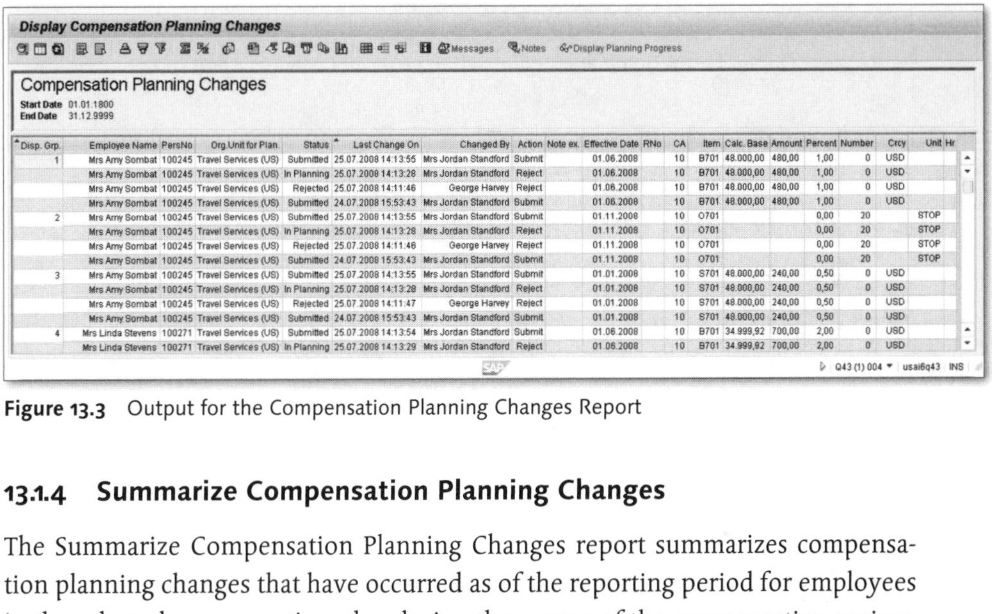

Display Compensation Planning Changes

Compensation Planning Changes

Start Date 01.01.1800
End Date 31.12.9999

Disp. Grp.	Employee Name	PersNo	Org.Unit for Plan.	Status	Last Change On	Changed By	Action	Note ex.	Effective Date	RNo	CA	Item	Calc. Base	Amount	Percent	Number	Crcy	Unit	Hr
1	Mrs Amy Sombat	100245	Travel Services (US)	Submitted	25.07.2008 14:13:55	Mrs Jordan Standford	Submit		01.06.2008		10	B701	48.000,00	480,00	1,00	0	USD		
	Mrs Amy Sombat	100245	Travel Services (US)	In Planning	25.07.2008 14:13:28	Mrs Jordan Standford	Reject		01.06.2008		10	B701	48.000,00	480,00	1,00	0	USD		
	Mrs Amy Sombat	100245	Travel Services (US)	Rejected	25.07.2008 14:11:46	George Harvey	Reject		01.06.2008		10	B701	48.000,00	480,00	1,00	0	USD		
	Mrs Amy Sombat	100245	Travel Services (US)	Submitted	24.07.2008 15:53:43	Mrs Jordan Standford	Submit		01.06.2008		10	B701	48.000,00	480,00	1,00	0	USD		
2	Mrs Amy Sombat	100245	Travel Services (US)	Submitted	25.07.2008 14:13:55	Mrs Jordan Standford	Submit		01.11.2008		10	O701			0,00	20		STOP	
	Mrs Amy Sombat	100245	Travel Services (US)	In Planning	25.07.2008 14:13:28	Mrs Jordan Standford	Reject		01.11.2008		10	O701			0,00	20		STOP	
	Mrs Amy Sombat	100245	Travel Services (US)	Rejected	25.07.2008 14:11:46	George Harvey	Reject		01.11.2008		10	O701			0,00	20		STOP	
	Mrs Amy Sombat	100245	Travel Services (US)	Submitted	24.07.2008 15:53:43	Mrs Jordan Standford	Submit		01.11.2008		10	O701			0,00	20		STOP	
3	Mrs Amy Sombat	100245	Travel Services (US)	Submitted	25.07.2008 14:13:55	Mrs Jordan Standford	Submit		01.01.2008		10	S701	48.000,00	240,00	0,50	0	USD		
	Mrs Amy Sombat	100245	Travel Services (US)	In Planning	25.07.2008 14:13:28	Mrs Jordan Standford	Reject		01.01.2008		10	S701	48.000,00	240,00	0,50	0	USD		
	Mrs Amy Sombat	100245	Travel Services (US)	Rejected	25.07.2008 14:11:47	George Harvey	Reject		01.01.2008		10	S701	48.000,00	240,00	0,50	0	USD		
	Mrs Amy Sombat	100245	Travel Services (US)	Submitted	24.07.2008 15:53:43	Mrs Jordan Standford	Submit		01.01.2008		10	S701	48.000,00	240,00	0,50	0	USD		
4	Mrs Linda Stevens	100271	Travel Services (US)	Submitted	25.07.2008 14:13:54	Mrs Jordan Standford	Submit		01.06.2008		10	B701	34.999,92	700,00	2,00	0	USD		
	Mrs Linda Stevens	100271	Travel Services (US)	In Planning	25.07.2008 14:13:29	Mrs Jordan Standford	Reject		01.06.2008		10	B701	34.999,92	700,00	2,00	0	USD		

Figure 13.3 Output for the Compensation Planning Changes Report

13.1.4 Summarize Compensation Planning Changes

The Summarize Compensation Planning Changes report summarizes compensation planning changes that have occurred as of the reporting period for employees in the selected compensation plan during the course of the compensation review. Comparisons are performed between the amount (or number) first planned and the current amount; and the guideline and the current amount. This report uses the contents of the employee history Table (T71ADM_EE_HIST) for its summary. This report is only relevant if you use the new multilevel approval process.

Its program name is RHECM_SUMMARIZE_CHANGES and can be accessed via the SAP Easy Access menu by following the path Human Resources • Personnel Management • Compensation Management • Enterprise Compensation Management • Compensation Planning • Monitoring • Summarize Comp. Planning Changes. Figure 13.4 shows the output of the report.

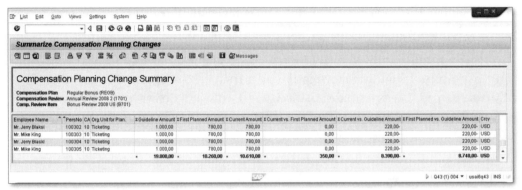

Figure 13.4 Output for the Summary Compensation Planning Changes Report

The following three queries are available for salary survey participation.

13.1.5 Salary Survey Participation

The Salary Survey Participation query provides an extract of relevant employee and compensation data to support participation in salary surveys. The query name is AQZZ/SAPQUERY/H0ECM_JPR_01 and is discussed in detail later in the chapter. The Transaction code is PECM_QUERY_SURVEY, which you can access via the SAP Easy Access menu by following the path HUMAN RESOURCES • PERSONNEL MANAGE-MENT • COMPENSATION MANAGEMENT • ENTERPRISE COMPENSATION MANAGEMENT • JOB PRICING • EXTRACT DATA FOR SURVEY PARTICIPATION. In Figure 13.5 you can see the selection screen of the query.

13.1.6 Data Extraction for Salary Survey Participation

Another query for extracting data for salary survey participation is the Data Extraction for Salary Survey Participation query. The query name is AQZZ/SAP-QUERY/H0SALSURVEY_EXT. The Transaction code is S_PH9_46000228 and can be accessed via the SAP Easy Access menu by following the path HUMAN RESOURCES • PERSONNEL MANAGEMENT • COMPENSATION MANAGEMENT • INFORMATION SYSTEM • REPORTS • SALARY SURVEYS • DATA EXTRACTION FOR SALARY SURVEY PARTICIPATION. Figure 13.6 shows the output of the query.

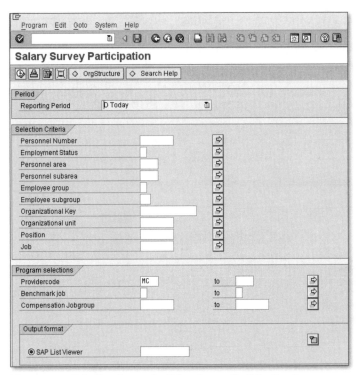

Figure 13.5 Selection Screen for Salary Survey Participation Query

Data extraction for salary survey participation

Org. Unit	Org. unit name	Job	Job Titles	BM	Number of employees	Personnel No.	Last year's annual salary	Currency	Current annual salary	Currency	Min.Pay Grade/Level	Cu
50000051	ABC Corporation	60000014	Chairman and CEO	No	1	00001000	210,000.00	USD	210,000.00	USD	85,000.00	US
50000051	ABC Corporation	60000008	Executive Assistant	No	1	00001001	42,639.00	USD	42,639.00	USD	20,000.00	US
50000052	Global Sales	60000012	Senior Vice President, Sales	No	1	00001002	175,000.00	USD	175,000.00	USD	85,000.00	US
50000052	Global Sales	60000012	Senior Vice President, Sales	No	1	00001002	204,000.00	USD	204,000.00	USD	65,000.00	US
50000053	Global Human Resources	60000009	Senior Vice President, Human Resources	No	1	00001003	200,000.00	USD	200,000.00	USD	65,000.00	US
50000052	Global Sales	60000008	Executive Assistant	No	1	00001006	44,823.00	USD	44,823.00	USD	20,000.00	US
50000052	Global Sales	60000008	Executive Assistant	No	1	00001006	62,399.00	USD	62,399.00	USD	20,000.00	US
50000053	Global Human Resources	60000008	Executive Assistant	No	1	00001007			25,667.00	USD	20,000.00	US
50000053	Global Human Resources	60000008	Executive Assistant	No	1	00001007	30,000.00	USD	30,000.00	USD	20,000.00	US
50000051	ABC Corporation	60000008	Executive Assistant	No	1	00001007	30,000.00	USD	30,000.00	USD	20,000.00	US
50000054	Global Finance	60000015	Chief Financial Officer	No	1	00001009	200,000.00	USD	200,000.00	USD	65,000.00	US
50000054	Global Finance	60000008	Executive Assistant	No	1	00001010	70,719.00	USD	70,719.00	USD	20,000.00	US
50000101	Corp Finance	60000015	Chief Financial Officer	No	1	00001011	45,000.00	USD	45,000.00	USD	25,000.00	US
50000055	Global Marketing	60000010	Senior Vice President, Marketing	No	1	00001012	160,800.00	USD	160,800.00	USD	25,000.00	US
50000100	WW Compensation & Benefits	60000007	Director, Compensation	No	1	00001013	135,000.00	USD	135,000.00	USD	65,000.00	US
50000100	WW Compensation & Benefits	60000008	Executive Assistant	No	1	00001014	46,000.00	USD	46,000.00	USD	20,000.00	US
50000100	WW Compensation & Benefits	60000008	Executive Assistant	No	1	00001015	72,555.00	USD	72,555.00	USD	20,000.00	US
50000101	Corp Finance	60000008	Executive Assistant	No	1	00001016	70,719.00	USD	70,719.00	USD	20,000.00	US
50000057	Global Supply Chain 1	60000025	Vice President, Supply Chain	No	1	00001017	213,600.00	USD	213,600.00	USD	65,000.00	US
50000057	Global Supply Chain 1	60000008	Executive Assistant	No	1	00001018	49,919.00	USD	49,919.00	USD	30,000.00	US
50000056	Global Information Technology	60000018	Chief Information Officer	No	1	00001019	108,000.00	USD	108,000.00	USD	65,000.00	US

Figure 13.6 Output for Data Extraction for Salary Survey Participation Query

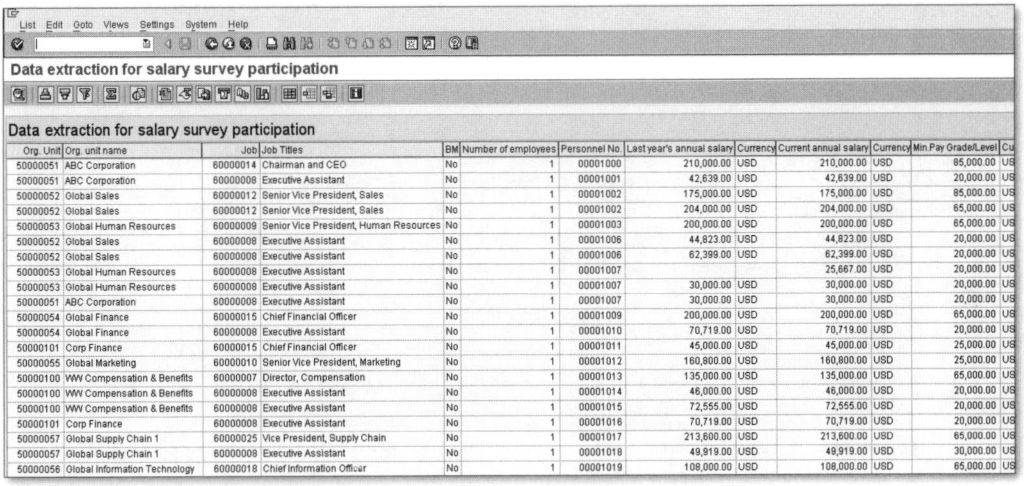

13.1.7 Hay PayNet: Data Extraction for Salary Survey Participation

The Hay PayNet: Data Extraction for Salary Survey Participation query is specifically designed for customers using HayGroup® for their salary surveys. The query name is AQZZ/SAPQUERY/H0SALSURVEY_HAY. The Transaction code is S_PH9_46000227, which you can access via the SAP Easy Access menu by following the path HUMAN RESOURCES • PERSONNEL MANAGEMENT • COMPENSATION MANAGEMENT • INFORMATION SYSTEM • REPORTS • SALARY SURVEYS • HAY PAYNET: DATA EXTRACTION FOR SALARY SURVEY PARTICIPATION. in Figure 13.7 you can see the selection screen of the query.

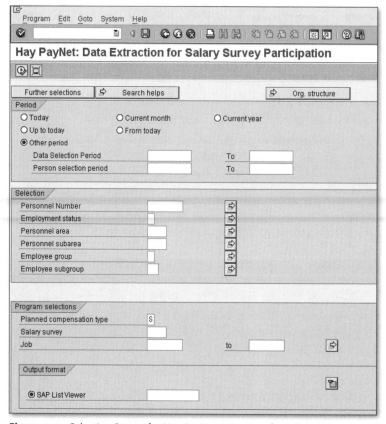

Figure 13.7 Selection Screen for Hay PayNet Extraction for Salary Survey Participation Query

The following two reports are relevant to pay scale reclassification. Pay scale reclassification, which we discussed in Chapter 5, is an important part of compensation practices for those employees on collective agreements and step progressions.

13.1.8 Defaults for Pay Scale Reclassification

The Defaults for Pay Scale Reclassification report displays the next standard pay scale reclassification for individual employees. You can use this report to determine whether you have missed reclassifying an employee or to determine when and who is due for a reclassification in the future.

Its program name is RPLTRF10. The Transaction code is S_AHR_61016357 and can be accessed via the SAP Easy Access menu by following the path HUMAN RESOURCES • PERSONNEL MANAGEMENT • COMPENSATION MANAGEMENT • INFORMATION SYSTEM • REPORTS • EMPLOYEE COMPENSATION DATA • DEFAULTS FOR PAY SCALE RECLASSIFICATION. Figure 13.8 shows the selection screen of the report.

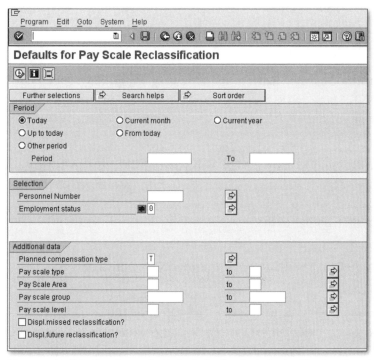

Figure 13.8 Selection Screen for Defaults for Pay Scale Reclassification Report

13.1.9 Time Spent in Each Pay Scale Type/Area/Group/Level

The Time Spent in each Pay Scale type/area/group/level report provides the duration of an assignment to a pay grade/scale or level for an employee. The report provides the date as along with years and months since entering their current grade/level.

Its program name is RPLTRF00. The Transaction code is S_AHR_61016356. You can access it by following the path HUMAN RESOURCES • PERSONNEL MANAGEMENT • COMPENSATION MANAGEMENT • INFORMATION SYSTEM • REPORTS • EMPLOYEE COMPENSATION DATA • TIME SPENT IN EACH PAY SCALE AREA/TYPE/GROUP/LEVEL, and you can see the output in Figure 13.9.

13.1.10 Compa-Ratio Analysis

The Compa-Ratio Analysis report provides a report of all of the compa-ratios for a given selection. The employee's compa-ratio is calculated by taking his base salary and comparing it to the midpoint of the salary range of his grade. The system takes the employee's capacity utilization percentage (from Infotype 0008) into account. The equation for calculation is:

Compa-ratio = (100/capacity utilization level) * (base salary/reference salary)

The reference salary can be manipulated by implementing BAdI HRCMP00COMPA_RATIO. Method GET_REFERENCE_SALARY is another way of generating the reference salary for an employee.

Its program name is RHCMPCR0. The Transaction code is S_AHR_61018799, which is accessed via the SAP Easy Access menu by following the path HUMAN RESOURCES • PERSONNEL MANAGEMENT • COMPENSATION MANAGEMENT • INFORMATION SYSTEM • REPORTS • EMPLOYEE COMPENSATION DATA • COMPA-RATIO ANALYSIS. Figure 13.10 shows the output of the report.

13.1.11 Compare Actual Base Salary to Planned Compensation

The Compare Actual Base Salary to Planned Compensation report provides a comparison between an employee's base salary and Infotype 1005 (Planned Compensation) attributes on their job (or position). The program first looks at the employee's position for any Infotype 1005 override records. If the system cannot find any records at the position level, it will retrieve Infotype 1005 from the employee's job.

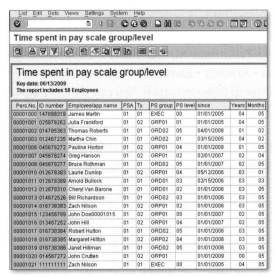

Pers.No.	ID number	Employee/app.name	PSA	Ty.	PS group	PS level	since	Years	Months
00001000	147899319	James Martin	01	01	EXEC	00	01/01/2005	04	05
00001001	025879262	Julia Frankford	01	02	GRP01	01	01/01/2005	04	05
00001002	014785363	Thomas Roberts	01	01	GRD02	05	04/01/2008	01	02
00001003	012467235	Martha Chin	01	01	GRD02	01	03/15/2005	04	02
00001006	045678272	Pauline Horton	01	02	GRP01	04	01/01/2008	01	05
00001007	045678274	Greg Hanson	01	02	GRP01	02	02/01/2007	02	04
00001009	045678277	Bruce Rothman	01	01	GRD02	02	01/01/2007	02	05
00001010	012678383	Laurie Dunlop	01	02	GRP01	04	05/12/2006	03	01
00001011	012678389	Arnold Bullock	01	01	GRD01	03	02/15/2006	03	03
00001012	012678310	Cheryl Van Barone	01	01	GRD01	02	01/01/2006	03	05
00001013	014672526	Bill Richardson	01	01	GRD02	03	01/01/2006	03	05
00001014	016738383	Zach Nilson	01	02	GRP01	02	01/01/2006	03	05
00001015	123456789	John Doe00001015	01	02	GRP01	00	01/01/2007	02	05
00001016	013467252	John Hill	01	02	GRP01	04	01/01/2007	02	05
00001017	016738384	Robert Hulton	01	01	GRD02	05	01/01/2006	03	05
00001018	016738385	Margaret Hillton	01	02	GRP02	04	01/01/2006	03	05
00001019	016738386	Janet Hillman	01	01	GRD02	05	01/01/2006	03	05
00001020	014567272	John Crutten	01	02	GRP01		01/01/2009	00	05
00001021	111111111	Zach Nilson	01	01	EXEC	00	01/01/2005	04	05

Figure 13.9 Output for Time Spent in Pay Scale Group/Level Report

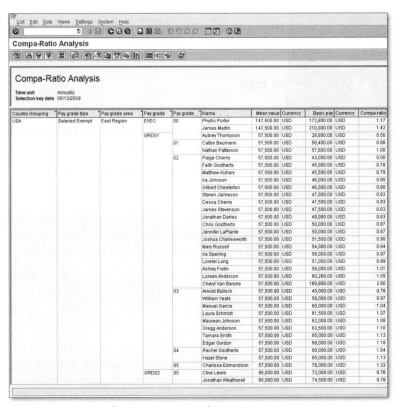

Country Grouping	Pay grade type	Pay grade area	Pay grade	Pay grade	Name	Mean value	Currency	Basic pay	Currency	Compa-ratio
USA	Salaried Exempt	East Region	EXEC	00	Phyllis Porter	147,500.00	USD	172,800.00	USD	1.17
					James Martin	147,500.00	USD	210,000.00	USD	1.42
			GRD01		Aubrey Thompson	57,500.00	USD	28,800.00	USD	0.50
				01	Catlyn Baumann	57,500.00	USD	50,400.00	USD	0.88
					Nathan Patterson	57,500.00	USD	57,600.00	USD	1.00
				02	Paige Cherny	57,500.00	USD	43,000.00	USD	0.00
					Faith Gootherts	57,500.00	USD	45,000.00	USD	0.78
					Matthew Kuhary	57,500.00	USD	45,500.00	USD	0.79
					Ira Johnson	57,500.00	USD	46,000.00	USD	0.80
					Gilbert Chesterton	57,500.00	USD	46,000.00	USD	0.80
					Steven Jaimeson	57,500.00	USD	47,000.00	USD	0.82
					Dessa Cherny	57,500.00	USD	47,500.00	USD	0.83
					James Stevenson	57,500.00	USD	47,500.00	USD	0.83
					Jonathan Davies	57,500.00	USD	48,000.00	USD	0.83
					Chris Gootherts	57,500.00	USD	50,000.00	USD	0.87
					Jennifer LaPlante	57,500.00	USD	50,000.00	USD	0.87
					Joshua Charlesworth	57,500.00	USD	51,500.00	USD	0.90
					Mary Russell	57,500.00	USD	54,000.00	USD	0.94
					Ira Sperling	57,500.00	USD	56,000.00	USD	0.97
					Lorelei Long	57,500.00	USD	57,000.00	USD	0.99
					Ashley Frelin	57,500.00	USD	58,000.00	USD	1.01
					Loreen Anderson	57,500.00	USD	60,260.00	USD	1.05
					Cheryl Van Barone	57,500.00	USD	160,800.00	USD	2.80
				03	Arnold Bullock	57,500.00	USD	45,000.00	USD	0.78
					William Yeats	57,500.00	USD	56,000.00	USD	0.97
					Manuel Garcia	57,500.00	USD	60,000.00	USD	1.04
					Laura Schmidt	57,500.00	USD	61,500.00	USD	1.07
					Maureen Johnson	57,500.00	USD	62,000.00	USD	1.08
					Gregg Anderson	57,500.00	USD	63,500.00	USD	1.10
					Tamara Smith	57,500.00	USD	65,000.00	USD	1.13
					Edgar Gordon	57,500.00	USD	68,000.00	USD	1.18
				04	Rachel Gootherts	57,500.00	USD	60,000.00	USD	1.04
					Hazel Stone	57,500.00	USD	65,000.00	USD	1.13
				05	Charissa Edmondson	57,500.00	USD	76,000.00	USD	1.32
			GRD02	00	Clive Lewis	95,000.00	USD	72,000.00	USD	0.76
					Jonathan Weatherall	95,000.00	USD	74,500.00	USD	0.78

Figure 13.10 Output for Compa-ratio Analysis Report

353

Its program name is RHCMPCOMPARE_ACTUAL_PLANNED. The Transaction code is S_AHR_61018798 , which is accessed via the SAP E … ol-
lowing the path HUMAN RES … ON
MANAGEMENT • INFORMATION … •
COMPARE ACTUAL BASE SALARY … ut
in Figure 13.11.

Not authorized

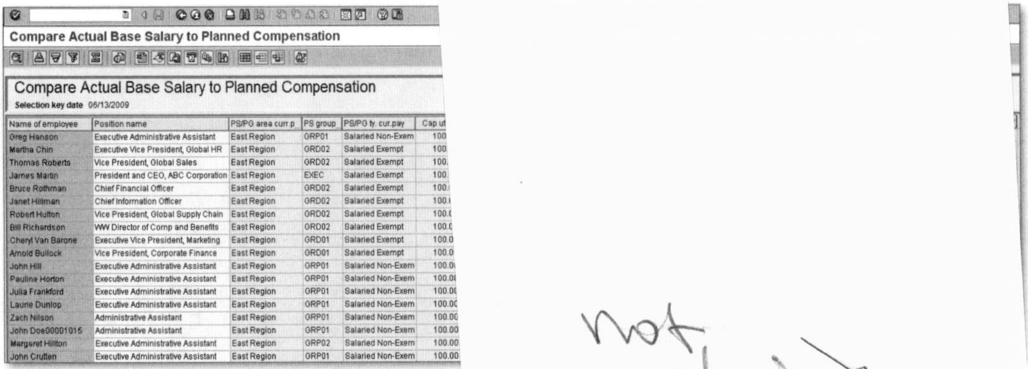
Compare Actual Base Salary to Planned Compensation

Compare Actual Base Salary to Planned Compensation

Selection key date 06/13/2009

Name of employee	Position name	PS/PG area curr.p	PS group	PS/PG ty. cur.pay	Cap ut
Greg Hanson	Executive Administrative Assistant	East Region	GRP01	Salaried Non-Exem	100
Martha Chin	Executive Vice President, Global HR	East Region	GRD02	Salaried Exempt	100
Thomas Roberts	Vice President, Global Sales	East Region	GRD02	Salaried Exempt	100.
James Martin	President and CEO, ABC Corporation	East Region	EXEC	Salaried Exempt	100
Bruce Rothman	Chief Financial Officer	East Region	GRD02	Salaried Exempt	100.
Janet Hillman	Chief Information Officer	East Region	GRD02	Salaried Exempt	100.
Robert Hulton	Vice President, Global Supply Chain	East Region	GRD02	Salaried Exempt	100.
Bill Richardson	WW Director of Comp and Benefits	East Region	GRD02	Salaried Exempt	100.0
Cheryl Van Barone	Executive Vice President, Marketing	East Region	GRD01	Salaried Exempt	100.0
Arnold Bullock	Vice President, Corporate Finance	East Region	GRD01	Salaried Exempt	100.0
John Hill	Executive Administrative Assistant	East Region	GRP01	Salaried Non-Exem	100.0
Pauline Horton	Executive Administrative Assistant	East Region	GRP01	Salaried Non-Exem	100.0
Julia Frankford	Executive Administrative Assistant	East Region	GRP01	Salaried Non-Exem	100.0
Laurie Dunlop	Executive Administrative Assistant	East Region	GRP01	Salaried Non-Exem	100.0
Zach Nilson	Administrative Assistant	East Region	GRP01	Salaried Non-Exem	100.00
John Doe00001015	Administrative Assistant	East Region	GRP01	Salaried Non-Exem	100.00
Margaret Hillton	Executive Administrative Assistant	East Region	GRP02	Salaried Non-Exem	100.00
John Crutten	Executive Administrative Assistant	East Region	GRP01	Salaried Non-Exem	100.00

Figure 13.11 Output for Compare Act…

not authorized

13.1.12 Pay Grade Structure f…

The Pay Grade Structure for Jo…
structure including pay grade typ…
to view or edit additional info…
tion Result), Infotype 1051 (Sur…
(Description). Selection can be m…

Its program name is RHCMPJOBPL …
and can be accessed via the SAP Easy Access menu by following the path HUMAN RESOURCES • PERSONNEL MANAGEMENT • COMPENSATION MANAGEMENT • INFORMATION SYSTEM • REPORTS • PAY STRUCTURE • PAY GRADE STRUCTURE FOR JOBS. Figure 13.12 shows the output of the report.

13.1.13 Display Pay Grade Structure

The Display Pay Grade Structure report provides a list of pay grades, ranges, and other information from Table T710. Please note that you can change the default layout from the standard to display fields such as average, range, and differential of the pay grade level.

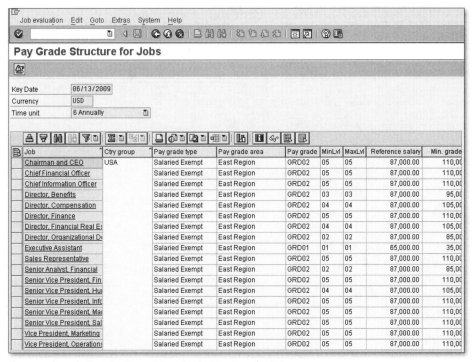

Figure 13.12 Output for Report Pay Grade Structure for Jobs

Its program name is RPLCMP01. The Transaction code is S_AHR_61015554. You can access it via the SAP Easy Access menu by following the path HUMAN RESOURCES • PERSONNEL MANAGEMENT • COMPENSATION MANAGEMENT • INFORMA-TION SYSTEM • REPORTS • PAY STRUCTURE • DISPLAY PAY GRADE STRUCTURE, and you can see the output in Figure 13.13.

13.1.14 Display Pay Scale Structure

The Display Pay Scale Structure report looks similar to the "Display Pay Grade Structure" report except that it provides a list of pay scales, ranges, and other information from Tables T510 and T510N. The entire pay scale structure is output including the pay scale type, area, group, level, and employee subgroup grouping for collective agreement provision.

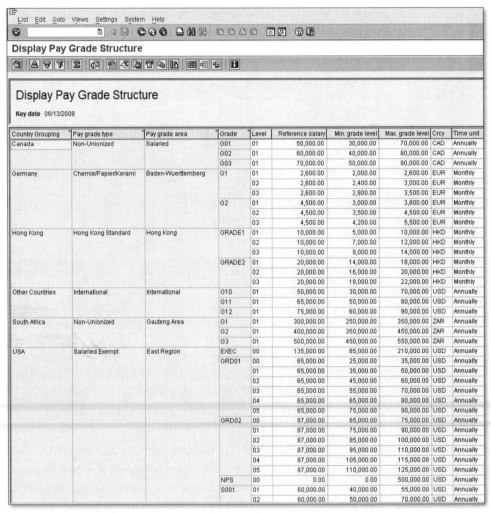

Figure 13.13 Output for Display Pay Grade Structure Report

Its program name is RHPAYSC0. The Transaction code is S_AHR_61015556, which is accessed via the SAP Easy Access menu by following the path HUMAN RESOURCES • PERSONNEL MANAGEMENT • COMPENSATION MANAGEMENT • INFORMATION SYSTEM • REPORTS • PAY STRUCTURE • DISPLAY PAY SCALE STRUCTURE. Figure 13.14 shows the output of the report.

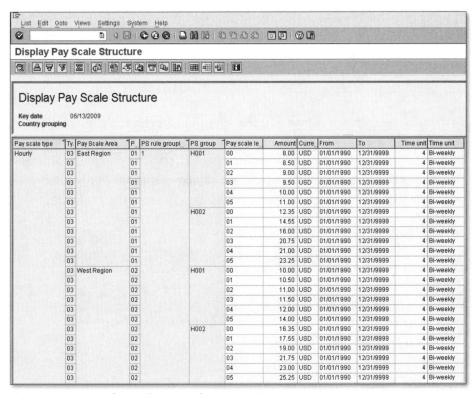

Figure 13.14 Output for Display Pay Scale Structure Report

13.1.15 Planned Labor Costs

The Planned Labor Costs report calculates the planned compensation per position for one or more organizational units. The planned compensation information is retrieved from Infotype 1005 at the position level (not the job). The following options are available on the selections screen:

► If X is selected for Reporting along a structure, all positions from that organizational unit down are evaluated. If left blank, only the positions in the specified organizational unit are evaluated.

► The maximum, minimum, or reference salary can be used for comparison by selecting the appropriate option in the Values field.

► Comparisons can also be done with a time unit via the Periodfield.

► An alternate currency can be specified and conversion type can be specified (default is M).

Its program name is RHXSOLO0. The Transaction code is S_AHR_61015558 and can be accessed via the SAP Easy Access menu by following the path HUMAN RESOURCES • PERSONNEL MANAGEMENT • COMPENSATION MANAGEMENT • INFORMATION SYSTEM • REPORTS • PAY STRUCTURE • PLANNED LABOR COSTS. Figure 13.15 shows the output of the report.

By default, the evaluation path SOLLBE (position overview along organization structure) is used by the program. However, if an alternate evaluation path is desired, then select the Standard selection screen checkbox and run the program. This takes you to program RHSOLO00, which allows you to specify a different evaluation path.

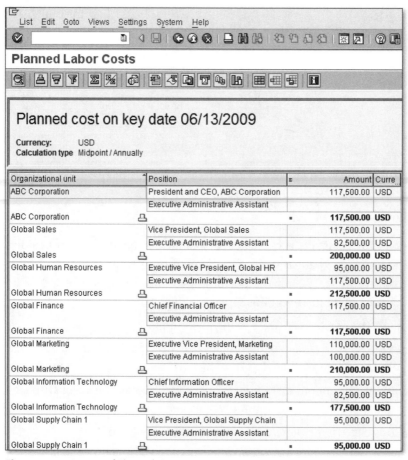

Figure 13.15 Output of Planned Costs on Key Date Report

This concludes are review of the available ABAP reports for compensation management. As with other reports in SAP, if any of the standard reports do not completely satisfy your business requirements, then custom ABAP reports can be created. This is common — particularly within the compensation function — because no two companies have the same data or do the same type of analysis. Expect to build 5 - 10 custom ABAP reports with varying complexity to support your typical ECM implementation with average scope. We have seen implementations that go live with a powerful planning and approval tool but suffer from a lack of reporting capability.

The next type of reporting within compensation management is via the ad hoc query tool.

13.2   Ad Hoc Query

SAP's ad hoc query tool enables users to create a query "on the fly" using a flexible, robust user interface. Frequently used queries can be saved and executed at a later time. Because most of your compensation data is stored at the employee level within infotype records, queries can be created to return this data to the user. The ad hoc query is a very powerful tool and is often underutilized at most companies.

The ad hoc query is good for more straightforward reports. Although more complex logic can be included within the tool (by adding additional fields), it's best to use the query tool for what it is best at: quickly and easily extracting information. More complex reporting can be achieved through custom ABAP-developed reports.

> **Note**
>
> More information on setting up and managing ad hoc query can be found at: *http://help.sap.com/printdocu/core/Print46c/EN/data/pdf/BCSRVQUE/BCSRVQUE.pdf*.

There are several components to the ad hoc query. All of the pieces are important for understanding the full breadth of available query functionality for compensation. These include:

▶ Transaction — the transaction shortcut to the query tool with the default user group.

▶ User group — the functional grouping of infosets, also serving as a point of access control.

▶ Infoset — the group of infotypes available for inclusion within a query.

▶ Query — the report that is created by the end user, which can be saved for later use.

All of these concepts play a critical role in the development and deployment of the ad hoc query. Let's first discuss how to access the query tool.

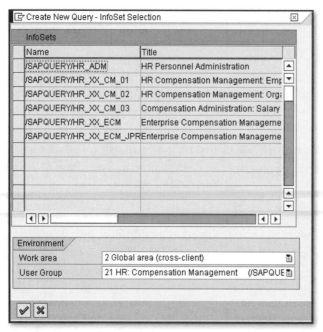

Figure 13.16 List of Queries within User Group /SAPQUERY/H0 from Transaction S_PH0_48000509

13.2.1 Transaction

Transaction S_PH0_48000509 (Ad Hoc Query) is available to create new queries within Compensation Management. You can reach this transaction via the SAP Easy Access menu by following the path HUMAN RESOURCES • PERSONNEL MANAGEMENT • COMPENSATION MANAGEMENT • INFORMATION SYSTEM. Figure 13.16 shows the pop-up box that is displayed when the user first executes this transaction. Queries can also be accessed via Transaction SQ01 (you can reach this transaction via the SAP Easy Access menu by following the path HUMAN RESOURCES • INFORMATION SYSTEM • REPORTING TOOLS • SAP QUERY). If you use Transaction SQ01, you must first check to see whether you are in the right query area and infoset.

13.2.2 User Group

User group /SAPQUERY/H0 (HR: Compensation Management) is reserved for compensation management. It is within this user group that all compensation management infosets are located. This user group can be found within the global area (cross-client) query area, which means that the query is available system-wide in all clients (versus the standard area, which is client specific). User groups can be maintained via Transaction SQ03. In this transaction, you can assign infosets to user groups and maintain a user's access to a user group. Figure 13.17 shows the user maintenance screen for user groups.

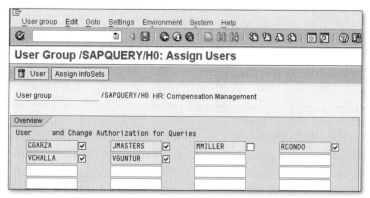

Figure 13.17 Maintenance of Users within User Group /SAPQUERY/H0

Let's now discuss infosets, which form the critical piece of ad hoc query.

13.2.3 Infosets

Infosets allow you to group related infotypes. This allows the SAP system to organize and group infotypes with similar functional purpose. For example, the same or similar infotypes are needed when reporting on compensation data. You can bet that Infotypes 0007 (Planned Working Time), 0008, 0758 (Compensation Program), and 0759 are found in most ECM infosets.

SAP provides a number of standard-delivered infosets. The standard infosets can be copied into your customer namespace and enhanced according to your business requirements. The following are the standard compensation-relevant infosets available to query from:

- /SAPQUERY/HR_ADM (HR Personnel Administration)
- /SAPQUERY/HR_XX_CM_01 (HR Compensation Management: Employee Data)
- /SAPQUERY/HR_XX_CM_02 (HR Compensation Management: Organizational Data)
- /SAPQUERY/HR_XX_CM_03 (Compensation Administration: Salary Survey Data)
- /SAPQUERY/HR_XX_ECM (ECM)
- /SAPQUERY/HR_XX_ECM_JPR (ECM — Job Pricing)

Two infosets are standard within ECM: infoset /SAPQUERY/HR_XX_ECM and infoset /SAPQUERY/HR_XX_ECM_JPR. Both infosets are based on logical database PNPCE (versus logical database PNP), which means that it considers concurrent and global employment data if activated in your system.

Infoset /SAPQUERY/HR_XX_ECM has the following Infotypes available for query: 0000 (Actions), 0001 (Organizational Assignment), 0002 (Personal Data), 0006 (Address), 0007, 0008, 0014 (Recurring Payments and Deductions), 0015 (Additional Payments), 0041 (Date Specifications), 0267 (Additional Off-Cycle Payments), 0758, 0759, 0760 (Compensation Eligibility Override), 0761 (LTI Granting), 0762 (LTI Participation), and 0763 (LTI Participation Data).

Figure 13.18 shows infotypes from logical database PNPCE within infoset /SAPQUERY/HR_XX_ECM.

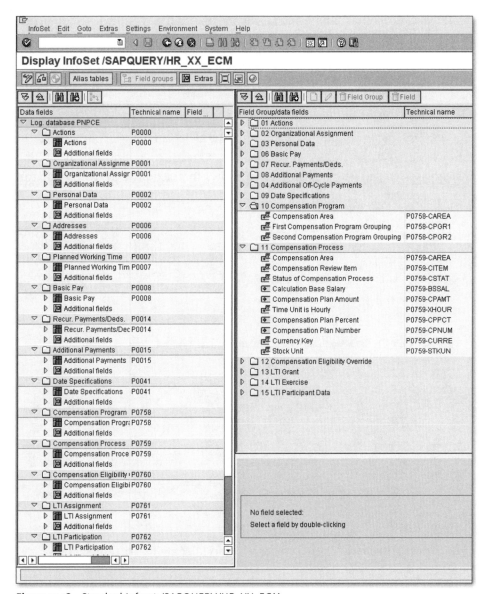

Figure 13.18 Standard Infoset /SAPQUERY/HR_XX_ECM

Infoset /SAPQUERY/HR_XX_ECM_JPR has the following Infotypes available for query: 0000, 0001, 0002, 0006, 0007, 0008, 0041, 0267, 0758, 0759, 0760, 0761, 0762, and 0763. The infoset also brings in the matched survey job and survey market data including: provider code, survey job code, survey job level job match percentage, and job grouping code stored in the job pricing tables.

The infosets form the foundation of your query. Let's review the query next.

13.2.4 Queries

Queries provide a way for end users to create quick and easy reports based on infotype data defined within an infoset. When creating a query, you specify the selection screen and output. Figure 13.19 shows Transaction SQ01, where you can maintain queries.

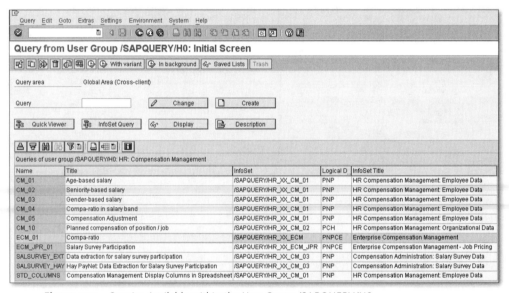

Figure 13.19 Queries Available within the User Group /SAPQUERY/H0

The following two queries are standard within ECM: ECM_01 (Compa-ratio) and ECM_JPR_01 (Salary Survey Participation).

Query ECM_01 provides standard selection screen elements (such as personnel area, personnel subarea, employee group, and employee subgroup) and fields such as pay type, area, grade, level, and compa-ratio. Output, shown in Figure 13.20, contains the fields Name of employee, Pay Grad, LV, CpRt, Min. grade level, and Max. grade level.

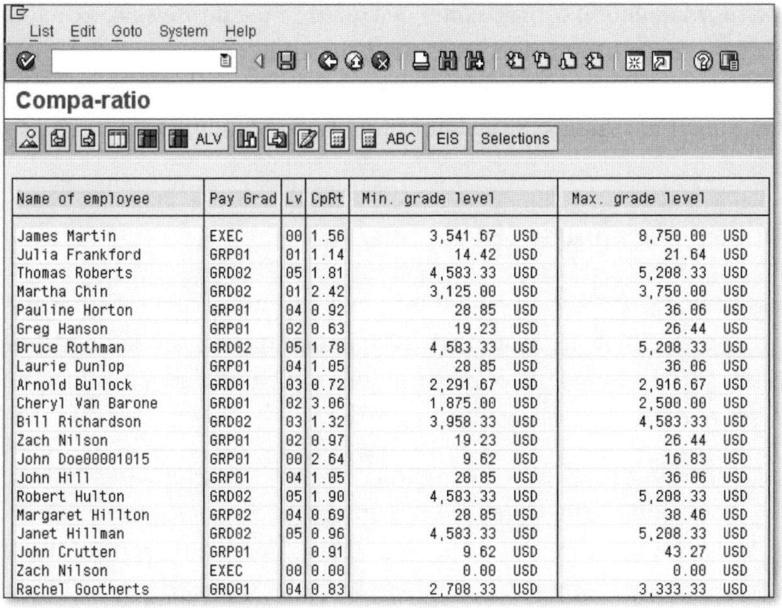

Name of employee	Pay Grad	Lv	CpRt	Min. grade level		Max. grade level	
James Martin	EXEC	00	1.56	3,541.67	USD	8,750.00	USD
Julia Frankford	GRP01	01	1.14	14.42	USD	21.64	USD
Thomas Roberts	GRD02	05	1.81	4,583.33	USD	5,208.33	USD
Martha Chin	GRD02	01	2.42	3,125.00	USD	3,750.00	USD
Pauline Horton	GRP01	04	0.92	28.85	USD	36.06	USD
Greg Hanson	GRP01	02	0.63	19.23	USD	26.44	USD
Bruce Rothman	GRD02	05	1.78	4,583.33	USD	5,208.33	USD
Laurie Dunlop	GRP01	04	1.05	28.85	USD	36.06	USD
Arnold Bullock	GRD01	03	0.72	2,291.67	USD	2,916.67	USD
Cheryl Van Barone	GRD01	02	3.06	1,875.00	USD	2,500.00	USD
Bill Richardson	GRD02	03	1.32	3,958.33	USD	4,583.33	USD
Zach Nilson	GRP01	02	0.97	19.23	USD	26.44	USD
John Doe00001015	GRP01	00	2.64	9.62	USD	16.83	USD
John Hill	GRP01	04	1.05	28.85	USD	36.06	USD
Robert Hulton	GRD02	05	1.90	4,583.33	USD	5,208.33	USD
Margaret Hillton	GRP02	04	0.69	28.85	USD	38.46	USD
Janet Hillman	GRD02	05	0.96	4,583.33	USD	5,208.33	USD
John Crutten	GRP01		0.91	9.62	USD	43.27	USD
Zach Nilson	EXEC	00	0.00	0.00	USD	0.00	USD
Rachel Gootherts	GRD01	04	0.83	2,708.33	USD	3,333.33	USD

Figure 13.20 Output for Compa-ratio Query

Query ECM_JPR_01 provides standard selection screen elements (such as personnel area, personnel subarea, employee group, and employee subgroup) and fields such as provider code, benchmark job, and compensation job grouping. Output, shown in Figure 13.21, contains the fields Organizational Unit (ID and name), Job (ID and name), Job group (ID and name), Pers. No., Provider code, Survey Job code, Survey Job level, Job matching, bonus award with currency, base salary award with currency, total compensation with currency, and time unit.

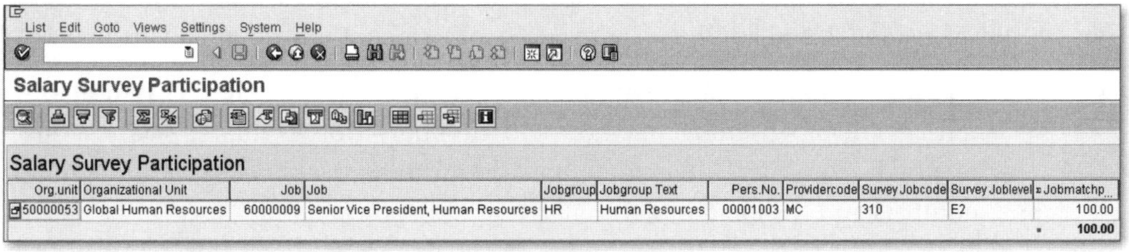

Org.unit	Organizational Unit	Job	Job	Jobgroup	Jobgroup Text	Pers.No.	Providercode	Survey Jobcode	Survey Joblevel	Jobmatchp...
50000053	Global Human Resources	60000009	Senior Vice President, Human Resources	HR	Human Resources	00001003	MC	310	E2	100.00
										100.00

Figure 13.21 Output for Salary Survey Participation Query

Although the standard solution contains only two queries, the infosets provide you with the ability to create an unlimited number based on your business requirements. Now that we have covered the query capability within compensation, let's review the functionality within SAP's BW solution.

13.3   Business Warehouse (BW)

If your company owns SAP BW, you can perform more robust analytical reporting on compensation data. There are more than 30 standard queries available within SAP's NetWeaver 7.0 BI content. Also, these queries can be used as a baseline for any customer-specific BW reports you need to create.

The roles, queries, and infosets packaged within SAP BW come grouped in four major content areas for BI content related to compensation management: Compensation Administration, Long-Term Incentives (LTIs), Budgeting, and Job Pricing. Each of these areas is discussed next, along with the standard pre-packaged queries.

13.3.1   BI Content Area: Compensation Administration

The first BI content area available for ECM is Compensation Administration. In this content area, planned compensation adjustments can be compared against guidelines and compa-ratio (and position in range), calculations can be evaluated, and forecasts on new compensation can be displayed. Much of this information is sourced from Infotypes 0008, 0758, and 0759.

The following standard queries are available within the BI content area for Compensation Administration:

▸ **Planned Compensation Amounts or Numbers vs. Guideline Defaults** — retrieves compensation amounts and numbers (for example, salary adjustments, bonuses, or LTI grants), and the difference between these amounts/ numbers and the guideline defaults.

▸ **Planned LTI Grants vs. Guideline Defaults** — retrieves the compensation numbers (compensation category LTI Grant), and the difference between these numbers and the guideline defaults.

▸ **Number of Participants vs. Eligible Population** — compares the number of employees eligible for a compensation plan with the number of employees who actually participate in the plan, that is, employees who are granted a salary increase, a bonus, or an LTI grant.

▸ **Compensation Amounts according to Guidelines** — simulates the effect of different guideline setups. It can be executed before managers begin the planning phase and displays the amounts that would be spent if everybody was paid according to the guidelines.

▸ **LTI Grants according to Guidelines** — simulates the effect of different guideline setups. It can be executed before managers begin the planning phase and displays the numbers that would be spent if everybody was granted LTIs according to the guidelines.

▸ **Compa-ratio** — retrieves employees belonging to one or more organizational units and calculates their compa-ratio.

▸ **Percent in Salary Range** — retrieves employees belonging to one or more organizational units and calculates the percentage of their salary according to the salary range of their pay grade.

▸ **Planned Changes to Annual Salaries** — retrieves planned changes to employees' salaries due to salary adjustments.

▸ **Planned Compensation Amounts vs. Guideline Minimum** — retrieves the compensation process amounts (that is, salary adjustments or bonuses) and the difference between these amounts and the guideline minimum.

▸ **Planned Compensation Amounts vs. Guideline Maximum** — retrieves the compensation process amounts (that is, salary adjustments or bonuses) and the difference between these amounts and the guideline maximum.

▸ **Planned LTI Grants vs. Guideline Minimum** — retrieves the compensation process numbers (LTI grants) and the difference between these numbers and the guideline minimum.

▸ **Planned LTI Grants vs. Guideline Maximum** — retrieves the compensation process numbers (LTI grants) and the difference between these numbers and the guideline maximum.

This concludes the list of standard queries within the Compensation Administration BI content area.

13.3.2 BI Content Area: LTIs

The second BI content area available for ECM is LTIs. In this content area, information on granted and awarded stock can be reported on. Much of this information is sourced from Infotypes 0761 and 0762.

The following standard queries are available within the BI content area for LTIs:

- **Awards Exercised in Period** — retrieves the number of awards that have been exercised within a specific period and the exercise price and the fair market value on the exercise date.

- **Awards Vested in Period** — retrieves the number of awards that have vested within a specific period.

- **Awards Granted in Period** — displays the number of granted LTI awards within a specific period.

- **Open Awards on Key Date** — retrieves the number of awards that are either still open (unexercised or forfeited) or exercisable (that is, already vested but neither exercised nor forfeited) on a key date.

- **Awards Expired/Forfeited in Period** — displays the number of forfeited/expired LTI awards within a specific period.

- **Exercisable Awards on Key Date** — displays the number of exercisable awards on a key date.

This concludes the list of standard queries within the LTIs BI content area.

13.3.3 BI Content Area: Budgeting

The third BI content area available for ECM is Budgeting. In this content area, allocated and spent budgeting data from the organizational unit and budget unit structures are available.

The following standard queries are available within the BI content area for Budgeting:

- **Amounts Spent per Budget Unit** — lists the spent amounts per budget unit, drilled down to the level of single employees.

- **Numbers Spent per Budget Unit** — lists the spent numbers per budget unit, drilled down to the level of single employees.

▶ **Monetary Budgets** — displays the budget hierarchy for a selected budget period and monetary budget type.

▶ **LTI Budgets** — displays the budget hierarchy for a selected budget period and nonmonetary budget type.

That's it for the list of standard queries within the Budgeting BI content area.

13.3.4 BI Content Area: Job Pricing

The fourth BI content area available for ECM is Job Pricing. In this content, data on job matches, salary survey market data, composite market data, and salary structures is available. Due to the high volume of salary survey market data in most organizations, allowing compensation specialists access to this data is a significant boost to their analytical capability.

The following standard queries are available within the BI content area for Job Pricing:

▶ **Salary Survey Market Data** — allows for a search of market results for jobs of survey providers.

▶ **Employee Pay Categories** — displays the different pay categories for your employees.

▶ **Composite Market Data** — view and analyze the existing composite market data for internal jobs.

▶ **Compare Employee vs. Composite Market Data** — allows you to compare the market data and the pay categories of the employees and displays the differences between the values.

▶ **Job Matching** — displays the existing job matches for internal jobs to external provider jobs and the weighting of that match.

▶ **Salary Structure** — displays the existing or planned salary structure values.

▶ **Salary Structure Comparison** — compares two salary structures.

▶ **Comparison of Salary Structure Against Market** — compares planned or actual salary structure values against market composite data.

Figure 13.22 shows the output of the standard Composite Market Data BI query.

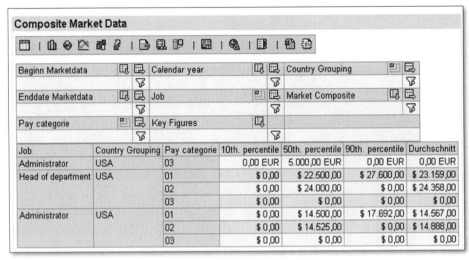

Figure 13.22 Output of the Standard Composite Market Data BI Query

This concludes the list of standard queries within the Job Pricing BI content area.

Note

You can find more information on BW roles, queries, and infosets within ECM on the SAP Help website at: *http://help.sap.com/saphelp_nw70/helpdata/en/e5/e37661ce-a89e4794fb6dc1282d000d/frameset.htm*.

Keep in mind that there is no delivered BI content to support the bonus process (i.e., short-term incentives). This is because most organizations create a custom SAP application (program) to calculate this type of compensation because no two companies typically have the same bonus plan design. Depending on the plan design, you may be able to use some of the same roles, infosets, and queries from the content areas explained previously because you may be saving your bonus awards as Infotype 0759 records. This analysis would need to occur during the project's blueprinting sessions.

13.4 Summary

Throughout this chapter we reviewed the reporting components within SAP ERP HCM ECM. As with other areas within HCM, the ECM functionality offers standard ABAP reporting via the SAP backend system, SAP query capabilities with delivered user groups, infosets, queries, and BI content via SAP BW. With SAP ERP 6.0 enhancement package 4, significant backend reporting capability has improved the robustness of the reporting within the system. New reports are now available to compensation and HR professionals to assist them during the compensation planning, approval, and calibration processes.

In the next chapter, we will review some lessons learned from our past experiences implementing ECM.

If you always approach things the same way, you will always end up with the same result. If you learn from your experiences and apply what you learn to new projects, you can achieve better results. In this chapter, we share some of the lessons we learned as we implemented Enterprise Compensation Management (ECM) over the years.

14   Lessons Learned

In this chapter, we explore some lessons we learned implementing ECM both by itself and as part of larger SAP HCM initiatives. We have singled out those lessons that apply across more than one implementation so that they are more relevant. Certainly, not all projects are the same but the lessons covered in this chapter should apply to most typical ECM implementations.

The following lessons learned should not be considered a comprehensive list. Each lesson should be reviewed within the context of your own implementation and applied with its own merit. Depending on your company's size, culture, and global reach, some lessons will inevitably mean more to you than others. You might want to review these items with the project team at the project's blueprint stage to ensure you have considered these elements in your design and operational model.

The following lessons learned are an important guide to ECM functionality and compensation processes based on our experiences.

Ensure a Solid Definition and Application of Eligibility

Eligibility is an important aspect of compensation administration. Employees showing incorrect eligibility can become a maintenance nightmare for the Compensation department. Managers and Human Resources (HR) can become frustrated as they may not immediately realize the issue, because it could be data related, configuration related, or development related.

The difficulty in managing eligibility is compounded if the rules are complex or if employees have to be overridden so that they are eligible (due to exception). After defining the business criteria and incorporating the logic into the system, it is best to execute eligibility queries (before the compensation process starts) to determine if there are any issues with data cleanliness or eligibility logic.

We also suggest that you define a clear approach for overriding eligibility. Infotype 0760 (Compensation Eligibility Override) should only be used when necessary. Placing overrides at the employee level does allow flexibility in the solution but also permits exceptions to be condoned. Managing a large pool of exception cases becomes a liability if not justified and addressed appropriately.

Another area of concern with eligibility rules is being able to correctly validate all business scenarios during testing time. To assist in the testing, we recommended that the functional requirements relating to eligibility rules are clearly documented and include specific scenarios describing exactly when an employee becomes eligible/ineligible for each plan. We have seen instances where the testing team was not able to effectively test the eligibility rules. The result was an unruly amount of exceptions during the administration process.

Limit the Amount of Employee Movement During the Compensation Cycle

Changes in the reporting structure during the compensation planning cycle can result in issues with budget allocation. Based on employee movement, the budget allocation originally intended to support manager planning needs to be adjusted every time there is a change in position outside the manager's span of control. (This assumes that you do not participate in a "freeze.")

Let's use the administration of a merit plan during compensation planning as an example. In this scenario, you have set up your budget to allocate 3% of each eligible employee's meritable pay. Using standard SAP budgeting, the budget allocation rolls up through the managers' organizational unit hierarchy so that individual and overall budgets are established after initialization. If an employee is transferred from manager A to manager B, the budget allocation does not automatically change (without manual intervention or a customized automated process). Without addressing the movement, the transfer results in manager B not having enough allocated budget to compensate the employee while manager A has a budget surplus. Manager A might mistake the additional allocation as available dollars/units that he can use during the planning process to allocate to other employees.

As discussed in Chapter 4, Compensation Budgeting, custom functionality can be developed that allows you to dynamically recalculate budget allocation and spend amounts. Depending on the approach you take, you may or may not leverage the standard SAP concept of budgeting.

One of the ways to mitigate this issue is to limit the number of transfers during the period that compensation is being planned for. If limited, you can add some additional steps to the transfer process that take the compensation process into consideration and require the user performing the transfer to also update the budget allocations for the affected organizational units. Depending on the size of your organization and the frequency of transfers during planning time, this approach may be sufficient.

Keep It Simple — Avoid Adding too Many Columns to the Planning Worksheet

A natural design tendency with the compensation planning worksheet is to add as much data as possible to let managers administer compensation plans efficiently. Based on experience, additional columns can add a lot of value to the process but can become overbearing when done excessively. Too many columns end up overwhelming managers and complicating the process. As an example, take compensation concepts such as compa-ratio, percent in range, and percentiles. If managers are not educated on what these terms mean, they can easily become confused and disinterested.

Managers also become increasingly frustrated if they have to scroll to the right to see additional information on the worksheet. Sometimes it is inevitable that the planning worksheet contains additional columns that may cause a manager to scroll right. If you believe your worksheet extends too far to the right, we recommend that an additional column be added (in the middle or at the end of the worksheet) to display the employee's first/last name (again). This approach prevents the manager from having to scroll back to the left to determine which employee he is working on.

Adding too many columns also has a negative impact on the tool's system performance. Companies with 20-plus columns on each tab of the worksheet run the risk of poor performance. Because the information from the tool is being sourced from SAP in real time, there are potential issues with latency if not tested properly. We suggest a performance (stress) test be performed on the worksheet and integrated into your overall test plan.

Keeping the manager experience as simple as possible goes a long way with user adoption and process acceptance. The amount of columns is a great example but there are other ways to improve user experience, such as reducing the number of available buttons, reducing the amount of content on the screen, and making the navigation on the portal and within the application (iView) intuitive.

Implement an iView That Enables Managers to Print Employee Compensation Statements Once the Process is Completed

When considering the tools available to a manager during the administration of compensation — and looking at the process end to end — we consistently see a requirement to allow managers to print compensation statements on the portal so that they can be delivered to employees. Sometimes employee access to these letters is also desired. Not addressing this gap leads to an inefficient process. Compensation statements must be created and distributed in an efficient and timely manner. Doing this "closest to the source" (i.e., by the manager, from the portal) is usually the best way to deliver them.

To give managers more control over the process, we implemented functionality that enables managers to selectively print compensation statements directly from the portal. Once the compensation process has been completed, managers can go into the portal, select one or more employees in their span of control, and print a customized statement with the employee's compensation. The statement is usually an Adobe PDF document branded with the company logo.

In most implementations, we add data such as the employee's performance rating, date of hire, guidelines, proration information, and position information. This is especially useful when both the employee's performance and compensation are delivered in one "pay-for-performance" conversation. The statement can be geared to support one type of compensation (e.g., merit) or it could incorporate all types for that review (e.g., merit, bonus, and equity).

The compensation review statement, mentioned earlier, should not be confused with a Total Compensation Statement (TCS). A TCS lets employees view all of their rewards (compensation, benefits, training, etc.) on the portal. Like the compensation review statement, the form is typically delivered via PDF. A standard Employee Self-Service (ESS) for the TCS is available from SAP's ESS Business Package.

> **Note**
>
> For more information on ESS, check out the SAP PRESS book, *Implementing Employee- and Manager Self-Services in SAP ERP HCM*, by Jeremy Masters and Christos Kotsakis.

Statements usually contain some fine-print disclaimers at the bottom of the document specifying that the information contained therein is not legally binding. It should also indicate when (i.e., date and time) it was printed. This verbiage is there to protect the company from any legal issues if the statement is somehow incorrect in any way. Disclaimers are an important part of the statement and should be reviewed by your legal and compliance teams to ensure they provide the necessary protection.

Establish Controls to Safeguard Information During Implementation and Mask Sensitive Data During Testing

Do not underestimate the effort in defining and managing security and access control during the implementation. The sensitivity of compensation data is a key consideration when involving HR and other departments during the project. Many implementation teams do not place the right level of importance around the sensitivity of compensation data and often overlook the need to mask data when creating testing scenarios and validating results. Depending on the testing plan, the testing team, and the countries/regions being tested, the appropriate level of safeguarding should be established to ensure there are no data privacy issues.

As a general rule, we recommend that you mask compensation data when testing your system. This is not a simple process because you want to maintain some level of realistic data integrity to test your calculations, including guidelines and proration. Simply masking the employee's name is not a way to protect information. Personnel number scrambling is also something that is risky and not recommended. When the right level of security is built and validated, only then should you introduce real test data into your testing cycle (presumably copied down from your production system).

If you choose not to mask compensation information throughout the testing cycle, the resources conducting the integration tests must be authorized to view the compensation data being tested. Also, any information that is produced from the system (such as datasheets, spreadsheets, report output, etc.) should be destroyed after validation.

Ensure a Smooth Calibration Process and Determine Who Will Perform Updates (and Validate Those Updates) in the System

Effectively implementing the planning worksheet supports the decentralized collection of compensation recommendations, but can also introduce a challenge when results need to be changed during and after calibration. *Calibration* refers to the process of comparing the recommendations for individual employees to their peers based on established criteria. The process is designed to equalize the recommendations across the organization so that key employees are rewarded and inappropriate recommendations are invalidated.

If your organization goes through a process of formal calibration, you need to consider how the calibrated adjustments will be input back into the system to reflect the final compensation adjustments. There are several options on how to accomplish this task:

▶ **Manager Entry:** Once the calibration is completed for the organization, revised adjustments are sent to the individual managers for them to perform the updates in the system. Having the manager update the system with the revised adjustments serves a dual purpose. First, the manager becomes more aware of the revised adjustments so that he can communicate more effectively to the employee. Second, the manager — who is closest to his employee's data — completes the updates directly in the system (via the compensation planning worksheet) and thereby reducing the oppotunity for error.

Although this approach has worked well, we have had to execute validation reports in SAP for the compensation team to ensure that updates were actually getting entered (and entered correctly).

▶ **Compensation Team Entry:** Once the calibration process is completed, the revisions are updated in SAP by the Compensation team. If there are only a few changes, the team can easily update the system mnually via Transaction PA30 and then communicate those revisions to the corresponding managers. If there are bulk updates, an upload program can be created to perform a mass update of infotype records.

Most organizations use this option but it really depends on the size of the Compensation team and the amount of employees that are receiving compensation through the process. Consider a broader compensation process (merit, bonus, and equity) with global scope for a Fortune 100 company; both the calibration process and revisions can become labor-intensive for the Compensation group at a time when they need to be focused on a number of other priorities associated with the process, including assisting the manager with decision support.

▶ **Automated Calibration Process:** For some larger deployments, we implemented a custom SAP application that conducts the calibration process online and does not require reentry of the data. Using an application such as this reduces the effort required in creating reports and spreadsheets for the calibrations meetings.

This is more costly from a build perspective but does provide cost savings over time.

Provide Managers with Guidelines

One of the key features of the compensation application in ECM is its ability to use preconfigured logic to provide managers with suggested guidelines for compensation recommendations. This functionality has a positive impact on user experience, as it supports the decision-making process that managers face.

One drawback that we experienced is related to how guidelines interplay with the budget. Depending on how the budget is calculated, guidelines may suggest adjustments, for example, that automatically put the manager over budget. Managers may feel that they were not given enough budget allocation to properly compensate employees. This makes the most impact for those managers who have a lot of high performers within their organization because the guideline typically exceeds the allotted budget percentage.

In past deployments, we had to specifically communicate to managers that guidelines are for reference and should be used as a guiding rule. Managers need to realize that all recommendations need to be considered within the overall budget before any final decisions can be made.

Avoid a Complicated Approval Process for Annual Planning

In some organizations, multilevel approval during compensation planning is regarded as a necessary control mechanism for regulatory compliance. Having the ability to drive approvals based on the organizational structure is a key benefit of using ECM. When organizational structure updates occur, approval routing can be updated automatically. Simple one-up approval — though not as common — is also available using the same infrastructure.

That said, introducing a complicated approval scheme only makes the process more difficult. Requiring an additional one, two, or three levels of formal work-flow approval does not always guarantee the results expected. In fact, many times additional layers of approval can be a distraction from the process. This *does not* mean that managers "up the chain" should not have visibility to recommendations within their entire span of control. However, it does place importance on the fact that many approvals are done in haste and without consideration to the impact on the organization.

Requiring excessive approvals also slows the process down due to manager delays with the review. Because the planning period has a short window (typically 2 - 3 weeks), the approval process needs to happen quickly. Otherwise, top-level managers will not be able to plan effectively for their organization because they are not aware of the recommendations from their lower-level staff.

Requiring one-up approval — or even no formal approval — streamlines the planning process and forces managers to be more collaborative. Using this approach, higher-level managers need to understand from lower-level manager where they are in the process. This inevitably leads to more discussion and eventually better decisions. We are not suggesting that no approval is the right approach — only that it is an option to consider if internal audit and compliance agree on the terms.

Allow Proxy Access to Facilitate Planning, but Ensure the Necessary Controls Are in Place and Continuously Monitored

Although not as common as for forms and process requests, proxy functionality for compensation management is desirable for many organizations. Enabling an employee to act on the manager's behalf (for planning or approval) is often seen as a common business requirement. Although delegation for processes like compensation management (and performance management) is not as common, proxy capability is frequently incorporated or built into the ECM applications.

There are a few guiding principles that we typically see for proxy design within a compensation management context. These include:

- allowing managers to search for and select the proxy on the portal;
- providing a life span (start and end date) for the proxy assignment;
- prohibiting the proxy from updating his own record; and
- prohibiting the proxy from updating the proxied manager's own record.

While the authors do not necessarily agree (philosophically) with giving proxy access to employees for compensation activities, we appreciate the need and have found companies that use it a lot. As with your workflow approval design, you should engage your legal, audit, and compliance teams to obtain their feedback and incorporate it into the design.

Master Data is King

Without clean master data, compensation processes will fail. We have built world-class, enterprise-level solutions close to failure due to the condition of the data. The integrity of the data within your system truly dictates whether your configured business logic can be incorporated into ECM successfully or not.

Common reasons for bad data include the following:

- Incorrect salary grade
- Incorrect salary or wage type amount
- Incorrect capacity utilization level
- Incorrect work schedule
- Missing or incorrect date type (Infotype 0041 (Date Specifications))
- Missing or incorrect action or action reason
- Incorrect employment or customer status
- Incorrect position, job, or organizational unit

As you can see, most of the reasons originate from Infotypes 0000 (Actions), 0001 (Organizational Assignment), 0007 (Planned Working Time), and 0008 (Basic Pay). If data within these infotypes are missing or incorrect, eligibility, guidelines, and proration will all be compromised.

Putting together a small master data taskforce is a good idea for preparing the system before go-live. This group is responsible for extracting data through various utilities and doing the appropriate comparisons to verify that the data is correct. The magnitude of effort depends on the project scope and the amount of employees/data being handled.

14.1 Summary

This chapter provided some lessons learned from previous ECM implementations. We hope these lessons provided some ideas on how best to deliver a robust solution with a high rate of adoption. We encourage you to use these lessons learned — and connect with other companies that have implemented ECM — to gain a better understanding of how you can improve your process and streamline your system implementation. We believe the main objective when implementing compensation management is to provide an intuitive, compliant process with supporting technology that provides managers with the necessary information to effectively administer compensation within their organization.

In the next chapter, we discuss recommended resources (such as websites, information resources, and user communities) that may help you gain a better understanding of ECM.

Knowing where to look for answers is perhaps one of the single most important skills of a project team. Resourcefulness is crucial in implementations such as Enterprise Compensation Management (ECM). This chapter looks at some of the important resources available to you before, during, and after your implementation.

15   Resources

This chapter details recommended websites, information sources, and user communities that may help you gain a better understanding of SAP's ERP HCM ECM functionality. You can use these resources before, during, and after your implementation.

15.1   Solution Documentation on SAP Service Marketplace

Solution documentation for ECM is available for registered users on SAP's Service Marketplace website. For those that do not have a Service Marketplace username and password, speak to one of your project leaders or Basis resources on how to obtain one. A lot of good solution documentation for ECM is available in the Media Library sections of the Service Marketplace.

To download ECM product documentation from the Media Library, do the following:

Go to *http://service.sap.com/erp-hcm* (see Figure 15.1) and log in with your Service Marketplace username and password.

On the left navigation panel, follow the path SAP ERP • SAP ERP Human Capital Management • Talent Management• Enterprise Compensation Management, and click on Media Library to access the following documents:

▶ Collaterals, such as solution brochures

▶ Detailed Documentation, such as configuration, comparisons between the older compensation management and newer compensation management functionality, reporting, budgeting, and job pricing

▶ Detailed and brief overview presentations on functionality

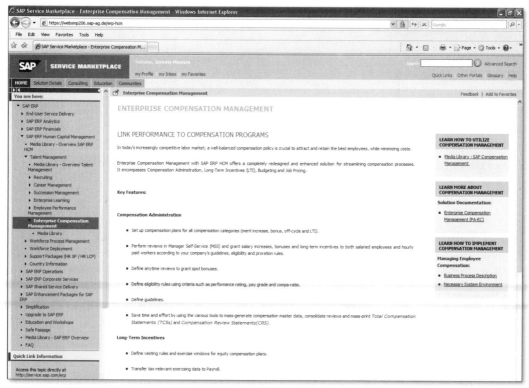

Figure 15.1 ECM Home Page within SAP's Service Marketplace

We recommend that you bookmark this site and refer to it regularly, because SAP posts useful documentation here.

15.2 SAP Online Help

SAP's online help site is often overlooked as a great resource for documentation. It is always helpful to ground yourself with the standard documentation from SAP. SAP posts the latest, revised help documentation on this site. To read the documentation on SAP's help website, do the following:

Go to *http://help.sap.com*.

On the SAP Solutions tab, click SAP ERP.

Open the documentation by clicking on the language of your choice. (The latest documentation as of this book's release is *ERP Central Component, Release 6.0 SR1, SP14* available in English and German.) If you are on an Enhancement Package, click on the SAP ERP Enhancement Packages link underneath SAP ERP Central Component and navigate based on your package level.

Another window will launch with the SAP Library. Click SAP ERP Central Component in the left navigation panel.

Expand the Human Resources folder in the left navigation panel.

Expand the Talent Management folder in the left navigation panel.

Expand the Enterprise Compensation Management folder in the left navigation panel.

The help is organized into the following high-level topics:

- Compensation Administration
- Long-Term Incentives
- Budgeting in Enterprise Compensation Management
- Compensation Budgeting Using PCP Tools
- Job Pricing

For portal-related documentation for ECM including employee and manager self service components, do the following:

Go to *http://help.sap.com* in your web browser.

On the SAP Solutions tab, click on SAP ERP.

Open the documentation by clicking on the available language you prefer. (The latest documentation as of this book's release is *ERP Central Component, Release 6.0 SR1, SP14* available in English and German.). If you are on an Enhancement Package, click on the link underneath SAP ERP Central Component and navigate based on your package level.

Another window will launch with the SAP Library. Click on the SAP ERP Cross-Application Functions link in the left navigation panel.

Click on the Cross-Application Components folder in the left navigation panel.

Expand the Self-Services folder in the left navigation panel.

Click on the Business Package for Employee Self-Service (SAP ERP) 1.x1 folder to open up the help documentation for compensation-related ESS, or click on the Business Package for Manager Self-Service (SAP ERP) 1.x1 to open up the help documentation on Compensation-related Manager Self-Services (x is the Enhancement Package number). Navigate to the appropriate compensation-related iView(s).

15.3 SAP Notes on SAP Service Marketplace

The SAP Notes section of the Service Marketplace is where SAP customers usually go when they are looking to troubleshoot an issue. This site, previously called Online Service System (OSS), provides important bug fixes for SAP customers and consultative advice on workarounds for known product issues. It is the lifeline to a lot of project implementations.

The SAP Notes section of the Service Marketplace can be accessed directly by going to *http://service.sap.com/notes*. You will be prompted for a username and password and you need to be a registered user.

Most ECM SAP Notes are categorized under application area PA-EC. Under the PA-EC application area, subapplication PA-EC-AD is for Compensation Administration, PA-EC-BD is for Compensation Budgeting, PA-EC-JP is for Job Pricing functionality, PA-EC-LT is for Long-Term Incentives (LTIs) and PA-EC-TC is for the Total Compensation Statement. Figure 15.2 shows the hierarchy within the SAP Service Marketplace.

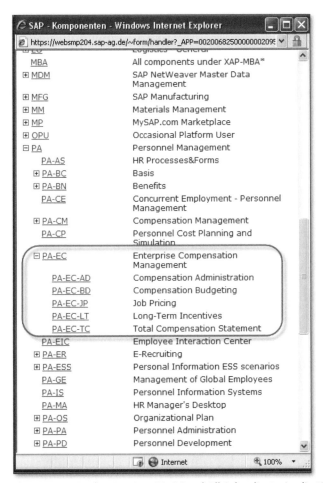

Figure 15.2 Application Area PA-EC and All Subordinate Application Areas

At the time of this book's writing, there are fewer than fifty SAP Notes on ECM functionality (PA-EC). The following list represents the SAP Notes under category PA-EC:

▶ SAP Note 1326618 — Workflow Task 04000013 is missing from the transport

▶ SAP Note 1323177 — Shortdump in the Planning Overview NAV_OBJECT_ NOT_FOUND

▶ SAP Note 1321449 — Employees not detected if org. unit has no manager position

▶ SAP Note 1319740 — Reinitialization of org. units not possible

▶ SAP Note 1312154 — Notifications not sent on approval of planning

▶ SAP Note 1306483 — ECM: Attributes for Planning Overview cannot be saved

▶ SAP Note 1275480 — Planning Overview: Org. unit status not set to Planned

▶ SAP Note 1275189 — FORM alv_log_fill_fields

▶ SAP Note 1273925 — Extractor 0HR_PA_EC_01: Error in currency conversion

▶ SAP Note 1268574 — Job Pricing: No further development

▶ SAP Note 1258114 — Integration compensation management for performance mgmnt

▶ SAP Note 1257437 — Planning Overview: Status wrong or wrong EEs selected

▶ SAP Note 1239178 — Infotype 0761: Subtype check in Transaction PA30

▶ SAP Note 1171157 — Infotype 0759: Subtype check in Transaction PA30

▶ SAP Note 1164142 — Extend Package Iterface PAOC_ECM_ADM_BL

▶ SAP Note 1158093 — Business Function Documentation not displayed

▶ SAP Note 1141686 — Incorrect data is displayed in the TCS

▶ SAP Note 1137668 — Adobe Forms HR_CMP_TCS and HR_ECM_CRS

▶ SAP Note 1121960 — Extension of help text for Anytime Review flag

▶ SAP Note 993694 — Budget don't roll up if org. unit has more than one manager

▶ SAP Note 979171 — Missing print data in HECM_PRINT_CRS in reverse order

▶ SAP Note 907456 — Compensation Specialist overview page

▶ SAP Note 893626 — Test Run flag in ECM reports

▶ SAP Note 880572 — Expiry date default for large plan term doesn't work

▶ SAP Note 879720 — FAQ Enterprise Compensation Management

▶ SAP Note 877638 — PECM_UPD_0008_1005 does not check ESG for CAP

▶ SAP Note 843631 — Infotype 0759 overview screen: Currency decimal places

▶ SAP Note 801586 — Error in Transaction PECM_CHANGE_STATUS for French employees

- ▶ SAP Note 780795 — Authorization groups for ECM database tables missing
- ▶ SAP Note 772687 — Missing translation in Budgeting and Job Pricing BSP
- ▶ SAP Note 746585 — Correction system alias in portal iViews
- ▶ SAP Note 729261 — Check Indicators for ECM transactions missing
- ▶ SAP Note 726423 — PA-EC: 726423 Documentation enhancements II
- ▶ SAP Note 726421 — PA-EC: 726421 Documentation enhancements I
- ▶ SAP Note 694731 — Incorrect calculation of date shifts
- ▶ SAP Note 685280 — Extractor Corrections in Enterprise Compensation Management
- ▶ SAP Note 682867 — Inconsistent evaluation of hire and leaving date
- ▶ SAP Note 580425 — Exits in HR core for Compensation Management

There is no composite SAP Note for ECM functionality, but for frequently asked questions SAP Note 879720is available.

Compensation-related MSS SAP Notes are categorized under application area EP-PCT-MGR-HR with keyword search "compensation." There are over sixty SAP Notes at the time of this book's writing. Some important SAP Notes include the following:

- ▶ SAP Note 1306265 — ECM Save does not save data to infotype
- ▶ SAP Note 1304578 — ECM Clear Entries does not clear Amount field
- ▶ SAP Note 1268065 — Missing budget information when currency mix detected
- ▶ SAP Note 1259751 — Incorrect currency format in Compensation Adjustments iView
- ▶ SAP Note 1259748 — Incorrect currency format in Salary Development iView
- ▶ SAP Note 1148555 — Salary development iView in MSS returns an RFC exception
- ▶ SAP Note 1022764 — MSS: ERP compensation (ECM) cannot partially reject
- ▶ SAP Note 985643 — Business Package for MSS 60.1: SP corrections
- ▶ SAP Note 804608 — Business Package for MSS 50.4/60.1: SP corrections
- ▶ SAP Note 569839 — MSS compensation: Status change in allowance scenario

► SAP Note 565371 — MSS compensation: Error in the approval workflow

► SAP Note 556050 — MSS: Configuration of UWL and launch handler

You can search for these and other SAP at *http://service.sap.com/notes.* Figure 15.3 shows a screenshot of the website's main search page.

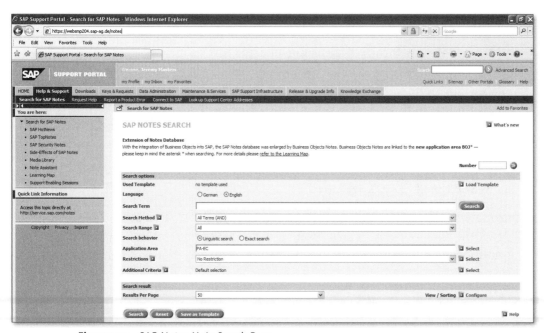

Figure 15.3 SAP Notes Main Search Page

15.4 SAP Developer Network (SDN) — SAP Community

SDN is an online community and network of SAP practitioners, developers, configurators, and other project team members. SAP is now branding SDN within the larger SAP Community Network because the site has a lot of resources to offer — and not just to developers. The website is *http://sdn.sap.com* and registration is free. Members can post, respond to, and view questions found in the forum. Although the forum is the most popular spot on the site, there are other great features including free eLearning classes, blogs, and downloads.

The majority of the threads on ECM can be found in the ERP HCM (HR) forum. Figure 15.4 shows a screenshot of the ERP HCM (HR) forum with a search result for ECM.

Figure 15.4 Forum Search on the SDN SAP Community Network Website

15.5 HR Expert

Wellesley Information Services, producer of *SAP Insider* events and publications, publishes *HR Expert* — a magazine that covers essential SAP HCM concepts, tips, and Best Practices. There is a focus on case studies and real-world" experiences in the articles. You can find a lot of good material on the website as well (it is a paid subscription). The website is *http://www.hrexpertonline.com/*. Figure 15.5 shows an example article on Job Pricing.

Figure 15.5 Example Article on the HR Expert Website

Table 15.1 lists several articles in the *HR Expert* archive that are relevant to ECM.

Article	Volume # / Issue # / Month
Easily Tie Compensation to Targeted Performance by Integrating SEM's Balanced Scorecard with HR	Volume 04 / Issue 01 / January and February
How to Administer an SAP Compensation Administration Plan	Volume 02 / Issue 03 / April
How to Design an SAP Compensation Administration Plan	Volume 02 / Issue 01 / January
Remunerating Multi-Rated Employees	Volume 01 / Issue 2 / May
SAP Compensation Administration Application Supports a Total Compensation Strategy	Volume 04 / Issue 08 / December
SAP Job Pricing Part 1: Set Up the Foundation for Market Data Analysis	Volume 04 / Issue 09 / November
SAP Job Pricing Part 2: Compare Your Salaries to Market Rates	Volume 05 / Issue 01 / January and February

Table 15.1 List of HR Expert Articles Pertinent to ECM

15.6   Annual Conferences

The two most popular conferences for SAP HCM practitioners are the annual SAP HR conference and ASUG/SAPPHIRE.

Every year, Wellesley Information Services sponsors the HR conference where SAP partners, exhibitors, and customers come to listen to speakers, share Best Practices, and see what new functionality may be available. The conference is a great place to network, hear what others are doing, and have fun. The website for the HR 2010 conference is *http://www.sapinsiderhr2010.com*.

Also, SAP annually hosts a combined ASUG/SAPPHIRE event that is geared for both current and prospective clients. It is an opportunity for SAP to show their cutting-edge solutions to its customer base. As you might expect, the ASUG/SAPPHIRE event includes speaker presentations, demos, and an exhibitor area. For more information on the conference, visit *http://www.sapsapphire.com/*.

15.7   User Communities

Two SAP HCM user communities are popular for networking events, knowledge sharing/harvesting, and roundtable discussions:

Americas' SAP Users' Group (ASUG) is a customer-driven community of SAP professionals and partners. There are more than 75,000 individuals and 2,017 companies represented within the community. It is a great place for networking. Visit their website at *http://www.asug.com/*.

The Society for Human Resource Management (SHRM) is the world's largest association devoted to HR management. Founded in 1948 and representing more than 250,000 individual members, SHRM currently has more than 575 affiliated chapters and members in more than 140 countries. Visit their website at *http://www.shrm.org/*.

15.8   LinkedIn

LinkedIn (www.linkedin.com) is a business-oriented social networking site launched in May 2003 that is mainly used for professional networking. The site has some excellent groups to subscribe to for registered users. Membership is free. Of particular interest to SAP compensation management professionals is the SAP Talent Management group at *http://www.linkedin.com/groups?gid=152688*. This group is dedicated to sharing ideas, trends, and Best Practices within SAP's talent management space including performance management, compensation management, succession planning, E-Recruiting, and E-Learning. Check it out!

15.9 Internet Search Engines

Don't forget about your Internet search engines! Google, Yahoo, and Microsoft Live, among many others, provide a great tool for finding answers to your SAP questions. You know what to do! Simply type in your question or keyword and see what you get — you might be surprised! Just be sure to give proper credit if the material is not in the public domain.

15.10 Summary

There are many resources you can embrace to research answers to your ECM questions. Some of these resources, such as the SDN SAP Community, SAP Service Marketplace, and Internet search engines, are absolutely free and provide a wealth of information at your fingertips. Just remember: if you are stuck on something, there are probably other SAP HCM practitioners who are struggling or have struggled with the same or similar challenge. Go out there and take advantage of all of the wonderful resources at your disposal!

The Authors

Jeremy Masters is an author, a speaker, and an SAP ERP HCM subject matter expert. He is also the Cofounder and Managing Partner of Worklogix, which provides SAP ERP HCM professional services and software solutions to Fortune 1000 companies. He has been an SAP HCM practitioner for over 11 years, spending his early years with Price Waterhouse, PwC Consulting, and IBM Global Business Services. He has been involved in over 20 projects, many of them global in scope.

In addition, he has been helping clients implement HCM talent management and self-service solutions for the past 11 years. Besides implementing Enterprise Compensation Management, he has worked with much of the new Talent Management functionality, including Performance Management, Succession Planning, and E-Recruiting, and self-service functionality including Employee Self-Service and Manager Self-Service. You can reach him via email at: *jmasters@worklogix.com*

Christos Kotsakis is an author, a speaker, and a subject matter expert on self-service applications. He has worked on transformation projects for over twelve years and has extensive knowledge of self-service applications and related technologies. In addition, he was an Associate Partner in the HCM practice at IBM Global Business Services where he led the design and implementation of large-scale, global HCM transformation projects using SAP HCM. Over the past 10 years, he has managed more than a dozen project teams, spanning across HCM functionality, including Performance Management, Compensation Management, and E-Recruiting. He also has extensive experience in software development and enterprise portal implementations including the SAP NetWeaver Portal technologies. You can reach him via email at: *christos.kotsakis@emedianet.com*

Index

U

V

W

Z

Strategy, conception, and implementation made easy

With numerous real-world examples, customization tips and critical success factors

2nd, updated and completely revised edition for SAP ERP 6.0

Richard Haßmann, Christian Krämer, Jens Richter

Personnel Planning and Development Using SAP ERP HCM

This completely updated and revised second edition provides a detailed overview of the SAP ERP HCM functions for personnel planning and development processes. Based on real-world technical requirements, you'll be introduced to strategies, concepts, and the mapping of processes in HCM systems. Everything, from organizational management to skill management and development planning to E-Recruiting and personnel cost planning is covered. And, you'll learn how to implement, optimize, and customize SAP ERP HCM effectively. Numerous real-life examples and critical success factors are used throughout.

approx. 550 pp., 2. edition, 69,95 Euro / US$ 69.95
ISBN 978-1-59229-187-8, Jan 2010

>> www.sap-press.com

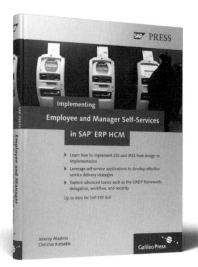

Provides an overview of ESS and MSS

Covers the fundamentals of implementing SAP ESS/MSS

An overview of Duet™

Uses ECC 6.0 and SAP NetWeaver Portal 7.0

Jeremy Masters, Christos Kotsakis

Implementing Employee and Manager Self-Services in SAP ERP HCM

Written for HR managers, power users, IT professionals, and consultants, this is the first comprehensive guide to what Employee and Manager self services (ESS & MSS) are all about. Not only does it explain ESS & MSS, but it also teaches how to implement an effective strategy in SAP ERP HCM. The book details the baseline ESS/MSS functionality in SAP's latest release (ECC 6.0) using NetWeaver Portal (EP 7.0. It also covers more advanced topics like developing self-service applications with the Floor Plan Manager, authorization management (i.e., security), workflow, and delegation.

431 pp., 2009, 69,95 Euro / US$ 69.95
ISBN 978-1-59229-188-5

>> www.sap-press.com

GOLF

THE GOLDEN YEARS

A PICTORIAL ANTHOLOGY

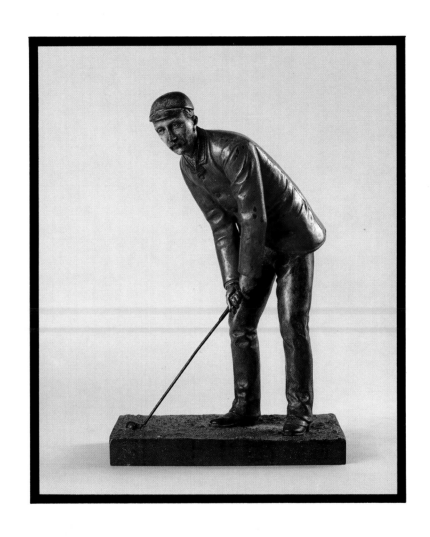

GOLF
THE GOLDEN YEARS

A PICTORIAL ANTHOLOGY

COMPILED BY

SARAH BADDIEL

STUDIO EDITIONS
LONDON

FOR MY LATE FATHER, MY MOTHER AND MY FAMILY

GOLF: THE GOLDEN YEARS
First published 1989 by Studio Editions Ltd.
Princess House,
50 Eastcastle Street,
London W1N 7AP

Copyright © Morgan Samuel Editions 1989
Reprinted 1990, 1992, 1994

ISBN 1 85170 320 9

This book was edited and designed by
Morgan Samuel Editions, London

Typeset in 10/13pt Garamond
by Peter MacDonald Associated, London
Separations by Scantrans, Singapore
Printed and bound in Singapore

CONTENTS

FOREWORD

THE PSYCHIATRIC TEXT BOOKS DO NOT identify collecting as a specific mental disorder. If they did they would not call it anything so straightforward as collecting, because all the learned professions know very well that incomprehensible gibberish is the key to bamboozling the lay public in preparation for the extortion of fat fees. Collecting would therefore be called something like "Acquisitive-Obsessive Behavioural Syndrome", contracted to AOBS for the sake of completing the confusion.

A significant proportion of golfers suffer from AOBS, more and more virulently than other sports, I fancy. This is partly explained by the fact that golf artefacts are more attractive in their own right than the impedimenta of, say, cricket or baseball. A long-nosed driver can transcend craftsmanship and be enjoyed as a work of art. The literature of golf, at least up to the time that Henry Longhurst stopped writing, is rich. Fine artists such as Harry Rowntree found inspiration in golfing subjects.

But there is more to this AOBS than collecting objects which are eminently worth collecting. Golf creates nuts, another word not to be found in the psychiatric text books, and once a nut gets the collecting bug then you have a prime candidate for raging AOBS. I once went down with incipient AOBS and found myself seriously debating whether the nest egg which had caused my family such deprivation for a down payment on our house might not be better invested in a signed Gourlay feathery ball. I managed to arrest the progress of the disease, and by following a strict routine I keep it under control. The essence of my AOBS management is to collect nothing but rubbish. My books are therefore all seriously foxed; my pictures are cheap prints and my hickory-shafted clubs are from the era that qualifies them for pea sticks.

For this reason I envied the professional dealers in golfiana. In my maladjusted state I imagined that their lives consisted of a sequence of meetings with impoverished widows.

Impoverished widow: "Good morning. This golf stick was the pride and joy of my late husband. I wondered if by chance it had any pecuniary value?" *Produces early Philp putter in pristine condition.*

Dealer: "Let me take a look. Oh yes, a clumsy counterfeit by an unscrupulous and not very gifted club-maker. The country's flooded with them."

Impoverished widow: "Oh dear, I was hoping it might be valuable ."

Dealer: "I am afraid not, madam. Tell you what, I am a fool to myself but to save you the trouble of throwing it away I will take it off your hand for you, plus I will give you this nominal sum of money. Can't say fairer than that."

Exit impoverished widow, sobbing with gratitude at the nobility of the human race. Dealer takes Philp putter to his back room and adds it to his private collection.

Over the years, I have come to realize that such a scenario is seriously wide of the mark, although in one particular it is true: dealers are all collectors. They suffer from galloping AOBS even worse than their customers. The only difference is that they collect for a living rather than as a hobby. A dealer would not dream of selling you a first edition Badminton unless he already had another one, and in better condition, in his own collection.

Sarah Baddiel is known throughout the world of golf as a dealer in golf books and artefacts, but, as explained above, she is essentially a collector critically stricken with AOBS. She would never contemplate selling her treasures, not that most of us could afford the prices commanded by golfing rarities these days. So I am sure that I speak for many frustrated AOBS victims in welcoming her enterprise in compiling this volume, which is itself a collectable. For we can enjoy the fruits of her collecting, and her scholarship, without all the expense and inconvenience of fitting burglar alarms and taking out massive fire insurance.

But this book is more than collecting by proxy. It enables us to become time travellers, going back to 1895 and the Victorian missionary zeal which took golf to every corner of the civilized world. Those pioneers did not know what they were starting, but Sarah Baddiel has chosen well in her title "The Golden Years" and we can now appreciate through her work how the great sporting and social revolution progressed.

Peter Dobereiner

Peter Dobereiner

INTRODUCTION

LAYING OUT THE COURSE OF GOLF
Bernard Darwin, *Pall Mall*, 1931

If I live to be very, very old and correspondingly untruthful I shall probably tell my listeners, if I can get any, that I saw the beginnings of golf. They will not believe me of course, for they will have read in their history books that people were playing golf in Scotland in the fifteenth century – I shall however have been misunderstood and shall explain that I meant the really important beginnings of golf, the general subjugation of England by the Scottish game. Then I shall not be thought quite so outrageous an old liar because by that time 1884 will seem a very long time ago and my memories do go back to that year.

In the early 1880s golf was, if I may so term it, a much cosier game than it is now, because there were so many fewer people playing it that they all had something of a fraternal sentiment towards one another.

Golf is essentially a friendly game even now, but it was in the nature of things friendlier then. The few golfers made pilgrimages to the few golf courses sure of a welcome for the single reason that they were golfers.

In 1863 an apparently quite unimportant event occurred. In that year a certain Mr. Gossett, the parson at Northam in North Devon, had a cousin to stay with him, General Moncrieffe from St. Andrews, and when the General was taken out for a stroll on Northam Burrows, he made this historic remark, now almost as famous as that of Archimedes, "Providence evidently designed this for a golf links." A year later the providential design had been fulfilled, the Westward Ho! links existed and in due course there was bred to the game on it a small boy called Horace Hutchinson. Five years later Hoylake was made, and there was bred another small boy called John Ball.

It was in the eighties that the first real boom came when people began to make jokes about golf and draw pictures of golf and middle-aged England woke up to the fact that here was the ideal game to amuse it, and keep it slim and young.

In the first place I think there were in England few young people playing it. Now there are boy golfers by the thousand. Then I arrogantly felt myself to be one set apart by a special dispensation. To see another small boy on the links was a surprise and not altogether a pleasant

Golf in the 18th century: a cigarette card from a series on the origin of games by Nicolas Savony & Co.

GOLF. 18TH CENTURY

8

Andrea Kircaldy
and Willie Park, *far
left*, at St. Andrews
in 1890. *Left*,
Kircaldy, Tom
Morris and others
in 1902.

A. Kirkcaldy.   Willie Park. *Champion 1887. 1889.*

Tom Morris.   Archie Simpson.   A. Kirkcaldy.   Ben Sayers.   A. Herd
(Champion 1902)

one; we looked at each other stiffly like strange
dogs. As to ladies, they had tea at the club house
certainly and perhaps walked round, but I have
no recollection of ever seeing one play. I fancy
that my memory is here quite correct for it was
still six years before the Badminton volume on
golf came to be published and therein Lord
Wellwood, posing as a most enlightened man,
welcomed ladies' links as "a kind of Jew's
quarter." They should, he thought, include some
putting holes and some longer ones "admitting
of a drive or two of seventy or eighty yards." He
did not doubt that ladies were capable of driving
even longer distances, but he added, "We must
observe that the posture and gestures requisite
for a full swing are not particularly graceful when
the player is clad in female dress."

So the players were all grown men, not very
young and not, I suppose, very good for the most
part, though there were exceptions and Mr.
Mure Fergusson, then, as for years afterwards,
one of the best amateurs of the day, used to come
to Felixstowe fairly often. Many of them played
in red coats. To do so was supposed to mark
some very mild standard of proficiency. A man
would treat himself to a red coat as soon as he had

gone round or said he had gone round in under a
hundred. Nobody as far as I recollect every
played a four ball match.

Foursomes, on the other hand, were played
regularly after lunch, much more than they are
to-day, and it seems to me that there was a
pleasant feature about those foursomes which
has now almost vanished, namely that the
professional constantly took part in them.

Where there were a few good amateurs and so
many novices the professional was a truly heroic
figure, a being altogether apart. The other day,
turning over some old letters, I came across one
written to me by my father when I was quite
small. He had been visiting some other links and
said, "The lies are so good that I think a
professional could take his driver anywhere."
That sentence is to me extraordinarily
characteristic of its time for two reasons. First
there is the looking up to the professional as a
godlike creature and, second, there is the
insistence on the quality of the lies. Nowadays

An Art Deco watercolour of 1920: Fashion and Motoring, by Noel Vargetta.

we regard a good lie as a right, but then, unless I am mistaken, we thought of it more humbly and gratefully, as a gift from heaven. I doubt if courses were very much better kept then than they had been thirty-five years before when the Dunns played Allan Robertson and Tom Morris at North Berwick, and the two sets of partisans raised loud cheers according as their champion's ball had the better lie. No doubt, too, the greens were nothing like so smooth and trim as they are nowadays, but the change has been so gradual that this is a matter of inference rather than positive recollection. On the other hand the turf

was the real seaside thing, fine and delicate, sometimes bare and sandy, whereas to-day much feeding and treating has almost wiped seaside turf off the face of the links. The exquisite thrill of getting back to it after a spell of inland mud is one which I can never hope for again.

It is essential to lay stress on that contrast, because those who have been brought up on the beautiful inland courses of to-day, the courses of sand and heather and fir trees, do not at all realise what inland golf was like in the eighties. There were a few courses with more or less light soil and more or less good turf, such as Wimbledon

Common, or on the downs such as Eastbourne, but the vast majority of inland courses were made on clay, hard as a rock in summer and unspeakably squelchy in winter. Moreover nothing like the best was made out of that most unpromising material. Courses were laid out by a few Scottish professionals, excellent men within their own limits but with small powers of thought or imagination. They had failed to grasp – probably they had never tried – what were the qualities, apart from seaside sand and turf, which went to make the merits of their own native links, and so were incapable of reproducing them even imperfectly. Their intellects could not soar beyond rectangular rampart bunkers at set intervals, and these they dotted in dismal profusion about the country. To say this to-day is, I know, to be wise after the event. I do not think that many of us who played on those courses realised how infinitely better they might have been made. We just accepted them as the only available substitutes for the real seaside thing and made the best of them.

Inland golf was in the eighties and early nineties generally odious, and so the making of the first sandy inland courses is really a great landmark in golfing history. It would be rash to assert which precisely was the first. I do know that when I went up to Cambridge in October

1894, the nine-hole course of the Royal Worlington and Newmarket Club was in full swing and was a revelation.

Then about 1901 or so came Sunningdale and every since there have grown up more and more such courses laid out by men who are genuine artists. So good are the courses now that I have even heard a distinguished professional, lacking an excuse for bad play in the Open Championship, exclaim, "I can't play on these beastly seaside courses."

Now let me turn to the great men. The English professional had not had time to come into being in the eighties. The professional was always a

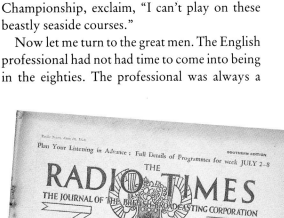

Far left, J.H. Taylor driving, in a postcard of unknown date, but probably around 1915. *Near left*, the cover of the *Radio Times* for June 30, 1933.

Tom Morris.   Mr H. H. Hilton.   Mr J. L. Low.
Famous Golfers. Valentines Series   *Amateur Championship.*

Open Championship.—J. H. Taylor driving.
Famous Golfers. Valentines Series

H.H. Hilton, Tom Morris and J.L. Low, *near right*, from the Amateur Championship of 1895; *far right*, J.H. Taylor at the Open Championship, probably of 1908.

Scot and by no means always the smart, respectable and self-respecting person that he is now. He was a feckless and reckless creature, not infrequently cursed with a taste for drink, but he was often amusing and essentially a "character". There were some very fine players – to whom these remarks do not apply – Willie Park and Willie Fernie, the Kirkaldys and Simpsons, Willie Campbell, Ben Sayers and Douglas Rolland, perhaps greatest of them all though an uncrowned king, but it seems to me, as an Englishman, that the golfer was an English amateur, Mr. John Ball, of Hoylake. He was beyond all doubt a very great, as he was a very picturesque, golfer, with a swing, to my mind at least, the most perfectly graceful ever seen, and he put England completely on the golfing map. Mr. Horace Hutchinson had done much towards it by winning the first two amateur championships. But Mr. Ball, an Englishman and an amateur beat all the Scots professionals for the Open Championship. That was in 1890. Two years later another amateur from Hoylake, Mr. Hilton, did the same thing, racing round Muirfield in his white shoes with his trail of cigarette smoke behind him, and that too was a mighty feat. But Mr. Ball had been the first and he remains still a unique figure in our golf. If the greatness of a player depends on the greatness of

his followers' devotion then I do not think there can ever be anyone like him again. To see him on a big occasion with his bodyguard of Hoylake fishermen in their blue jerseys, followed by rosetted stewards and trampling crowds was to see hero worship such as brings a lump to the throat.

Mr. Ball and his contemporaries, in their youthful prime, were famous, but they were so only among golfers who were still a comparatively small body. When in our history we reach the middle nineties we come to champions who were known, not only to a much larger band of golfers, but also to people who did not play the game. A man need not now be a cricketer to know the name of Hobbs, and in the nineties thousands who called a club a stick yet knew the awe-inspiring name of Harry Vardon.

No one else could start, as he did in 1899, so firm a favourite for an Open Championship, that the chance of any other player was hardly considered.

Everything to do with him was gaped at and talked about, the more so as he had a very distinct style of his own which is now accepted as almost ideally elegant, but was then regarded as breaking many venerable rules. He acquired an added romance from being the first professional to wear knickerbockers. Bobby Jones has

12

appealed, of course, to a much larger public, on two continents instead of in one country, but he has not produced intenser excitement than Harry Vardon did at his devastating best.

Now I must leave the champions and come back again, in my rather desultory way, to the man in the street. In 1902 a great change came over golf which affected all golfers and the humblest perhaps the most. It came too with extraordinary suddenness and swiftness. In May of that year the Amateur Championship was to be played at Hoylake and before it there was to be the first international match between England and Scotland. I had hopes of being chosen to play in it and so set out some days beforehand. At Euston Station I met a friend from Lancashire who said, "Are you going to play in this match? If you do you ought to play with a Haskell ball"; and I answered, "What is it?" When I got to Hoylake a few players had got the new American ball, but there were no more to be had. So I played in the match with a gutty and lost by one hole in thirty-six to a Scotsman armed with a Haskell. As he might well have beaten me by more in any case, I was not greatly impressed, but the ensuing Championship was won by a man of fifty-three and a grandfather at that, Mr. Charles Hutchings, and the ball he used had come to stay. Within a week everybody was

THE OPEN CHAMPIONSHIP AT MUIRFIELD, JUNE 1906.
JAMES BRAID (CHAMPION)

Above, Bobby Jones on the cover of the *Chicago Sunday Tribune*, August 26th 1928; *left*, James Braid, winner of the Open Championship at Muirfield, June 1906.

13

trying to buy Haskells at fancy prices, and one that was old, scarred and paintless was a gift fit for a king. There were a few stalwarts, who will always be honourably remembered, who foresaw that the game of golf would be robbed of some of its finer points and fought hard to have the intruder barred; but their voices were drowned in the acclamations of thousands who had never hit a ball so far in all their lives before and, for good or ill, the rubber-covered ball arrived.

It is often said that it was the new ball that gave golf its second booming and made it the world-wide game it now is. I have heard it cogently argued on the other side that its popularity was at that very moment increasing rapidly and that the new ball had very little to do with it. However that may be, there is not much doubt that the average unyouthful, unathletic and unskilful player began to get more fun out of the game than he ever had before. All things are relative and it may be that the good player got no more pleasure out of hitting the rubber core 220 yards than he had got out of hitting the gutty 170, though I am not so sure about that. The poor player got more pleasure if only because he no longer so constantly topped his tee shot into a bunker in front of his nose. Even if he did not hit the new ball very cleanly, away it soared somewhere and he watched it ecstatically against the blue sky. Moreover he gained a new sense of power and that is one of the joys of any ball game; the untamed savage in man likes to hit hard and far, for the sensual joy of doing so; he has a sense of domination which goes to his head like wine.

1902 seems a good long time ago now, but nothing like the revolution of that year has happened in all the years that have gone since. The two outstanding features of those twenty-nine years have been, I suppose, the triumph of the Americans and the tremendous development of ladies' golf. In 1903 a team of the Oxford and Cambridge Golfing Society made a memorable tour in the United States and on their return Mr. John Low, the captain, warned complacent Britain against the young American champions to come. "Already," he exclaimed prophetically, "I hear the hooting of their

A tous les âges de la vie, l'HEMOSTY

steamers in the Mersey." All the world knows now how true a prophet he was. Francis Ouimet, little more than a schoolboy, staggered us in 1913 by beating Vardon and Ray in a historic tie for the American Championship, but the real American domination began after the war, when a team of their amateurs beat the best that we could produce at Hoylake in 1921. It is true that in the Championship which followed the invaders were surprisingly beaten, but that first international match had been nevertheless the writing on the wall. The first Walker Cup match was played next year and whether in our country or theirs the Americans have always won it. Moreover in 1921 Jock Hutchison, a born Scot but a nationalised American, first won our Open Championship at St. Andrews, and from that day to this the cup has lived beyond the Atlantic

Mr. Bobby Jones is of course a game playing genius that occurs only once or twice in a century, such as W. Grace was at cricket, but he

Docteur ROUSSEL donne des forces.

is different from the other American golfers only in degree, not in kind. There will be more and more young players almost as good as he and some day, we may presume, one will arise who is quite as good as he was, though we who saw him at his zenith shall never admit it.

As to the ladies, their advance has been astonishing and here at least we can hold our own. Miss Wethered is fully as outstanding a genius as Mr. Jones, but leaving her on one side it seems to me that our lady golfers have something more of the earnest American spirit that longs, passionately for self-improvement than our men have. It may be a shameful confession, but I do not know that I want our men to have it; one must admit however it is the way to "deliver the goods." An observant friend of mine says that the mystery has departed from golf and perhaps it has; the game has become an ordinary part of daily life and everyone understands at least something of its language; a stymie is as well known as a crab or a yorker. Still it is very pleasant as it is. As an old Scottish golfer wrote in his parting benediction, "Golf, thou art a gentle sprite, We owe thee much."

A collection of golfing medals, *below left.* Top row: BGC (possibly Brighton Golf Club) monthly medal of 1892; middle row, from the left: a Masters pin, Swanston Golf Course, and Prestwick Golf Club's Edinton Medal; bottom row: DGC (possibly Deal Golf Club), founded 1891, but made in Berlin.
Below right: a Gerz whisky flask, c1910.

15

SECTION ONE

GREAT MOMENTS, GREAT COURSES

Playing in the Road * The World's Most Testing Finish
* Kings and Queens of Scotland * How John Ball Won *
The Home of Golf * Designed by Providence * Sixes
and Sevens at St. Andrews * My Caddy * The Artificial
and the Natural * The Oldest Club * The Great Divide *
A Stage for Leading Ladies * The Golfer's Blend * The
Golfer's Alphabet * A Hole in None * The 6,000ft Drive
* Playing in the Bar * A Half in One * Pilgrimage to St.
Andrews * The Prestwick Links * The Great Charge.

PLAYING IN THE ROAD
Bobby Jones on Golf, 1926

The seventeenth hole at St. Andrews is the famous Road Hole, and the most historic in golf. It was on that hole that John Henry Taylor, needing only a six and a five, I think, to win the Open Championship, played over into the road and took thirteen strokes.

Watts Gunn and I collaborated at this same hole in one of the most terrifying bits of golf I have ever seen. It was in the Walker Cup matches in 1926 and we were playing Tolley and Jamieson in the Scotch foursomes, which means that each partner plays alternate strokes on the same ball.

Watts and Jamieson were driving. The drive here is supposed to go straight over the middle of a barn, which is out of bounds. Watts just got over, while Jamieson hit the building plump in the middle, and Tolley had to play three off the tee. Cyril, made cautious by his partner's mistake, pulled his drive over in the first fairway.

It was now my turn and I played a conservative spoon shot short of, and in front of, the green. Jamieson topped the fourth for his team and Tolley, in an heroic effort to reach the green, went over into the road. That was five for our opponents and, being in the road, they would do well to go down in eight!

Watts and I looked certain to twin the hole. But nothing is ever certain on the seventeenth at S. Andrews. Watts had to play a run-up to the very narrow green between the bunker on one side and the road on the other. He shanked into the road. Now, we were in the road in three, they in five.

Jamieson played a beautiful shot up twelve feet from the hole. That looked bad for us, for our ball was lying in the hard road. The hole was only fifteen or twenty feet away; the green was dry; and the terrible bunker was just beyond the flag. Watts and I put our heads together and indulged in a little mental arithmetic. We finally decided that if I should play down toward the brook behind the green, Watts could pitch back on so that two putts would give us a seven and a half, if Tolley holed his putt. We felt that we would be thankful for anything now.

We did get our seven. Tolley rimmed the long one, and we won the hole, but not until we had used up all our shots and most of the little brains we had.

Bobby Jones, *right*, at the golf course at the Shenvalee Hotel, Virginia, in 1930.

SHENVALEE HOTEL, NEW MARKET, VIRGINIA. This beautiful hotel was just opened to the public on Sept. 1, 1930. It has 20 rooms, large dining room, locker rooms, and full equipment to supply every need of the traveler. The nine-hole golf course is a popular part of this equipment. This view shows Bobby Jones, world famous golfer, exhibiting his skill before a crowd of Valley golfers and visitors. Rates are moderate—rooms $2 and up, dinners 75c and up. For information, write Manager, Shenvalee, New Market, Va., or call 73.

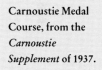

Carnoustie Medal Course, from the *Carnoustie Supplement* of 1937.

THE WORLD'S MOST TESTING FINISH
Golf, 1937

Carnoustie is commonly regarded as possessing the most difficult finish of all the courses in the world. At the last two holes, the Barry burn (which we should have found no difficulty in avoiding at the earlier holes) becomes a formidable hazard, whose serpentine meanderings leave us the minimum of space in which to place each shot.

At the 428-yard seventeenth the drive has to be 'placed' on a long, narrow island of fair turf, enclosed by a bend of the stream, and anything of the nature of a hook will take the ball into the water, while the stream has again to be carried with the second shot.

The eighteenth is even stiffer. Not only is it some twenty-five yards longer, but here the burn – which at this point attains the dimensions of a small river, twenty-five feet from bank to bank – flows right across the front of the green.

With the wind against the players, as it was during play for the last Open Championship contested there, the carry becomes a formidable undertaking even for the champions. The difficulty of the hole, moreover, is enhanced by the fact that the player dare not go 'all out' for an exceptionally long drive, in order to make the second shot easier.

The drive itself has to be placed upon an exiguous peninsula of turf, a trifle under fifty yards wide, enclosed by another of the convolutions of the ubiquitous stream, and beyond that the fairway is still hemmed-in by the boundary railing on the left.

Coming at the end of the round, when the difference between a 4 and a 5 may mean the difference between being Open Champion and merely one of the 'also rans,' it is a hole which calls for the most careful weighing of chances.

Not very long ago, I was discussing this hole with Percy Alliss, who in the last Open Championship played there was one of the most unlucky of its victims. In the fourth and last round it happened that Alliss was one of the earliest players out, and he therefore did not know what he required to do to win. But he

19

Bobby Jones
(wearing white
plus-fours), from a
print by William C
Palmer of 1939.

could hazard a shrewd guess at the figure that would be needed, and at this eighteenth hole he determined to 'go for' the 4.

In this, it may be said, events proved him entirely in the right, for a 4, as it turned out, would just have enabled him to tie with Tommy Armour for first place.

Unfortunately, Alliss' ball was not lying quite perfectly, and though his brassie shot carried the hazard all right, he had put just a trifle of 'draw' on the ball in nipping it out of a slightly heavy lie.

The ball actually landed on the green, but that bit of draw took it through the railings on the left – out of bounds.

Alliss had to drop another ball, found a perfect lie this time, and put his ball a few yards beyond the flag. But the stroke and distance penalty left him a couple of strokes behind the leader.

I was greatly pleased to find that, in spite of this bit of bad luck, Alliss was of the opinion that the hole was a perfectly fair one, giving the stronger player the chance to save a stroke by getting home to the green in two, provided he was willing to take the risk of the carry.

In practice, of course, the majority of the professionals, against the wind, were content to play short of the burn with their second, and to

rest any hope of a 4 upon getting down from there with a chip and a putt. But to the supermen, with the world to win, it gave the chance of a 'death or glory' shot that made the hole a test of tactical judgment and of nerve, as well as of skill.

In every class of golf there is a time to go out for things and a time to play safe. But although public opinion is always severest on the errors of judgment that bring players to disaster through taking risks, my experience is that a majority of championships are thrown away through players trying to play 'safe.'

The trouble about this sort of safety tactics is that it lowers the player's golfing vitality. The man who comes to the last nine holes of a championship three strokes behind the leader has all to gain, and nothing to lose, by going out for everything, and comes home in a burst of fireworks that beats the other man on the post.

Let the same player face the last four holes requiring nothing better than par at each hole to take him home, and experience has proven that the task of 'fighting against the figures' is nearly always too much for him. In an unconscious effort to 'play safe,' he tries to steer the shots, instead of playing them, with disastrous results.

It is the same, gentle reader, with duffers like you and me, in our friendly matches. With two good swipes we leave our ball fifty yards short of the green at a par 5 hole. Our opponent has made a hopeless mess of it, and the hole is already as good as ours. The poor mutt, in fact, is playing his fifth, from a long way short of the green. But let him lay the fifth, by luck or good guidance, a foot from the flag and the whole situation is changed.

It goes for nothing that we have still three strokes for the hole, and that three, from where we are, is an ample allowance. The realization that the other man is safely home, while our task is still to do, that our vague but adequate advantage is reduced to a definite number of strokes, strikes cold about our hearts, and we have to summon up all our fortitude to play the three simples shots that are needed to win the hole. The same soul-shaking effect, magnified a hundredfold, must be felt by the super-golfer, left to score two 4's to finish at Carnoustie.

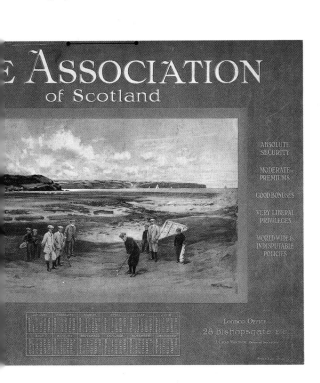

21

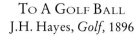

Top right, two Christmas Dunlop Golf Ball boxes, from the 1930s; *middle right*, two silver golfing trophies of the 1920s; and, *bottom right*, golf ball boxes and a tin of golf ball paint from 1920 to 1930.

TO A GOLF BALL
J.H. Hayes, *Golf,* 1896

Long ago, when first I bought you,
You were white and fairly round,
And a little gem I thought you,
Teed upon the teeing ground.

But, alas! the months have vanished,
And, if I must speak the truth,
They have altogether banished
The resemblance to your youth.

For I've "pulled" you and I've "sliced" you,
And you've lain in banks of gorse,
And I've temptingly enticed you
From the cart-ruts on the course.

So, though quite devoid of beauty,
I would claim you as a friend
Who has nobly done his duty
From beginning to the end.

and receive my thanks unsparing,
That you've heard with dumb assent,
The perhaps too-frequent swearing
Which I've used, though never meant.

22

KINGS AND QUEENS OF SCOTLAND
TRAVELLER, *The American Golfer*, 1928

There are in Great Britain to-day one thousand, seven hundred and thirty-five golf courses. More are in process of construction, of which some are on the point of completion.

Very many of these are really famous. Some for their great age and traditions – they have been playing continuously on the Royal Dornoch Links, for example, since 1609; some because of their difficulties and fearsome hazards – the rushes at Westward Ho! "the Himalayas" at Prestwick, the seventeenth on the Old Course at St. Andrews – and because many a Championship has been won and lost there; and some because of the beauties that nature has bestowed upon them.

All the famous courses have marked characteristics peculiarly their own. Many of the little known are as delightful to play over as the illustrious ones. But, in my humble judgment, no keen golfer's education is quite complete – if it ever is! – until he has played upon the King's Course and the Queen's Course at Gleneagles in Perthshire, Scotland.

This somewhat superlative statement is not made without good reason. We in the United States pay a great deal of attention and respect to the opinions of Scottish Professionals; partly because most of us have at some time or another learned the rudiments of the game at their patient hands, and also because they appreciate good golf when they see it. Therefore, one of the reasons why every golfer visiting Scotland should visit Gleneagles is because many Scotch Professionals whom I have spoken to about it have given it as their considered opinion that the King's Course represents one of the finest courses in the world.

It must be a very material, unimaginative player not to find his or her attention wandering here and there from the matter of the score in hand to the lanscape and all that it offers. A dozen larks rise throatily and sombre blue-grey mountains tower above you. Trout rise with a 'plop' in streams to your left. Purple and canary heather stretches away and away to your right.

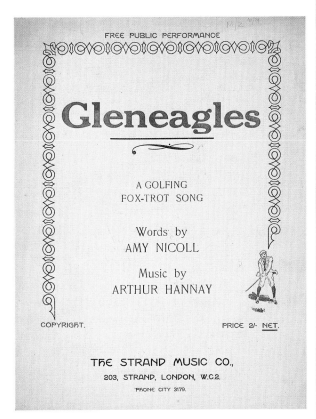

Beneath you is the billiard green grass. Beyond is the forget-me-not blue sky, with a white powder puff or cloud drifting vaguely across. And before you are fresh holes of a fascinating nature to conquer. Behind you are regal holes that, alas, have conquered you.

Never at any time during the unforgettable round are you harried by the propinquity of your fellow creatures. So planned is the place that each hole seems a thing apart. Men and women appear upon the sky line here and there, but never to your discomfiture; you scarcely notice them.

You may play a good round or a bad; bad if you are temperamental and "subject to scenery;" good if you can steel your eyes and your hand to the business of the moment, which is to do justice to these grand golfing holes, and to the card that allows you 80 of a score. You wander back to the little grey stone club house, or to the hotel itself, to the well earned lunch, thinking over some of the gems and how you handled them. Holes, for instance, like "The Whaup's

The cover of the music for *Gleneagles* – a Golfing Foxtrot, from 1923.

23

Nest," one hundred and sixty five yards only, and how you insisted on the Jigger, disbelieving the caddies who proffered the driver because of the head wind, and how woefully short you were! And "The Wee Bogle," another little fellow, the littlest, one hundred and twenty five yards only; a perfect mashie shot which must be pitched well up. You were short, and the voracious bunker swallowed it. But heavens! what a superb hole.

Then the quiet afternoon on the Queen's. Shorter, but with all the feminine subtleties. Elated by a goodish morning card you set out to vanquish her the more easily. Beware of her guile. For she has devilments of nerve-shattering nature. The "Witches' Bowster," for example, where you can – and did – slice into the loch. The "Lover's Gait," where she offered you a 4 and you squandered a scuffling 6 upon her. The "Needle E'e" ... The "Heather Bell;" they were all as pleasing as their names imply. What a day; what golf; what an evening and a night to come!

Yes, because the sun is now upon its golden journey down towards the sage green and ebony-black of the great hills. Pompous enough they seemed by day; very regal and dignified and sad have they now become. *The Nunc Dimittis* of the day is at hand. Fling wide your bedroom window and gaze upon its pageantry, the like of which you have never seen.

No matter what manner of man or woman you are, you will, and must, be impressed beyond mere speech. The whole barbaric splendour of Scotland appears to be spread before you. Fifty miles of her fair country is presented to your gaze. Mysterious mountain, wandering moorland, gingling burn. And brooding over all that peace of evening, everything is very still. The world seems to have stopped. Colour merges into colour. Here great stains of olive-green gorse; there orange and purple splashes of heather; an infinity of greys, umbers and duns, with the black knife-edge of the mountains cutting into the rose-pink and silver of the skies.

And then there is the faint tinkle of a plate from some remote nether region, recalling you to the mundane matter of food, preceded by the delicious ritual of the "after exercise" bath and the settling into the cool dress shirt. The cocktail in the American Bar, an interesting place where one is prone to linger. Dinner: a dance or two; complete contentment.

It is supposed, and in most cases very readily – but I cannot help thinking, and indeed I have heard widely travelled Americans say – that there is little further one can go on the road to "100% efficiency" than the appointments and administration of this gargantuan railway Golf hotel resort. It is certainly an example to all Europe. Sumptuous is a fitting term for its appearance, and its achievement. There's a prevailing note of cheerfulness, and a quiet undercurrent of perfect service.

Further, you will get something else as well; something peculiarly your own, which cannot be imitated or surpassed. You will get, in the pearly, early morning, at the height of blazing mid-day, at sunset, and under the benediction of pale moons that wonderful and ever changing picture of Scottish scenery at its best; than which there is surely nothing more impressive?

HOW JOHN BALL WON
The American Cricketer, 1912

The final was not the first meeting of Ball and Mitchell, for the veteran had severely beaten the Cantelupe player at Hoylake in 1910. The morning was misty and oppressive and the afternoon round was played in a down-pour. At the end of the morning Mr. Mitchell enjoyed a

A railway poster, 4ft high, advertising golf in Tunis, from the early 1930s.

25

lead of three holes, but Mr. Ball, playing with great determination, reduced it to one at the turn in the afternoon. The tenth witnessed a remarkable recovery on the part of Mr. Mitchell. Mis-hitting his tee shot, because of a slipping grip, he landed in thick rushes, but a mighty niblick saved him, for he landed his next hole high and then holed a long and treacherous putt for a half in 4.

At the eleventh crisis of the match occurred. Mr. Ball pulled into the rushes and had to lift and drop. He made a magnificent recovery and got a hard half in 5, his opponent, after reaching the green in his second, failing to get down in 2. The unexpected saving of this hole was a godsend for Mr. Ball; had Mr. Mitchell secured this hole it would have made a tremendous difference.

Mr. Ball gained the lead at the fourteenth for the first time in the match but he lost his advantage on the next, the 33rd of the match, by laying himself a stymie.

The next hole, the 16th, provided the sensational shot of the match which merits particular record. Both players found the right-hand pot from the tee. Mr. Ball playing the odd got well out beyond the far edge of the

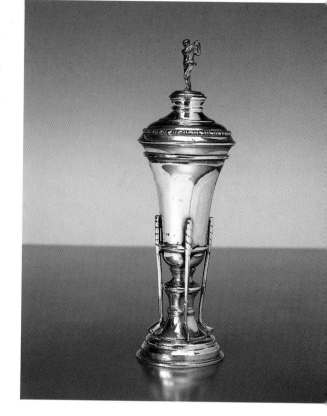

An English golfing trophy in silver, *above right*, 5in high, from 1919.
The cover of Colliers magazine, *near right*, for August 18, 1934.

green, Mr. Mitchell getting out even better, only being a few yards past the hole. Mr. Ball then ran his ball within 2 feet of the hole. Mitchell made a fine putt, the ball stopping on the tip of the hole and actually overhanging it, an apparently dead stymie. For Mr. Ball to hole his putt seemed absolutely impossible. He examined the position most carefully and seemed to consider it comical, for a broad smile lit up his face. Finally Mr. Ball decided to use his ordinary aluminium putter. He had noted the lie of the land and perceived the possibility of the favorable fall of the ground giving him a 1000 to 1 against chance of bringing off the coup. To the amazement of the crowd, he managed, like a wizard, to pull his ball past Mr. Mitchell's without touching it and get it down. The most infinitesimal graze must have sent Mr. Mitchell's ball right into the hole. It was a master stroke.

The 17th found Mr. Ball in difficulties with his 2nd, which he failed to get up enough to clear the bunker, and, although he made a gallant effort, Mr. Mitchell gave him no chance of recovery, for he got a faultless 5 and thus became dormy one.

When the tee shots and seconds had been played, both duellists being on the green, and

26

A lady golfer, *far left*, sculpted in silver in about 1908, hallmarked, by Hal Ludlow, accompanied by a silver tankard; *near right*, a biscuit barrel hand-painted with a golfing theme.

after they had run their long putts up within a few feet of the hole, the Championship of 1912 seemed safely in the keeping of Mr. Mitchell. Evidently the fairy that presides over Mr. Ball's career at golf decided otherwise and determined as a reward for his 16th hole achievement to give him another chance. Mr. Mitchell had a putt of about 4 feet to execute in order to become Champion. Mr. Ball lay 3 feet off and must have needed nerves of iron to watch his adversary addressing his putt and preparing to send it securely to the bottom of the hole. He may have had a glimmer of hope, owing to the many putts of that length which Mr. Mitchell had missed and owing to the curly nature of the putt. Conversely, Mr. Mitchell's feelings may be imagined. No doubt he was trembling with the apprehension of making one more faux pas.

A roar of mingled surpise, disappointment, and relief went up when it was realized that he had missed the putt, and when Mr. Ball had sent his safely down the crowd rushed helter skelter up the course of the 1st hole. It was some time before the course could be cleared for the continuation of the match. At the 37th hole both slightly pulled their tee shots but lay clear. Mr.

Ball pushed his 2nd into the right-hand guarding bunker where he lay well and in the middle. Mr. Mitchell tried to reach the green, but got a slight pull on and found dreadful trouble in the watery ditch behind the bunker to the left of the green, whence it looked impossible for even his mighty wrists to get the ball out. When Mr. Ball got his ball beautifully out to the green the match seemed over. But Mr. Mitchell by a superhuman effort dunched his ball almost on to the green and almost holing the next got a hard half in 5.

The end came at the 38th, where Mr. Ball got away a perfect tee shot, while Mr. Mitchell topped his and got behind the bank not far from the tee. He got his next over, and then in endeavoring to recover lost ground gave a mighty pull, and found another horrible ditch. Mr. Ball seeing the prize, for which he had fought such a bitter and exhausting fight, in his grasp, clinched matters by sending a lovely 2nd to the foot of the green. Mr. Mitchell made an effort, like a man, to get out of his trouble, but when he saw that the ball was not coming out, he caught it as it was falling back, in sign of surrender to his great antagonist.

Miss D. Campbell, *near right*, driving from the first tee during the Ladies Open Championship at St. Andrews in 1908; and, *far right*, the clubhouse and 18th green at St. Andrews in 1905.

THE HOME OF GOLF
R. Barclay, *Batch of Golfing Papers*

In a book about Golf no apology is required for introducing some remarks upon St.Andrews. Golf without St. Andrews would be almost as intolerable as St. Andrews without Golf. For here are the head-quarters of the 'royal, ancient, irritating sport.' Here Tom Morris holds his court, his courtier, the clubmen and the caddies; his throne, the evergreen links; and his sceptre, a venerable putter. Here the children make their entrance into the world, not with silver spoons in their mouths, but with diminutive golf-clubs in their hands. Here the Champion is as much a hero as the greatest general who ever returned in triumph from the wars. Here, in short, is an asylum for golfing maniacs and the happy hunting-ground of the duffer, who, armed with a rusty cleek, sallies forth to mutilate the harmless turf.

Here, there, and everywhere Golf is spreading: almost every day we hear of Tom Morris opening a new green and declaring it (with a faithless regularity) to be 'the finest green in the country' – though he will occasionally modify the statement to this extent, that it is 'second only to St. Andrews.'

There are links which are sporting, and links which are long: links which have good putting greens, and links which have none at all: links which have no hazards, and links which are all hazard: but place any of them beside St. Andrews, and – oh, the difference! In short, St. Andrews is the home and nursery of Golf.

In St. Andrews are the hopes of the golfer fixed. The very air seems to be impregnated with the spirit of the game. At the tee with the brave old towers behind, the rolling waters of the Bay to the right, and in front the mounds, and hillocks, and levels of the links, one feels that he has reached the end of his pilgrimage to the Shrine of Golf. A new glamour is thrown about

the game: the Golfer's "spirit leaps within him to be gone before him then": he may foozle on the green under the critical eye of a by-standing professional, but "his heart's his own, his will is free." And standing at the end hole with his round half accomplished, he can survey the towers of the ruined Cathedral and the ragged masonry of the Castle, and the grey old city itself with the feelings of one who has found life worth living and Golf a game for men.

Designed By Providence
Bernard Darwin, *Club Brochure*, 1935

Far away in the early sixties General Moncrieffe from St. Andrews came to stay with Mr. Gosset, the Vicar of Northam. He was taken out for a walk, as Mr. Hutchinson tells us, "across that stretch of low-lying common ground known as Northam, or Appledore Burrows, to the famous Pebble Ridge and the shores of Bideford Bay." And when he came to the region of noble sandhills he broke forth in the historic words above quoted.

Those words must have been echoed by thousands of golfers since then, for, though the course is now very different from what it was in 1864 when the Royal North Devon Club was founded, it still appears as if it had been laid out wholly by the hand of nature. It is one of the merits of Westward Ho! that it is not only beyond all cavil one of the great golf courses of the world but that it looks the part so superbly. There is no finer view of golfing ground anywhere than that which bursts upon us as we stand on the fourth tee confronting the carry over the biggest bunker in the world. Away in front of us there stretches a tangle of sandhills

and broken, undulating ground and the fearful, spiky rushes that belong to nowhere else. And what beautiful turf!

There is so much turf that we can walk on it practically the whole way from the little town of Westward Ho! to the club house, banging a ball before us as we go. Some years since, when there was a big professional tournament at Westward Ho! a distinguished player remarked that he could not see, as he played his approach shot, which was fairway and which was putting green. He meant it as a criticism: he wanted to see a putting green quite clearly marked. But to me he seems to have been praising one of the great charms of the place. The turf is so fine and the links so natural that the fairway does melt imperceptibly into the putting green. Of course there are features there which are artificial, as there must be on any course. There are bunkers that have been cut by the hand of man, especially in places where the forests of rushes have been somewhat diminished. Nay, there are even

plateaux that have been if not built up, at any rate improved upon by art. The art being mainly that of Mr. Herbert Fowler, and his designs having been skilfully carried out they look entirely "designed by Providence."

Westward Ho! is essentially "big" golf. When the tees were put very far back for the Daily Mail Tournament in 1920 it was very big indeed and Duncan's score of 291 for four rounds, but three over an average of four, will remain one of the standing wonders of the golfing world. But though long hitting is of immense value there, the course does not, I think, overpower the moderate driver. There are not crushing or impossible carries from the tees. He will get just as much fun – possibly more – in getting his fives, as will the more slashing and ambitious in going for fours and taking perhaps sixes. Moreover he will probably have the enjoyment of hitting what is for him a long way. There is every encouragement to good driving. The turf, for one thing, supplies the good lies for it, and then

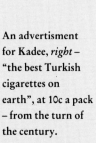

30

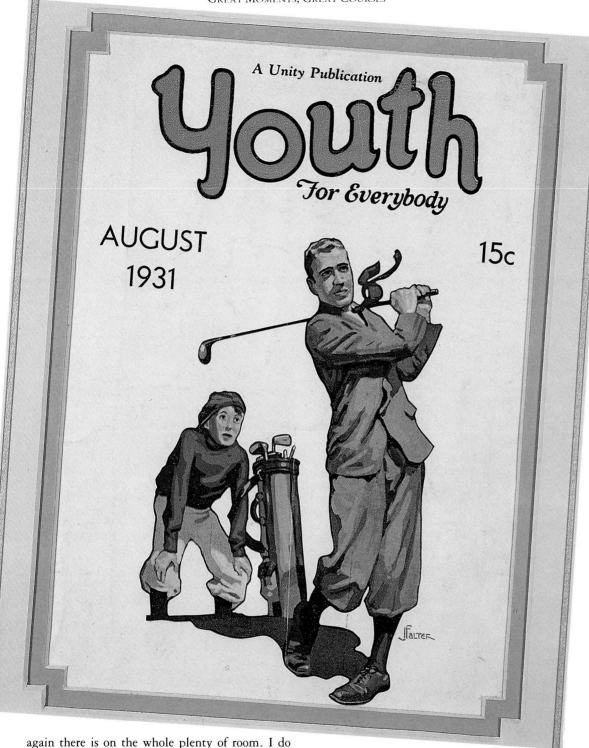

The cover of *Youth Magazine*, for August, 1931.

again there is on the whole plenty of room. I do not mean that he can drive where he likes, but save now and then, when the rushes come formidably crowding in on him, he need never feel cramped and frightened; he can open his shoulders with a reasonably light heart.

Again, he will have plenty of variety. He certainly cannot complain of a mere sameness of slogging. There is a flat land near the club house, there is the hilly land further out; there are the holes that have rushes and those that have not; there are plateau greens — more than there used to be — comparatively flat and open greens and a green or two lying in hollows such as the 4th; there is perhaps the best short hole in the world, the 16th, and certainly one other very attractive one the 5th; finally there is a burn, without

which no course appears quite complete, and as is right and proper, it guards the home green and terrifies the uncertain pitcher who is all square with one to play. Here altogether is a rich and varied feast of strokes and there is nearly sure to be a wind to make them more varied still, sometimes almost painfully so.

Westward Ho! has what is, I think, almost a virtue: certainly it is not a vice; it begins slowly and breaks us in gradually. We do not come to the golf in all its fullness till we have warmed to our work and swung off our early morning stiffness. Thus the first two holes lie on the comparatively flat and marshy ground. They are far from being dull holes: they are of a fine length and there is plenty of trouble, but there are no hills and no spiky rushes to speak of. We begin by driving over the burn with a ditch on our right to catch a sliced shot. There are also bunkers to right and left as there are in front of the green. Indeed the opening is a fairly narrow one and two very long straight shots are wanted if we are to begin with a four. The second is likewise a good two shot hole, with no very outstanding character, yet all the character it has is sound.

So far we have been driving straight ahead of us at the Pebble Ridge, a great barrier of stone that hides the waters of Bideford Bay from us, and also, which is more important, prevents them from pouring over the links. When we get near the Ridge we turn sharp to the right to play the third hole, yet another fine "two-shotter" with a narrow way in to the green beleaguered by various bunkers. By this time we are getting into the supremely golfing country and have left the flatness behind us. At the fourth we face a colossal bunker, with a black-boarded edge. The carry at the widest part must be a full 170 yards, but there is a merciful little promontory or cape of turf that comes jutting in at one point and makes the carry shorter for weaker brethren. With a gutty ball this was a mercy indeed, and there were worse fates than to hit the black boards and bound back on to the turf at the bottom; but now, with the rubber cored ball the terror of this bunker is more apparent than real. If we hit a respectable shot we shall sail over it and enjoy at the same time the sensation of having done something rather splendid. Once

The *Almanach des Postes des Telegraphes*, for 1923, *above right*; *below right*, a selection of golfing board games from 1900 to the 1930s.

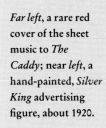

& DES TÉLÉGRAPHES

over, a good firm straight iron shot takes us on to a pretty green in something of a hollow, and we may hope to break into fours after taking, very likely, three fives for the first three holes.

At the fifth we should have a three, for it is a short hole. It is, however, also a very difficult one. We turn partially back and play up into the sandhill country. The green is long and narrow, surrounded by sand, but it has this compensation that it slopes upward and, the ball, if hit clean, may also be hit with reasonable boldness. After this we have two glorious tee shots to play at the sixth and seventh – real seaside golfing shots if

Silver King Golf Balls

Far left, a rare red cover of the sheet music to *The Caddy*; near *left*, a hand-painted, *Silver King* advertising figure, about 1920.

33

ever there were any – both struck from high places into a stretch of undulating country, where are bent grass and sand and all the best sorts of trouble. In each case, the green used to be low lying and not very interesting, but now there are, instead, two plateau greens. At the sixth the second will need the very finest shot we can hit; at the seventh it will be a dexterous pitch and in either case the hole is a little dog-legged and we turn rather to the left for the second shot.

The eighth may hearten us up and improve our score with another three. It is a comparatively long short hole if the tee is far back, well guarded by bunkers on the left hand side, and then comes a really grand hole; the ninth. Here is a noble opportunity for shoulder-opening from the tee; there is plenty of room and yet it is really most important to be straight, for bang in front of the hole, which is perched on a plateau, there is a bunker. If we drive to the correct spot, something to the right, we may then play a second with just a little hook, and the ball will climb the bank and come curling round the bunker, run down the green and lie, perhaps, dead. It is a beautiful dream and a beautiful hole,

Austrian "Schwarzburg" pottery with a golfing theme, *near right*, **dating from around 1915.**

A silk picture of a lady golfer, *above left*, dating from 1910; *below left*, the cover of *Motor Magazine* for July, 1927.

and the cold, prosaic truth is that we shall probably take five to it.

After the turn we are in the country of rushes. There is a perfect sea of them, five feet high or so, as thick — with a little poetic license — as the shaft of a club and desperately barbed at their tips. We have to drive over them now at one of the very best of dog-legged holes. If we cut off a very big chunk of them with a little draw on the shot, we may pitch comfortably home on to a narrow gully of a green guarded by a cross bunker. If we are more cautious, so much longer and more difficult is our second. If we are too cautious and drive too far to the right we shall be trapped, and it will serve us right.

There are more rushes at the eleventh and twelfth; on both sides of us at the eleventh, and to our left at the twelfth. This twelfth takes us far away into the flat country, which is by comparison uninteresting. We are still on it when we turn back in our tracks to play the thirteenth and fourteenth — the one a long hole, the other a short. Both have bunkers clustering round the green, and the plateau at the thirteenth has been trimmed and sloped off with remarkable skill and judgment. Good holes all these four, but without quite the real Westward Ho! thrill. That thrill we get in full measure at the fifteenth and sixteenth. At the fifteenth there is an alarming hedge of furze to frighten us from the tee, and a fine high iron shot over a bunker is wanted to put us on the green. The sixteenth I regard as the most agitating of all short holes, even taking into account the high hole coming in at St. Andrews. There are bunkers all round, and the green is a little "cocked up." You may think you have played a shot that is good enough, but behold there was just a little hook or cut on it. Away breaks the ball and runs gently but quite firmly down a little slope and there it is in the bunker after all.

After that hole, the seventeenth for all its length, its big bunker to carry for the second and its well guarded green, seems almost easy and yet it is a good hole and in the right place, just at the crisis of match. The eighteenth is also the right hole in the right place, just as are the last holes at Hoylake and Muirfield. There is the burn in front of the green, an inevitable hazard: you

An early publicity photograph, *right*, for the Holy Island Links, produced by the London and North Eastern Railway Company in around 1900.

cannot play round and must go for it, even though you do so by instalments. You may play sufficiently short with your second and then pop the ball in with the mashie. Let us rather hope, however, that you carry boldly home in two and get your four. If you have done anything near eighty you may be thoroughly pleased with youself unless you are a very eminent person indeed.

Perhaps I may add that, though the Royal North Devon Golf Club is of such distinguished antiquity, and its course is a championship one, the visitor need not be in the very least frightened of it. The Club is always glad to see visitors, and every effort is made to get a match for anybody who has not got one. In short Westward Ho! welcomes the stranger within its gates and there are no pleasanter gates within which to be.

SIXIES AND SEVENS AT ST. ANDREWS
Bernard Darwin, *The American Golfer*, 1934

The other day I chanced to mention in an article the great foursome played over three greens in 1849 – Allan Robertson and Tom Morris against the two Dunns. This brought me a letter from a gentleman at St. Andrews who is hard on ninety years old. In looking through some family papers he had found a letter from an uncle of his written to a brother in India giving the scores of the match at St. Andrews. He kindly sent me a copy of it and it thrilled me to the marrow. Even to my readers who do not know St. Andrews – and most of course do not – I think the scores will be illuminating and so I set them down:

First round
Allan and Tom
Out – 6 5 6 5 5 5 5 4 4 – 45
Home – 6 4 5 5 7 7 4 6 6 – 50
    95
The Dunns
Out – 6 5 4 6 6 6 4 4 5 – 46
Home – 5 3 5 6 5 5 5 6 6 – 46
    92
Second round
Allan and Tom – Out – 5 5 7 5 6 4 6 3 5 – 46
    Home – 3 4 5 5 6 6 5
The Dunns – Out – 6 6 5 5 8 5 4 4 4 – 47
    Home – 4 4 4 5 8 5 5

Allan and Tom won by three up and two to play.

For those who do not know the course I may just add that the two short holes are the eighth and eleventh and the two long ones the fifth and fourteenth, that the par of the course today is 72 and that the only hole played by either side which today would be deemed under par is the three which Allan and Tom did at the tenth.

Bear in mind that here were the four unquestionably great players of the day and they were taking well over ninety to get round a course which as regards the position of the greens was much what it is today, from shorter tees. Yet what an utterly different course, infinitely narrower with gorse creeping right in on the player in places which are now perfect fairway, with all manner of bad lies, with greens which were known for their different bad qualities – one for its roughness, the next for its sandiness, the one often for its heather roots all over it. The holes were probably too big, unless indeed, they were freshly cut for the match, since in those days there were no tins and the holes grew bigger as hand after hand dived into them for a pinch of sand to tee the balls. That big hole was the only conceivable average those old heroes had and they had to get a feather ball into

it and not a very round one. The gutty had just come in at the time of the match, but it is certain that Allan Robertson would not have played with it, for it was on this rock that Allan and Tom split a few months after.

I can sit and pore over that score and try to imagine how it was done – how in the name of goodness did they halve the last hole in six? At that hole, once the burn right in front of the tee is crossed, there is nothing in the way. A drive and a pitch and run is all that is wanted. Mighty hitters have driven the green with a wind behind and ordinary mortals can get into the hollow short of it. How did those champions take six? I suppose there was a strong wind against them in which case they could not nearly get home in two. Perhaps they needed three full shots; perhaps they took three putts apiece. I wish I could see it.

As to the two eights that the Dunns took at the two long holes no doubt the gorse had something to say to that and I am sure there must have been a fierce wind for it is to be remembered that Allan once holed St. Andrews in 79 and that is a very different thing from 92, isn't it? The fives doubtless represented good play, for, with a gutty, most of the St. Andrews holes needed two wooden club shots, and with a heathery they must have needed two and a bit. It is all terribly difficult to imagine.

An O'Hara Dale stein, with an Indian on its lid, made in Waltham, Massachusetts in about 1900.

Golf must have been an exciting game to watch with the best of players taking sixes and sevens. There must, as I fancy it, have been so much more hope for the man who was playing the one off two; the other fellow might always get a really bad lie or a series of them. That is what we must always remember – the character of the lies for indeed even I can remember the time when one remarked "I've got a good lie", where today one only comments on a bad lie.

The cover for the sheet music of "The Caddy", right, published in America in 1900.

My Caddy
Maurice Noel, *Golf*, 1891

Who daily comes to meet my trap,
And – touching jerkily his cap –
Seizes umbrella, clubs, and wrap?
    My Caddy.

Who makes a little sandy tee,
And, down upon his bended knee,
Adjusts the Golf-ball carefully?
    My Caddy.

Who, if I make a decent hit,
Is sure to let me hear of it?
Who flatters me a little bit?
    My Caddy.

Who, when the balls erratic fly,
Can always an excuse supply,
"The Stance was bad," or else "the lie"?
    My Caddy.

Who, if to pieces I should fall
And top, and pull and slice the ball,
Knows better than to talk at all?
    My Caddy.

Who, when from hazard blind and bad,
He telegraphs the signal glad –
"All clear," becomes "a clever lad"?
    My Caddy.

But who, if it should come to pass
The ball is lost in whins or grass,
Too frequently becomes "an ass."
    My Caddy.

DURING A STRIKE OF CADDIES.

Who, if I suffer from "a rub,"
Or badly lie in sand or scrub,
Had *better* hand the proper club?
    My Caddy.

Who, when I'm down a hole or two,
Has sometimes all that he can do
A weary task to worry through?
    My Caddy.

Who, though I hurry through the green,
Should ever at my heels be seen,
Attentive, tireless, and keen?
    My Caddy.

Who, when the foe walks proudly in,
Is heard to swear through thick and thin
That luck alone has let him win?
    My Caddy.

Who, ever anxious to defend
My interests from end to end,
Ought to be treated as a friend?
    My Caddy.

A music cover for Millie – The Caddie's Song, *left*, published in America in 1901; *below*, a British caddie figure in lead from the 1930s.

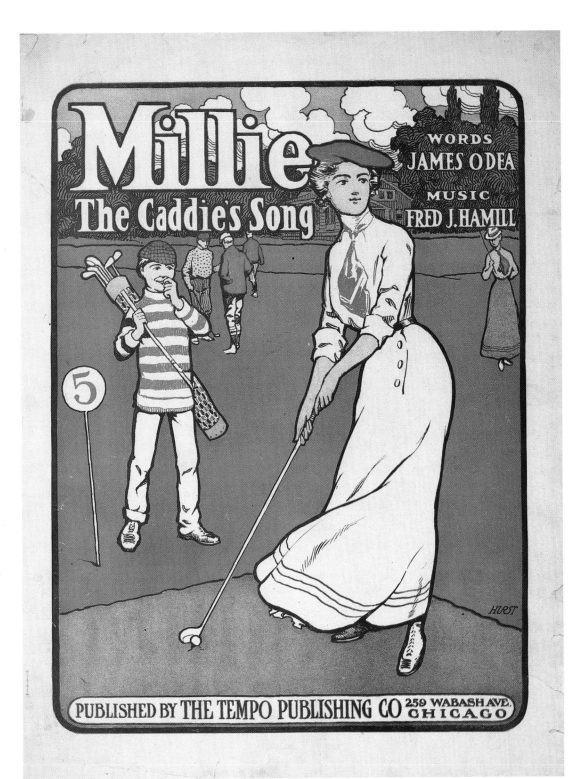

THE ARTIFICAL AND THE NATURAL
Bobby Jones on Golf, 1926

The difference between the golf courses of America and of Great Britain can best be expressed by the two words "artificial" and "natural"; and that means a whole lot more than the mere presence or absence of the fabrication of man. The difference begins at the front of the tee and extends to the very back edges of the green, and it is a difference which a player cannot conquer by mechanical proficiency alone. To combat it requires judgment, experience, and, as O.B. Keeler would express it, "something between the ears."

To begin with, let us play a round upon the average first-class American course. American architecture allows practically no option as to where the drive shall go. To the expert, there is always the evident desirability of placing the ball on one side or the other of the fairway, but, as a

rule, he is much more concerned with avoiding bunkers and long grass along the sides. There is only one safe place for the ball, and it must be put there. The shot is prescribed by the design of the hole – it must be in exactly a certain direction, and, usually, as long as possible.

Suppose, then, that we have made a good drive and our ball is lying nicely in the fairway. From this situation, one of two shots is required – either a long wallop with a brassie with the hope of getting close to the green, or an iron or pitch shot designed to reach the green itself. The brassie shot, being simply an occasion for the application of a strong back, may be dismissed.

The iron shot, like the drive, leaves the player little choice. The green is usually well defined and sloped up toward the rear. Further, it is almost always well-watered, so that any shot with fair height will not go over if it pitches onto the green. The problem is to hit the green, and if that is done, it matters little what spin the ball may have. The soggy green takes the place of the perfect stroke.

Now, let me ask what manner of golfer will be developed by courses of this nature? The answer is – a mechanical shot producer with little initiative and less judgment, and ability only to play the shot as prescribed.

Take this man and put him down for the first time on a British seaside links, and watch the result! There the fairways are wide, and the greens are watered only from the skies. The greens are quite unartificial, usually flat or even sloping away from the shot. Bunkers do not surround the green defining the target. In a word, there is no prescription. It is left entirely to the judgment and conscience of the player as to what route he will choose. If the greens are soft, the flag still offers a target, and our shot-making machine will not fare badly. But let there be dry weather for the real show!

I came to like this seaside golf just as any lover of the game must come to like anything which adds zest to the play. Variable conditions afford ample opportunity for the display of any strategic talent we may possess, and preserve in the most human of games that fascinating personal element which is its chief attraction.

Right, a Californian advertising postcard of the 1930s.

GOLF ALONG CALIFORNIA'S COAST
Where out-door sport reigns all the year 'round.
Reached via Southern Pacific.

PETERHEAD

TWO 18-HOLE GOLF COURSES
Illustrated Guide from Town Clerk, Peterhead, or any
L·N·E·R Enquiry Office

A large railway
poster, 5ft high, *left*,
from the LNER in
about 1930,
advertising golf at
Peterhead.

A paperweight produced by Hawtree & JH Taylor, golf architects, *below right*, in the 1930s, with a mother-of-pearl golf scorer of 1910.

On an American course we play – indeed, we are forced to play – one stroke at a time. If we played the same hole twice a day for months, we should always be striving to play it in the same manner, usually straight away from tee to cup. We should never change tactics because of wind, rain or dry ground. We should rarely have a choice, or an opportunity to think. Now, British seaside golf cannot be played without thinking. There is always some little favor of wind or terrain waiting for the man who has judgment enough to use it, and there is a little feeling of triumph, a thrill that comes with the knowledge of having done a thing well when a puzzling hole has been conquered by something more than mechanical skill.

And let me say again that our American courses do not require, or foster, that type of golfing skill. Our men have to learn it in England or Scotland, and that is the big reason they cannot play there without experience.

THE OLDEST CLUB
Bernard Darwin, *Club Brochure*, 1933

The Royal Blackheath Golf Club is, as all the world knows, the oldest golf club in the world.

It would be superfluous for me to enlarge on the historic glories of the club. The tradition – and who would dare to doubt it – that James I

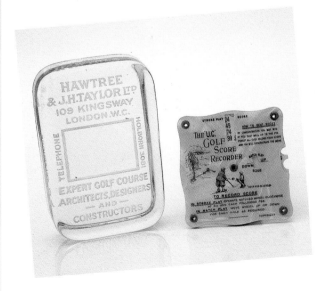

and his Scottish Courtiers played on the heath, the certain fact that the Silver Club was presented by Mr. Henry Foot in 1766, the dinner that the golfers eat at the Chocolate House and the Green Man, the epaulettes that decorated the Captain-General, the fine turtles and the haunches of venison, the marriage noggins and the rest – are not these and many other delightful things written in Mr. W.E. Hughes's delightful book, *"Chronicles of Blackheath Golfers"*?

From the actual heath itself the glory has now departed. Roads, lamp-posts, pedestrians, herds of football-playing boys, the ever-increasing outward thrust of London have conspired together to make golf impossible, and the classic seven holes, one of them the longest in the world, are cut no longer by the Club hole cutter on that dear, barren flinty expanse. But the glory of the club itself survives.

longer and, in addition, the bunkers have taken on a far better and more modern shape and guard the greens much more closely than they did.

We begin with a cheering drive rather down hill which should get us well on our way, but it is not a particularly easy shot, for there are bunkers in the offing and rough grass both to right and left as, generally speaking, there is at all the holes on the course. It is a good long hole – 450 yards – and wants two good long shots, so that a five will not be seriously amiss and a four will be very satisfactory, a remark which applies to both the next two holes. The second strikes me as a really excellent two-shotter. We turn back towards the club house and go slightly up hill this time. The tee shot must be laid down between two sentinel bunkers, and the second shot must not be sliced. The third hole takes us away from the club house (these three holes are the only ones that have a suspicion of the old parallel character), and if it possesses no particularly dramatic qualities, it is sound, of a good length, and wants playing.

The fourth is a one-shot hole of 200 yards which calls for real accuracy at such a range, for the bunkers crowd in round the green very menacingly, and then we come to an entirely new hole of Braid's, which shows him in a most skilful and merciless mood. The length is that of a

It is "park golf," but not in any excessive sense; that is to say, the trees do not unduly obtrude themselves, they stand there as sentinels, but they do not interfere with the golfer unless he makes a very crooked shot, and, which is equally important, they do not stifle him on a warm summer's day. At the same time, the course has the merits of park golf in the shape of old, seasoned turf which produces excellent lies and the smoothest, truest, and best of putting greens. The ground is in parts perhaps a trifle flat, but the holes are good sound holes of a good length, repaying sound golf.

Moreover, the course has lately been very much improved since James Braid was called in to remodel it. It was a fair criticism in earlier days that the holes ran on too definitely parallel lines. The player had a sensation of "about turn" and so over the old ground again. That exists no

A selection of golfing pamphlets from around the world, *above left*; and an American cobalt blue vase with silver overlay, *below left*, accompanied by a glass decanter with silver overlay: both of the 1920s.

43

drive and an iron, but what a frightening drive: On the right is the railway line – out of bounds; that would not matter so much if there was plenty of room to pull far to the left in a cowardly manner, but then there is not. There is remarkably little room, because on the left is a solid line of remarkably solid trees. To hit the ball straight down the middle provides the maximum of self-satisfaction. The sixth is a long hole of 475 yards with a tee shot between the trees, standing like goal-posts on either side of a not too wide fairway, and the seventh is a good drive-and-iron hole with a charming wooded background. Drive well to the left and all should go well; slice, and all will go ill.

We now walk through a belt of trees, and if we have been hitherto a little confused between the old and new holes, this strip of ground remains an old familiar friend. The eighth is a short hole of 162 yards, not of an alarming appearance by having bunkers on either side of the green, so that when the ground is hard and slippery the shot can be a ticklish one. The ninth wants a good drive and iron to something of a plateau green near the club house. It is quite a good hole in itself and, coming where it does, has the advantage of dividing the course into two loops of nine holes apiece with alternative starting places. The tenth (350 yards) is just a little shorter and possesses a hazard to be carried for the second in the shape of an innocent-looking pond which annually engulfs the balls of many players,

who cannot imagine why they should be frightened of it.

A short walk past the end of the belt of trees takes us to the eleventh tee. There is something attractive about this hole for the green lies tucked away in a pretty corner, and if the approach shot is to be easy, the drive must be laid down with some nicety to the right. Twelfth is another one-shot hole; so you see you will get a fair number of threes if you play your iron properly. The green is not far from the seventh, and there is a well-placed oak tree to catch you if you slice; there is also a young plantation (one of several in various parts of the course) and heavy rough to catch you if you hook.

You had better get your three here for you will now be kept very hard at work for some time in trying to get fours. You will not get one at the thirteenth, for this is a really long one of 507

44

yards. After avoiding a pond in front of your nose you must drive straight between two bunkers, then play your second straight and then pitch or run-up straight between two more bunkers. You may get your four at the fourteenth, for it is only 360 yards long, but the green has a narrow entrance. So has the green at the fifteenth (350 yards), and this hole has an entertaining or, as you may find it, an alarming tee shot over a grassy mountain with bunkers on the slopes of it. As a *surcease* after such hard hitting there now comes an engaging mashie-shot hole with another pleasant background in the form of a lake. There is no fear of going into the lake, but this hole is not such a very simple three, as the ball must be pitched high over cross-bunkers and made to stop quickly.

After that we turn our noses finally towards home. The seventeenth is a hole that everyone remembers because of the tall, grassy rampart that guards the green. I remember that in ancient days with a gutty ball it was a cause of justifiable pride to carry home in two. To-day the task is less formidable, but the hole is over 400 yards in length and the rampart is still there with the flag fluttering beyond it: we must play a good long shot, and, if we have a promising medal score, we shall be glad to be safely over. If we have that good medal score we shall certainly play the last hole on the instalment system, a safe drive out to the right and a pitch home over the dyke to the green right in front of the club house windows. If, on the other hand, we are in a dashing or despairing mood we may go straight for the hole over the top of a pollarded tree, skirting all manner of horrors on the left. The hole measures 290 yards, and if – it is rather a big if – we can carry right home there are few more satisfying shots. It is a shot to send one in to lunch with a real appetite.

THE GREAT DIVIDE
Bobby Jones on Golf, 1926

The British play golf as and when the spirit moves them; the Americans golf in the light of greater study and with higher ideals of golfing possibilities. If success is founded on the winning of team matches or championships our system is infinitely better. To the best of the British golfers, a possibility remains too often just that; to the best American players the possibility is carefully studied until it takes the form of a probability.

Another reason why American golf is sounder and productive of a high class, ever-increasing army of players is our courses. We spend so much money on them; we trap them so profusely; we make greens of such enormous size and the entrances so narrow that it is not essential to rely on Nature's breezes, as is done so frequently abroad. On a check-up just finished, of a dozen courses near Edinburgh and a dozen close to New York, I find the American layouts to have an average of twenty more traps, and to be three hundred yards longer. All our new golf courses have length, they are wickedly trapped, and the greens are usually large and undulating. The good players and all professionals have their games immeasurably helped by these circumstances.

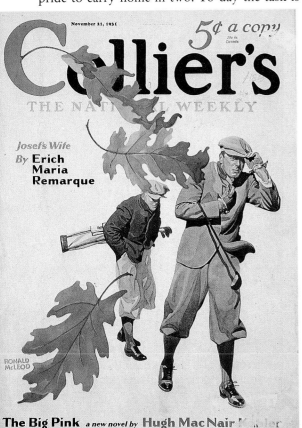

The cover of *Colliers* magazine, *left* for November 1931.

The cover of the *Saturday Evening Post Magazine*, *above right*, for July 8, 1916; *below right*, the cover of the sheet music for "The Wannamoisett Waltz", published in America in 1915.

A STAGE FOR LEADING LADIES
Bernard Darwin, *Green Memories*, 1928

I must call a halt somewhere, but there is one more match that must be mentioned, a match not between men but between ladies, the final of the Ladies' Championship at Troon in 1925 between Miss Joyce Wethered and Miss Cecil Leitch. It contained every possible dramatic element except the international one. It was perhaps as well that this was absent. As it was the crowd was so great and so much excited that the player had scarcely finished her stroke when she was swallowed up in a hot seething mass of humanity.

From the very beginning of the Championship this match had been anticipated. Miss Leitch had been for a long time the undisputed queen of golf, but then an even greater than her had arisen in Miss Wethered. She in her turn had reigned since their meeting at Prince's in 1922. Now that Miss Wethered was in one half of the draw and Miss Leitch in the other there was a chance of another final between them. Both parties have the power of inspiring almost fanatical enthusiasm among their supporters, and excitement was at boiling point. Yet on the eve of the final it was difficult to imagine that the match would really be a match at all. Miss Wethered's progress had been a series of executions carried out with merciful swiftness. Round after round she had clung to an average of fours on this long and testing course. Miss Glenna Collett, the American champion and a very fine player, had held her for a while, but in the end had been overwhelmed like the others by that remorseless accuracy. Miss Leitch, on the other had, had not been herself at all. She had never touched her proper form, she had only got through by her great powers of fighting and because some of her opponents had been so terrified at the chance of beating her that they could not take what the gods gave them; she had appeared ill at ease and anxious, always brave but never confident.

And then on the morrow all was changed and a new Miss Leitch appeared, calm and serene, having reached the place that she had set out to reach,

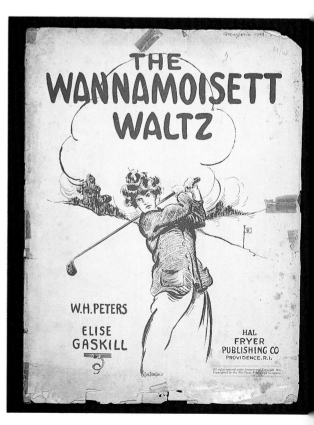

Above left, the cover of *Modern Priscilla* for October 1925; a brass ashtray of the 1920s, *below left*.

MODERN
Priscilla

Good Things
In This
Issue:-

The New "Pin-Me-Up" Dresses

Lamp Shade Making

Butterfly Embroideries

Christmas Handkerchiefs

New Fall Hats and How To Make Them

Toys You Can Make for Christmas

Fascinating Cut Paper Work

Making Your Own Gloves

"My Ideal Home" by Bruce Barton

Housekeeping or Homemaking—Which Shall It Be?

Silver for The October Bride

Business Women's Menus

October
1925
Twenty
Cents

"Her cares dropped from her like the needles shaken from out the gusty pine."

She was ready to do battle for her life, and she did it so magnificently that, though in the end she lost the match, it was she rather than her conqueror that was the heroine of the day. Everybody knew that she would rise to the occasion and make a great effort, but hardly anyone, I think, expected quite such a great one.

From the very beginning of that match Miss Leitch played like her best self, confidently and boldly. As for Miss Wethered, though she did not wilt under the fierce attack, something of the divine fire had temporarily departed, and so at the end of ten holes we were faced with the almost incredible situation that Miss Wethered was three down. Then, however, she made her great push. She played grandly and finally holed a long putt on the home green to be home in 35 and square the match. Miss Leitch had never weakened for a single moment: she had played as well as ever and had given no openings. To lose three holes to such golf was almost inevitable and probably any other lady golfer would have lost several more.

They were at it hammer and tongs again after luncheon, with the same fine golf. Any notion of Miss Wethered's going right away had long since been dispelled. Going to the ninth hole she was one down and there came one of the crises of the match. Miss Wethered had a putt for the hole, but she was stymied. To go for the shot and knock her enemy's ball in would be to be two down and that would be a very serious situation indeed. To go for it and bring it off would not only mean the gain of a valuable hole but would almost inevitably have a moral effect. She took the brave risk, lofted the shot perfectly, won the hole and squared the match.

The moral effect was palpable enough. For the next six holes Miss Wethered dominated the play. She was two up with three to go; if she could put a fairly long iron shot on to the sixteenth green she would in all human probability win the match by 3 and 2. This was the type of shot that she had been playing better perhaps than all the rest. Every one had so intense a belief in her that even at this most critical moment hardly a soul doubted that she

A Wills Gold Flake cigarette advertising card, *above right*, of the 1920s; and a Cavanders cigarette advertisement, *below right*, of March 22, 1919.

would put the ball bang in the middle of the green. For once, however, she was not straight, but hooked the ball into the rough mounds on the left of the green. The hole was halved and Miss Leitch was still alive.

Again the moral effect was obvious. Miss Wethered for once played two weak holes in succession, played them as if she was shaken and tired. Miss Leitch metaphorically leaped on her like a tigress and, aided at the last hole by a little of that fortune that aids the brave, most gloriously squared the match. And that ought to be the end of the story. A half was the right ending the greatest thirty-seventh hole in the world must have seemed a pity. However, they had to go on, someone had to win, and the someone was Miss Wethered, who laid a very long putt stone dead at the thirty-seventh. It was a fine effort and deserved victory, but every one who saw that match will always wish that there could for that year have been two queens on twin thrones of exactly equal splendour.

THE ILLUSTRATED LONDON NEWS, March 22, 1919.—4

Peggy: We're both playing like a book. Jack you're on the Green again—must be these New Clubs.

Jack: No, dear Old Thing, it's the Old Clubs—Army Clubs—stick to Army Club Cigarettes and you can't go wrong.

"CAVANDERS'
ARMY CLUB"
CIGARETTES.

Sold by the leading Tobacconists and in all the Canteens.

20 for 1/1
50 ,, 2/8
100 ,, 5/4

THE GOLFERS BLEND
The Manchester Golfer, 1910

THE Tobacco for the Links.
Does not fritter away in the wind.
Does not burn the tongue.
Does not fall to ashes half-way through your
    pipe.
Does help you to keep that calm temper
    without which you wil be useless at the tee,
    and worse than useless on the green.

The Golfer's Blend, 6½d. per ounce

Smoked by many of the most prominent
    golfers in and around Manchester.
Ask for it at your Club.

Felix S. Berlyn, 34, King Street, Manchester.
And Branches.

A selection of
golfing match-
holders and strikers,
left, from 1900 to
1935.

Right, a hand-painted, terracotta Austrian figure, of around 1898.

The Golfer's Alphabet
K.V. Kenealy, *Golf*, 1898

A is for Andrew, the Saint of the game,
B for the Bunker that made him profane.
C is for Caddie, inscrutable Sphinx,
D for a bad word they use on the links.
E for the Expert by whom links are laid,
F for the Fluke that the *other* man made!
G is for Golf, the game "Ancient and Royal,"
H is for Hazard, the golfer to foil.
I th'Infatuation when once you've begun,
J is the Joy when you've "holed out" in one.
K is the Kilt which all weather defies,
L is for Lofter to make the ball rise.
M is for Morris, the famous Golf Veteran,
N must be Novice, I can't find a better 'un!
O's the Opponent, on winning so keen,
P is the Putter he wields on the green.
Q for the Queries to drive editors wild,
R the Replies so kindly and mild.
S is the Score that you make on the Links,
T is for Tee (*not* the kind that one drinks!)
U the Ubiquitous "Bogey" we fear,
V is for Vardon, the "crack" of the Year.
W is the Drink which to Scotch Golf conduces,
X the 'Xpletive a "Foozle" produces!
Y is the Yell in which you cry "Fore,"
Z is the Zenith of joy when your score
  Has beaten the record of "Bogey" by four!

50

A British Christmas card, *left*, of 1905.

A HOLE IN NONE
Golfer's Handbook, 1939

A hole for which the score 0 was properly entered on the card was returned in the Middlesex Alliance four-ball medal competition at Northwood, 1934. D. Fraser of Pinner Hill, six handicap, holed his tee shot, with an iron, at the 15th hole, which measures 150 yards. Fraser received a stroke allowance at that hole, so his net score was 0, an unprecedented incident in a competition.

THE 6,000-FT DRIVE
Golfer's Handbook, 1939

Long drives have been made from mountain peaks, from the Pyramids, high buildings in New York, and on many occasions a golf ball has been driven into a passing train, and after travelling long distances been duly restored, but these are essentially freakish, and have been repeated so often that even the strangest need not be

accorded a place in the authentic records of the game. As an illustration of such freakish "drives" a member of the New York Rangers Hockey Team, from the top of Mount Edith Cavell, 11,033 feet high, drove a ball which struck the Ghost Glacier 5,000 feet below and bounced off the rocky ledge another 1,000 feet. A total drop of 2,000 yards.

PLAYING IN THE BAR
Golfer's Handbook, 1939

1854-5 – Park and Morris played in all of their six £100 matches, and honours were about evenly divided. In the fifth match at Musselburgh the spectators interfered with Morris's ball repeatedly, and the referee stopped play. Morris and the referee, Bob Chambers, an Edinburgh publisher, retired to a nearby public house. Park waited for some time and then sent a message to Chambers and Morris that if they did not come out to play to a finish he himself would play the remaining holes and claim the stakes. Morris and

A postcard advertising Svale Kite Golf Balls, *near right*, dating from around 1910. *Far right*, "The Nineteenth Hole" – A Royal Doulton plate of about 1920.

Chambers remained in the public house, and Park completing the round, was subsequently awarded the stakes.

A HALF IN ONE
Golfer's Handbook, 1939

On Sunday, 9th August, 1925, Mr. W.S. Evans and Mr. R.L. Matthews halved the 14th hole at Clarement Golf Club, Swinton, in one stroke. The feat is well authenticated, and was witnessed by four club members. The normal length of the hole is 133 yards; on this occasion it must have been nearer 140 yards, as the pin was well towards the back of the green. The green was quite clear when the shots were taken, and the four fellow-members present were able to see the green clear. The players immediately called up the four non-participants before touching the pin, or approaching nearer the hole, as, realising at once the tremendous odds against such an occurrence, they desired to have unassailable evidence of the fact.

PILGRIMAGE TO ST. ANDREWS
J.A., *Golf*, 1892

It has frequently been observed that St. Andrews is to the golfer what Mecca is to the Mohammedan. The comparison is apt in many respects. The Mohammedan turns his face towards Mecca when he prays, and gives utterance to words expressive of his belief in the Prophet. The golfer turns his thoughts towards St. Andrews. Each of their kind holds his city to be sacred in the eyes of true disciples. Both places too are reached by a certain pilgrimage, and, when the desired haven is attained, the happy pilgrim forgets all but the supreme delight of the moment.

St. Andrews having been reached, and the gauntlet of the younger fry of the caddie tribe having been run, the first thing to do was, of course, to visit the shrine of that deity of the place, Tom Morris, who received his visitors with the genial cordiality which has made him more than esteemed by all who have come into contact with him.

Gold and silver jewellery with a golfing theme, *left*, from 1910 to 1938.

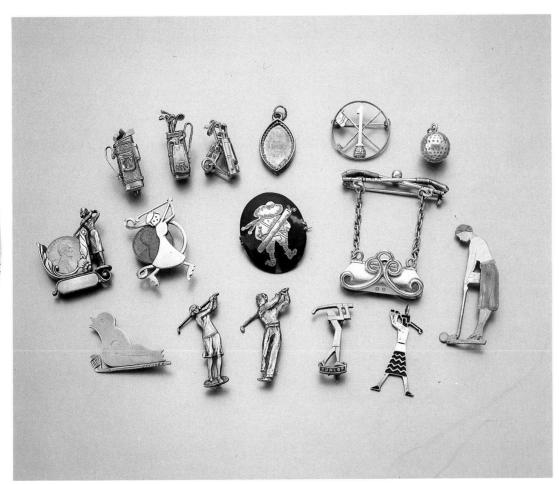

To play Golf well at St. Andrews requires an intimate knowledge of the course. Many hazards are quite unseen from the tee, and after playing what appears to be a beautiful shot the ball may be found trapped in one of the numerous bunkers with which the links is honeycombed. But the bunkers are by no means to be condemned. St.Andrews without its bunkers would be as a jewel without its setting. They greatly add to the zest of the game, yet, unless one knows beforehand exactly where the bunkers lie, the best and steadiest playing the world may result in a tall score. This is probably true of all greens, but it is specially applicable to St. Andrews. Again, there is hardly a hole where a hazard requires to be carried from the tee, and where it is not better and safer to "dodge" it. It is, no doubt, a fact that long and straight driving may save a stroke at some holes; but is not this more than compensated by the risk of being caught in some bunker and losing more than the advantage gained?

St. Andrews men have always been more noted for long driving than for anything else, and the green encourages the cultivation of this part of the game. There are a good many holes where two long shots should lay the globe near the disc and where a weaker driver would require an iron shot in addition; but this is bound, to some extent to cramp iron play, and more than one golfer has remarked upon the absence of the necessity for good iron play at most of the holes. The hard putting-greens, too, are rather against approaches pitched up, rendering it difficult to make the ball fall dead.

St. Andrews has been justly described as a "heaven" of Golf. Every advantage has been taken of the great natural capabilities of the green. Its beautiful velvety turf has been carefully tended and fostered; and seldom indeed is a bad-lying ball to be got even at the end of the year.

Who has not heard of the bunkers? And who, after having visited the place, is not acquainted

A British Christmas card, *right,* **of 1910.**

even to St. Andrews and the Royal and Ancient. As compared with the antiquity of the Royal and Ancient it is, of course, a comparatively modern institution, but during three of the four decades of its existence it has kept pace with its elder and larger rival in maintaining, promoting, and encouraging the game of Golf. St. Andrews is the Mecca of the golfer, but Prestwick is the Medina, and no enthusiast would consider his pilgrimage complete who had not visited the last named placed as well as the former.

It is invidious to make comparison sometimes, and I am not anxious to set off Prestwick against St. Andrews, especially to the disadvantage of the latter. But everything in this objective world is comparative, and one must have some approximate equivalent to set one's comparisons against. There is one circumstance that gives Prestwick the advantage over St. Andrews, the circumstance that a considerable portion of the links is the property of the club. Lord Wellwood has aptly written that "A fine day, a good match, and a clear green... make up a golfer's dream of perfect happiness." The last essential here is always a feature of Prestwick links. The familiar "Fore" is a word that is almost unknown there.

with their terrors? All sizes and shapes are there, and most of them are deep, necessitating strong and skilful play to extricate the unfortunate gutta entombed in their depths.

St. Andrews was a prominent place in Scottish history. It teems with objects of interest; but those who are interested in subjects of this kind should go and glean for themselves – not forgetting to take their clubs.

THE PRESTWICK LINKS
J. M'Bain, *Golf*, 1891

As a centre of Golf, Ayrshire occupies in the West of Scotland the position that Fifeshire does in the East. It is now, and is likely to remain, the chief seat of Golf in the West, and it contains more Golf links and more golf clubs than all that remains of the West of Scotland placed together. And what St. Andrews is to Fifeshire and the East, Prestwick is to Ayrshire and the West, the richest in incident and the most important in the recent annals of Golf. In respect of historical records within the last thirty years Prestwick with its premier club occupies a place not second

A 6ft-high railway poster, *left*, advertising the Caledonian Railway, from about 1910.

A selection of silver
golfing spoons,
above right, dating
from 1910 to 1937.

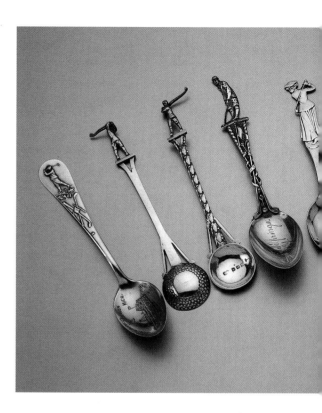

The club has the exclusive rights in an arbitrary way. Needless to say that they are not in the habit of warning pedestrians off the ground, or of refusing the use of the greens to applicants for a day's Golf, still the private character of the links is a guarantee against any outside interference, and the casual pedestrian, aware that he is on the ground by the goodwill of the club, takes care not to interfere with their game.

Prestwick Golf club came early to the front as a promoter of the game. In 1860, it instituted the Open Championship, an institution which has lasted till the present day, and is now likely to be permanent. For eleven years this important event was played over Prestwick alone; but in 1878, as is well known, young Tom Morris by winning the championship belt three times in succession became its possessor; and after being a year in abeyance the meeting was reconstituted under its present conditions, these conditions providing for the event taking place in rotation over Prestwick, St. Andrews and Musselburgh.

Prestwick has always taken a leading part in the settlement of important professional matches. The links are as eminently adapted in every way for these contests, and provide as good a test of Golf, as the best links in the kingdom. There is no living golfer of repute among the professionals who has not played in important matches over the ground. Old Tom Morris was custodian of the green for thirteen years, till he was transferred to St. Andrews.

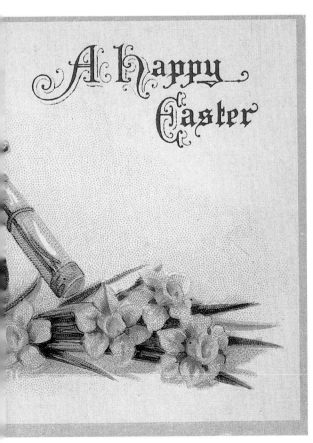

Many of Tom's most important triumphs were won over Prestwick, including the winning of the championship four times. Young Tommy, who was brought to Prestwick from St. Andrews when he was only a few weeks old, was initiated into the mysteries of the game at Prestwick, and when at the early age of thirteen he left it he was beginning to make his mark as a player. His subsequent career brought him often back to Prestwick, and his most important laurels were won over the ground where he first began to handle the clubs.

The links are situated on the Ayrshire coast at Prestwick, a well-known West of Scotland watering place three miles north of Ayr. So far as convenience in the matter of being easily got at is concerned, Prestwick is the most favourably situated links in the Kingdom. The town is for all practical purposes situated on the main line, and all the expresses north and south pick up and set down passengers there. The club-house door is within thirty yards of the station platform, and the first tee is within the same distance. The club has a private entrance from the station, so that in this respect the links could not be more favourably situated. As originally laid out, the round consisted of twelve holes, the space within which they were included forming a compact area with clearly defined boundaries. The boundaries were the railway on the east, the Pow Burn and "The Wall" on the north, the Sandhills on the margin of the sea on the west, and the public road on the south. The enclosure constitutes what may be called the classic portion of the present links, that portion over which some of the most memorable contests in modern golf took place. More recently the links expanded to the north, over "The Wall," the burn was crossed, and the club strayed into "meadows green and pastures new."

When "The Wall" is crossed the Golf is of a somewhat different character from what it is on the older portion, not unlike the new ground that was added to North Berwick, though a good deal more varied. Indeed the links is one of the most diversified I know, and contains every species of hazard, with the exception of rabbit holes. There is not a rabbit on the whole ground nor the signs

A British Easter card, *below left*, of 1924.

57

The cover of *The Elks Magazine*, right, for April 1933.

of one, although the newer portion was at one time a warren, and is so styled in the title deeds of the property.

THE GREAT CHARGE
"Observer", *The American Golfer,* 1932

Gene Sarazen broke more records at Sandwich to win the last British Open than any golfer ever broke before in a single championship. In the first place, he toured the long Princes links in 283 strokes for seventy-two holes, two under Bob Jones' record at S. Andrews which led the list. In the second place he set another record by playing the seventy-two holes in thirteen under par. No one had ever approached this mark in any other national championship. In none of the four rounds did he go a stroke over par when the final summing up was made.

There were several remarkable features hooked to this British Open which are worth noting here. One is the fact that Sarazen started at least six weeks before the battle of Sandwich with the same system of training that a fighter or a football player might use. He went on a more simple diet, which helped him to take off eight or ten pounds, eating only two meals a day. He swung a thirty-ounce driver fifteen minutes a day to strengthen his arms and hands and wrists. He played at every chance on cold, windy and rainy days in case bad weather should blow in from the sea. He would also pick out small targets one hundred and eighty or two hundred yards away with a cross wind blowing and hammer away at these with wood and iron to help perfect his control.

As a rule, this heavy schedule of training is inclined to develop staleness for golf on the mental side. In the case of Sarazen it left him fit and ready, replete with confidence in every club.

"I've done everything I can," Sarazen said before leaving, "to be ready for this championship. My main point now is to see that my concentration stays on the job from the first stroke to the final putt. That is the hardest job of all. But I've been working on that side, for concentration can be developed and improved just as much as anything else."

The remarkable side of Sarazen's showing was the third round. He opened with a 70-69, miraculous golf against a par of 74. After two such rounds as this, it invariably happens that something has to bend, if not to break. A razor edge of this sort can't last long. It is entirely too keen. Now, the third round of an open is the hardest test for those still left with a good chance. When Sarazen came to this round, he knew that it meant the big story of the week. There were too many crowding him to permit any faltering. But in place of slipping up to a 74 or a 75, Sarazen came tearing through with another 70. He had been four under par for his first round, and five under par for his second. Now he was back again at the crucial spot with another par-shattering attack. With his first three rounds set at thirteen under par, he still had enough left to match par on his final swing.

Gene Sarazen achieved a burning ambition in winning the British Open Championship. His total is the lowest ever scored in the history of the competition covering a span of 60 years.

59

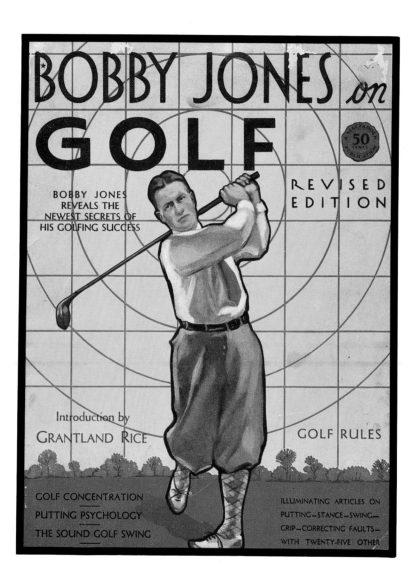

SECTION TWO

Great Characters

The Father of Golf: Tom Morris * An Old Friend * The
Slashing School * John Ball * Harry Vardon * H.S.C.
Everard * Alexander M'Kellar * Horace G. Hutchinson
* A Golf Pipe * Won at the Last Hole * Dorothy
Campbell-Hurd * A Superior Set of Men * Bobby Jones
* Golfluenza * It's a Rough Lie * In the Springtime.

THE FATHER OF GOLF: TOM MORRIS
H. Everard, *Golf*, 1891

This 15th day of June, 1891, appears to the writer a suitable one on which to take pen in hand, and scratch a few commonplaces about one of the best-known men in Scotland – Tom Morris. To expand him into Thomas Morris would be improper, a solecism to be looked for among the profane and vulgar, an equivalent to eating peas with a knife, or any other barbarity which shocks our refined sensibilities; to the brotherhood, therefore, let him be as he is, Tom Morris, or better still, the ever-popular favourite, Old Tom.

Tom's golfing career began at an early age. Being a native of St. Andrews, his profession might, perhaps, have been anticipated, but as a matter of fact it was only determined by a haphazard remark of old Sandy Herd, who asked him why he did not get himself apprenticed to a club-maker. Negotiations with Allan Roberston followed, the upshot being that he took Tom into his employment, and taught him the trade with which his name has been identified for half a century. For our hero in good sooth is a man whom his warmest admirers would hardly characterise as a living embodiment of order and method.

Tom's name will ever be associated with the great match for £400 between Allan Roberston and himself against Willie and James Dunn, played in 1849. This match has been admirably described in a little book recently published by Mr. Peter, who was an eye-witness. The match is ancient history, but the narrator invests it with such interest that one feels almost as if one were present to share the enthusiasm which animated the crowd. Tom and Allan were, to all intents and purposes, beaten, as much as twenty to one being laid on their opponents at a time when the latter were 4 ahead and 7 to play. But one after another these holes dropped off, till the match stood all square and 2 to play; but the penultimate hole must have been a trying one to the layers of the aforesaid odds. Allan and Tom had played three more, and were, besides, in a bunker; but the Dunns had come to grief at the back of a curb-stone on a cart track off the course.

Here they seem entirely to have lost all judgment, the last vanishing traces of which were indicated by a request on their part that a spade should be sent for and the rock of offence removed. When this was negatived by the umpire, they alternately kept missing the globe, by reason of the iron glancing off the stone, until one off three became the odds, when it occurred to them to play the ball out backhanded. Had they done this at first they must have won the hole, and, most probably, the match; instead of which they lost both. Mr. Peter, it is satisfactory to see, records his opinion thus, "I think it only just to say that, in my opinion, the winning of the above match was due to Tom Morris, who played with pluck and determination throughout." Elsewhere he adds: "Who has ever handled a club and does not know him, his genial countenance, dark, penetrating eye (his eye, however, is a blue-grey in colour), which never failed to detect a cunning road to the hole; imperturbable temper, unflinching courage, and indomitable self-control under circumstances the most exasperating."

Tom has won the open championship four times the scene of his victories being Prestwick on every occasion – in 1861, 1862, 1864 and 1867. His scores were 163, 163, 160, and 170, his most formidable antagonist being Park, who was never more than a stroke or two behind. On one occasion at Perth they tied at 168, but in playing off Tom won by fourteen strokes, Park being utterly at sea in the putting, which was very keen and difficult. Quite a unique feature in Tom's career is the extraordinarily fine game he has displayed almost continuously since his sixtieth year. Since then he has won two professional competitions, and on his sixty-fourth birthday holed St. Andrews Links in 81, compiled with nothing above a five.

His services are in frequent request where new greens have to be exploited. Among those he has already laid out are Prestwick, Westward Ho! Luffness, Dornoch, Tain, Callander, Cheltenham, and the Honourable Company's new green at Muirfield.

Long may he live, this grand old golfer! All golfers may be proud of numbering Old Tom among their friends. His the native dignity which

A signed photograph of Tom Morris, *left*, dated 1901.

63

outweighs all factitious advantages; his the pleasant demeanour, courteous without servility, independent without aggression, which affects favourably to all, and renders the possessor the master of circumstances on every occasion. We may fitly conclude with an echo of the sentiment by Tom's favourite poet, page upon page of whom he delights in quoting:-

"The rank is but the guinea's stamp,
The man's the gowd for a' that."

AN OLD FRIEND
L.A. Monkhouse, *Golf,* 1897

Years ago I bought this driver
Which you hold now in your hand.
Dear it seemed at seven shillings;
Golf I did not understand.

Time, alas! has spoilt the varnish,
Cracked the head in pieces twice,
Worn away the maker's trade-mark;
On the shaft there is a splice.

Yet was ever club so supple?
Give it just one gentle swing,
Whizz! the ball went swiftly flying,
Clearing walls and everything.

True, its working days are over,
But it hangs still on the wall –
Souv'nir sweet of days long vanished,
Gone forsooth beyond recall.

A polydrone bronze figure of John E. Laidlay, *near right,* **about 16.5in high, signed by G. Gonnella of Dundee, about 1880.**
Far right, **a selection of glass with a golfing theme, some items hand-painted, from 1910 to the 1930s.**

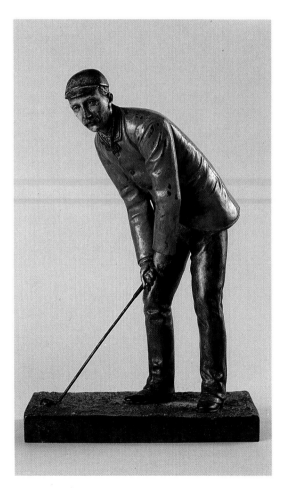

64

OLD TOM

THE SLASHING SCHOOL
L. Latchford, *The Young Man*, 1903

The world of golf has some outstanding personalities – amateur and professional – titanic figures which loom vast on the golfing horizon, men of whom all devotees of Royal and Ancient speak with bated breath. There is Tom Morris, the doyen of golf, the W.G. Grace of the game. "Auld Tom" the custodian of the links at S. Andrew's the Mecca of all true and faithful golfers.

His fame is world-wide, for the name of Tom Morris has gone to all four corners of the earth. He is the oracle of the game – par excellence the final authority upon all knotty points of law and etiquette.

Four times "auld Tom" won the open championship belt at Prestwick, and then his own son – "Young Tommy," of pathetic memory – captured the trophy from his sire and, holding it three consecutive years, won the prize outright. Golf has evolved since the days when "auld Tom" was in his glory. The "slashing" school of long drivers has flung the old style of play into obscurity, but "auld Tom's" reputation as a player survives while his lofty character has earned him the esteem and admiration of three generations of golfers.

Another interesting personality is Mr. Horace G. Hutchinson, the first Amateur Champion and the foremost expositor of the game. But his pre-eminence is as a writer upon golf. The service he has rendered to the game by his facile pen is incalculable. He was responsible for *The Badminton Golf*, and in that excellent library of sport there is no single volume which gives evidence of more editorial sagacity, lucid exposition and graceful writing than the volume bearing Mr. Horace Hutchinson's name.

Greater than Mr. Hutchinson as a player is Mr. John Ball, junior. It is significant of much that both men are Englishmen. Mr Ball's record defies recital in a brief magazine article. He was the first amateur to win the blue ribbon of the golf links – the open championship. Up to 1890 the Champion Cup had gone as if by a fixed process of inevitability to a professional, but Mr. Ball captured the trophy at Prestwick and in the

A postcard of Tom Morris, *left*, from 1900.

same year won the Amateur Championship on
his own club green at Hoylake. This achievement
is quite unique.

Equally famous, and no less deservedly so, is
another Hoylake amateur, Mr. Harold Hilton, a
Liverpudlian, not yet half way through the
"allotted span" of life, but with a sheaf of
victories to his credit. Twice he has been Open
Champion and twice Amateur Champion. On
his own familiar green at Hoylake he is almost
invincible with his amalgam of strength and
accuracy, and his well-nigh weird knowledge of
every trick and manoeuvre of the game.

By far the most attractive personality is Harry
Vardon, of Totteridge, "a Napoleon of the
game," as he has often been called. Vardon is a
Jerseyman, who learnt his golf, of all places, in
the Channel Islands. He came to England as a
sort of invading conqueror and bewildered
English golfers by a sensational series of
triumphs over all comers and in all quarters. His
genius was his steadiness. Nothing daunted him,
nothing disturbed his equable temperament. The
personification of all that is graceful and elegant,
Vardon set a new standard for English golfers.

Of quite another school of golf is J.H. Taylor, the exponent above all things of mechanical accuracy in all departments of the game. Taylor has almost reduced golf to an exact science. Straight as a die goes his ball from the tee, and almost straighter and truer go the balls from his mashie in approaching. His three championships are of course his signal triumphs, but the wonderful consistency of his ordinary tournament play deserves even greater credit. Much of Taylor's sustained and consistent brilliancy may be traced to the moral qualities of the man. His is a reposeful nature – he is as imperturbable as the proverbial Hindoo. Whether winning or losing he plays steadily, doggedly on – giving no suggestion of consciousness of the position of the game.

JOHN BALL
Manchester Golfer, 1911

When golf in England was but a name and played only by a few scattered and exiled Scots, and when Hoylake was but a small and unknown fishing village, there was growing up there a young English schoolboy who was destined to make history in the world of golf, and to make a name for himself which will endure as long and wherever the game of golf is played.

In those far-away days "Johnnie" was known officially as "John Ball, Tertius," and his name first appears in the records of the Royal Liverpool Club years before the vast majority of present-day golfers were born.

It is a long cry back to the year 1872, yet that was the year when the oft-times champion won his first notable victory in the golfing arena, when at the mature age of eleven he annexed his first medal. The boys' medal is played for annually at Hoylake, and as the age limit is 15 it is not improbable that the embryo champion was playing against boys who were almost twice his age.

Since those far-away days many stars have risen in the golfing firmament, but none have shone with greater or more constant brilliancy than the subject of this sketch, for from that day to this John Ball has been continually electrifying the world of sport by his multitudinous

victories. His medals are as the sands of the sea for number; no one knows how many he has won, and least of all does he himself know. I dare say he could tell you pretty accurately how many championships he has won, but as to cups and medals they would require a statistician to number them.

Such a being as an English golfer was an anomaly, and as a consequence Scotsman after Scotsman journeyed south to put the aspiring young Sassenach in his rightful place, but they one by one returned defeated to tell the tale to others. For it was in 1888 that Mr. Ball started winning championships, and since that date the habit appears to have grown upon him; and as it is quite a good habit, his friends and admirers – the terms are synonymous – are hopeful that he will still keep it up, and not lapse into less glorious ones.

Mr. Ball was the first amateur to seriously threaten the proud and apparently unassailable position of the professionals. There were always amateurs who played in the "Open

A pot metal barometer with a golfer, *left*, of 1910.

67

A Johnnie Walker
Whisky
advertising
cigarette case,
right, from 1910.

Championship," and even at the age of 14 the Hoylake player occupied a high position in this competition, but it was not till 1890 that he succeeded in placing himself in the unique position of being in one and the same year "Amateur" and "Open" champion.

It was at Prestwick that Mr. Ball won his first championship, and it was on this same Ayrshire course that he won the Open Championship; it was here, also, that he played that never-to-be-forgotten final with the late Lieut. F.G. Tait.

One characteristic which has always been a dominant feature of Mr. Ball's has been his grit and pluck, and never was this more emphatically demonstrated than in the Championship at Prestwick in 1899, a few months before both he and Lieut. Tait found themselves fighting their country's battles in South Africa.

In the first round the Scot was in the happy position of being three holes to the good, and the prospects of the Championship coming to England were remote indeed; but those who thought so forgot that it only needed these

adverse conditions to bring out all those qualities which we admire so much in Mr. Ball's play. He stuck grimly to his redoubtable opponent, squared the match, and won it by a wonderful three at the 36th hole. Freddy Tait was undoubtedly the idol of the Scots as Johnnie Ball is the idol of we Southerners. No two finer amateur golfers ever lived; they were good friends and honourable opponents, each having great respect for the prowess of the other. When they met it was indubitably a battle of the giants.

Mr. Ball is popular wherever he goes, his quiet unassuming manners have endeared him to all with whom he has come into contact. His name is a household word with golfers and all classes of sportsmen the world over; even the Scots have only one thing against him, and that is that he was born on the wrong side of the border.

He has been made a life member of no one knows how many golf clubs, the Royal and Ancient Club being of the number who paid him this honour – an exceptional one in their case, and one previously only conferred upon members of the Royal Family.

HARRY VARDON
Golf, 1897

Harry Vardon, the young Jersey professional, now resident at Ganton, Scarborough, won the Open Championship at Muirfield. As some misstatements have been made with regard to the new Champion's age, it may be well to say that the accurate statement is twenty-six years, he having been born at Grouville, in the Island of Jersey, on May, 9th, 1870. He is entirely a self-taught golfer; that is to say, he has had no lessons from anybody. His game is the result simply of imitation of a style which he fancied.

His success is made all the more remarkable by his golfing history. He was a caddie for a year or two, but went to gardening when fourteen years of age. He was a member of the workmen's club at Grouville, and was able to play on the fine eighteen-hole course there, as well as on the sands. It was not until he was about twenty-one years of age that he took up Golf as a profession, so that he has only been following the game exclusively for five years. Yet in that short time he has climbed to the topmost rung of the golfing ladder. He used to drive a longer ball before he strained his back in the Championship meeting at Prestwick in 1893.

When he went up to the Championship, his putter seemed to be a regular snare to him, so he sold it, bought a cleek, put a short shaft into it, and straightway went and putted in truly championship form with it. A round of 76 seemed to be practically a matter of child's play to him. His record for the course is 70, and that of Mr. Broadwood, 72.

Harry Vardon is one of seven brothers, five of whom are good golfers. The youngest, Alfred, is in his brother's shop at Ganton, and although only fifteen years of age, he is already equal to a round with an average of 5 a hole. Harry Vardon plays with short and light clubs, and, for driving, stands with the right foot well forward, though not so far advanced as Taylor's stance. He grips very tight for putting, and tight for mashie strokes. His grip of the driver is in the "interlocked" fashion – the thumb of the left hand down the shaft, the left hand being partly

A stein, *left,* an oil lamp and a whisky flask, all by Lennox from America between 1894 and 1901.

interlocked in the right – which was supposed to be a fashion peculiar only to the ex-Champion. Vardon has always held his driver in this way, except when he formerly kept both thumbs down the shaft.

It could be told at once that Vardon is not a St. Andrews man. His style is one which would not be greatly admired on that course, unless it were accompanied by the prestige of a Champion. Still, let it not be thought that he has failed to find admirers in Scotland. After the Championship meeting at Muirfield, one of the most distinguished, and most experienced of Scottish amateurs – himself the possessor of a style which is the picture of grace – was asked to say who was the best golfer of the day. He prefaced his answer by saying that he knew his opinion would cause some surprise. The company were all old golfers; most of them had known and played with young Tommy Morris, and Taylor was high in favour. But our authority knew his own mind, and declared it. "Vardon," he said, "was the player of the day." This opinion need not be criticised. It is mentioned only to show that in Scotland the Champion finds ardent appreciation. Yet may it be said that, at first, he does not impress one as being the player he is. His swing is comparatively slow, and it is a little slack. It is, in short, more amateurish than professional.

There are some professionals who say that they always putt for the back of the hole. It is a good maxim, but it requires to be tempered with discretion. If a player putts consistently for the back of the hole, the chances are that he leaves himself too much to do, and, against Vardon, a game of that kind would not pay. It is not implied, of course, that the Champion does not know the value of a long steal. To see him on the green is to know that he always plays with the hope of one. A characteristic attitude of his is that which he assumes just before putting. He sits down, extends his putter along the line of putt, as if taking aim at the hole; then, gripping his club very low, he sends off the ball with a wonderfully true and accurate run. If he does not get down, he is invariably within a foot of the hole, on days, that is to say, when he is in Championship form.

One other point in his play should be noted.

His temper, it is certain, helped him largely at Muirfield last year. He is a self contained gentlemanly player, so, though not insensible to momentary vexation – that is to say, he is human – keeps himself well in hand, and never allows temper to put him out. In this, Harry Vardon, the self-taught champion from Jersey is, or at least should be, a model for all players: professionals and amateurs alike.

H.S.C. EVERARD
F.G. Tait, *Golf*, 1892

With perhaps the solitary exception of Mr. Horace Hutchinson there is no contemporary golfer who is known to a wider circle of golfers than the subject of this sketch. His stalwart form is as well known on St. Andrews links as that of old Tom; he is one of the institutions of St. Andrews; and, by means of a racy, picturesque, and scholarly pen, he has appealed through our columns and through other journals to golfers all over the world, imparting instruction and amusement to a subject whose interest is as perennial as the eternal hills. Did Mr. Everard know how the editor has been bombarded for over a year by golfers in all sorts of nooks and crannies in the country, asking the plain question "When are you going to have Mr. Everard in?" he would at least feel how clamant was interest in his golfing personality, though perchance his modesty would be somewhat distressed.

It, therefore, gives us peculiar satisfaction to meet the wishes of those readers now, not only account of the intrinsic merit of Mr. Everard as a player, but also because he is one of the best known and most brilliant exceptions, to the second postulate, at least, of that time-honoured maxim, "To play Golf well one must begin young and stick to it." He is recognised everywhere as one of the shining lights of the large and ever-increasing body of English golfers, though he did not begin to play Golf regularly until the age of 25. Handicapped, however, as he thus was, he may now claim to rank among the best amateur golfers of Scotland.

Mr. Everard was born at Claybrook Hall, in Leicestershire, a county which at that time did

An advertising card for Footform shoes, *left*, from Britain in the 1920s.

not boast of a Golf course. His earlier years were spent at Langton Hall, near Market Harborough, situated in the centre of one of the finest hunting counties in the Midlands. Mr. Everard begun his public school life at Eton in 1860. During the summer holidays of the next two years he paid his first visits to St. Andrews, where, under the able tuition of the well-known Watty Alexander, and a caddie of the name of Martin (no doubt some relation of the ex-professional champion, Bob Martin), he received his first instructions in the game at which he was afterwards to be so famous. Mr. Everard utilised to the full extent these two summers at St. Andrews, and, as old Tom Morris and Jamie Anderson were then at the zenith of their fame, he had ample opportunity of seeing the game played as it should be.

During the next few years, Mr. Everard appears to have neglected Golf altogether. Whether his studies at Christ Church, Oxford, were too onerous, or his love for cricket left him

little or no time for a game requiring so much practice, it is difficult to say; but it is certain that even at the age of one-and-twenty he did not devote much time to the Royal and Ancient game.

While at Christ Church, Mr. Everard was considerably interested in athletics, and he won sundry prizes in that field, his special line being as a thrower of the cricket-ball, and a walker. During the next eleven years, Mr. Everard occasionally played Golf, but most of his spare time was devoted to tennis, racquets, and cricket. At all of these games, especially the last named, he showed that skill and precision which now characterises his play in the more important game of Golf.

It was not until 1880 that Mr. Everard began regularly to play Golf. He, however, made a capital beginning by marrying the eldest daughter of the well-known and enthusiastic golfer, Colonel Boothby. This lady is almost as keen a player as her husband. Since his marriage

Two postcards, *right*, dating from around 1905.

Mr. Everard has been a most enthusiastic player, and, extraordinary as it may seem, gets better and better year by year.

In medal and tournament play Mr. Everard's successes have been numerous, and so distributed over a number of greens that it is a matter of difficulty to know where to begin our account of them. But, as he has played over St. Andrews more frequently than any other course, we may as well start with his achievements there. The Calcutta cup has been won by him on two occasions, the first of which will long be remembered as one of the closest finishes ever witnessed. Mr. Everard, after a succession of exciting finishes, almost all of them depending on a putt at the last hole, had to meet Mr. J. Robertson Reid in the final. To this gentleman he conceded the large handicap of six holes, and, further, by losing two out of the first four, stood in the precarious position of 8 down and 14 to play. The round, however, was halved; nor was it until after a second round had been played next

day that the cup finally came into Mr. Everard's possession, the latter winning, amidst much excitement, by one putt.

Mr. Everard's successes are by no means confined to his Home green. In an amateur competition at Montrose, in 1888, he beat a strong field, including Mr. Alexander Stuart, Captain Burn, and others of note. At Troon he has been almost uniformly successful, having on three occasions won the Duke of Portland's medal with a remarkably low score.

In the amateur championship Mr. Everard has been somewhat unlucky, for although on many occasions playing a game that would have brought him easily into the final, he has constantly met an opponent who, recording a phenomenally low score, has made the pace too hot for him.

Mr. Everard, besides being a high class golfer, is well known to the public in the capacity of an author. He has written a number of exceedingly interesting articles and biographies for *Golf*, and

"The Mashie" and "Putting" from around 1905.

A metal
match-holder and
Lady-golfer inkwell,
right, both from
around 1900.

for various other books and magazines which treat of the game; and in fact it may well be said that he is as judicious and effective with his pen as he is with his "iron." Mr. Everard has also been the performer of a very curious feat. He is the only player who has holed the short hole at St. Andrews five times in one, three times going out, twice coming in. The advantage of putting this noteworthy performance to one's credit, however, is doubtful when it is stated that Mr. Everard has had to pay five bottles of whisky to the caddie!

Mr. Everard drives a low and very straight ball, a habit particularly useful against wind. His play on this account is not much affected by a gale; it is then that he is really seen at his best. The most noticeable and telling part of his game however, is his iron play. With that useful weapon he has a happy knack of laying the ball dead from very remarkable distances; and finally he usually holes out with considerable certainty.

Mr. Everard is a most efficient partner and an equally dangerous antagonist; and it is to be hoped that the success which has till now attended his efforts may long continue to follow him.

ALEXANDER M'KELLAR
Golfer's Handbook, 1939

Alexander M'Kellar was probably the most enthusiastic golfer who ever lived. He spent the whole day on Bruntsfield Links, Edinburgh, and at night would practise putting by lamplight. Even in winter, if the snow was frozen, he would be seen enjoying his round alone if he could not persuade any one to join him. His absorbing predilection for the game annoyed his wife, and one day she tried to put him to blush by carrying his dinner and nightcap to the links. She arrived at a moment when M'Kellar was hotly engaged, and, failing to see the satire of his wife, he observed she might wait if she chose, for at present he had not time for dinner. He died at Edinburgh in 1813.

HORACE G. HUTCHINSON
H.S.C. Everard, *Golf*, 1891

We are all familiar with old maxim about familiarity, but the greater our familiarity with the Golf of Mr. Horace G. Hutchinson, or personally with that gentleman himself, the less do we feel disposed to regard it and him with aught but feelings of respect.

Few names are so well known as his in connection with the nationalisation of Golf; not only is he one of the finest living exponents of that game, but he has taken up his pen in the cause, and given to the world the benefit of much valuable advice. As a player, few can boast a larger measure of success; his earlier years were passed at Westward Ho! where he was almost alone among his schoolfellows in his keen pursuit of the game.

He was not beholden to any of the professionals for his success in this particular, for he struck out a line of his own, and putted on a system which certainly produces surprising results in his case, a system which he has since advocated in the Badminton Book, as an alternative to that practised by professionals and other good players generally. For these usually stand half-facing the hole, with the ball somewhere about opposite the right foot whereas Mr. Hutchinson places himself quite square to the hole, the ball half-way between the feet, or rather nearer to the left foot, gives his wrists free play, and lets his putting iron swing as much like a pendulum as possible. So wonderfully accurate did he become, that putts of twelve feet or so were almost always stone dead for him, nor did he ever appear to fail at that shorter and inglorious distance of a club length or under, which is frequently productive of such wailing and gnashing of teeth.

The first requisite of successful putting on Mr. Hutchinson's plan would seem to be as he says, an iron putter – preferably as nearly as possible a facsimile of the one used by him. He who writes was once fortunate in procuring such a copy, with which, he tried to put the new theory to a practical test, he struggled on in season and out of season. Never in this world was seen such execrable putting, the resultant of opposing forces; neither short putt nor long one ever found its way into or near the hole by any accident, from which we may infer that what is one man's meat is another man's poison.

Though the short game is perhaps Mr. Hutchinson's strongest point of all, he is a really beautiful approacher, combining as he does very great power and control over difficult distances with an artistic lightness of touch at the shorter lofts, which cannot be excelled. He is a very long driver with an iron; at one time, too, he used to carry a cleek which had a play-club shaft, and a light head, such as is used by boys. This was an excellent idea, and wonderfully long shots could be driven with it; but the head, being deficient in weight of metal, would not withstand the continued hard hitting, and was apt to become too concave. Mr. Hutchinson is one of the few players who appear to immense advantage in driving against the wind; he appears to have some knack of hitting the ball by which he communicates a strong forward rotation round a vertical axis, the effect is which is apparent in increased running power when the ball alights. Some of his shots in these circumstances may well be classed as sensational.

Character is a factor not to be lightly esteemed, and as to this, Mr. Hutchinson is well endowed; there is about him an air of quiet good-humoured determination, accompanied by a cool composure, which gives him a great advantage over players whose temperament is to be described of an opposite or more mercurial order. Careful and calculating he is, yet not so much so as to prejudice his chances by undue sacrifice of all brilliancy, but when the critical point arrives, as it does in most encounters of importance, perhaps in the shape of a six-foot putt to be holed for a half, three holes from home, with the match all square, none are more likely to rise to the occasion than him.

Altogether Mr. Hutchinson has won over forty medals and prizes on his home green, his former home green one should say, as Eastbourne now more properly answers to that description. Among his performances, it may be mentioned, that from 1881 to 1888, both years inclusive, he was the winner of the Prince of Wales gold medal.

Three silver golf
trophies, *right*, from
the first half of the
century.

From 1882 to 1888, both inclusive, he held the Lindsay Bennet gold challenge medal for united scores, his average for fourteen rounds coming out at about 80½. "Good wine needs no bush," and the mere mention of such consistently brilliant play is all-sufficient without further comment.

He has twice won the amateur championship, and played in the final on a third occasion. St. Andrews was the scene of his first victory, in 1886, where he played the final with Mr. Henry Lamb; the succeeding year saw him the conqueror of Mr. John Ball, jun., by one hole, on the latter's own green at Hoylake.

It will be apparent that Mr. Hutchinson's position resembles somewhat that of Alexander; perhaps, almost surfeited with success, he has turned his attention to the world of literature, being fully bent on proving himself as able with the pen as with the putter. Still it is not be said that he suffers his game to deteriorate. "I want to write a novel, and here I go fooling about the country playing Golf," as he recently remarked; but he won the medal, and has since written the novel besides. A good novel too, "*Creatures of Circumstance*" its title, which the lover of Golf and of cricket and of fresh Atlantic breezes would do well to read. His *Badminton Book*, and "*Hints on Golf*, are too well known to need further notice, while he is besides, a prolific contributor to various magazines.

Mr. Hutchinson's influence on Golf is, in the writer's opinion, very distinctly traceable in the marked improvement in amateur play which has taken place during the last few years. In this he is to be associated with Messrs. Laidlay and John Ball, jun. These three stars may be regarded as a brilliant constellation; they have shed such a bright light upon the game that previous illumination becomes by comparison quite crepuscular. For in the times, the good old times as some would call them, anterior to their arrival on the scene, any score of 90 or thereabouts over a decently arranged green was a nearly sure win for any medal, and the old first-class player was content to go jogging along at about the form which that steady-going and respectable number represents. But not these players, being about on a par with the best professional talent of this or

any age, and being able to knock ten strokes off that number, have administered a salutary stimulant to the rest of their brethren, who naturally have no wish to be left farther behind than they can help, and on many occasions they manage to hold their own fairly well.

In taking leave of Mr. Hutchinson, it is fitting and a pleasant duty to pay tribute to the social qualities which make him a popular favourite with a large circle of friends. He has many strings to his bow; he is as much at home on the cricket field as on the links: a member of the Zingari, of the Free Foresters, and of M.C.C., whether on a cricketing tour with an eleven, or on a golfing tour on his own account, he is an ever-welcome guest, a friend whom the majority of us would like to honour.

A silver Dunlop hole-in-one trophy of 1924, *above right*, with a bramble ball, and another silver hole-in-one trophy of the 1930s.

Below right, a silver matchsticker by G.W. Turner & Sons of 1895, and a handpainted matchsticker with a portrait of Tom Morris.

A GOLF PIPE
Golf, 1892

This is the latest novelty which has been brought out for the benefit of the golfing community. The wonder is that the thing has not been attempted before, seeing how readily the implements of the game lend themselves to miniature reproduction, not only in jewellery but in other forms of ornamental and decorative art. The Golf Pipe is elegant in appearance and practical in use, as it can be smoked with or without the long stem, and the Golfer who indulges in the fragrant weed will be able to enjoy a long pipe while reading, or a short one at cards or billiards. The stem of the pipe is an exact reproduction of the club, but of course, proportionately smaller, and the bowl, which is made of briar or meershcaum, resembles a Golf ball, both in size and appearance.

The pipe can be obtained through any tobacconist from the makers of the well-known brand of Pipes. Judging from the specimen now before us, the makers seem to have produced this interesting novelty in material of excellent quality and high finish of workmanship. We cannot imagine a more suitable prize for competition than the long Golf Pipe with meerschaum bowl, and handsome case covered with Russian leather. The short briar pipe will be found a useful addition to the Golfer's outfit.

A silver golfing
match-striker, *left*.

79

A British silver pin cushion and a silver golf notebook from Britain, and a silver match-striker from America, *above right*, all from the 1920s. *Below right* silver and mother-of-pearl cutlery with a golfing theme, from the 1920s.

WON AT THE LAST HOLE
Review, *Golf*, 1893

By M.A. Stobart... 1s 6d

This is an amusing story of love and Golf, two ingredients which mix well in our daily cup of enjoyment. A bachelor betakes himself, in search of rest and recreation, to Golfstone-on-Tees. His golfing stock-in-trade consists of a driver and a mashie tied together by a piece of string, and on arriving at the station he finds himself in the midst of a band of cheery golfers, each laden with a bag of clubs. Attempts are made by his companions to break through the outer crust of reserve which had enveloped Mr. Brown, and naturally the conversation drifted into the channel of Golf. Mr. Brown was asked what handicap he received, to which question he cautiously replied: "I played at Sandwich, and

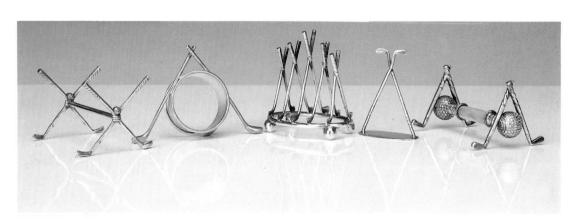

Loving Greeting

An American
Valentine Card, *left*,
of 1910.

81

A Success Glass oil lamp, *above right*, in the "Gone With the Wind" style with a pot metal American reading lamp from the 1920s; *below right*, golfing ephemera from the 1920s and 1930s – items of the type that are frequently thrown away.

they didn't give me anything." He was, of course, put down as a scratch player, and when he got to the links Mr. Brown was matched with another scratch golfer. He was saved from a ludicrous situation by the appearance of a friend, Mr. Thornton, just in the nick of time. Mr. Thornton and Mr. Brown become rival suitors for the hand of the same lady, a Miss Burrows, who plays Golf pretty well. A good many diverting episodes take place before it is finally arranged between the gentlemen that the result of a foursome should decide who shall have the privilege of asking the lady. Mr. Brown, by the aid of Miss Burrows herself, wins the match by a heroic putt at the last hole, and so the tale ends as it should do. It is capitally told, and the illustrations of Major Hopkins lend added charm to a racy, bright, amusing golfing tale.

DOROTHY CAMPBELL-HURD
J. Dey, *The American Golfer*, 1934

At the age of fifty, Dorothy Campbell Hurd plays eighteen holes of golf over an orthodox course in 69 strokes. It is the best score this golfing grandmother ever has made, although she cards under 80 almost as often as above. It is an apogee at which she has star-gazed all her life.

At the age of fifty-five, the Hon. Michael Scott, a son of the fourth Earl of Eldon, wins the British amateur championship for the first time, becoming the oldest champion in the tournament's history. This prize is perhaps the most difficult of atttainment in all golf.

It is a fascinating if garbled summary – 105 years scoring their first 69 and winning their first major championship.

A British golfing trophy, *left*, 4.5in high, of 1919.

Then, H. Chandler Egan, a greybeard of forty-nine, Amateur Champion in 1904-05, throttles the reigning Open Champion, Johnny Goodman, in the first round at Cincinnati. Max R. Marston comes back to be national finalist at the age of forty-one, ten years after winning the title.

John D. Rockefeller on his ninety-fourth birthday plays his usual nine holes. Two mile walks are carefully avoided by many of today's youngsters. "Let's ride," they parry. Poor Youth! Where is thy serving? Or so it would seem.

Those facts, all of 1933 date, constitute not so much a case against Youth as a commentary on an athletic game in which it is possible to scale the heights despite advanced age. Further, they embody a sketchy introduction to the outstanding character in women's golf – a player who, at the half-century mark, is even more skilful than when she was champion of the world, who is yet a match for anyone, who, in fine, is the epitome of the "old guard" in its unbudging, stand against Time.

Presenting – Dorothy Iona Campbell Hurd, a member of the Merion Cricket Club, Haverford, Pennsylvania.

Golf critics, although perhaps less prone to splurge with superlatives than other sports experts, have been applying to Mrs Hurd the label "wonder woman" at intervals spanning more than two decades.

They first had occasion to use it twenty-three years ago when Mrs. Hurd completed the **unprecedented and still unequalled feat of** winning the American, the British, the Scottish and the Canadian women's championships.

In 1924 they cast conservatism overboard again. After a twelve-year hiatus in which she had been denied a major championship, Mrs. Hurd came back with a reformed, modernized swing, recaptured the United States title, and set up an all-time record of having won eleven national championships in four countries. She was then forty-one.

In 1926 she established a new world record for putting, using but nineteen putts in an eighteen-hole round. Once more the air was florid with adjectives.

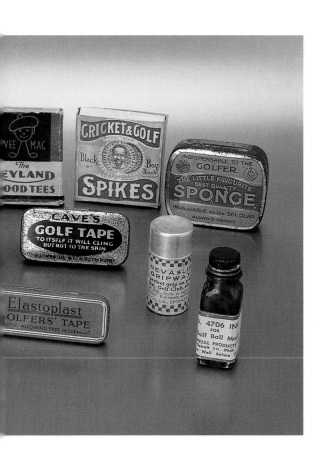

Last spring she celebrated her fiftieth birthday by scoring a 70 over the Belmont Manor course in Bermuda; a few weeks later, on the same course, she recorded the best score of her life, the 69. Belmont Manor is 6,172 yards in length and has a men's par of 70. Three months thereafter, in July, Mrs. Hurd qualified for permanent possession of the Griswold Trophy by defeating a field of younger, capable players for her third victory in the Shenecossett Country Club's annual invitation tournaments at New London, Conn. Then, in September, she won the classic Berthellyn Cup and created an all-time record of four triumphs in the series of invitation events conducted by the Huntingdon Valley Country Club, Abington, Pa.

A Royal Doulton Burslem pot, *below,* **from around 1890.**

So today, after thirty-four consecutive years as a scratch-handicap player, Mrs. Hurd still is the game's "wonder woman".

It is characteristic that she is blissfully unaffected by the pretty things said and written of her. She is a human encyclopaedia on golf, unstinting in advice and encouragement to fellow-players; but beyond a certain pardonable pride, she is rather girlish in her naive outlook on her accomplishments. She disclaims the "wonder woman" title and is convinced that Joyce Wethered is the greatest feminine golfer of all time.

On the course, Mrs. Hurd is thoroughly businesslike; off it, quite unassuming. Once she has finished a day's play, she invariably discards her clubs in favor of knitting needles, retires to a quiet corner of the club-house veranda, and looks as if she might be a mother but mildly interest in golf waiting patiently for her daughter to finish a round.

Mrs. Hurd is not "just a golfer." She is a omnivorous reader, a clever writer, an enthusiastic theatregoer, and a diverting conversationalist. One of her two chief complaints is that she never achieved her ambitions as a singer and a pianist. The other is that her golf swing is not stylish.

After she defeated Florence Hezlet in the final of the 1909 British championship at Birkdale in Lancashire, she was about to enter the enclosure where the prize-giving was to take place, when her way was barred by a six-foot commissionaire with a row of medals on his chest.

"Are you," asked this pompous individual, with a supercilious stare, "a golfer?"

"I don't think so," was the completely serious reply, "but I believe they will want me inside to receive the championship cup."

Nor is Mrs. Hurd a relentless playing machine, but a very human being. Defending the Philadelphia women's championship last year, she started by breaking the qualifying-round record with a 79. She won her first match, then in a second round met a young clubmate, Mrs. John J. Mitchell, 3d. Although a tyro at championship play, Mrs. Mitchell began brilliantly and was four up after seven holes.

At this point, the match acquired a gallery, in

the form of a lone reporter. Mrs. Mitchell suddenly became self-conscious. She lost the next two holes and at the turn was but 2 up. She was faltering fast.

Thereupon, Mrs. Hurd whisperingly suggested to the one-man gallery that he make himself scarce. "I'm afraid your presence is disturbing Mrs. Mitchell," she explained. "This is her first match of any importance and she's unaccustomed to playing before anyone. She should be given every fair opportunity to win."

The reporter took the hint and departed. Mrs. Mitchell did win, 1 up in nineteen holes. ...

Almost a quarter-century has passed. Still Dorothy Campbell Hurd goes on, with a constancy that a Tennysonian brook might envy. She is yet able to compete on a level footing with younger, more vigorous players.

How does she do it? What is the secret of golf's "wonder woman?"

The observer would note these points: golf is a rarity among athletic games in that it does not tend to "burn out" the player in the concurrent advance of age and participation; Mrs. Hurd has kept pace by readjusting her swing from time to time, conforming it to effective modern ideas; her ability to concentrate, to wipe out all memory of a bad shot; her sedulous execution of the principle that practice makes perfect.

Mrs. Hurd herself confesses ignorance as to the reasons for her protracted success, "unless," she said, "it's merely because of my short game and the fact golf is almost second nature to me since I have played it all my life."

A carping critic might quibble with the statement she has been playing golf all her life, so for the sake of strict truth it must be admitted she had attained the ripe old age of one and one-half years before she first swung a club. However, the family background of her golf extends far beyond a half-century. Her paternal grandfather as well as her eight uncles all played the game over the links at North Berwick.

"Since I lived in such an atmosphere of golf," she says, "I took to the game at a very early age. To this day I vaguely remember my first little club, a six-penny club lacking the bone and the lead then commonly used, purchased in a toy shop in the High Street of North Berwick.

"One day when I was on the links with my nurse I swung my little club so hard I lost my balance and fell flat on my face. Robert Chambers, the publisher, was passing. Seeing this strange performance, he predicted to my mother that because I had swung so energetically I 'would be a great golfer some day.'

"I played my first match when I was five years old, and a memorable contest it was. Two of my six sisters, Madeline, then eleven, and Muriel, ten were partnered against me and Arthur Dewar, a young man whose family owned the Scotch whisky interests of the same name. Mr. Dewar, of course, 'carried' me – and 'carried' has both a colloquial and a literal significance. For one thing, he made most of the shots that counted heavily for our side. Furthermore, by the time we reached the fifteenth hole I was so weary I could hardly walk, so Mr. Dewar picked me up,

placed me on his shoulder, and transported me until we arrived at my ball."

Fortunately for little Miss Campbell, she grew stronger of limb as she became older. It was well for her that she did, else when she formallly "grew up" at the age of eighteen she might not have been able to lug around the heavy tweed skirt she was required to wear. The skirt stopped just one inch short of the ground. In those Victorian days it was considered immodest to appear in briefer attire. In retrospect, Mrs. Hurd cannot comprehend how she and her contempories swung clubs in such tent-like habiliment, which not only was cumbersome of itself but became quite heavy in rainy weather or when sand collected in the hem. The golf hats of the period also were not practical. They were large and full-brimmed, tilting at disconcerting angles with every fresh breath of breeze.

Nineteen years intervened between Mrs. Hurd's first and her last national championship conquests. Over that period she gained countless honors. She became the only player ever to win the four major national championships of women's golf. All told, she captured national titles eleven times; the American thrice, 1909, 1910, 1924; the British twice, 1909, 1911; the Canadian thrice, 1910, 1911, 1912; the Scottish thrice, 1905, 1906, 1908. She and Gladys Ravenscroft are the only foreigners who have won over here.

One of the proudest of all Mrs. Hurd's distinctions is that she once held simultaneously three of the four national championship trophies, the American and the Canadian, won in 1910, and the British, gained in 1911.

The cover of *Woman's Home Companion* magazine for September 1933, *near right*, showing Charlie Chaplin; and a ceramic hand-painted Donald Duck golfer, *far right*, of about 1930.

THE DUNLOP CADDIE

"THE GOLFER'S SYMBOL OF GOOD LUCK"

probably plays Golf, but not better than a second-class amateur. There is a batch of such men at Musselburgh. They are mostly very illiterate, but in their own way very respectable and deserving of respect.

My usual caddie, Flinn, is one of the same lot. He carries well, knows his employer's game, and almost never needs to be asked for a club – he has always the right one ready. His employer's clubs he keeps in good order. He is always sober during the day – at least, nearly always.

These men have no wish to do anything more than earn a living. Neither Flinn nor 'Fiery' attempt to sell balls, nor offer to remake them. They simply carry. They will have nothing to do with caddies who have ever been in gaol for theft, etc. Neither Flinn nor 'Fiery' would beg. They often starve. 'Fiery' is a very reticent man. No one knows more than that he is a bachelor, and lives in a lodging. No man ever saw him with his cap off, nor knows why he refuses to let his head be seen. He and his lot are quite heathens. They look on churches as for their betters, just as much as clubs. (This statement of Sir Walter's requires

A Dunlop caddie brooch, *above left*, on its original cord, and a penfold pin, *below*, both British from the 1920s.

A Superior Set Of Men
J.Kerr, *Golf*, 1893

It is your caddie's business to find out how far you drive with each club, and since a life-long experience will have taught him the exact relative position to the hole of each blade of grass on the links, he ought to be always able to put into your hand the right club, almost without your asking for it. He will also know the idiosyncrasies of your play, to what extent he may allow you to 'greatly dare,' out of what lie you may be permitted to play with a brassy, and all such little niceties.

Almost since he was born (in the year 1847) 'Fiery' has been connected with Golf, and it is a proof of his excellence as a caddie that young Willie Park has had him for helper in all his famous tournaments. He is one of those caddies who rank as high as the best professional, but who are purely carriers and coaches. 'Fiery'

PENFOLD

some qualification. Some of them, we happen to know, are good churchmen.) They would as soon expect to be invited to lunch in the one as to worship in the other.

I believe that in their own way 'Fiery' and his set are most reliable men... Whether 'Fiery' is better educated, or merely more intelligent, than most of his set I don't know; but he is a man of suave and polished manners. Yet he and two other caddies to whom we once gave a glass of champagne at St. Andrews because we happened to have no whisky unpacked, all said they have never tasted wine before. 'Fiery' alone seemed to appreciate it. He disagreed with the others who did not wish to taste it again, and said he 'could see that men might come to like that, but for his part he did not think it had 'eneuch o' grip.'

Prints of William Gunn (Caddie Willie), a curious character of the golf links, are familiar in Scottish club-houses. One of the strangest peculiarities of this eccentric ancient caddie was the way in which he wore his clothes, and the extraordinary profile he presents in the prints of him is accountable to the fact that he continually carried his wardrobe on his back. All the clothes he got he put on his back, one suit above another. To admit of his wearing three or four coats at once, he had to cut out the sleeves to let them on. True to the uniform which invariably distinguished golfers in those days, an old red coat was always worn outside of them all. He also wore three or four vests, an old worn fur one being outermost. It was the same with his trousers – three or four pairs on, and the worst outermost; and three bonnets, sewed one within the other. He had his quarters at Bruntsfield, renting a garret.

Willie was very honest, paying his rent regularly, and for his bread and milk as he got it. He lived entirely on baps and milk, never having a warm diet or a fire in his garret, even in the coldest winter. 'Caddie Willie' was a Highlander, and could only speak English imperfectly. He was in the habit of tramping from Edinburgh to his Highland home every autumn when the golfing season closed. In 1820 he left Bruntsfield. From that journey poor Willie never returned, and all the inquiry golfers made never elicited his fate.

BOBBY JONES
H.B. Martin, *50 Years of American Golf*, 1936

At the age of 28, Robert Tyre Jones, Jr., of Atlanta, Georgia, – better known as Bobby Jones of all points North, East, South and West – stood upon the highest pinnacle of golfing fame, looking back on the most marvellous stretch of achievement ever reached by a golfer on either side of the Atlantic. There was nothing ahead left undone, no championship title that had escaped his attention; and anything that he might do in the years to come could only be an anticlimax to what he had just accomplished that summer. As far as he could see along the distant horizon from his lofty height nothing could be discerned but waste barren land that held no promise of a future.

With no more worlds to conquer the Atlanta barrister decided to put away his famous "Calamity Jane" that had done such devastating work, along with the rest of his golfing weapons and call it a day.

In the spring of 1930 Bobby sailed for England, with seven other prominent young American amateurs, seeking another victory in the Walker Cup matches. Jones had other ideas in his mind that involved bigger game. For years he had been gunning for the British amateur championship but it had always managed to move out of range of his deadly fire each time. Those who had gathered at the dock to see the boys depart and wish them *bon voyage* – and a bit of luck on the other side – centered their hopes in Jones and expressed the wish that he might return with both British championships. Bobby's reply to his well wishers was that he would be quite satisfied with the amateur title and that there would be plenty of time to talk about the open after he had successfully landed the first plum.

It is a matter of history that he had a close call in that first event, at the hands of an American and fellow teammate, George Voigt, but he managed to get away with it and that was all that mattered. Once snaring the elusive amateur title, he found it even less difficult to annex the open and he set sail for home with both of these cherished possessions in his golfing kit.

PORTRAIT MADE IN HOLLYWOOD AFTER RETIREMENT FROM COMPETITIVE GOLF

Bobby's golfing dream was realized when he came back to American shores and completed his "grand slam" by winning both the amateur and the open titles, making a clean sweep of the four important major events in one year. This has all been too recent in golf history to warrant a detailed recital of what happened. All four of these championships, each one an achievement in itself and all the more remarkable when they came in a cluster, could not actually be counted the best golf that he had every played. In analyzing each event we find that not one of them showed exceptional golfing skill or outstanding play beyond the Jones standard, but they did show a tremendous amount of courage and fortitude and a display of nerve that has never been equalled. As he neared his goal the strain must have been intense. But the stout hearted young Georgian never faltered; he was bent solely on accomplishing his aim and determined to see it through.

Not Bobby Jones nor anyone else will ever again do as fine a thing in golf. Realizing full well that the records set down in this volume will last for generations to come, it is safe to predict that Jones' achievement will never be equalled. "The impregnable quadrilateral of golf," as George Trevor so aptly termed it, has been quite enough to place Jones on a lasting pedestal of fame; but Bobby, aside from this, occupied a pretty secure position in the world of golf in 1929. His record previous to the "big event" will bear the closest scrutiny. Starting life as a boy wonder, Bob Jones was forced to take what came his way and make the best of it. Even as a youngster the impeccable Mr. Jones of Georgia had many successes and many bitter disappointments which even to a boy didn't seem to be a square deal at the hands of Fate.

The earliest records of Bob Jones can be found in an old copy of *The American Golfer* printed in 1910, chronicling the deeds of a young lad by the name of Bobby Jones who at the age of eight had just won a golf tournament in Atlanta. Skipping over a few years we find this same young chap at the age of fourteen seeking national honors in the

amateur championship at the Merion Cricket Club in Philadelphia in 1916. It is a strange coincidence that Bobby should have started his tournament career at Merion, won his first amateur title there and returned to play in his last national championship on these same links.

The youngster from Atlanta was a sensation at Merion in 1916 in more ways than one. His golf stood up for two rounds after the qualifying test but his golfing disposition came in for much criticism from the beginning. "The kid wonder," as we golf writers called him, could play golf like a man and he could also swear like one when things went wrong. It was quite some time before he was able to master an uncontrollable desire to throw clubs at random and to use language unbecoming a gentleman, even allowing for liberties that the golf links are supposed to license. The golfing world had much time to speculate and wonder about the future of this precocious youngster in the next three years, since no major championships were played during the time we were engaged in the World War.

Bobby filled in his time playing in Red Cross matches and improving his game. He attracted attention wherever he appeared and his performance was highly satisfactory. He was a match for anyone, amateur or pro. Long Jim Barnes stopped off at Atlanta one day and played in an exhibition against Bobby in which the latter astonished Jim by his ability to throw clubs and otherwise disport himself like a spoiled child. Jim, in telling about his experience with the boy a few weeks later, remarked that there was nothing wrong with Bobby's disposition. "Any golfer," said Jim, "who is as determined to play topnotch golf and win matches as he is will make a champion some day. Mark my words, the kid is there and we are going to hear a lot about him in the next few years."

Bobby turned out to be a terrible disappointment to those who had figured that his golfing temperament would ruin him, and had thought that if he ever did succeed in winning there would be no living with him. In 1919 when he was runner-up to Dave Herron at Oakmont there was a complete change. Here was a modest little chap taking his beating in the final in a

championship that he would have loved to win, and not grumbling about it. In the next few years he had learned to take it on the chin, even though he didn't exactly relish the idea of not being able to win one of the big major events. But he was becoming dissatisfied with his lot.

There was a time when Jones seriously considered giving up the game, and had it not been for his victory in the open at Inwood in 1923 he would have been lost to golf. His greatest disappointment came in 1922 at Brookline. He was the outstanding favorite to win this amateur championship, and when he was turned back by Jess Sweetser in the semi-finals by the highly decisive margin of 7 up and 6 to play it was a bitter pill to swallow. O.B. Keeler, who always had Bobby's confidence, remarked at the time that it looked like the beginning of the end for the Atlanta youngster.

"Bobby has had several shots at the amateur championship," said Keeler, "and if the old dame who guides the destinies of golf champions is going to treat him like it did here he will be among the missing next year. Bobby has ambitious plans for a business career, and these plans do not include any golf. I wouldn't be surprised but what you have seen the last of us in golf championships. When Bobby quits I will quit too."

Two Bobby Jones "Flick Books", *right*, from the 1930s.

PHOTO EDWIN LEVICK, N. Y.

Left, Bobby Jones on the cover of *The Boy's Life of Bobby Jones* by O.B. Keeler, 1931.

There were times when Jones had to take the bitter with the sweet and profess to like it. As we look back on these upsets now they appear of minor importance. One disturbance was the distressing defeat at the hands of Walter Hagen in Florida in '26 by the rather humiliating score of 12 and 11. It was just Walter's time to shine, and there was nothing Bobby could do about it. Another occasion that was none too pleasant was when, under the sunny skies of California in 1929, he was stopped in the first round of the amateur championship at Pebble Beach by Johnnie Goodman. Bobby's admirers and well wishers were really more disturbed over this than he was, as he admitted he had never really seen an amateur championship before from a spectator's standpoint.

There is always one achievement that stands out in a champion's mind as his own pet stellar achievement. Bobby knows which tournament he got the greatest kick out of winning. It was the open at Scioto where he scrambled under the wire a stroke ahead of Joe Turnesa. It was a great victory because he was forced to do something worth while to win it. With nine holes to play it was seen that Jones could beat the score just turned in by Turnesa if he could manage the rest of the journey home in par figures. His march home that day was something long to be remembered, so seldom does the winner come to the home hole in a blaze of glory. Usually the stretch-running is where the hopes of many golfers are dashed to the rocks. Instead of being able to deliver their best, the players find a signal to fold up and become lost in the general scramble.

Jones didn't falter for a single instant that afternoon. Once he had his work laid out for him he went about the task like a master workman, and when he had finished there was just that one stroke that told the story. In the locker room that afternoon the pros held an indignation meeting, each blaming the other for letting Bobby come through. Hagen told the boys what he thought about it and he didn't mince words. "Every time I happen to be going badly," said Walter, "all the rest of you quit on the job. If we don't stop this lad he will be walking away with all our championships. Amateurs have won our open

five times now, out of the last twelve tournaments, and that is just a few times too many."

There is hardly any question but what Jones had become a threatening menace to the pros. He was an additional hazard in every championship and one that wrecked the scores of many players with chances for victory in sight. Hardly a pro could be said to be scot-free of the Bobby Jones complex. Some pros admitted it openly, others stumbled into the pit unconsciously; but one thing is certain, at one time or another they all fell, and it was not an easy task to scramble to their feet. Usually during the progress of a tournament the cry from one end of the links to the other was "How is Jones going?" Most of the players were so busy worrying about the entry from Atlanta that they had no time to concentrate on their own games. This made Jones' task doubly easy and often paved his way to victory when it might have been otherwise.

It was charged that the governing body had something to do with making Bobby's life a happy one on the links. The pros were whispering around that Jones was getting all the breaks. He could pick his own partner and had the choice of the starting time. If there were special rules to be interpreted a bevy of friendly officials were on hand to perform this function. Always he carried a bodyguard of officials on and off the links. This was beginning to be a sore spot with the entire professional brigade and it meant an additional worry.

The U.S.G.A. may have favored Jones, consciously or unconsciously, but usually there was some good reason. The increased galleries when the Atlanta barrister was at his height is explanation enough to clear up the mystery. Jones was drawing the crowds and the people's interest had to be looked after. It was a one man show for a while and it was a profitable performance. Naturally the star is entitled to the best dressing room and the breaks of attention up and down the line. If any of the other actors didn't like it all they had to do was to step in and steal the show. It was not so easy to do as a rule, but sometimes it happened.

Bobby Jones' career was all too short to allow any correct opinion of what he might have done

in later years. That he was truly a very great artist there can be no doubt, and whatever he has done he has left an indelible impression upon the minds of golfers who knew him during his tournament days. To be compelled to write about one so young in the past tense is difficult, for there is always the possibility that he may burst out at any time and start a new career. This seems unlikely when one knows the former youthful prodigy as well as the author – but stranger things than that have happened in golf.

Jones was a stylist, with scarcely a blemish in a swing that appeared to the onlookers to be absolutely perfect. He had a habit, like all great artists, of concealing his art, which made his golf look so ridiculously simple and easy that one could rarely hope to benefit from watching his play.

Jones was an impatient youth with a desire to surge ahead and accomplish great things before he had learned the most important lessons of golf discipline. In the beginning he played competitive golf two different ways. His strongest asset was medal play and his success at this method easily carried him to the top. Yet in his early amateur championships he was guilty of

"playing his opponent," generally to an unsuccessful conclusion. It was only after he had learned the true art of match play – which is really medal play, playing one's own game and permitting the opponent to handle his own situation the best he can – that Bobby became a consistent victor. Jones was methodical, he was a student of good form and never failed to check up on himself to see that the clubhead was kept swinging in the right direction with the correct rhythm. This led some to remark that "Only a genius can play to a timetable and keep just a fraction ahead of the field."

Jones was popular abroad where they had accepted him as one of their own. Long before he had won a major championship his fame had travelled to England and they were anxious to see the boy wonder – and when they did see him perform they were not disappointed.

Jones' most spectacular feat abroad was at Sunningdale in 1926 while qualifying for the Open championship. He hit top form by going around this difficult course in 66 and 68 for a total of 134, which opened the eyes of the British. This was Jones at this best and he was so pleased with his score that he remarked that he would like to wrap up the course and take it home with him as a souvenir.

Albert F. Free of New York, who has seen more major championships, both here and abroad, than any other American, has said many times that the Jones performance at Sunningdale was the best golf he had ever seen played. He is positive that America has never seen Jones at his best. There seems to be something in this statement, because outside of his first fling at the British open at St. Andrews, where Bobby became disgusted and in a moment of thoughtlessness tore up his card, he has averaged a higher percentage of victories over there than in this country. Out of only four British Opens in which he competed he has won three of them. Out of four attempts to win the British amateur title he was successful once, making the phenomenal average of .500 on British soil. In twenty-four major championships he has played in over here he has been successful nine times which would give him a percentage of .375 on his home links. Jones has played in thirteen amateur

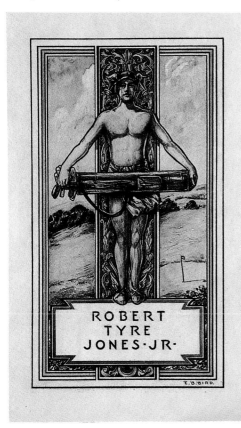

ROBERT
TYRE
JONES·JR·

A bookplate of Robert Tyre – "Bobby" -Jones, *left.*

Right, Charles Blair MacDonald, *The American Sportsman*, 1928, by Richard B. Adams, an original painting.

championships, including all of the events played from 1916 to 1930, and he has won five amateur titles. He has taken part in eleven Opens from 1920 to 1930 and has won four of them.

Never was there an athlete imbued with a truer spirit of amateurism than Jones who steadfastly refused to listen to tempting offers to join the professional ranks. Once in Florida Bobby finished fourth in the Miami Open. The author was conducting the tournament and was pleased to present the Atlantan with a Gladstone bag. Bobby refused it and asked if the value of the bag might not be added to the prize money for the pros. He was always like that, leaning over backward sometimes to make sure of his position in the game.

However, there came a time when the temptation was too great and the prize, a princely fortune, too much to be spurned. After Jones made his clean sweep of the major championships in 1930 the moving picture companies and other interests deluged him with offers that simply could not be refused, so Jones became a business man golfer and regretfully left the amateur ranks.

H.H. Ramsay, former president of the U.S.G.A., in commenting on Bobby Jones after he had made his grand slam, said: "Time and time again he has demonstrated that he had remarkable courage, determination and courtesy. All of these qualities would be nothing if he had not within him a spark of the undying fire, the glowing flame of character without which no man can be a real champion. As the poet says, 'When the fight begins within himself, a man is worth something.' As with all men of character, his greatest victory has been himself."

GOLFLUENZA
L. Latchford, *The Young Man,* 1903

Golf is not a mere game; it is a disease, infectious and contagious, which once acquired cannot be shaken off. Once a golfer always a golfer – there's no help for it!

The game exercises a spell, a thrall over the man who has once swung a club. You begin promiscuously and experimentally. A golfing friend casually hands you a driving iron and asks you to have a "whang" at a golf ball. Well! you "whang" and your fate is sealed. You are a golfer from that moment. Most likely you missed the ball and, like the man who ordered another pound of beetle powder, vowing that "he'd kill that confounded cockroach before he'd done," you mutter between your teeth that you'll go on whanging till you knock that ball into the next field. Or you, by the veriest chance (as you discover later), give the ball a fine swinging smack and to your delight see the lively bit of white gutta-percha soaring in the air to alight a full hundred yards off.

Then with a mild chuckle you hand back your friend his iron and exultantly observe that you think this game would "suit you" thoroughly. Whatever your luck – whether you hit or whether you miss – you are a golf-infected person. The incipient stages of the disease are rapid. You buy a set of clubs, clandestinely and ill-advisedly, seeking no advice, and probably acquiring tools which indeed prove "ill adapted for putting the little balls into the little holes." Then you sally forth covertly to practise and to fret away your soul in vain endeavours to "drive." You practise "putting" – which looks so easy, but is so tricky – on your lawn, and you fume and perspire at your own ineptitude.

Thenceforward you are known to talk of nothing but mashie strokes, bunkers, long putts, stymies and cuppy lies. A course of golf reading almost inevitably follows, the quality of the golf

Henry Cotton, *near right*, at Ashridge, and a Spaldings Advertisement, *far right* of the early 1920s.

Henry Cotton, with the Ashridge Golf Club-house in the Background

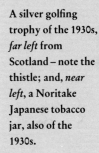

links decides for you your summer holiday resort, you betake youself to see the professional tournaments, you talk familiarly of Harry Vardon, Braid, Sandy Herd and Jack White, and you breathe the name of "auld Tom Morris" with caressing veneration. Then you are fully ensnared – the royal and ancient game is your fowler.

IT's A ROUGH LIE
P.S. Anderson, *The American Golfer,* 1928

It's rough when you're out of the fairway,
It's fair when you're out of the rough,
And the fairer it is, in the fairway
The rougher it is, in the rough.
When you bounce off a shot from the fairway,
And watch it hide out in the rough,
You feel it is really no fair way
To treat a good lie. Golf is tough!
And when you get out of the fairway
It takes a sweet shot from the rough
To recover the fight through the fairway,
For every shot counts – That's no bluff.
And every man's shot in the fairway
Is longer than one in the rough.
so try to hole out through the fairway
And keep out of that hole in the rough!

A silver golfing trophy of the 1930s, *far left* from Scotland – note the thistle; and, *near left*, a Noritake Japanese tobacco jar, also of the 1930s.

's Golf Player.

ON THE LINKS

The pleasure and benefit of healthful exercise are increased and made more permanent by the bath which follows. Ivory Soap, because of its purity, its mild creamy lather and the comfortable feeling of perfect cleanliness that results from its use, is the soap most generally preferred for the bath. It floats.

Right, a Proctor & Gamble soap advertisement from 1889.

IN THE SPRINGTIME
I.A. Monkhouse, *Golf,* 1897

Come and see the Golf links
On an April day,
Hawthorns are in blossom,
Lambs, too, are at play.

Scarlet coats are flying
In the balmy air,
Sailor hats are nodding
Over faces fair.

Old and young have turned out,
Wielding club and ball,
Some for competition,
For enjoyment all.

On the green are old men
Busy holing out,
Golf is their elixir,
Warding off the gout.

By a silv'ry streamlet
Wander "he and she,"
Other links, they dream of
In futurity.

Naught we feel beyond us
On a day in Spring,
E'en to break the record,
Seems an easy thing.

A hole-in-one silver holder, *left,* of around 1900 with a featherie ball.

99

SECTION THREE

A Golfing Bag

Golf Balls and Boys * A Sight for the Gods * The Love Ticket * Cooking With Golf Balls * The Appliance of Science * That's My Excuse * Measure for Measure * A Caddie's Story * In Defence of Caddies * The Ghost of Colonel Bogey * Putting the Ladies Right * Golfing Ladies * Disposing of Tommy * The Haskell Ball * Bobby Jones in Close-Up * Instructions in Etiquette * Redressing the Balance * Driving to Destruction * Dictionary of Golf * Flocking to Carnoustie * Warding off the Brain Storm * From Marbles to Golf Balls * What's the Use of Worrying * A Raphael at Golf * The Necessary Evil * Plain and Simple * Beyond the Bounds of Reason * Bicycle Skirts and Sailor Hats * Golf in the Year 2,000 * A Little Abstinence * A Golfing Holiday * Packing Up Your Golf * Spoons, Niblicks and Stymies * A Traitorous Handicap * A Worm's Paradise * The Core of the Problem * Golf in the Old Country.

GOLF BALLS AND BOYS
Bernard Darwin, *The Winner For Boys Book*, 1920s

If this article had been written a certain number of years ago it would have begun, I suppose, with the statement that Golf was a game played almost entirely in Scotland on pieces of waste land near the sea, that the balls were made of gutta-percha and painted white, and the instruments, called clubs, consisted of long thin wooden shafts having heads spliced and bound on to them with twine. Fortunately, it is not now necessary to begin like that, because Golf is played everywhere, and everybody plays Golf. I shall assume, then, that if any boy reads this article, he knows what Golf is, has seen it and perhaps played it to some extent, that he has near him some kind of a golf-course or a field or a garden where he can play, and that he can get some clubs.

That clears the ground, but I may say a little more about his clubs, and it will be easiest if I address him in the vocative sense. *Puer* I will say to him, as in the Latin sentence book, "O Boy." First of all then, O Boy, you need not have many clubs, and indeed you will probably do better if you have not, for you will then learn to be master of the few you have, by discovering that they can be made to do all sorts of different golfing jobs. I think, if possible, you had better have four. To begin with, of course, a wooden one, and I should have a brassey rather than a driver. All sorts of distinguished people, including many of the best American players, drive off the tee with a brassey nowadays, and it will do the work through the green for you as well. I should have it a little lofted, because it will thus be easier to get the ball well into the air. That is encouraging, and if you are not frightened of topping, you will swing the club more easily and freely. After that comes some sort of driving or medium iron, a

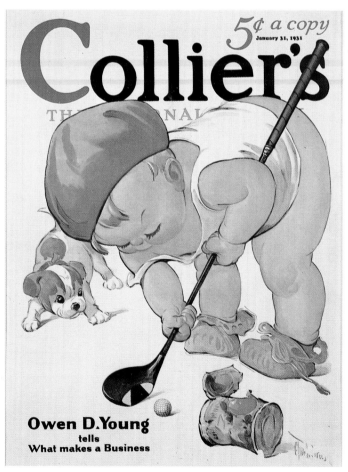

5¢ a copy
January 31, 1931

Collier's
THE NATIONAL

Owen D. Young
tells
What makes a Business

mashie or a mashie-niblick – the former for choice, and a putter.

People will very likely tell you that you do not want a putter, and that you can learn to putt just as well with your iron, but if I were you I should stick out for a real putter of you can possibly get one.

Having got your clubs, you are going to set to work to play with them, and the best way to learn is by watching very carefully and then imitating as well as you can. Fat old gentlemen cannot imitate: they have to be pushed or prodded into the right attitudes and taught how to move their bodies bit by bit; but you can twist yourself about quite easily and copy the way in which somebody else twists himself. But, of course, it is desperately important to imitate the right person and not the wrong one. Fathers are, for instance, excellent people, to be imitated and looked up to in perhaps every other way, but they do not always play golf very gracefully or very well. I have seen dutiful little boys trying to

ruin their golf for life by playing in just the same styles as their fathers; and those fathers were either as stiff as a pair of compasses, dressed up in a coat and trousers, or else danced on their toes like a cat on hot bricks – neither of them good plans. So when you take a model be sure it is a good one – a professional if possible, or a really good amateur, or another boy who is a friend of yours, if he has a good style. Then watch your model very hard, try to see how he holds his club and where he puts his feet and swing the club as like him as you can.

One thing you want to be on your guard against. The professional seems to take up his club very fast and hit with a tremendous swish. He seems to be able to throw himself about just as he likes. That is because he is used to it, and always doing it, and has the knack of balancing himself. When you first see him and try to imitate what he does, you will be inclined to swing too fast or too far and to tumble about. So take another look at him and you will see that for all he swings so fast and appears so free and easy, he really keeps wonderfully still. His head hardly moves at all; and to keep your head still is probably the most important thing in golf, because it makes you keep your balance and stops your body from tumbling about. His body does not tumble about – his shoulders turn, but they turn on an axis which keeps steady. His feet do not move much – he does not dance on the tips of his toes – and his knees do not bend much. He looks perfectly free, but all his movements are kept very well under control.

On the other hand, look at a bad player, and look at our friend the fat old gentleman. He doesn't look free, he looks cramped and tied up like a stuck pig. Yet if you take another and more careful look at him, you will see that really he is moving and moving all over the place: his head bobs about and his knees crumple under him. This always seems to me one of the funniest things about golf that the player who appears at first sight all movement is really keeping still, and vice versa. And so I say again, don't take just one look at your good player and then go away and swing yourself into a complicated knot, because that is not really the way he does it at all.

Left, portrait of Bobby Jones, from the Bobby Jones Trust.

103

As to putting, you can practise that on the floor of your room if you want to, and if this is not so good as a real green it is much better than no practice at all. Only remember this, that it is very easy to hit the leg of a table or a chair if you only hit hard enough, and that which is very easy won't do you much good. So try to putt with the proper strength as you would do at a real hole when you are afraid of running past it out of holing. And don't be content with just hitting the table leg. Try to learn to hit the ball smoothly and to take the club back straight and to stand still. If you can do those three things you will be a good putter, which is the way to win matches.

Finally, if I were to try to give you one comprehensive bit of advice about playing golf, it would be: "Don't hurry." The ball is there waiting to be hit, and it will go on patiently waiting: it won't run away. It is not like a cricket ball which will be past you and in your wicket if you don't make up your mind at once what to do with it. At games with a moving ball you are often too late for it, but very, very few people hit a golf ball too late. Ninety-nine bad shots out of a hundred and more than that are missed because the player hits too soon. He gets his club back properly perhaps, and then he suddenly gets anxious and rushes at it, and just as he is in too much of a hurry to hit it, so he is in too much of a hurry to see where he has hit it, and so he takes his eye off the ball. This is as true of the shortest putt as of the longest drive. So don't hurry, and if

you never do I think I can promise you that you will be a very remarkable golfer and a very happy one.

A SIGHT FOR THE GODS
Some People We Meet, 1900

The man "wot" golfs is as well satisfied with himself as a newly feathered turkey. He likes to be thought an ardent player and continually interlards his conversation with such words as "Bunkers," "Tees," "Clicks," and other dreadful sounding things. His costume consists of a tweed coat and knickerbockers of an alarming pattern, with stockings conspicuous a mile off, a shirt loud enough to startle a township, and new orange-yellow boots. A sight for the gods, he fussily lugs towards the links a bright leather bag – on which his initials are painted, about a foot to a letter – full of curious looking implements, the bulk of whose names he doesn't even know, but which appear to him to be the correct thing to carry. He strides over the turf as though all Southampton belonged to him, shouts out your name across the field, wanting to know "'ow many you've made," swears volubly and "muffs" everthing. The men avoid him; the ladies keep at a respectful distance, whilst the "caddie" with visible difficulty suppresses an emphatic opinion concerning his skill. He is single, and has a keen desire to move in society.

A selection of Carlton Ware ceramics, *right*, of the 1920s.

Life

10¢

May 8
1931

The cover of *Life*
magazine, *left*, for
May 8, 1931; *below*,
a Noritake Japanese
tobacco jar of the
1930s.

THE LOVE TICKET
Irish Golfer, 1933

Basil Haddon could play golf. It was pretty well the only thing he attempted in life. Such devotion to a game may mean good luck or disaster. In his case it was the latter. His job – not a wonderful one – left him, though many would have said he left it. So he found himself one day with about fifty pounds and no possibility of securing further employment.

Possessed of good looks, a bright disposition, and not too much brains, he looked about him and thought hard – where he could golf and blow his money. He was quick in deciding the line of a putt, and he was nearly as quick in deciding on making for Ballysand, the glorious links on the Atlantic. He would go and have a jolly good time for a few weeks and let the future look after itself.

Ballysand is a little village on the west coast of Ireland consisting of an old-fashioned hotel, two churches, twenty-seven public houses, and about thirty private houses. The golf course laid out among the sandhills had earned what fame Ballysand possessed.

Haddon on arrival found he had the place more or less to himself, but that did not upset him, as he could spend money playing with the professional. The latter was genuinely impressed by Haddon's undoubted golfing talent, and a week passed pleasantly enough.

Perhaps not so pleasantly as Haddon might have wished. The result of a big sweepstakes draw had been published and there was no mention of the ten tickets he had taken. But who would bother about a trifle when fine weather and Ballysand links called to one so cheerfully? Haddon didn't.

He came back to lunch one day to see an intriguing sports car outside the hotel and became mildly excited. Perhaps it contained golfers. In the dining-room he was slightly disappointed when he saw only a woman had arrived. That she was remarkably pretty and possessed of rather beautiful wandering eyes did not greatly interest this youth who only lived to win golf championships. Still even he began to hope she was staying. Stay she did, and Haddon

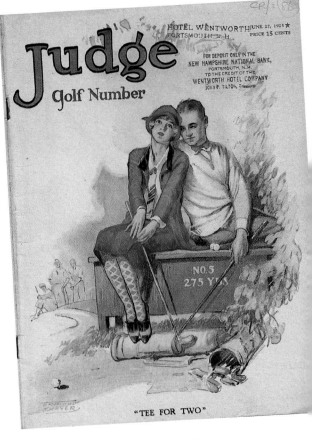

"TEE FOR TWO"

and she progressed wonderfully well because she was a golfer, too, and fully understanding.

They played much golf together. He had heard of her before, for as Pamela Birdey she had also won fame on the links. Young people to-day lose no time and soon they were Pamela and Basil to each other. Old inhabitants of the village shook their heads at modern ways when they discussed the two most striking visitors at the hotel.

"I was so disgusted over the sweep draw that I felt I must get right away and play golf," Pamela told Basil.

In between tremendous golf matches the two motored in her car, and she had quickly become a "divilish sensible girl" when she let him do most of the driving. Incidentally, she was quick to see he was a good driver.

One day they went to see some wonderful cliff scenery, and as the car drew near it the road narrowed to a boreen and climbed steeply.

"Heavens! Will we ever be able to turn?" Pamela exclaimed as they climbed slowly on.

"Probably not," was the nonchalant answer. "But who wants to go back?. I don't."

"Pleasant lad! Brain failing as the Atlantic air becomes stronger."

Basil was feeling thrilled and, if the car had not been on such an incline, might have descended to sloppiness. The air, the gallantly climbing car, both got into his blood, and he became a totally different Basil. This she "sensed," as modern writers so horribly express it, and she forbore to say more. Also she was becoming slightly anxious.

They reached the end of the climb and the road and with that huge stone wall. Turning the car was an impossibility, the moving of the stone wall nearly so. Brakes full on, they looked in each other's eyes, then laughed – rather nervously, it is true. It stopped when he jumped out to put big stones behind the rear wheels.

"Nearly two miles of a reverse down a bally awful hill," he said returning to her. "You had better walk down while I manage the car."

"Never desert my ship in a storm. But I thought you said you didn't want to go back."

"I don't. Life's splendid here with you and only the noise of the sea in our ears."

"H'm; no golf, no meals, no bed – not for me," declared Pam. "Still it's nice of you to say so, and all that."

He broke into a declaration of love, which she did not restrain, and they talked and other things for an hour or so. He had no money, nor had she, so she said.

"Look here, Basil, we'll take a ticket in the next sweep together. If it's lucky, we'll get married."

"Never won anything in my life."

"Never mind, you may this time."

Youthfully they chatted till the descent was made most skilfully by Basil. It was a touch-and-go descent on a desperately bad surface, which seemed to roll down with the car.

"A wonderful recovery from a hanging lie," declared Pamela laughing, when they were on the flat again.

"I'd like a lot of such lies," said Basil gallantly.

That night she told him she had to go away in the morning. The sudden announcement upset him far more than he ever anticipated, and for the rest of the evening he was glum.

"It's no good, Pam, I'll never do any good except on a golf course. Better forget me – and Ballysand."

Two American Valentine cards, *left and below*, from 1910; and the cover of *Life* magazine, *bottom*, for August 29, 1929.

The cover of *Ladies Home Journal* magazine, *right*, for July 1929.

"Don't be an idiot! I'll get that ticket and we'll win. You've got enough to keep you going till the next draw. Then together we'll win championships and have a jolly good time. Dear old Ballysand, how I love you! We'll have our honeymoon here," said Pamela, getting up to retire to bed.

"Wish we could," he said lighting her candle.

"We'll call it 'The Love Ticket,' and it will never let us down," laughed Pam, though she was near tears.

Pamela had come to Ballysand because she had drawn a horse in the sweep that ran second in the Derby, and she wanted to escape all the fuss aroused by her good luck.

Luck stood to her again, as the "Love Ticket" drew a horse that ran third in the Cambridgeshire.

Once again at Ballysand at bed-time.

"Dear old boy, do you remember your depression when I was here before and how I told you the 'Love Ticket' would be lucky?"

"You were an optimist," he said lighting her candle.

"Now you'll be able to blow it out," she said with a laugh as she ran upstairs.

COOKING WITH GOLF BALLS
J.D. Dunn, *Bulletin of the USGA*, 1900

This article is more particularly written for the benefit of golfers in out-of-the-way places where there is no professional or dealer to do the work. And again, some enthusiastic amateurs may come to look upon it as a pleasant pastime for a winter's evening.

Purchase a can of lye, costing fifteen cents. Half a can of lye in a pail of water will take the paint off six dozen balls in about six hours. Ball-makers use a very strong solution of lye, which they put in an apparatus similar to a washing-machine. This brings off the paint in short order and does not injure the gutta-percha. Amateurs should stir the balls up in the lye occasionally.

After the balls have been in the lye about six hours, take them out with a vegetable strainer. Place them in some lukewarm water, and then brush off the old paint with a nail-brush.

The balls must now be placed in a pot of water that is almost on the boil. Don't have more or less than half a dozen balls in the pot at one time, and always keep replacing them by others. It is not

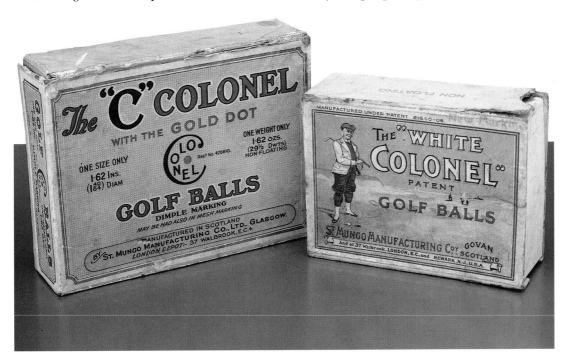

Two Colonel Golf Ball boxes, *left.*

109

Silver and mother-of-pearl cutlery, *right*, with a golfing theme, from the 1920s.

necessary to let the balls get heated right through. Take the ball out of the pot with a table-spoon and work out the cuts, if any, with your thumb. Roll the ball around in your palms until it is slightly egg-shaped. Do not keep the ball so long in your hands that the outer surface gets cold, or the gutta-percha will not take the impression of the marking. Should the balls be sticky in the hands a little water or linseed oil may be used as a preventive.

When the ball is in the mould squeeze it up in a press. It is not absolutely necessary to have a regular ball press. A book press or vise will do almost as well, and the expedient brings the cost down considerably.

For very little additional cost you can have your initials on the mould. This will save you the trouble of marking your ball before playing in a match, and settles all disputes about ownership.

Allow the ball to remain in the mould about a minute, then put it in a pail of cold water. You can afterwards cut off the "fin" with a sharp knife. On a large scale this is turned off on a machine somewhat like a lathe. The same machine also makes an impression similar to the rest of the marking on the ball. This is not necessary, although it looks better.

The next operation is to paint the balls. This is best done by putting some paint in the palms of one's hands. Rubber gloves may be bought for this work, although they are not nearly so good for the work as the bare skin. The paint does not do any harm and it will wash off easily in warm water. The paint should be put on in four very thin coats. Only the second coat should be rubbed into the marking. After painting, the balls should be stood on a wooden frame to dry.

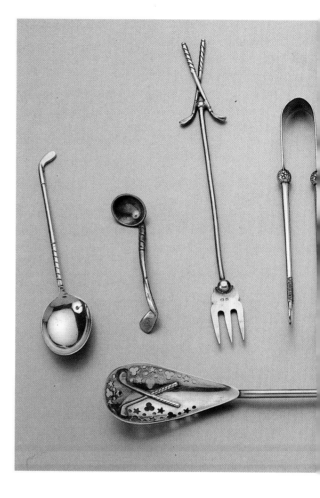

THE APPLIANCE OF SCIENCE
Golf, 1893

At an ordinary meeting of the Royal Society of Edinburgh, held on June 5th, Professor Sir Douglas Maclagan presiding, Professor Tait read a paper on the "Approximate determination of the path of a rotating spherical projectile." The point which he discussed, and which he demonstrated by means of a model, was that a rotating spherical body in moving through the air is deflected in the direction towards which its front rotates. Thus if a ball is thrown to a distance, with a rotatory motion along a vertical axis in the direction of the hands of a watch, the ball, instead of following a straight path, will curve away to the right, the explanation being

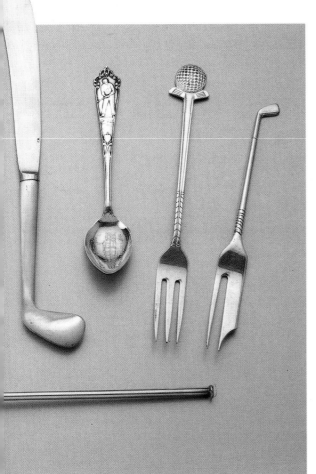

right or left according as a rotary motion was imparted to it in a right or left handed direction along the vertical axis; and if a player under-cut a ball, and there was no gravity, it would turn away upwards. He had often seen "slicing" having the effect of making a ball change its direction through nearly a right angle before it reach the ground.

If they assumed that anything could be done in the way of under-cutting, so that the front of the ball as it went forward was ascending, then they could account for the fact that even with moderate speeds, such as 400 yards initial velocity, they could get a range of 200 yards. If they assumed an initial velocity of 400 feet per second, and that the ball was projected, but without rotation at a tangent of one in four, the range would be about 400 feet, and at a tangent of one in eight, it would be about 320 feet. Keeping the same initial velocity, but with a slight amount of rotation, the range of the ball, at a tangent of one in four, would be about 500 feet. Keeping the

that a greater pressure by the air is exerted upon the ball upon the side to which the motion of rotation takes place.

Applying this fact to the question, how it is possible to drive a Golf ball to so great a distance as say 200 yards, with the moderate speed which human strength can give, Professor Tait said it seemed to him that if a player trusted solely to overcoming the resistance of the air with so light a projectile, it would be necessary to give a tremendous initial velocity – some 700 or 800 feet per second. It occurred to him, therefore, that the rotation of the ball must have something to do with it. He had observed that the path of a well-driven Golf ball was sometimes markedly concave upwards. There must be some cause to produce this ascensional tendency, and the only possible cause was to be looked for in the form of rotation of the ball, so that as it went forward its front was always going upwards. In the same way was to be explained the deflection of a ball to

MARCH 1900 TEN CENTS

THE LADIES' HOME JOURNAL

THE CURTIS PUBLISHING COMPANY, PHILADELPHIA

The cover of *Ladies Home Journal* magazine, *left*, for March 1900.

The cover of *Leslie's* magazine, *above right*, for July 16, 1913; *below right*, a collection of lead figures from 1920 to 1935.

same initial velocity, but with a slight amount of rotation, the range of the ball, at a tangent of one in four, would be about 500 feet, and at a tangent of one in eight over 400 feet.

Finally, if they gave a large amount of rotation, and started the ball with an initial velocity of 400 feet per second, at a tangent of one in eight, it would, at the outset of its flight, follow a path which was concave up, and reach its greatest height at a distance of three-fourths of its total range, dropping with a greater amount of inclination at a distance from the starting point of about 560 feet. If it were started off without any inclination at all, it would gradually achieve a height, and have a range of 520 feet. In reply to Lord M'Laren, Professor Tait said that his impression was that the rotation of the ball was only slightly diminished in the course of its flight, and after landing it might still be seen spinning with extreme rapidity.

THAT'S MY EXCUSE
Bulger, *Echoes From the Links*, 1924

The average golfer is prolific in excuses. No doubt, as the number of his bad strokes decreases, he will indulge in fewer explanatory remarks. From the persistent way in which players proffer excuses, we must infer that this "escape of steam" has an ameliorative effect upon their tempers.

I have seen a golfer of a choleric temperament striving manfully to keep calm. It was a not uninteresting spectacle. All went well for a few holes, until, after a succession of poor shots, he would give way to a horrid imprecation, and then fling his club after the ball. Other men, in similar circumstances, occasionally hit the ground savagely with their clubs until they break them. Such manifestations of the natural man are regrettable, but they are rather uncommon.

While the number of excuses is legion, perhaps the most popular is a sudden attack of indigestion. A winning player has rarely anything to complain of. Not so the man who is holes behind, and likely to remain so until the match is over. If he happens to be playing very badly, he will speedily remark, "I'm out of form to-day. I've been suffering from indigestion for

JULY 18, 1912

Leslie'

THE PEOPLE'S WEEKLY

"F o r e"

several days." His opponent smiles inwardly, if that is a possible feat; but vocally he is quite sympathetic. "Indigestion is a most troublesome thing," he will admit, and then he may go on to describe one of his own recent attacks.

The married man – more especially the young married man – has an excellent reason for his bad play. His excuse has done duty a thousand times, and it is not in the least likely to be dethroned from its position of favouritism. The baby is often restless at nights, and the loving husband, anxious to conserve his darling wife's strength, willingly attends to "the bottles." This labour of love interrupts the husband's slumbers, and, if it should occur on a Friday night, its effects are

seen next day in the erratic strokes from the tee and the faulty pitches to the green. "I had a disturbed night," is a good phrase, and one that is thoroughly understood by every Benedick.

Dogs frequently afford legitimate excuses for a poor stroke. A terrier will sometimes dash in front of a player who is about to strike the ball, and, if a foozle is made in the circumstances, the golfer's complaint is obviously well-grounded. The "meh" of a sheep has often an unsteadying influence. I have seen a player interrupted three times by a sheep, which coolly and, as it seemed, deliberately raised its voice in protest, just at the very moment that the club was about to be drawn away from the ball.

A collection of W.H. Grindley & Co porcelain, *left*, with teddy bear motifs, 1910 to 1930.

Most of us make bad strokes at golf – some more, some less – but the impaired digestion, the bad night's rest, and the yaup of the mongrel have not so much to do with the unsatisfactory results as some players imagine.

If the lie of the ball were studied more, and the distance to the hole carefully measured by the eye, I am convinced there would be fewer weak approaches.

What is called playing "wi' the heid" is simply using one's eyes and judgment to the best advantage. The thoughtful, observant player will make greater progress at the game than the man who plays it in a happy-go-lucky manner.

An early American country store broomstick holder of the 1880s, *right*, with a selection of clubs.

MEASURE FOR MEASURE
Harry Fulford, *Golfing,* 1909

K. Richard -
We are amaz'd; and thus long have we stood
To watch the fearful bending of thy knee.
Because we thought ourself that it were right;
And if we be, how dare thy joints forget
To do their rightful duty in our presence?
If we be not, show us again the swing
Lest we dismiss thee from thy post;
For well we know, as you have shown us oft
We grip the handle of our driver right.

Romeo -
Boy, give me my mashie, or the lofting iron.
And now take heed that thou movest not,
See thou betrayest not thy presence
By word or deed, upon thy life I charge thee
Whate'er thou hear'st repeat it not.
And do not speak to me upon the course.
Why I consent to play upon these links
Is, partly to confound Capulet,
Who hath a record, complished.
I am not jealous, but by Heaven
It rankles in mine bosom. Though
If I may trust the feeling that's within me,
This day will see an end to my revenge.

Hamlet -
To tee, or not to tee, that is the question:
I have oft heard it said that he
Who scorneth sand, wherewith his ball
May be brought closer to his reach,
Is tempting providence. Inasmuch
He causeth it to ascend unduly.
Therefore it behoves us, Horatio,
To take heed of this precept.
It is mine honour.
And being, as I trust, most honourable,
It will enhance mine honour
To keep my passion within bounds,
Lest in the losing of it, I lose my match.

(He strikes) -
'Tis sad. Despite my most careful attention
It has flown, to the country from whose bourne
No ball returns.

A CADDIE'S STORY
H.M.F., *Golf*, 1898

Tim was a caddie at the Highwater Golf Club, and was much sought after by reason of his unswerving interest in the game, his integrity, civility, and general quiet demeanour. He was only twelve years old, and small for his age, though, his old grandmother, with whom he lived, and whom he carefully tended, would say, "There's a power of use in him."

But Tim had a weakness, and it was this.

There was another boy, Jack Peterson by name, the smartest caddie on the links, and considered the best player among them. This lad was Tim's hero. He was three or four years Tim's senior, and treated him with the condescending patronage that a retriever might be expected to show to an admiring kitten. That his hero could ever be in the wrong never entered into the little lad's calculations, and to be allowed to fetch and carry for him constituted his highest pleasure in life.

Now, Tim was no mean golfer himself, though he could not drive as far as Jack, with his long slashing drives, and would-be-professional style, yet his neat approaches and steady putting made him a formidable opponent.

A caddies' competition was organized during the summer, and as usual, Jack and Tim played round together. Now, it happened on this occasion that Tim's putting was at fault, and his score mounted up while Jack played a steady as well as a brilliant game, and was doing an excellent score. Tim was in raptures, and could hardly suppress his excitement. All went well till they came to the seventeenth hole, where the green was guarded by a yawning bunker. Here, approaching from a distance, Jack's ball was seen to reach the edge of the bunker and disappear, Tim's ball following in the same direction.

"One of us is in!" cried Jack in an annoyed voice, as they drew nearer and found only one ball visible.

Tim was seized with an inspiration, "It's me," he said, "I saw it go in," and though he had the grace to colour up at what he knew to be a perfectly untrue assertion, he pointed to the other ball lying just to one side of the bunker, and began hammering away at the ball in the sand, as if his very life depended on it. Jack played the other ball without giving it more than a casual glance, as he had no wish to discover the mistake, if such there was.

An Austrian match-striker caddie, of 1910; and a collection of Royal Doulton Series Ware, *left,* **from 1911 to 1932.**

115

The cover of *The Saturday Evening Post* magazine, *right*, for July 18, 1936.

"Just a bit lucky" commented he, taking the two balls out of the hole, "I thought as I was done for that time, it 'ud 'ave taken me a week to get out."

Of course Jack proved the winner, and was congratulated and envied by all, except Tim, who rushed off home as soon as he could, the other boys thinking he was annoyed at not winning himself.

But his depression continued the next day, and increased as the week went on, especially when the lad who came in second, and who had always been very kind to him, told him what bad luck he had had in losing his ball, which had prevented his coming in first. Jack, too, seemed to avoid him, and was always cross when the competition was mentioned. At last Tim's tender conscience worked him up into such a state of mind that he became quite ill, for worst of all was the harrowing thought that perhaps Jack had known all the time.

Finding how thin and ill he was getting, his grandmother made him stop in bed one day, and seeing the curate of the parish pass she asked him if he would come in and see Tim. The curate, who was a golfer, and Tim's especial patron, willingly complied, and was surprised to see the change in the boy during the last few days. After chatting with him for a little while, he asked if he had anything on his mind, at which Tim burst into tears, and reluctantly confessed the whole of his duplicity. Naturally, the whole tale had to come out, and it transpired that Jack had known perfectly well all the time that he was playing with the wrong ball, and what is more, it turned out, as these things will upon examination, that it was not the first time that he had managed to come in first with the help of a little manoeuvring of his own.

The Committee of the Club thought that it was a pity to let the lad continue in the place of his temptation, so they got him a berth at sea, where he proved himself entirely satisfactory. Tim eventually realized the height of his ambition by being apprenticed as a club-maker, and if, as is expected, he becomes a first-class professional, the lesson he learnt as a boy as to the frailty of human nature will not have been wasted.

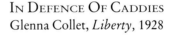

In Defence Of Caddies
Glenna Collet, *Liberty*, 1928

"There are no good caddies; some are worse than others!"

This golfing maxim was salvaged, it is said, from the testimony of a choleric duffer on trial for homicide after the mysterious disappearance of the small boy who had carried his bag. The youngster, who had a habit of whistling around the greens, was last seen fleeing into a thicket closely pursued by his employer, who was brandishing a mid-iron.

A jury of golfers who had never broken a hundred, and who therefore were quite familiar with the perversity of caddies, brought in a verdict of acquittal. The district attorney, chairman of the caddie committee at his club, stated privately that he thought a finding of justifiable homicide would have been more in keeping with the facts, but that, nevertheless, he felt the ends of justice had been served.

The cover of *Life* magazine, *above left*, for April 21, 1927.

The cover of *Ladies World*, magazine, *right*, for September 1900. *Below*, an Austrian ceramic caddie, 4.5in high, of about 1910.

abused the greens committee. "Gimme a mashie niblick and stand over there. Quit moving. Don't rattle that bag."

From hole to hole he abused the boy. "Get back, you're casting a shadow," though the heavens were clouded and the sun hidden. "Stop that chattering," although the boy was silent. "Put that flag down," when it was down.

Finishing the nine holes in 54, he took the bag waved the caddie aside. "Go back to the clubhouse and tell the caddie master you are not satisfactory. I'll carry my own bag. That's all."

Yet this boy was known as the best caddie of a club near Yonkers. Goodness in a caddie, like beauty, seems to lie in the eye of the beholder.

Caddies in the United States, according to some estimates, earn $10,000,000 a year in fees – and if there are many golfers like the one just described they are underpaid.

I have never had an impulse to do away with my caddie. I have had impulses, to be sure, but they have been somewhat less drastic. But perhaps I have been fortunate in my bag carriers.

Why are there bad caddies? Well, here is a true sketch of a golfer: On the first hole he sliced into the tall grass and burst into a flood of imprecations. He dropped another ball and took an eight. On the second tee he lectured the caddie. "I am not here to do your work," he said angrily. "Now keep your eye peeled."

His drive was dubbed, most likely because of his anger. He called the caddie with a snarl and yanked out a mashie, throwing the driver at the caddie's feet. A short putt missed cost a seven on that hole. "Stand off the green when I am putting," he snarled at the caddie.

On the third his drive rested in a divot scar, and, unable to fix responsibility on the boy, he

118

THE GHOST OF COLONEL BOGEY
Long Spoon, *Golf,* 1897

There is a "Colonel Bogey" at every Golf links in the kingdom. Some golfers in their ignorance regard him as a mythical personage, who we play against in order that he may play with us – as a cat does with a mouse. Nothing of the kind. He is the spirit of a departed golfer.

Have you ever noticed a golfer whom everyone knows, and yet no one knows? His past history is obscure, but his present and future are painfully patent. He is a golfer who has taken up the game late in life, and has been bitten with the craze in its deadliest form. Some golfers escape his fate because they die, or commit suicide, or are dragged to Bedlam. Better that, than the end waiting for this poor wretch. Sore stricken with the mania, he struggles round the links weekly, daily, hourly. His days are one long foozle, his nights a hideous nightmare.

Then a change comes over the scene. The iron has entered his soul. Heaven save the mark! Better a thousand times that he had remained a guileless, foozling, Christian old gentleman. His game improves by leaps and bounds. Simple golfers are astounded, but the wise grow fearsome. He becomes, if not the best player in the club, the most deadly. The handicapping committee are nonplussed, he carries everything before him. He does not smoke or drink, and he only swears in obscure parts of the course, and in tones deep and guttural and in language strange to human ears. Hanging lies have a fascination for him, and he revels in a stymie.

And so he plays on, regardless of the tender feelings of the handicapping committee, winning gold medals galore, scooping the half-crowns of the ardent novice, and breaking records right and left until – until what? Until the end comes and his spirit leaves the clay, to fly to the newest links – inland by preference, where his ghost becomes the "Bogey" of the green. Why do we top our drives, foozle our iron shots, miss ridiculous putts? Because his spirit is always with us annulling our best efforts.

Do you see that irascible-looking golfer on the last green? He has got an eighteen-inch putt, to save the match. If he holes the ball his wife and children will have a week of blissful happiness. If he misses – why, heaven help them! His caddie hands him his putter. It is a momentous occasion, and the silence of death falls on the little group. Wise men shake their heads, they recognise that he is fighting with an unseen force. Slowly he squats down and takes his line. Only eighteen inches separate his ball from the hole, and the green is as level as a billiard-table. But he sees a hog's back, four worm casts, and a tricky slope. Back goes the putter and then forward, there is a faint click, the ball speeds forwards towards but (alas! for his wife and children) not into the hole. Both men swear, the loser with savage emphasis, the winner, out of assumed sympathy and softly as if he was pronouncing a benediction. Some men there are who escape the fascination of this demon. These men are dull-witted or imbecile, or men who never drink water, or pray, or go to church, or men possessed of a handy trick of blasphemy.

A MacIntyre Burslem cup and saucer of 1895, *far left*; a Spy cartoon of King Edward VIII of Britain, *near left*.

119

PUTTING THE LADIES RIGHT
E.M. Boys, *Badminton Magazine*, 1908

There is a theory extant that the 'weaker sex' is (if one may use such a paradox) the stronger at putting; but, after some years' experience, I must candidly confess that I have always found women painfully erratic putters. Of course, there are brilliant exceptions; but, speaking collectively, I have not found women to be much superior in this respect to men. The few really good putters are, curiously enough, generally weak in their play through the green or in their driving, and one rarely meets a player who is proficient in all three. 'Putting is an Inspiration,' we are told, but I am more inclined to agree with the man who so sapiently said, 'Putting is the Devil!' On days when every putt goes down, no matter how remote you may be from the hole, you are ready to say proudly, 'Putting is an Inspiration,' but on other days, when you are losing hole after hole through atrocious putting, you would fain proclaim aloud the other sentiment.

A Bovril advertisement, *right*, of around 1910; *below*, an Edmund Dulac print, also of around 1910.

G was a giddy young girl,
With a gaudy green hat and a curl.
    She was not commonplace,
    And displayed so much grace
While playing at golf with an earl.

BOV

FOR HEALTH STRENGTH AND BEAUTY

An envelope for a
hair-net, *above left*,
of around 1910.
Harry Vardon ladies'
silver spoon, and
a hand-painted
pottery fairground
figure, *below*, of the
1920s.

121

A blotter print of a lady golfer, *near right*, by T. Earl Christy in around 1910; *far right*, the cover of *The Saturday Evening Post* magazine for April 22, 1933.

GOLFING LADIES
E.M. Boys, *Badminton Magazine*, 1908

Golfers – I refer to ladies – might be divided into three classes: the Sportswoman; the Enthusiast, or Pot-Hunter; and the Ignorant. Let us try to briefly describe them.

A Sportswoman is one who loves sport for itself, and not for what it will bring. As golfers, sportswomen are a judicious blend of keenness and sense. Content to play once or twice week, their play seldom suffers from staleness; they never play, if they can avoid it, in rain or in a gale of wind, and when they get 'off their game, ' wisely refrain altogether ffrom playing for a few days. They take a keen interest in their home club, and are always eager to assist their captain in her efforts to promote inter-club matches and the interests of the club in general; and it is among the ranks of these sportswomen that the best golfers are to be found.

On the other hand, the Enthusiasts, or Pot-hunters, play, if possible, every day of the

URDAY
G POST

Weekly
enj. Franklin

10c. in Canada
(INCLUDING TAX)

5cts. THE COPY

C • WALTER D. EDMONDS

week, and in all weathers; in fact, they are quite oblivious of rain, and playing during a gale of wind is only considered good practice, with the result that many of them break down. It is by no means uncommon to hear of a lady straining herself, and being obliged in consequence to give up golf entirely for some months, or contracting a bad chill from a thorough wetting, which may settle on her lungs if she is delicate. 'Pot-hunting,' or what has more aptly been termed 'the Cult of the Biscuit Box,' is rapidly ruining golf – and, for that matter, all games – from a sporting point of view. There are a regular set, belonging to this 'Cult,' who go from open meeting to open meeting, 'pot-hunting,' and appear to regard the game only as a means to that end. They will unblushingly try to keep their handicap up to have more chance of achieving their ambition, and I have even heard a golfer of this class regretting that she has been unfortunate enough to win a monthly medal just before a spring or autumn meeting, and, in consequence, lowered her handicap, and so reduced her chance of winning 'pots.'

Possibly the worse trait in their character is that they have no genuine esprit de corps, but will unhesitatingly throw their captain on the

Stay young

playing Golf in Germany

information and Handbooks from all Tourist Agencies and Travel Bureaus

Left, a railway poster of around 1930.

123

A Gerz pottery stein, *right*, German, from around 1910.

horns of a dilemma by refusing to play in an inter-club match if another engagement of a more fascinating description is suggested to them at the last moment.

We now come to the members of the 'Ignorant' class, or in other words, the beginners, who, one might say, always remain beginners, the despair of professional instructors and the bugbear of every club. They chip along the course, cutting up the grass, day after day, never doing any hole under double figures, and yet cheerfully enter any competition for which they are eligible. Their chief characteristics are unfailing good nature from utter indifference and a dogged determination, which makes them go on, though they never improve.

DISPOSING OF TOMMY
R. Browning, *The Stymie by "Han-Kan"*, 1910

According to the definition, when two persons playing one ball between them contend against a third person playing his own ball, the match is called a "threesome." I explained all this to Milly on the way to the first tee. For on the principle that a beginner's enthusiasm is more likely to be encouraged by a real game than by any amount of practice, we had agreed that Milly's first lesson should take the form of a match between us two on the one side and her youngest brother on the other.

Milly was rather huffy at the start because I picked out the oldest and dirtiest ball I had got to tee up for her. But I know what ladies' golf is. You would think that they don't swing the club with any strength at all, and yet I have seen a girl, playing for the first time, cleave a brand-new Haskell to the mid-riff in a manner that Ivanhoe himself might have envied.

However, her first shot – I mean the first one she hit, for, of course, we were not counting misses – was such a rattling good one that it made her quite pleased again. We were on the green in two to Tommy's three. "Do you know," said Milly, as she held out her hand for the putter, "I think women, though, of course, they can't hit as far as men, should be able to do the wee shots on the green better." I admitted that a delicate touch was everything in putting; and pointing to a spot

about half way between the ball and the hole, "You try and play it to there," I said.

Milly laughed – she had a particularly nice kind of laugh – and asked me if I thought she knew no more about golf than that. "Well, if you're going to play for the hole," said I, " be sure not to hit too hard. The ball flies off far faster than you are apt to think." "Oh, I know," said Milly, and played the ball straight for the hole. It was a longish putt, but I believe if she had hit the ball with just about one-quarter of the strength it would certainly have gone in. As it was, I was able to play the ball back on to the putting-green again with my next, but Milly's second putt was so timid that we had never any chance.

After that, we wrestled along pretty comfortably until the sixth hole, though Milly never came near repeating the succes of her first shot. But at this point I had to help Tommy to hunt for his ball which he had lost in a patch of whin, and when I got back to Milly I found that she had played her ball and had not the slightest notion where it had gone. All that she could say was that she thought it was a pretty far shot, although she had "hit the earth a little too." However, we hunted for it in vain.

At last I suggested that we might have a better chance of guessing whereabouts it had gone if she would take us back to where she played it from. Ye gods! she certainly had "hit the earth a little too." I would never have dreamed that so much strength lay in these slight wrists. For there lay a fine tough divot of about four inches by six, not taken clean out certainly, but folded over, for all the world like the lid of a milk-can.

"I don't think the ball would go very far, when you took the earth as heavily as that," I said, and stooped to replace the divot. Never was wisdom more quickly justified – for the ball lay underneath. All the same Milly need not have been so angry just because I laughed.

However, by the time we had played two holes more, and Milly was playing with so little heart that Tommy won both with ease, I saw that her enthusiasm for golf had pretty well evaporated. Yet if I suggested stopping I knew what a nuisance Tommy would make himself. It was a time for desperate measures. The way to

the tenth hole is bordered by a fence on the right-hand side, with a stretch of heather beyond. I teed a brand new two shillings' worth before Tommy's gleaming eyes, and adopting the stance which Vardon recommends for the player who wishes to slice, I sent the ball curving gracefully into the heather.

"Ugh!" said I, "there's small use in searching for it there!"

"You don't mean to say you're going to leave it?" – Tommy's youthful thrift was instantly in arms against such heedlessness. I explained that I thought it a bit too tiresome for Milly to wait while he and I hunted for a ball that we might never find. "But if you like to have a search," I added, as indifferently as I knew how, "you can hang on to it if you find it."

"Right-oh!" said he, "I've got my eye on just about the very place." And with that he was over the fence like a shot.

An Austrian Art Deco print, *far left*, of the 1920s; and, *near right*, a cover of *Fry's* magazine.

We left him still searching. But as I whispered to Milly on the road home by the Lochan, "Two is a match, and a threesome is none."

THE HASKELL BALL
Horace Castle, *House Annual*, 1902

The Haskell Ball was first really taken up at the Amateur Championship Meeting at Hoylake this year. Owing to a few good players at that time playing with them, it came into general use, and its advantages were for the first time really recognised.

The Haskell has still a few enemies who argue that the ball is no good to stop on a keen green and is a bad putting ball, also that it is a bad ball against a wind, and the length of the courses is spoiled.

As regards a putting ball, I ask is there any such thing? If a putt is hit properly, does it matter what ball is used? One often hears the exclamation of an exasperated golfer as his put lips the hole, "If that had only been a gutty, it would have been in," or some such nonsense. In my opinion, if cleanly and correctly struck, the Haskell is quite as good as the gutty on the green.

The great disadvantage of the Haskell, however, is the absolute ruin of the length of present courses; all the good length holes laid out for the gutty are spoiled by the Haskell. The good two shot holes which used to mean a well hit drive, and a good cleek or long iron, are now in the reach of a man who half hits his drive, and the whole beauty of the length hole is spoiled. This is a serious matter, and will have to be rectified in some way. Either the courses will have to be lengthened or the ball will be barred. This, to my mind, is the only great disadvantage, because the courses are made so tame, and this is

A collection of British silver, *right*, from the 1920s. From the *left*: a salt cellar; a mustard pot; and a pepper pot.

than a gutty, but on a seaside course a Haskell is a distinct economy, as it can be used, with fair treatment, for six or eight rounds and will never lose its shape, whereas a gutty will often be useless after one round, by reason of its being knocked square.

BOBBY JONES IN CLOSE-UP
Grantland Rice, *The American Golfer*, 1928

There are certain details connected with Bobby Jones' game that are beyond explaining. These include his complete coordination and his almost perfect smoothness that belong to genius. They are matters not be defined in words. They can be seen and followed, but they cannot be taken apart for any casual inspection.

But there are also simpler details of his swing which can be more accurately hung up for public view. Where one might never understand just how any mere mortal can keep hitting the ball in exactly the same way and hitting it almost perfectly round after round, one can at least understand part of the physical accompaniment.

One of the first points to notice in Bobby Jones' play is the closeness with which he holds his feet together, even on full shots. Even on the drive I don't believe his feet are more than a foot apart, certainly not more than fourteen inches.

The cover of the sheet music for "Follow Thru", *left*, published in America in 1928.

where the handicap man has the advantage over the scratch man, and there is no doubt that many of our crack players who play with the Haskell, out of self-defence, would be delighted to see the Haskell barred.

It is only natural the professionals should be down on the Haskell, because, of course, their profits are seriously interfered with, but very few of them play with the gutty. In fact, with these notable exceptions, viz.: Braid, Taylor, and Vardon, nearly every professional plays the Haskell. Braid has tried the Haskell, but he hits so hard that he splits them, and, of course, owing to his extreme driving power, he gets far enough with the gutty ball.

Vardon, as far as I know, has never given the Haskell a real trial; I suppose he could not play much better with any ball than he does at present, though I should like to see what he would do with the Haskell.

It is also adduced against the Haskell, that, it is an expensive luxury, and that only a rich man can afford to play with it. For a really bad player or for anybody who plays on a course where it is easy to lose a ball, it is, of course, more expensive

Right, a cartoon by
Victor Forscythe
from the *New York
Evening World*,
1926.

Frequently on his pitch shots there is less than six inches separating the heels. On the short chip shots his heels are closer still, while in putting they are almost touching.

It has been stated on several occasions that the straight left arm in golf is not necessary. It isn't. Vardon has a light kink in his left elbow at the top of the swing and other fine golfers have about the same bend. But in the case of Jones he uses a left arm as straight as an unbent rod of steel.

I watched him in practice at Brae Burn before his final match. For ten or fifteen minutes he hit almost every type of shot – drive, brassie, long iron, full pitches and short pitches – and without exception he called on the straight left for every type of stroke. If there was the slightest kink in Jones' left elbow, it was not visible to the naked eye. It was not caught by the camera. The marvel of his swing was the way he could cock his left wrist at the top without bending the left arm. He had reduced his swing to two main hinges – the left shoulder and the left wrist. The hinge at the left elbow is eliminated. Naturally this leads to greater accuracy – the more hinges, the more chance for trouble.

Jones gives the impression of left shoulder power and left shoulder control. You can sense a feeling of strain or torsion in this left shoulder for any full swing. He also has a marvellous amount of leverage or punch in his cocked left wrist. There is firmness here, but no sign of stiffness. You get the impression that it is controlling the whip of the club head with the right hand coming in for the final flip or crack or blow.

There is still another feature of the Jones swing worth some study. This is the way he turns his chin slightly to the right as he addresses the ball. This was a trick that Jerry Travers always

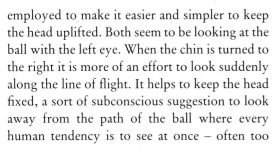

The cover of the sheet music for "Everything Happens to Me", *left*, published in America in 1939.

employed to make it easier and simpler to keep the head uplifted. Both seem to be looking at the ball with the left eye. When the chin is turned to the right it is more of an effort to look suddenly along the line of flight. It helps to keep the head fixed, a sort of subconscious suggestion to look away from the path of the ball where every human tendency is to see at once – often too quickly – just what has happened. This frequently takes place before anything has happened, before the club head has ever reached the ball.

The amateur champion says he makes no direct effort to keep his body still, fearing a feeling of stiffness. But the fact is that his body seems to be completely still on all shorter putts

from two to six or seven feet in length where the hands and wrists do practically all the work. So far as championship golf is concerned there has a never been a surer putter from three, five, or seven feet away than Jones.

He has a light, firm touch that is as smooth as velvet. It is his idea to get the ball just about to the cup, rather than ram for the back of the tin. For in the gentler putting system there is a wider target to hit – over four inches against a trifle more than two inches. A putt just getting up to the cup with only a slight run left will usually drop in from either side. But if hit too stoutly it must find the exact center of the cup. This can be overdone by not getting the ball up to the cup, but it accounts for the fact that you almost never see one of Jones' putts from shorter ranges hit in and then hop out, one feature of golf that wrings raw agony from the most stoical of souls.

These features of Jones' play are mere segments, taken from a swing that is largely genius. One might as well attempt to describe the smoothness of the wind as to paint a clear picture of his complete swing. The coordination between all working muscles and between these and the eye is uncanny in a game where coordination, even among the elect, so often crumbles up or goes upon a zigzag journey.

INSTRUCTIONS IN ETIQUETTE
Douglas Erskine, *Pacific Golf and Motor,* 1917

Etiquette is described in the dictionary as "the conventional rules or ceremonial observed in polite society; good breeding."

I have a friend who wanted to teach me golf and whose first lesson consisted of a dissertation on the value of golf as a teacher of etiquette.

"The game gives you the best idea of etiquette," he said. "Every golf player continually bears in mind the fact that he is playing a game which depends for its success and

Right, three book marks, produced by the Glasgow and South Western Railway, around 1900.

Left, a collection of
**Weller Dickins
Ware from the late
1800s.**

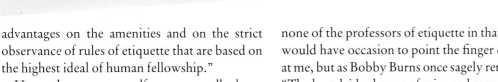

advantages on the amenities and on the strict observance of rules of etiquette that are based on the highest ideal of human fellowship."

He took me to a golf course, walked me around a couple of miles of up-hill-and-down-dale real estate, reduced me to a physical wreck and a mental derelict and it was all due to that etiquette of which he had boasted.

"Before you take a club in your hand," said this Chesterfield of the links, "I want you to come with me and watch a match between two good players. You will observe the courtesy with which they will act toward each other, the good fellowship that will prevail throughout the match, the cordiality with which the loser will congratulate the winner, and the heartiness with which the spectators will offer their felicitations to the winner and their condolences to the man who loses. And above all, you will notice with what superior consideration for the feelings of the players the gallery will act from start to finish."

I made up my mind to act in such manner that none of the professors of etiquette in that gallery would have occasion to point the finger of scorn at me, but as Bobby Burns once sagely remarked: "The best-laid schemes of mice and men gang aft agley."

Mine went agley before the match started.

One of the players took a bit of sand, placed it on the grass and gingerly planted his ball on the top of it. The gallery bent its gaze on the player with a collection of benevolent looks that would have done the young man a lot of good had he not been busily engaged in wiggling his stick and taking alternate looks at the ball and a point in the middle distance about 250 yards from where we were standing.

"Well, he's on his mark. Why don't the starter give the signal?" I asked.

My friend grabbed me by the wrist and a chorus consisting of the entire gathering whistled "Sh-Sh-Sh."

Right away I knew I was in the wrong and, with great presence of mind, I looked about as if to discover the culprit. But it was no use. From each

eye there shot a dagger right at me and the young man with the club stepped ostentatiously back from the ball and regarded me with a baleful gleam in each eye.

I could see that my remark showed ignorance of the rules and that the young man was extremely peeved about it. Evidently he had been used to playing before a deaf-and-dumb academy, so I said no more until he had sent the ball close to that point 250 yards away which had so attracted his attention.

I was relieved to notice, when the other player stepped up to take his turn at bat, that he was an old friend, with whom I used to play baseball when the belt he was wearing would have gone around him twice. I knew nothing would disturb him in his hitting. Hadn't I seen him knock home runs when thousands were shouting at him and calling him names, of which Fathead and Bonehead were the most flattering?

He wiggled his bat just like he used to do when he was trying to rattle the pitcher and I knew that the time for encouragement had arrived.

"That-a-boy, Bill," I yelled. "Slam it right over second."

One look at Bill's face showed me that etiquette had done its deadly work on him. That wild-running, reckless-sliding ball-player, who had ripped many a stocking with his spikes and opened wounds in umpires' feelings that never could be healed, glowered at me without a look of recognition.

A watercolour cartoon, *right*, of 1928.

"If the party with the raucous voice and the vacant mind will kindly remember that this is a gentleman's game, I shall feel greatly obliged to him," said Bill, and that gallery of etiquetters actually applauded.

Raucous voice, indeed! And that same Bill used to say I was the best coacher on the team because they could hear me all over the diamond.

Vacant mind! Why, I taught that big stiff all the inside baseball he ever knew.

"Now, will you be good?" said my companion. "You see what you get for failing to observe the rules of etiquette, which demand that deep silence prevail when the players are making their shots."

Etiquette and I got along fine together until they had the balls on the green. Then I got in bad again by laughing when Bill missed the hole when he only had to roll the ball a foot. Anybody would have laughed. It was so easy a man with two wooden legs could have kicked it in.

"Vacant mind, indeed! I don't see any jostling or over-crowding in his upper story," I remarked, loud enough for the etiquetters to hear. But I could see that they did not appreciate my resentment at Bill's remark to me.

"Hard luck," they murmured.

"Sure," I said. "The same kind of hard luck that makes a fellow fall for the hidden ball trick."

My instructor in etiquette had a busy time for the next few holes. I had to promise solemnly that I wouldn't say a word loud enough for anybody to hear, especially the players, and it

Copeland Spode ceramics, *right*, with a golfing theme, from around 1905.

was maybe just as well that I kept my promise. If they had heard what I was saying to myself I would have been eligible for every blackball in every etiquette club in the world.

By the time we got to the seventh tee, as my friend called it, Bill was "down." That's what they told me, and he looked to me as if he was down, and out as well. I could see that what he needed was support of some kind. So I determined that he should have it. Was my old side-kicker to lose because no one would show their faith in him? Not if I could help it.

"Come on, Bill," I shouted. "The lucky seventh. Here's where we knock one out of the lot."

Etiquette could stand no more. Bill showed that the new cult had him in its grasp.

"You will be doing me a great favor," he said, icily, I thought, "if you will get away as far as you can from this game and stay there. You have about as much idea of the usages of polite society on the links as a rabbit has of the internal economy of a greyhound's kennel. If you hurry you will be able to get to the ball park before the game starts and there you can get rid of that abundance of oratory which seems to be beyond your control. Mounted on a soap-box at a street corner, you might be all right, but on a golf links you are an anachronism."

Bill had the house with him and all I could do was to go. But before I went I wanted to show him that I forgave him.

"Well, I wish you luck," I said. "But you'll

never make the big league playing this game. You step back from the plate as if you expected to get beaned by the ball you're hitting and you'll raise dissension in the team with that mean disposition of yours. If I was the manager of this club, I'd release you and sign a busher."

Crushed by the coldness and indignant at the sneers of the gallery, I went off, aided by my friend, who stopped me from going back and telling them another hard thing I had just thought of.

Fortunately etiquette does not prohibit a member from buying his guest a drink, and I was *en rapport* for the first time that day when we got to the smoking room of the club.

I see by the papers that Bill won his match, but I'll bet he doesn't appreciate how much he owes me for my efforts on his behalf. He probably thinks he won on his etiquette.

REDRESSING THE BALANCE
Bernard Darwin, *The American Golfer*, 1928

If I may mention a personal detail of no importance, it happened to me the other day, out of sheer hard necessity, to buy a new pair of golfing shoes. On that occasion the urbane vendor and I discussed with becoming gravity how many nails there were to be, and exactly where they were to be placed. I tried to look as solemn as an owl and to express decisive views. Yet all the while I could not help wondering whether there might not be "a certain amount of tosh" about nails and shoes.

I recollected that once upon a time I used to play in button boots entirely void of nails, and that on one of the muddiest of all created courses. Perhaps it was not wholly of deliberate choice; I did not possess any with nails in them. There were indeed football boots with bars, and I remember having to put those on for a grand occasion, the annual scratch medal, on a half-holiday afternoon. However, as in my innocence I had already disqualified myself by practising putting "after twelve" in button boots, they were of small comfort.

I do not recall that I tumbled about any more in those nail-less boots than I do now with, comparatively speaking, all the resources of

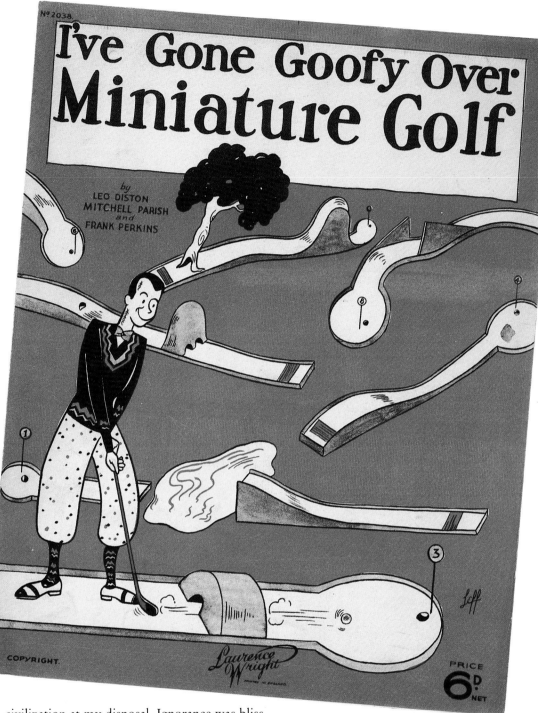

The cover of the
sheet music for
"I've Gone Goofy
Over Miniature
Golf", *left*,
published in Britain
in 1930.

civilization at my disposal. Ignorance was bliss, and I thought no more of them than I did of my stiff white shirt front. In the summer holidays no doubt I was more elaborate. The boots were then, I think, replaced by "sand shoes," such as may be seen hanging up outside sea-side shops among buckets, spades, and shrimping nets. I had seen pictures of the great Mr. Hilton playing in them (with his cap falling off); so they must be all right. His, it is true, were white, while mine were of a more clerical hue, but the principle was the same. Deliberate golfing shoes with nails in them only came later with one's own allowance and more sophisticated frame of mind.

I am sure that many boy golfers care no more for all these solemn things than I did, and three or four summers ago I watched some moderately grown-up ones reverting very successfully to their childhood's habits. It was at the time of the last amateur championsihp at St. Andrews. At

135

A fashion print for Arrow Shirts, *right*, from around 1910.

that sacred spot the light in May seems to last almost forever, and so after dinner a band of young warriors used to come out to play a few holes with one club apiece under some ingenious rules of their own.

They were dressed *cap-a-pie*; their shirt fronts were stiff and shiny, and so were their pumps. Yet they played shots which they would have been very glad to save up for their matches in the championship which was to begin a day or two later. They lashed out with a fine post-prandial freedom, and did not slip upon the dewy turf. And for that matter is it not on record that an amateur championship has been won by a golfer – the late A.J.T. Allan – who had no tackets in his boots?

This is not to say that we should all play just as well as or better than we do, if we were less portentous about our shoes. I am quite sure we should not, if only because we should be perpetually expecting to slip. All I do say is that the most nicely devised pattern of tackets is a poor substitute for the mysterious art or gift of balance. To some extent at least it is a gift. Who can doubt it, for instance, when he looks at Harry Vardon standing up to hit the ball with that particular little screwing movement of the right foot as he makes his one simple and rhythmical waggle?

There, as it seems to me, is instinctive balance personified. No doubt it is also an art that can be cultivated. I know one fine amateur golfer who

stands notably still on his feet. He used to be fond of skating, but gave it up because he thought it impaired his golfing balance. Cultivation could scarcely go any farther than that.

Be it a gift or art, most of us are very poor in it, and I imagine that half of our bad shots, which we attribute to other and more recondite causes, have this simple origin, that at the moment of our striking the ball anybody could knock us over with a peacock's feather.

DRIVING TO DESTRUCTION
J.C. Law, *The Irish Golfer*, 1902

If a good golfing temperament were not a *sine qua non* to success on the links, there would be many more players of first rank. Golfers there are by the score who are capable of playing the game with accuracy and power, and when things are going well of doing brilliant deeds; and yet they somehow or other fail when we most hope and expect that they will succeed. And this failure may, I fancy, not infrequently be laid at the door of mental rather than physical causes. The flesh is able, the muscles are fit, the eye is keen, the knowledge is sufficient, but the mind cannot control and govern the whole man. It has been said by one well able from experience both of life and golf to give a good judgment, that golf is a game which is always fighting against the player.

That golf is an irritating game anyone who has played it seriously knows, and recognises also that the man who loses his temper as a rule loses also the match. "I know it's only a damned game," shouted an eminent legal luminary as he snapped his croquet mallet over his knee and then hurled its head through the drawing-room window, but even games require some mastering or they will get the upper hand.

Nothing is more annoying than, after a good drive, to find one's self hampered for the next stroke by an unfortunate lie. Among the many ways of improving golf that have been suggested, a proposal that every ball should be "teed" seemed to me, at the time it was made, to be the most destructive. It was argued that this would

A group of Lennox ceramics, *left*: two silver-rimmed tigs, 5.5in and 3.25in high, and a jug 14.5in high – from 1894 to 1906.

make the game fairer and eliminate luck; and certainly the idea should have been welcomed by all bad-tempered golfers. But to overcome bad luck and come out triumphant in the end is the most satisfactory of enjoyments, the greatest of glories. Remove luck from the game and it loses one of its chief recreative qualities, and becomes, in fact, a game no longer.

If it be the bad lies that bring out the qualities of the player it will be found that it is the even-minded golfer who will overpower circumstances and surmount difficulty with success. The ball lies badly, then tackle the situation with all the ability you possess, and do not waste time and mind in thinking how different it would have been if things had been otherwise. Of course, had the ball been lying well it could have been played with great ease; the green might even have been reached had a wooden club shot been possible. But the ball does not lie well, so the best thing to be done is to make the most of the possibilities of the situation, to master within limits the work that has actually to be done. And yet this is easy to say, and hard to do; for the golfing mind is hard to concentrate, though concentration is vital.

If we think we are doing well success will probably follow; if we regard every misfortune as a catastrophe, every small failure as only one of many others sure to follow, then we are playing a losing game.

I like not the partner who assures me, after I have missed a short putt at the first hole that is is unlucky to win on the first green. I like better the man who says "Never mind, there are other holes to play." For this is true golfing philosophy, namely, not to look back on the milk on the ground, but rather go forward with a determination to observe more care.

There will probably happen in the course of a golf match things that may either be taken humorously or in anger, and the former attitude of mind will be found to answer the better. A lady may allow her parasol to be blown across the putting green just when a stroke is about to be made; a spectator may audibly ask the name of the player who is addressing the ball.

But what is most important, from the player's point of view, is that he should treat such incidents in a friendly way and not as pointed and premeditated insults to himself. Let him laugh at the matter for a moment, and then return with fixed mind to the business on hand.

The man who can fix his whole will power on every shot he plays, who is unconscious of what others are thinking of him, who cheerfully is determined to make the best use of every chance, be it ill-looking or fair, that man is not far from the perfection of golfing temperament.

The cover for Collier's magazine, *near right*, for May 18, 1919; *far right*, a Foley China tig of around 1910.

An H.M. Bateman cartoon, *left*, of the 1920s.

WIFE (*who has something "on" her husband*): "And mind, if he beats you, I shall do the same"

DICTIONARY OF GOLF
D. Irons, *Golfing Papers,*

BEGINNER — One who should be ashamed of himself, and generally is.

BUNKER — Quiet spot to which a player retires for purpose of making a few disjointed remarks.

BURN — Institution for adding to the uncertainties of the game, and the certainties of the ball-maker.

CADDIE — Gentleman of leisure, who for a consideration will consent to sneer at you for a whole round.

DRIVER — Most sympathetic of the tyro's instruments. When its owner loses his head it is apt to do the same.

GOLFER — Sort of cross between a martyr and a monomaniac.

GOOD STROKE — One that lands your opponent in a bunker.

HOLE — A cavity much smaller than the ordinary bunker, and much less enticing to the ball.

MATCH — Game arranged with a man you can beat.

PERFECT STROKE — One that plants your opponent's ball among the roots of a whin.

ROUND — A voluntary penance – best test of temper known.

ROUND OF EIGHTY — One that is generally done in the absence of a marker.

SHORT PUTT — Stroke often missed by a good player: by a beginner – never.

TURF – Grass carefully preserved by the layer for the beginner's benefit.

UNCERTAINTY OF THE GAME — What is suggested to you when M'Foozle manages to hit the ball.

Flocking To Carnoustie
T.T. Alexander, *Carnoustie Commentary*, 1937

Nearly forty years before William the Conqueror and his Norman Knights landed at Hastings and carved out a kingdom for themselves in the land of the Angles, Malcolm II of Scotland fought and defeated Camus the Dane on the Links of Barry.

The story goes that after the fight the Danes, furious and humiliated by their defeat, put a curse on the district.

They determined to have their revenge, and after a while they returned, but not to fight.

With them they brought thousands of crows, which they uncaged upon the seashore. The well-wooded country around was soon full of the birds, and from morning till night the incessant clamour of their cawing continued.

In course of time the inhabitants of the district got into the habit of called it "Craw's Nestie."

"Carnoustie" it became, but the original name is still preserved in the "Craw's Nest Tassie," the trophy of the Open Amateur Golf Tournament, which since 1927 has attracted the leading golfers of the world to the famous links at Carnoustie.

A hand-painted Loetz glass vase, *top left*, 14in high, made in Austria in around 1900.

Far left, a Carlton china figure – *"The Caddie"*, by Hassall, 1918; and, *left*, an Ed Wilson bronze, 19in high.

141

WARDING OFF THE BRAIN STORM
Frank C. Tone, *The American*, 1928

Silhouetted against the dusky sky-line of the seventeenth fairway was a lone figure. Although not positive, I felt certain I knew him, because only a few minutes previously I had caught a glimpse of him hurling a driver roughward off the tee. Ere long he pulled up at the home hole, where he hardly could resist wrapping a putter around a tree, then plodded slowly to the showers, his face bearing deep lines of mental anguish.

One year before that man could smile and joke at a score of 115. He had joined a golf club for recreation only. Having obtained that, his scores began to creep down into the 90s. Mistakes began to assume a much graver concern, until, after being magnified for several more months, they assumed the status of a calamity.

Yet, waste no sympathy on this chap unless you are immune from his failing. What he needs is not additional knowledge of golf, but an understanding of practical psychology as applied to the game.

No golfer can allow his game to be a worry to him and succeed as a golfer, any more than he could under similar conditions in his chosen profession. The golfer who finishes a sloppy round with a joke on his lips is the man to fear the next day.

Not long ago two golfers, close friends, were playing over a California course. A dispute over scores led to the fatal shooting of one and the committing suicide by the other. Physicians agreed that the man who did the shooting temporarily was insane. Yet, just how much of a gap existed between the mental status of the golfer who did the shooting and the wrathful fury many otherwise sane golfers allow to lay hold of themselves?

How many "dubs" have you seen in sand traps with hunted looks on their faces, slashing madly and wildly at balls which figuratively they could not see because of blind rage?

Warding off the "brain storm" which is wont to follow in the path of an inglorious trouncing in competition is not the easiest thing to do, but five minutes concentration devoted to the subject of the physical drain such a malady has upon man or woman sometimes will serve as a cure. "Nothing could have been lost, as nothing had been gained in that match." Is not that reasoning sound enough?

Why pay dues at a club for the privilege of working yourself into a fury? Get your money's worth!

FROM MARBLES TO GOLF BALLS
Harry Vardon, *My Golfing Life,* 1933

My first introduction to golf was along with many other boys. We were enticed to carry the clubs of the visitors. As far as I can remember we did not think very much of this new game, but after carrying a few times we began to see distinct possibilities in it. It was only natural that we should wish to try our hand at playing ourselves.

This, however, was a matter which required a good deal of thought. There were many difficuties to be overcome, as apart from not having any links on which to play, we had no clubs or balls. So keen, however, were we to play, that all these difficulties were eventually solved, and, as a start, we laid out our own course. This consisted of four holes, each one of them about fifty yards in length, and for boys of our age was quite good enough. When we had marked out and made our teeing grounds, and

A Silver King record: "Golfing Hints", by Archie Compston.

smoothed out the greens, one of our chief difficulties was definitely settled.

Then came the question of balls, and in the absence of real gutties we decided the most suitable article for us was the big white marble, which we call a taw, and which was about half the size of an ordinary golf ball. The question of clubs was a more difficult proposition, and caused a good deal of anxiety in our young minds. On reflection, I think great credit is due to us for the manner in which we disposed of this very important point. As nothing would be really satisfactory except a club which resembled as near as possible a real golf club, it was necessary to make many experiments before we were able to get the desired article. As a start, we decided that we must use as hard a wood as possible, and as the wood from a tree which we called the "Lady Oak" was suitable for our purpose, another important difficulty was satisfactorily overcome.

First of all, we cut a thick branch from the tree, sawed off a few inches from it, trimming this piece as near as we possibly could to the shape of the heads of the drivers of those players for whom we had been carrying. As splicing was impossible, it was agreed that we must bore a hole in the centre of the head, to enable us to fix in the shaft sticks. These were made of thorn, white or black, and when they had been trimmed and prepared to our satisfaction, we proceeded to finish off our club. To make a hole in the head we had to put the poker in the fire and make it red-hot so as to allow the shaft to be fitted in. Then after tightening it with wedges, the

operation was complete. All things considered, we were able to get a really long ball with this primitive driver.

After a time, as we grew more accustomed to making these clubs, we became quite expert young club makers. The brassies seen on the links had made a big impression on us, and as we had experienced some trouble with our oak heads, as being green they were rather inclined to crack, we eventually decided to sheathe the heads entirely with tin. This was not by any means an easy thing to do, and we were further troubled by the fact that our respective fathers declined to lend us their tools. This difficulty was overcome by borrowing them whenever the opportunity presented itself. These tin-plated drivers, which we called our brassies, were an enormous improvement over our original clubs. So expert did we become at making them that occasionally one which we made would stand out as far superior to the others. The reputation of the maker of this club was assured, and he did a good business in making clubs for others. A big price in marbles was demanded and paid to this expert club maker.

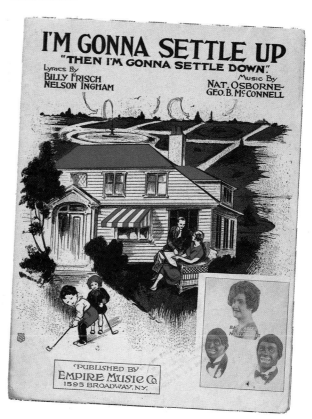

A photograph of a young child as a caddie, *above left*, and, *below*, the cover to the sheet music of "I'm Gonna Settle Up", published in America in 1927.

The cover of *Liberty*
magazine, *right*, for
August 10, 1940.

WHAT'S THE USE OF WORRYING
Bobby Jones on Golf, 1926

It has always been interesting to me to try to determine exactly what it is that makes it possible for a really good putter to experience days when he is as helpless on the putting greens as a babe in arms. I can understand how it can be that a first-class player will occasionally play lamentably poor golf from tee to green, for the long shots require a more complicated swing which demands nicer timing than the putting stroke. It is not surprising that even the best are sometimes off with the woods or irons. But the putting stroke is the simplest of all. I do not believe that there comes a day when the expert putter finds a defect which he cannot discover and correct in a few moments' practice. Yet he may go thirty-six holes putting like an old scrub-woman who had never seen a golf club.

I truly believe that a great proportion of putting difficulties is in the player's mind. There are days when one lines up a putt more accurately, particularly the long fellows, and days when the touch is nicer than usual. But when a putt of four feet is missed it is rarely because of a mistake in choosing the line. The mishap is almost always caused by mishitting the ball, either by striking it off line, or by failing to strike it cleanly.

Now the simplest stroke in golf ought to be that required for a four-foot putt. The backstroke need be only four or five inches in length, and there should be no temptation to look up, for the objective lies well within the range of vision all the while the stroke is being

played. There can be only one explanation for mishitting – that the player becomes uncertain and worried about the shot and his anxiety sets off tension which actually forces him to hit the ball off line. I have missed some short putts through rank carelessness, but these are very few compared to the number I have missed because I was scared stiff of them.

I always find myself more than a little annoyed – and I have heard many other competitors express the same feeling – when a missed putt of three, four, or five feet is greeted by "Oh's" "Ah's" and loud guffaws from the gallery. I am sure that many another struggling contestant has, as I have, wished devoutly for an opportunity to watch the author or authors of the loud noise attempt the same job under the same circumstances. I am certain that he or they should find that many short putts, when viewed

Hard to Replace Favorites

Have you ever stopped to think how peculiar and individual are the characteristics of a golf club, how difficult it is to replace an old favorite, or how silly you are to keep on acquiring and using new clubs when the old one still remains in serviceable condition?

A golf club in the hands of its owner is one of the most delicately sensitized implements in sport. It is fairly bristling with individual characteristics which are incapable of reproduction. The displacement of the balance by so much as a scant half inch, or even an infinitesimal reduction in the size of the handle, will make all the difference in the world in the "feel" of the club.

Yet how many times do we make allowance for these factors? Often a new club has such a friendly feel that we cannot resist trying it out. But rarely do we take accurate note of its construction to see if it is suited to the use we intend to put it to.

THE main thing to be considered in the club is the shaft, whether the amount of "spring" is proper for the capabilities and habits of the purchaser. Timing which is proper for one shaft will not be so for another no matter how nearly the same weight and lie of

which means that we must adapt our timing to the new implement.

To develop a new swing for every new club is quite a task in itself, especially for the business man golfer who has rarely time enough to perfect one swing. If he can get consistent results from the club he has he is doing very well.

The balance and feel of the club are of paramount importance, but I should advise never to try to use a club which does not appeal to the eye. A little clumsiness in the head or an improper line in the face is enough to ruin a club for me. I always find myself eyeing the defect in the club rather than looking at the ball.

PROBABLY I have been prompted to write all this by a desire to unburden my soul of all the grief that is in it. Recently, while I was in the locker room changing my shoes, an officious caddie either tried a swing with my pet driver or banged it over the head of one of his brothers, and succeeded in smashing the head clean off the shaft. That I could not discover who was responsible prevented a first-class funeral, but even that could have given me only momentary relief. It is odd, indeed, that a club which I have cared for like no other should be the very one to meet disaster in this fashion.

Clubs Part of Golfer's Game

The point of all this is that a golfer should be immensely careful with the implements of his trade. They are as much a part of his game as his knee action or his follow through. And

Clubs play an important part in every golfer's play. Deprived of a favorite, he is temporarily lost. Here are Bobby's favorites

(Wide World Photos)

when he finds a club that suits him, let him remember that no human hand can fashion another exactly like it. I have had eight copies of a defunct driver, a favorite of a few years ago, some made in this country and some in England, and have never found one I could use, although the original undoubtedly suited me better than any club I have ever owned.

...ch Club

...nably far is not im-
...; struck with the fact
...and timing with each
...to hit with a good deal

BOBBY JONES on GOLF

50 cents

BOBBY JONES REVEALS THE NEWEST SECRETS OF GOLFING SUCCESS

REVISED EDITION

...duction by ...LAND RICE

GOLF RULES

...CENTRATION
...YCHOLOGY
...GOLF SWING
...OF BACKSWING

ILLUMINATING ARTICLES ON PUTTING—STANCE—SWING—GRIP—CORRECTING FAULTS—WITH TWENTY-FIVE OTHER INSTRUCTIVE ARTICLES

from a competititve angle, assume a far different aspect than when seen from the outer reaches of the crowd by a person only mildly interested in the result.

Have you ever stopped to think how peculiar and individual are the characteristics of a golf club, how difficult it is to replace an old favorite, or how silly you are to keep on acquiring and using new clubs when the old one still remains in serviceable condition?

A golf club in the hands of its owner is one of the most delicately sensitized implements in

A Royal Doulton
Morrisian vase,
right, 12.25in high,
from around 1890.

caddie either tried a swing with my pet driver or banged it over the head of one of his brothers, and succeeded in smashing the head clean off the shaft. That I could not discover who was responsible prevented a first-class funeral, but even that could have given me only momentary relief. It is odd, indeed, that a club which I have cared for like no other should be the very one to meet disaster in this fashion.

The point of all this is that a golfer should be immensely careful with the implements of his trade. They are as much a part of his game as his knee action or his follow through. And when he finds a club that suits him, let him remember that no human hand can fashion another exactly like it.

A RAPHAEL AT GOLF
H.G. Hutchinson, *Golf*, 1893

In the museum at Venice there is a drawing, of which the accompanying print is a reproduction.

Apart from its artistic merits, which could not fail to be great, there are points of interest about this drawing. In all essentials, the swing is evidently the golfing swing. It does not matter by which name the game was called. It may have been the Italian equivalent of Golf, or it may have been *jeu de mail*. By the bye, in this *jeu de mail*, according to the old French book of rules, they played with a wooden ball through the green, as one may say, but when it came to the putting, they might change the wooden ball for a

sport. It is fairly bristling with individual characteristics which are incapable of reproduction.

To drive reasonably straight and reasonably far is not impossible with any sort of club but I was struck with the fact that I actually had to alter my swing and timing with each club, and in every case it was necessary to hit with a good deal less than full power. In other words, I had to control the club consciously rather than lash away with the assurance that I knew what would happen.

Now that is exactly the burden which a man puts upon himself when he discards an old club in favor of a new one. Golf clubs are like human beings in that no two are exactly alike.

The balance and feel of the club are of paramount importance, but I should advise never to try to use a club which does not appeal to the eye. A little clumsiness in the head or an improper line in the face is enough to ruin a club for me. I always find myself eyeing the defect in the club rather than looking at the ball.

Probably I have been prompted to write all this by a desire to unburden my soul of all the grief that is in it. Recently, while I was in the locker room changing my shoes, an officious

turning on the left toe, with the heel well off the ground, is as perfect as it could be.

This is all as it should be, and we may congratulate Raphael and his man. And even if his hands be thrown somewhat away above his shoulder, in a manner which does not suggest the best execution, may not this after all be attributable, perhaps, to the greater freedom of swing which must accompany such total freedom from garments. This, perhaps, is how we all do it in those practice swings, which we take when we get out of our morning tubs.

We shall not go far amiss, in our golfing aims, if we strive to realise, in our swings, this ideal of the great designer.

steel one; which, as they seem to have thought, putted better. They putted at a thing which was virtually a croquet hoop – not at a hole in the ground.

It is not very obvious what the exact shape of the head of the club may be with which Raphael's man (who seems, by the way, to have just stepped out of a Turkish bath) is playing. Probably it is a hammer-headed kind of thing, such as they used for playing *jeu de mail.*

The most interesting point to note is the correctness, judged by the modern golfing standard, of the swing. The most noticeable point of difference is the height to which the hands are raised above the shoulder. There is no fear of this golfer breaking his club on his right shoulder-blade; he has none of that vice of swinging the club round the shoulder, instead of over and above it. Rather we should say that his club had been brought up "ower straight," as the golfing professors phrase it, and that he would consequently bring it down "ower straight" also, and very likely slice the ball. But then we must always remember that neither this man nor Raphael, his maker, had had the inestimable advantage of reading the Badminton book on Golf, nor any other of the kindred works which teach the grammar of the noble game.

For the rest, however, Old Tom Morris would pass this Raphaelesque man sound enough. That

The Necessary Evil
Golf, 1892

The caddie is one of the necessities of Golf – as indispensable as the ball itself – too often he is the "necessary evil" which figures in all human enjoyments; but I wonder whether the influence of the caddie has ever been duly balanced by a thoughtful golfer.

This is not referring to the caddie's capabilities in the matter of advice or instruction, but I allude to his personal attributes and characteristics, what one might call his moral being.

A clean, cheerful caddie, who maintains an even demeanour, neither elating his master with undue praise, nor depressing him with an ill concealed scorn, is a rarity, and one to be cultivated and encouraged; but it must be

A CWS Tea advertising card, *above left,* from the 1920s; and, *below left,* a Royal Doulton pitcher, 10in high.

147

A Superoma pottery advertising figure, *below left*, of the 1920s; *below middle*, the cover of *The Delineator* magazine for June 1921; *below right top*, the cover of *The Saturday Evening Post* for March 21, 1903; and, *below right bottom*, a chromolith calendar of 1903.

admitted that the generality of the tribe have tricks and failings calculated to rasp the susceptibilities of the highly-strung golfer; and most golfers are highly strung when keen on the game, and materially influence his play.

There is the officious caddie, who offers gratuitous advice and criticism, too often from a slender stock of knowledge. He produces the club he thinks most suitable for a stroke, and looks supercilious if you select another which you fancy for yourself. He is conversational, and while patting up a tee imparts voluntary and undesired information.

This caddie may be endured on a day when your play seems all that you have longed for it to become, but on a bad day he is more aggravating than your play itself, and his conduct is conducive to manslaughter.

Then we have all met the languid and indifferent caddie, who fails to appreciate your most brilliant performances. He can never render a straight answer, being of an undecided temperament, and is a poor hand at "spotting" your balls.

The indifferent caddie is only a shade more bearable than his sympathetic brother. This individual condoles with one in way that is maddening.

"Seen you drive over that bunker very often, sir," he will remark when you have sent your ball into the cruel thickset furze. Later on he will tell you that Mr. Smith, whom you consider the worst player in the club, is not so much ahead of you after all. It is possible to ignore your butler, and even to despise your valet, but a caddie forces himself upon you, and you cannot overlook his presence.

There is no "probably, possible shadow of doubt," however, that a caddie is for all purposes of Golf a necessary adjunct, whether the evil be entire or mitigated; but there are a few points on which golfers might combine to reduce some of the evil. Principally they should, on no consideration, give the caddies more than the payment set down in the rules of club. If this be strictly observed, the evils consequent upon the system of "tips" will be done away, and greedy, avaricious caddies will cease to exist.

Plain And Simple
E.M. Boys, *Badminton Magazine*, 1908

Unfortunately all women do not realise the fact that good dressing means suitable dressing. Anything out of place, however good in itself, is bad taste; hence a woman donning London silks and delaines on a links or a moor is as much a fish out of water as a riverside maiden's boating costume is in Regent Street.

Golfing is like shooting – the simpler and plainer the style of frock the better. Thick tweed in useful colours, good serge, or any warm and light woollen material is suitable; but two other things are absolutely essential – short skirts and loose bodices. A skirt to the ankle does very well for a country walk, but it ought to be eight or ten inches from the ground for Golf.

Every woman does not like walking about in a short dress, except perhaps during the game itself, and for such the New Forest skirt is a joy. It is made in thick material (unlined, of course), and as simple and plain as possible. It is about twelve inches from the ground, and at the bottom has a deep tuck over the hem. Hidden away under the tuck are buttons some four or six inches apart. After the game is over, the wearer buttons on to the skirt an extra piece of cloth or leather about nine inches deep, and walks home in a skirt of ordinary conventional length. If the fair wearer is too modest to show her ankles even when playing she wears a leather bottom-piece during the game (which, when muddy, can be washed in exactly the same manner as the linings of shooting skirts), and when she gets back to the club-house, she puts on a dry cloth piece instead to match her skirt.

Skirt linings and petticoats must be avoided for Golf, and something far more practical and comfortable must take their place.

Now for the bodice. Of course tight-fitting tailor-made bodices look charming; but the very perfection of their fit makes them abominable to play in. A loose blouse, or a Norfolk jacket, is the best; but a loose cloth jacket with a shirt and neatly fixed tie will always hold its own.

Hats are always rather a trouble in windy places. Sailor hats in fine days, or tight caps, fitting to the head like a man's and made to match the dress, always look well.

Wind and Golf go together marvellously often, and everything fly-away in a woman's attire should be carefully eschewed.

Beyond The Bounds Of Reason
Saxon Browne, *Golf*, 1899

There are two sides to every argument. As Mr. Hutchinson says, "what seems common sense to one may seem uncommon nonsense to another." The particular argument which is engaging the attention of golfers at the present moment is distinctly two-sided.

When we get two such authorities as Mr. Hutchinson and Mr. Everard on different sides, it would be unwise to affirm that the balance of reasoning tended more to one side than the other.

Yet it seems to me that, apart from common sense, which is a dangerous commodity to handle when discussing laws and customs, the "out of bounds" question admits of prompt and satisfactory settlement.

To sum up, it is clear that there is no parallel between the case of a hole lost by a lost ball and the case of a hole lost by a ball out of bounds. In the one case the actual fact of the ball's being lost or not lost cannot be established in practice until after the second player has played; whereas, in the other case, the actual fact of the ball's being out of bounds or not out of bounds is established before the second player has played.

The mention of Mr. Everard's name recalls the extraordinary statement he made recently in the

A Staffordshire figure from the series of Blackheath Golfers, dating from 1900.

Two metal golf toys and a metal car mascot, *right*, from the 1930s; and, a Staffordshire figure of around 1900, from the series of Blackheath Golfers.

columns of " *Golf.* " Putting the imaginary case of a first player at St. Andrews driving into the Station-master's Garden, and thereby under the local rule losing the hole, Mr. Everard says: "If I were umpire in an important match I should not for one moment allow such a claim" – that is, the claim of the second player to win the hole without playing his tee shot – "and if asked my reasons in a court of appeal, I should reply that *such procedure is absolutely unsportsmanlike.*"

I have italicised the words I wish to refer to. Mr. Everard's knowledge of the game of Golf is probably equal to that of any man living; and he would be a bold man, not to say a fool, who lightly questioned that knowledge; but Mr. Everard's knowledge of the game and Mr. Everard's idea of the duties of an umpire are two different matters; and, unless the Golf umpire is a totally different breed of animal from any other umpire, I have no hesitation in saying that Mr. Everard is all wrong. It has never been the duty of an umpire to give an opinion of the question of sportsmanship; that is a matter which concerns two persons, and two only – the player and the opponent. The duty of an umpire at Golf is, I take it, to uphold the laws of the game, to decide disputes on questions of fact, and to see fair play. Between fair play and sportsmanlike play there is, alas! too often, a vast difference but it is a man's conscience which must decide for him what is sportsmanlike, and not the fiat of an umpire.

Precisely what Mr. Everard means by "a fair and honest tee shot" it would be difficult to say; but if a man is justified in playing short of a burn or round a bunker which he is doubtful of carrying, surely he is justified in tapping his ball off the tee to avoid a hazard, which the more vigorous stroke of his opponent has fallen into. And if the present agitation induces the authorities to render this "taking of the tee shot" compulsory by Act of Parliament, methinks this unsportsmanlike tap will become popular; at least, with ordinary golfers, who have, perhaps a larger stock of common sense than sportsmanship. But, as I have already remarked, common sense is a silly thing to air in an argument.

THE GOLFING GIRL

A
TRUE
LINE
DRIVE

THE GOLFING GIRL AND ALL HER
FRIENDS PLAY GOOD GOLF ON
ALL THE GOLF COURSES OF THE
DELIGHTFUL DISTRICTS SERVED BY

THE CALEDONIAN
RAILWAY.

DONALD A. MATHESON. GENERAL MANAGER

A Caledonian
Railway poster,
"The Golfing Girl",
left, from the 1920s;
and, *below*, a
French ceramic
bon-bon box of
arbout 1910.

151

A Traveller magazine cover, *right*, of around 1926; *below left*, the *British Girls Annual*, for 1923; and, *below right*, an Adventure magazine cover.

The Highland Traveler

YOUR RENDEZVOUS WITH SPRING
By G. M. DAVIDSON

The BRITISH GIRL'S ANNUAL

Stories of Life, Love and Adventure

September 1916
15 CTS

"THE SECRET WOLF"
A Complete Novel of Canada by
S. Carleton

W. C. Tuttle
Hapsburg Liebe
Gates Glen
S. B. H. Hurst
Kathrene and
Robt. Pinkerton
Paul H. Harris
Arthur D. Howden Smith
Leland Ward Peck
Henry Martel Gwynn
Geo. Warburton Lewis
A Serial of
The Ancient World

Bicycle Skirts And Sailor Hats
E.M. Boys, *Badminton Magazine*, 1908

There are some members of all three classes who bring lady golfers into ridicule by wearing as 'mannish' clothes as possible. They are to be seen with soft hunting ties, loose red shapeless coats, and the shortest and narrowest of bicycling skirts. Why bicycling skirts for golf? the reader may be moved to ask. Why, indeed? After giving the subject much thought, the only obvious explanation is that bicycling skirts are made to open at the sides, and are thus very adaptable for side pockets.

I must endeavour to draw a thumb-nail sketch of a golfer of this description attired in complete armour. Her hair is dragged up into a knot on the top of her head, on to which a man's cap is fixed (how, is not apparent); underneath is a tan-coloured face, from constant exposure to the elements without any of the protection which an ordinary sailor hat affords. A soft white hunting tie, fastened with a pin (an emblem of the game in some form or other), a loose red coat and a narrow bicycling skirt, into the pockets of which the wearer rams both hands when they are not required for golfing purposes; then, as a fitting climax, a pair of thick, clumsily made boots. It is needless to add that the attitudes and manners are quite as 'mannish' as the clothes.

Now, as no picture of this kind can be thoroughly appreciated without its antithesis, let me draw another.

A neat sailor hat, surmounting a head 'beautifully coiffeured,' every hair of which is in its place at the end of the round. A smart tight-fitting red coat, a spotless linen collar and tie, an ordinary tailor-made skirt, and a pair of well-made walking boots with nails in the soles.

Golf is by this time as much a woman's game as a man's, and ladies can and do look perfectly graceful when playing the game as it ought to be played. Let us all, then, take pride in raising golf as a game of our own, rather than in depreciating it and ourselves, by making it appear as if we were merely imitating man.

To play at Golf beneath the sea,
Is just as hard as it can be.
One cannot put, or drive, or tee
With very much facility;
The hazards are so hard you see.

A print of mermaids playing golf, *left* **from the 1920s.**

153

A REVIEW OF THE FUTURE
Golf, 1892

We have no wish to be unnecessarily harsh in our estimate of this book by J.A.C.K., – *Golf in the Year 2,000, or What We Are Coming To* – for whose excursion into literary pastures, as he tells us in the preface, himself shall hardly account, still, candour compels the admission that J.A.C.K., if the unpleasant pleasantry be allowed to pass, is not exactly a "ripper" in the arts and graces of authorship.

Like Rip Van Winkle, the narrator falls into a trance, and sleeps for a hundred and eight years, at the end of which time he awakes to find, not unnaturally, that he and his surroundings have "suffered a sea change."

Several wonderful things happen; shaving has been improved out of existence, in lieu thereof a magical depilatory removes the beard by touch; when dinner time arrives the table is found to be "made of three concentric circular pieces, and the middle one sank down through the floor, leaving intact the outer one, which formed the edge of the complete table;" "the dumb waiter portion reappeared, bearing two plates of soup on it."

The Chief Inspector when the time arrives for serious business, gives his guest the choice of a green on which to have a match ; "They are all equally convenient, from Thurso to Penzance; if you cared, we could even play a round on both of the greens I have mentioned." So by means of an electric tubular railway, they find themselves at St. Andrews almost before they have time to wink. Arrived there, it is necessary to procure a set of clubs, and a golfing coat, this latter a garment which subsequently develops unexpected, not to say alarming qualities. The starting is managed by phonograph, in conjunction with a board outside the window, on which board every man's name appears when his turn arrives. It is satisfactory to find that due sense of order and decorum prevails; in fact, no one is at the tee but the opponent.

The vagrom schoolboy, if under the age of fifteen, has no place in this economy, nor are there any caddies – none in the flesh, that is to say. As substitutes there are perpendicular rods about four feet high, weighted at the foot and hung upon wheels, the magnetic qualities of the employer's golfing jacket serving to keep them in tow, at a respectful distance of twelve feet. The clubs have advanced with the age, and are fitted with a dial apparatus for automatically registering every shot played, for there is a competition every day, and "we have got handicapping as near perfection as possible, for we have a record of every round a man plays, and by taking his average from day to day and from week to week, we soon arrive at this right figure."

Another automatic apparatus registers the length of every carry; the thickness of the grip can be altered at will in a moment, and the shape of the clubs, all made of steel in one piece, is such that they can be used either right or left-handed. The niblick is a work of genius; when swung over the shoulder its queerly-shaped double head begins to revolve on its own account with exceeding velocity, like a paddle-wheel, only faster, and ejects out of the bunker clouds of sand sufficient to keep "Old Tom's" greens going for a twelvemonth. Moreover, the golfing jacket shouts "Fore" every time a drive is made, to the detriment, until one becomes habituated to it, both of the stroke and of the temper.

Not without a touch of humour does the author allow his imagination free play in dealing with the future of the game, when match play shall have been almost improved out of existence, and the self-acting putter does everything short of telling you the line of your putt. The pity of it is that the ideas are clothed in such slip-shod English, grating on one at every turn, itself sufficient to mar the effect of the whole, however rich the imagination, or amusingly extravagant the general conception.

A LITTLE ABSTINENCE
Bernard Darwin, *A Friendly Round*, 1922

Not long ago I wrote rather bitterly of one who had given up golf. I do not wish to return to a subject so repellent, but would speak, not in reprobation, but rather of gentle pity, of those who for the good of their souls or their games try to abstain from playing golf for only a little while.

It is not, at the moment, my own case, because I have just played rather well and have beaten a Colonel, which is always a soothing sort of thing to do; but I have often tried at other times, and the ensuing agony can only be compared to that produced by temporarily giving up smoking. Everything conspires to lure one on to just one little swing, and in such a case the man who waggles is lost. Those who go to offices have at least a closed time every day when, if they have any regard for a reputation for sanity, they

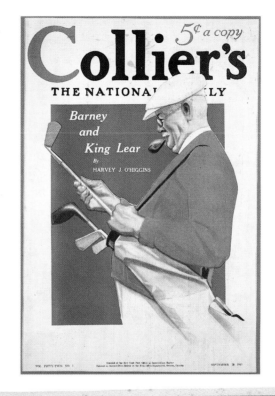

The cover for Collier's magazine, *left*, for September 20, 1913. *Below left*, a ladies fan, Horlicks advertising score-card and a postcard, all of around 1910; *below right*, a pamphlet advertising golf in South Africa of the 1930s.

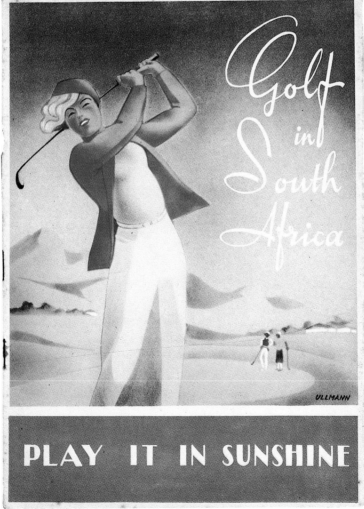

155

The cover of *Life* magazine, *right*, for September 5, 1926.

cannot swing; but for the home worker temptations lurk in every corner of every room. It is said that M. Clemenceau, when he gave up smoking, kept a box of peerless cigars open under his nose as he worked, every day for a fortnight. At the end of that time he had become miraculously proof against all temptation. Few people are strong enough for such a test.

At this moment as I write there stands a little sheaf of clubs within five yards of me. Now I had much better leave well along, because I really did drive that Colonel's head off – I believe I should have outdriven most Major-Generals – and yet there is a wooden club in the corner that is drawing me towards it like a lodestone. Those who were brought up on Mr. Shirley's leading cases will recall the prosperous baker of Liquorpond Street, who, having baked himself a fortune, undertook not to bake any more in the parish of, I think, St Andrew Undershaft, for five years. But the effort proved too much for him; "his fingers were itching for the pudding, and long ere the five years were out he was baking again as hard as ever." His fingers itch for the feel of the leather, and all too soon he is swinging again as hard as ever.

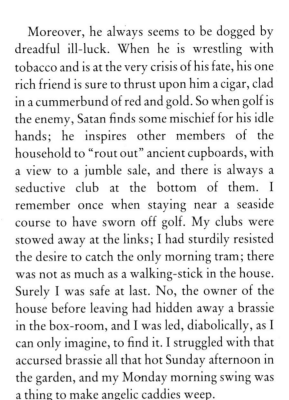

GOLF GIRL
COPYRIGHT 1907 D. HILLSON

Moreover, he always seems to be dogged by dreadful ill-luck. When he is wrestling with tobacco and is at the very crisis of his fate, his one rich friend is sure to thrust upon him a cigar, clad in a cummerbund of red and gold. So when golf is the enemy, Satan finds some mischief for his idle hands; he inspires other members of the household to "rout out" ancient cupboards, with a view to a jumble sale, and there is always a seductive club at the bottom of them. I remember once when staying near a seaside course to have sworn off golf. My clubs were stowed away at the links; I had sturdily resisted the desire to catch the only morning tram; there was not as much as a walking-stick in the house. Surely I was safe at last. No, the owner of the house before leaving had hidden away a brassie in the box-room, and I was led, diabolically, as I can only imagine, to find it. I struggled with that accursed brassie all that hot Sunday afternoon in the garden, and my Monday morning swing was a thing to make angelic caddies weep.

It is a depressing fact that, even when a vow of abstinence, whether from waggling, swinging, or actual playing, is successfully kept, the result is not always an improvement. Whether it is so or not depends, I think, upon the particular state of things that caused the taking of the vow. The player who is suffering from one or more clearly defined diseases will not cure them by ceasing to play. The bacillus of slicing or socketing is not killed thus, and may even be all the lustier and more rampageous for the rest. On the other hand, an attack of general golfing debility, in which sometimes one thing goes wrong and sometimes another and the whole game is a burden, ought generally to yield to a rest cure. In that delightful old book, *The Golfer's Manual* by a Keen Hand, it is stated that when the player's ball flies now to right and now to left "in a most unaccountable manner, he may safely conclude that there is something rotten in his state of play." I should rather suppose that in such a case there is something rotten in his own state, and that he had better repose a little. It is when the ball flies always to the right or always to the left that the state of play is at fault.

There are those, indeed, who can, and do deliberately, play themselves out of a fit of

157

A *The Ladies World* magazine cover, *right*, from 1905.

staleness. If we essay it, and the waters of bitterness do not quite close over our heads, we may emerge transfigured, playing perhaps better than we ever did before; but it is a painful and desperate remedy. When we are on a golfing holiday we are almost forced to attempt it, since to give up several days out of the limited number left to us requires a self-control that is more than human. But if staleness attacks us in the course of our everyday existence, when we can at least work on weekdays and take out the children on a Sunday afternoon, then we had better do as Mr Bob Sawyer and Mr Ben Allen did in Bengal after their fourteenth attack of yellow fever, and "resolve to try a little abstinence."

WIND AND WEATHER
Judith Ann Silburn, *Home Chats*, 1925

What shall we do for Easter? "It all depends on the weather," says someone shrewdly. That's just it, one never knows what this fickle jade of a climate of ours is going to give us, worse luck! Still, it is always safe to take a golfing holiday, as, unless the elements are exceptionally unkind to us, there is sure to be a round during the day.

There is no doubt that golf is the game par excellence for women of all ages, for it gives health-giving exercise in the open air without too much strenuous effort, but the golfer's wardrobe needs a little thought.

Golfing garments ought to be made of materials which will stand all weathers, and, above all, shoes should be strong and waterproof, and stockings should be of pure wool. By far the most serviceable kind of skirt is still the never-out-of-fashion tweed! There is one thing about a good Harris or Donegal tweed: it lasts for ages and keeps its cut, if tailored well, to its last days. Bright-coloured sports coats and woollen polo jumpers always look well on the golf course.

The golfing woman is not expected to sport a number of "changes," so that her wardrobe need not be a heavy one. Besides her golf "kit" all that

MARCH, 1905

THE LADI

S. H. MOORE

FIVE CENTS

'S WORLD

O., NEW YORK

she wants are a few pretty evening frocks, and perhaps one smart afternoon one, in case there is a very wet day and she has to stay indoors and play games.

By the way, a word about the sports girl's complexion. Wind and weather can play havoc with one's skin if care is not taken. The great thing is to protect the skin before going out, with some good pure oil, such as olive or almond oil. This prevents chapping and roughening.

The sports girl should never wash her face in hot water before going out. Hot water can be used in the evening when she takes her bath. The evening, you know, is certainly the best time to take a bath if one has been golfing all day.

If a little lemon-juice and peroxide of hydrogen be rubbed over the face before getting into bed it will remove any tan you may have got in the daytime. *

A GOLFING HOLIDAY
Bernard Darwin, *The American Golfer*, 1932

Let us begin with the packing of clubs which is on such occasions a labor of love. Of course we must take more clubs than we need; the reserve must be carefully searched and it is ten to one that we find an old friend that seems by a process of resting to have become an enchanter's wand. In any case it has played on our course so often

* The publishers wish to point out that the use of hydrogen peroxide on the skin is *not* advisable, and could be dangerous.

Near Left, an advertising fan, c. 1905.

159

A collection of gold, silver and precious stone golfing hat-pins from 1900 to 1930, *right*, in a silver hat-pin holder.

before that it would be churlish not to take it there again. There was that one hole it used to play so perfectly in a cross wind – and so that good and faithful servant goes into the bag, together with two or three additional putters, although of course we should not go off our putting – Perish the thought!

I say bag, but there are some people who have a case, a vast, black case, in the nature of a sarcophagus, in which their clubs travel. It is extremely convenient, but then it has to travel apart from its owner with the guard of the train and with soulless things like portmanteaus. I like my bag best because it is in the rack over my head

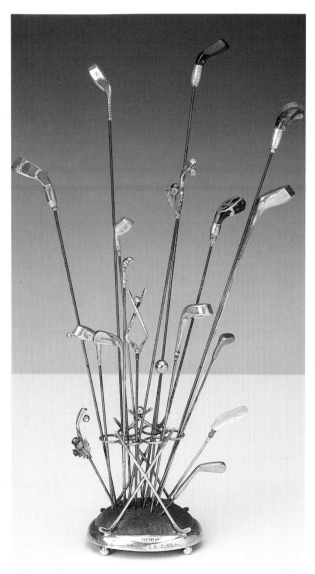

and I look up at it reassuringly now and then and hug to myself the knowledge that it is really there and I am really on my way.

That brings us to the journey and so comes the weighty question whether it is better to make it alone or in company of other travellers to paradise. Company is good and cheerful thing but for positive gloating it is almost necessary to be alone. "One of the pleasantest things in the world," says Hazlitt in a famous essay, "is going on a journey, but I like to go by myself." I am of Hazlitt's mind, or at any rate I like to start by myself.

Let me make a compromise, a concession to sociability. About half way or rather further to paradise there is a junction where some of my friends, coming from other parts of the country, may join the train. That is well, let them come! By that time, after several hours of solitary gloating, I shall be ready for them. One of the most agreeable parts of these festivals is their unchanging character and I know what we shall talk about: who are the other golfers that will be there, whether the course will be dry, whether all the projected bunkers have been made, and then, after an interval, whether we have reached a particular little station in the hills.

It is now evening and we peer out eagerly through the window into the dark for this is of great importance. After our engine has panted up that hill it tears and rushes down into the valley with only the sea now in front of it, so that we seem in advance to sniff the salt breeze of golf.

So much for the journey, and now for the arrival. Our very last stage is along the waters of a wide estuary, and when we stop it is on the very verge of the links. We can, if we are lucky, see the sandhills looming dark and vague, and there may be a light in the clubhouse window. We leave our clubs at the station, we commit our baggage to the same old carrier with the same old horse and then set out vigorously on foot – no carriers for us! – to stump up a steep hill. The same late tea has been kept for us with the same apple jelly. We are there at last!

Almost the best is over by then for nothing can be quite as beautiful as we expect it to be. Nevertheless it is quite beautiful enough to race down that steep hill next morning. We used to do

"topping" it after all. It requires practice and patience to acquire the "far and sure" stroke which is the motto of the best golf players.

Come, then, to the sandy links, as they are called. Their fellows in England are the undulating downs and grassy commons, a plain of fine green turf, diversified by knolls, furze-bushes, tufts of grass, hollows, and, may be, cart-ruts or pools of water. These form in golfer's parlance hazards, which are to be avoided if possible. The caddie is but the Scotch term for club-bearer, and he carries the somewhat miscellaneous appliances which the game demands.

Before, however, the game can be understood, some idea must be formed of the implements with which the game is played.

A pamphlet advertising golf in Italy, *far left*, from 1932; *below*, an umbrella with a silver handle in the shape of a golf ball, with a pencil contained in the handle.

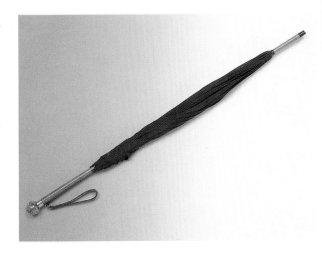

it on our feet and now I am afraid we do it in a motor car; some changes there must always be, but we get to the links and have our feet once more on that softest of seaside turf. And at the third comes that short hole over the mighty sandhill and the small caddie perched on his watch tower shouts "On the green" or sometimes he shouts "In the soup" and even that unnecessarily offensive statement does not make us very angry. We cannot get angry when we are playing golf in our own particular paradise at the start of a new year.

SPOONS, NIBLICKS AND STYMIES
Anon, *The Game of Golf*, c 1870

What chess is to draughts, what billiards is to bagatelle, what cricket is to trap-and-ball, so is golf to hockey. It is a game of skill, judgment, and science. It takes the player to breezy moors and healthful commons; it exhilarates without fatiguing him.

I well remember that inspiriting day when I accompanied those two old friends, members of the renowned and ancient club of St. Andrews, to witness their sport and to receive a few practical lessons on the art of avoiding hazards and getting out of a bunker. I well remember the smile of the attendant caddie as I swung the play-club as if I was going to send the ball the famed ten score yards, and only succeeded in

A collection of wooden golfing walking sticks, *left*, some with gold and silver bands, from 1900 to 1935.

The Ball is made of gutta-percha, about two inches in diameter, and painted white, so as to be easily seen. Formerly it was made of leather, stuffed hard with feathers. The price is about a shilling.

The Clubs are, however, the most important portion of the golfer's outfit. They are as various as the days in the week, and no good player would begin without a set of at least half a dozen. A fastidious player on an unknown ground would at least have half as many more, and would display with pride his (1) *play-club*, (2) *long spoon*, (3) mid-spoon, (4) *short spoon*, (5) baffing-spoon, (6) driving-putter, (7) *putter*, (8) *sand-iron*, (9) *cleek*, (10) *niblick*, or track-iron. Those most useful in ordinary play are printed in italics: indeed, the ground must be very difficult and full of hazards to require them all.

These clubs – for they all come under that generic name – are put to a variety of uses. The play-club is used for swiping, or driving the ball off the tee at the commencement of a game.

If the ball rests on a hollow, amidst rough grass or on uneven ground, then the long spoon is used. The mid-spoon is used for the same purpose, for short distances only. When near the hole, the short spoon comes into play: indeed it and the shorter baffing-spoon are used to elevate the ball for short distances only. As the cleek answers the purpose of the latter, it is generally used in preference.

The putter is more like a club that the croquet-player would appreciate, for it comes into use when the ball lies on the putting-green within, say, eighteen or twenty yards of the hole.

If the player could ensure the ball falling in pleasant green places, the foregoing clubs would suffice; but balls will fall at times in bunkers, as sand-holes are called, or fall in the whin-bushes, among the rushes and long bents, or among the rough stones of a road. Then the sand-iron is required.

The cleek is useful for driving balls over intervening obstacles lying between the ball and the hole near the putting-green. The niblick, sometimes called the track-iron is used to drive the balls from deep hollows, cart-ruts, or from among the stiff coarse stems of the furze or whin-bushes.

On reaching your ball, if it lies on the open turf, you may repeat the long swipe with advantage if you are not too ambitious. If in a sand-hole, you will require your sand-iron; if in a hollow of the turf, the long spoon; if in a rut, the niblick. You will find the bunker, or sand-hole, a hazard to be avoided rather than courted. It will require patience and perseverance ere the ball can be driven from its snug retreat on to the turf at one stroke.

At length your ball lies on the green itself, and the hole is temptingly near. You now want judgment and nicety of touch. You have to consider, not only the distance between your ball and the hole, but the possibility of a stymie.

A stymie is an ugly affair for a beginner, and it occurs when your antagonist's ball lies in a direct line between your hole and the ball, so that putting is out of the question. There is no other course open but to take the sand-iron and "loft" your ball over the stymie into the hole if you can. Stymies are sometimes play purposely, but it is not considered exactly fair to play them; but, whether played purposely or not, they often occur, and the young player should practise "lofting" with a view to overcoming stymies when they occur. Even without this obstruction, he has to consider the necessary strength to drive his ball safely in. He must also consider the nature of the intervening ground, whether up-hill or otherwise, and the best way of overcoming the difficulty.

"To putt" well ought to be the aim of every beginner; and, as he can practise it on any greensward, it is his own fault if he does not succeed.

A Traitorous Handicap
Harry Vardon, *Pacific Golf and Motor*, 1917

Very many golfers handicap themselves far more than they imagine by using implements which come into their possession in a more or less promiscuous way. They walk into the stores; see a club which takes their fancy; and emerge five minutes later with what they fondly regard as a treasure, but which ultimately proves to be a traitor.

Far right, the
**Moseley Hurst Golf
Club Challenge
Cup of 1912, and
the Corby
Challenge Cup
(1913 – 1927), both
by Royal Doulton.**
A fashion plate,
July 1927. *Near right*,
a Wedgewood
Kenlock Ware
Creamer c. 1900.

A WORM'S PARADISE
B. Radford, *Golfing*, 1910

"We believe that to charge as most clubs do three or four guineas entrance and a like subscription is ridiculous and unreasonable, and that there are scores of would-be golfers who are prevented from playing on the grounds of expense alone."

These are the remarks made by the chairman at a meeting called for the purpose of forming a golf club, and the meeting decided that, as 46 ladies and gentlemen had promised to become members, they would form a club, and before the meeting broke up they agreed that the entrance fee and subscription should be one guinea. They had already selected the ground on which to lay out a nine-hole course, and a committee was formed to enter into negotiations with the farmer.

Now, without wishing to damp the enthusiasm of these good people, I am of opinion that they are asking for trouble. They evidently know very little of the expenses connected with the making of a golf course, even on a modest scale. I know the ground that they propose to rent, and at the outset they are up against a stiff proposition in the person of the farmer. This same son of the soil had formerly let a portion of his land to a club, but having persisted in turning his cattle in, to the detriment of the greens, they had no choice but to shift their quarters. The professional who was attached to this club has

related to me the story of how on one occasion he turned the cattle off the links. This coming to the ears of the farmer brought him on the scene with a loaded gun. The timely warning of a caddie probably saved the pro's life, for when he arrived at the clubhouse the pro was nowhere to be found.

However small the club is, a nine-hole course cannot be brought into play under an expenditure of £250. The cost of labour, horse hire, machines, etc., would soon swallow up this amount, and there is always something required even when the committee think everything is in order. There are few, if any, courses that are as they were originally laid out, for it is not until they are played over that faults appear, and then begins the real work on a course. This bunker is in the wrong place, and that tee is dangerous, or it may be that more bunkers are necessary.

For a club with a membership of 200, possessing an eighteen-hole course, the subscription should be at least three guineas, for it is not possible to keep everything as it should be with a less sum, and when a club is formed the members should realise this, and not fix the entrance fee at a guinea as an inducement for others to join, for sooner or later they will awake to the fact that good golf cannot be obtained at this price, and if they do manage to rub along and keep the right side of the balance-sheet, the result will be seen in the condition of the course.

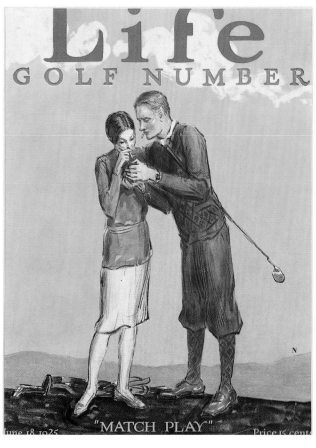

It is a curious fact that the largest and most exclusive clubs, such as Westward Ho! Hoylake, or St. Andrews, do not spend as much per year on the upkeep of the course as do some of the small Metropolitan clubs on the upkeep of the 90 acres usually known as a worm's paradise. It is on this type of links that greenkeeping is an art, and the seaside course calls for little skill on the part of the custodian.

To all enthusiasts I would suggest that before the club is formed they should see that from a financial point of view there is nothing to fear, and to get rid of the idea that good golf can be obtained for a subscription of one guinea.

THE CORE OF THE PROBLEM
H.B. Martin, *50 Years of American Golf,* 1936

Golf ball manufacturers had not taken the rubber-core seriously. They thought the dreadful "Bounding Billies" could never hope to become popular with the leading golfers. The Scotch players who dominated the game in America were certain that anything so silly as a rubber ball would never interfere seriously with the old traditions, and the principal one of these was that the game was to be played with a gutty. A rubber-cored ball, the Scotch insisted, was "nae gowf."

Arthur Tillinghast recalls showing old Tom Morris one of the new American balls made out of rubber and seeing him slowly shake his head in doubt. Probably it brought back memories of the old days when he parted friends with Allan Robertson over a similar dispute about the gutty

ball replacing the old feathery. Old Tom was a radical then, and his judgment proved to be right; but later he was reluctant to commit himself, although it did seem rather absurd to him to think that a ball that contained any amount of rubber would ever become popular. Yet Old Tom shook his head in doubt, probably wondering what those foolish Americans would do next.

French tobacco jar, *far left*, of around 1910; *near left top*, the cover of *Life* magazine for June 18, 1925; and, *near left bottom*, a Colonel Golf Ball box, and an advertisement for Colonel Golf Balls from *The Stymie*, of 1910.

165

A collection of tin golf games, *right*, from the first part of the century.

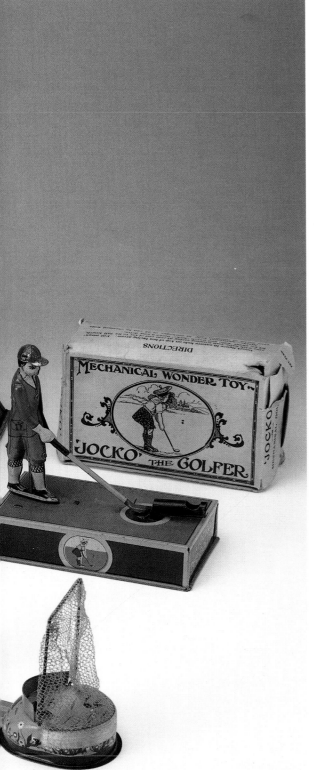

GOLF IN THE OLD COUNTRY
C.W. Whitney, *Harpers Monthly Magazine*, 1894

To the occasional or casual observer there appears in the Englishman's demeanor on the links no departure from his usual placidity. He stalks upon the grounds with habitual solemnity, and takes up the game in the same seriousness that has been associated with him at play. If the on-looker follows the player around the course, he seeks in vain for any visible sign of that joyous spirit which he, likely as not, has imagined fitting accompaniment to athletic contest.

But in golf the Briton is a contradiction. He gives no outward evidence of perturbation, though, to borrow topical opera slang, he boils within. It is only to his familiars in the club-house and around his own board that the Englishman reveals himself, and there, by the softening influences of good cheer, may you discover how hopeless a victim he is to the ancient and royal game.

Before he has finished his Scotch and soda he will play over again every stroke of that last round in which he was beaten a single hole, and then take up in elaborate detail certainly every

A collection of crested china, *right*, by Arcadian and others, dating from 1910 to 1930.

bunker and almost every brae on the course, until he has at length decided to his complete satisfaction on the identical stroke and spot that caused his downfall. I should be willing to give long odds in a wager on every golfing enthusiast in Great Britain being able to find, blindfolded, any given hazard on his home links, and the great majority of hazards on every course in England or Scotland. To hear them discuss strokes to evade, I was near saying, almost every bit of whin, and locate every sand dune is to gain some idea of the range and strength of golf mania.

I was prepared to find the country gone golf-crazy, but I found instead a condition bordering on what I have called golf-insomnia, though I should add that my observations were made from esoteric vantage-ground. At first I was disappointed, and ascribed the stories I had heard of the golf-furor to newspaper license; I had looked for some familiar token by which I might recognize the craze – signs such as in America indicate unmistakably that a boom is on. But my first visit to links so depressed me that I nearly reached a determination to pass by golf altogether in my pilgrimage – in the eventual failure of which resolution my readers have my heart-felt sympathy.

It was a disillusioning experience, that first sight of the much-heralded and antique game. Speaking retrospectively, I am not sure I have a very distinct recollection of just what I reckoned on viewing; I do not believe I expected to see players astride their clubs prancing about the teeing-ground in ill-concealed eagerness for the affray, nor a dense and cheering throng of spectators surrounding the putting-green of the home hole, nor triumphantly shouldered victors borne from the field amid hosannas and tumultuous applause by the populace.

Even as I write now I can feel again the dejection that came over me in successive and widening waves as I looked for the first time on the game that is reported to have converted in the last two or three years more disciples than any other in the old country. At first I thought I had gone on the links during a lull in the play. Then I persuaded myself that I had arrived on a day set apart for the convalescents of some near-by sanitarium, but as I discovered my error in the

ruddy imprint of health on their cheeks, my wonder grew that so many vigorous, young, and middle-aged men could find amusement in what appeared to me to a melancholy and systematized "constitutional."

Once recovered from the initial shock, I found amusement in the awful solemnity that enveloped the on-lookers about the putting-green, every mother's son of whom watched the holing out with bated breath. One, standing next to me in the crowd, and whose pleasing face gave encouragement, while the frequency with which he had trod on my toes seemed to me to have established a sufficient *entente cordiale* between us, bestowed upon me, when I asked why no one called the number of strokes each player had taken, so we would all know how they stood, such a look of righteous horror as I am sure would have caused any but an irrepressible American to wish the earth might open and swallow him. But being an American it simply increased my thirst for knowledge, and at the next sally I upset him completely by asking why a player, who was executing the "waggle" with all the deliberate nicety of one thoroughly appreciative of that important prelude to the

"What's wrong here?"

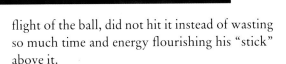

flight of the ball, did not hit it instead of wasting so much time and energy flourishing his "stick" above it.

To have alluded with levity to one of the rudimentary functions of the game was appalling enough in all conscience, but to have called a club a stick was too much for my neighbor, and he of the aggressive feet moved away from the tee with a pained expression clouding the open countenance that had tempted my golfing innocence.

Subsequent and solitary wanderings about the links brought but little solace to my joyless

sporting soul, for it seemed that at every turning I was challenged by loud and emphatic cries of "fore," the significance of which I did not understand, while the air appeared to be filled with flying balls that whizzed past at uncomfortable proximity, or alighted just behind me, after a flight of a hundred and fifty yards or so, with a thud far from reassuring. It does not seem probable such a situation could under any circumstances have a humorous side; but it may, and I have laughed until my head ached over the comical consternation of some luckless and obstinate duffer, who, instead of permitting, as courtesy and tradition teach, more skilful following players to pass him, continued on his laborious and turf-bruising way, driven into by those immediately back of him, and damned by every golfer on the links. Given an irascible and stubborn and indifferent (a combination that has been known to exist) leading player, with following balls dropping around him, and I fancy even an Englishman, if he is not playing, will acknowledge the picture mirth- provoking.

What broke the gloom of that first day of my experience, and turned indifference to a desire for knowledge, were the individual manoeuvres on the putting-green, which, sometimes

An English Christmas card, *right top*, for 1910; and, *right bottom*, and English Easter card for 1924.

grotesque, frequently picturesque, and invariably fraught with the weightiest meditation, convinced me that any game requiring such earnest play must improve on acquaintance. The putting-green presents a scene for the student of human nature, with its exhibitions of temperaments and varied styles of play: one will make a minute and lengthy survey over the few yards of turf that separate his ball from the hole, and attain the climax of his joy or woe by a short sharp tap with the club; another devotes his critical attention to the lie of the ball, followed by a painfully deliberate aim that seems never to quite reach the explosive point; some appear to acquire confidence by the narrowing of the human circle around the hole; others wave all back save their caddie, who, like a father confessor, remains at their side administering unction of more or less extremity to the last.

The duties of the caddie are manifold, including the responsibilities of preceptor, doctor, and lawyer. He will be called upon to devise means of escape from soul-trying bunkers, administer to the wounded pride of the unsuccessful, and turn legislator at a crowded teeing-ground; he must even at times serve as a foil to the wrath of the disconsolate player who has "foozled" a drive that was confidently expected to carry him safely beyond a formidable hazard. There are caddies and caddies, to be sure, but when of the right sort, no servants, I fancy, receive such marked evidence of their master's regard. Most of them are Scotch, and some of them the most picturesque figures on the golfing-green.

To obtain a full appreciation of the charms and difficulties of golf you should have acquired a settled conviction of its inferiority as a game requiring either skill or experience; you must have looked upon it with supreme contempt, and catalogued it as a sport for invalids and old men. When you have reached this frame of mind go out on to the links and try it. I never believed a club could be held in so many different ways but the right one until I essayed golf, nor dreamed it so difficult to drive a ball in a given direction. The devotion of the golfer to his game is only equalled by the contempt of him who looks upon it for the first time. You wonder at a great many

An iron umbrella stand, *left*, of the 1890s.

A blotter for The Sun Life Golf Club, *right*, for February 1932; and, *below*, an Aubrey Beardsley drawing on the cover of *The Illustrated American*, for 1894.

things when you first see it played, but your wonderment is greatest that a game which appears so simple should have created such a furor.

The secret of its fascination rests largely in the fact that it beats the player, and he, in his perversity, strives the harder to secure the unattainable.

The game is by no means easy; in fact, one of England's foremost players asserts that it takes six months of steady play to acquire consistent form. You must hit the ball properly to send it in the desired direction, and you must deal with it as you find it; you cannot arrange the ball to suit your better advantage, nor await a more satisfactory one, as in baseball and cricket. The club must be held correctly and swung accurately in order to properly address the ball, from which the player should never take his eye, while at the same time he must move absolutely freely, and yet maintain an exact balance. Besides which, it demands judgment and good temper,

and if you fail in the latter your play will be weakened on the many trying occasions that arise.

It is a selfish game, where each man fights for himself, seizing every technicality for his own advantage, and there is no doubt that to this fact its popularity may in a large measure be attributed. Unlike cricket, baseball, or football, one is not dependent on others for play. You can usually find some one to make up a match, or you may go over the course alone, getting the best of practice and fairly good sport, or at least there is always a caddie to be had for the asking, and the usual small fee.

172

TRUE LOVERS.

LINKS
do bind
his heart
of mine
Unto yours,
sweet
Valentine,

But they
are the
links of love,
Truer
than the
stars
above.

the ears, and set him putting into tumblers and whisking off the heads of daisies overnight, that in the morrow's play his aim may be the truer and his swing the deadlier.

An American Valentine card, *far left*, of 1910; *near left*, two luggage labels of the 1920s: one for the Hotel du Golf, Deauville, France; and one for the Hotel du Golf at Monte Carlo.

The exercise may be gentle, but whosoever fancies golf does not test the nerves should play a round on popular links.

I cannot say if the native views it in the same light, but I concluded before I had half finished my tour that the attraction of golf was as much due to the atmosphere of tradition on the links and good-fellowship in the clubs as to the qualities of the game itself. I doubt if we in America will ever be able to extract so much pleasure from it. Our dispositions, our temperaments, are not golf-like; we hurry through life at too rapid a gait; we have not the time to give golf in order to gain that responsive charm the game holds for the leisurely suitor.

What I have endeavored to show here is the breadth and depth of the spirit which has made the golfing widow an accepted national institution, seized the usually serene Briton by

173

A F T E R W O R D

BY SARAH BADDIEL

Compiling this anthology has been great fun for me, as I hope the end result is for you. But, more than just being fun, working on this book has given me the chance to reflect both on the history of golf and the way in which collecting golfiana has grown so quickly over the last twenty years or so.

In 1970, two American collectors, Joe Murdoch and Bob Kuntz, met at a golf tournament. Golf was played, good lunches were eaten and the odd gin and tonic drunk – as usual. But this time, something else happened: Joe and Bob formed the Golf Collector's Society. Its purpose was to allow collectors of golfing artefacts to meet and trade items, but not necessarily to sell them, and to produce a magazine for members called *The Bulletin*. The idea has been a tremendous success, and, in 1987, the British Golf Collector's Society was formed with Joe Murdoch as the President, and a journal called *Through the Green*, edited by David White.

Today, collectors of golfiana can be found all over the world – some of them, as Peter Dobereiner has said, suffering from AOBS; others using a small collection to remind them of gloriously successful – and sometimes less successful – days on the links. As you can see from the illustrations in this book, the term "golfiana" covers a wide range of items. This list, called COLLECTING BY THE ALPHABET, is from the March 1989 edition of *The Bulletin*, was produced by Fred and Shirlee Smith, to whom I am indebted for permission to reproduce it here.

Have a close look at this list – if you have just one item, you have the beginnings of a collection of golfiana!

But whether or not you decide to start a collection, I very much hope that you enjoy this book, and continue to enjoy your golf.

Sarah Fabian Baddiel

Sarah Baddiel
London, April 1989.

CONTACT ADDRESSES

USA Golf Collector's Society: THE GOLF COLLECTOR'S SOCIETY, INC
PO BOX 491
SHAWNEE MISSION, KS 66201, USA.

USGA: GOLF HOUSE,
FAR HILLS, NJ 07931, USA
Tel: 201-234 2300.

UK Golf Collector's Society: THE BRITISH GOLF COLLECTOR'S SOCIETY
PO BOX 843
SEAFORD, EAST SUSSEX, BN25 2HQ.

A
Ashtrays, Autographs

B
Bags, Balls, Book ends, Books, Buttons

C
Bag tags, Beer cans, Boxes, Button hooks, Caddy Badges, Clubs

D
Decanters, Deck of cards, Display, Door knobs, Door stops

E
Earthenware, Emblems, Ephemera, Etchings

F
Fancy face clubs, Featherie, Flasks

G
Games, Glassware, Golf carts, Gutties

H
Haskell balls, Hat pins, Hats, Hole-in-one medals, Humidors

I
Illegal clubs, Ink wells, Irons, Ivory items

J
Jackets, Jewellery, Jiggers

K
Key chains, Knickers, Knives

L
Lamps, Letter opener, Lighters, Lithographs, Lockets

M
Magazines, Manicure set, Markers, Match safe, McEwans, Medals, Miniatures, Moulds

N
Napkin rings, Needlework, Newspaper clippings

O
Open memorabilia, Orange ball, Ornaments

P
Paintings, Paperweights, Pencils, Periodicals, Philips poker chips, Photographs, Pipes, Plates, Players' badges, Postcards, Posters, Prints, Programmes, Punch boards

Q
Quaint carrying devices, Quivers

R
Rain gear, Reddy tees, Replicas, Rock

S
Scorecards, Sculpture, Society souvenirs, Spikes, Spoons, Steins, Stereo-opticon, Stock pins

T
Tape measure, Tees, Thimbles, Tie racks, Ties, Toast racks, Towels, Toys, Trademarks, Trays, Trophies

U
Umbrellas, Urquhart, USGA items

V
Vanity cases, Vases

W
Walking sticks, Wall plaques, Watches, Watch fobs, Woods

X
Xmas cards

Y
Year books, Youth clubs

Z
Zebra putter, Zippo balls, Zippo lighter.